The
OLD
TESTAMENT

RICHARD D. NELSON

The OLD TESTAMENT

Canon, History, and Literature

Nashville

THE OLD TESTAMENT:
CANON, HISTORY, AND LITERATURE

Copyright © 2019 by Abingdon Press

All rights reserved.

No part of this work may be reproduced or transmitted in any form or by any means, electronic or mechanical, including photocopying and recording, or by any information storage or retrieval system, except as may be expressly permitted by the 1976 Copyright Act or in writing from the publisher. Requests for permission should be addressed in writing to Permissions, Abingdon Press, 2222 Rosa L. Parks Blvd., Nashville, TN 37228-1306, or permissions@abingdonpress.com.

This book is printed on acid-free paper.

Library of Congress Cataloging-in-Publication Data has been requested.

978-1-4267-5923-9

Scripture quotations unless noted otherwise are taken from the Common English Bible, copyright 2011. Used by permission. All rights reserved.

Scripture quotations marked NRSV are from the New Revised Standard Version Bible, copyright © 1989 National Council of the Churches of Christ in the United States of America. Used by permission. All rights reserved worldwide. http://nrsvbibles.org/

Scripture quotations marked KJV are taken from The Authorized (King James) Version. Rights in the Authorized Version in the United Kingdom are vested in the Crown. Reproduced by permission of the Crown's patentee, Cambridge University Press.

Photos unless noted otherwise are from www.BibleLandPictures.com copyright © Zev Radovan. Used by permission.

Photo on page 275: Aramiaic. Marriage Document, July 3, 449 B.C.E. Papyrus, ink, mud, linen, Glass: 13 1/4 x 14 15/16 in. (33.7 x 38 cm). Brooklyn Museum, Bequest of Theodora Wilbour from the collection of her father, Charles Edwin Wilbour, 47.218.89.

CONTENTS

Preface · xxi

PART I: LAYING THE GROUNDWORK

Chapter 1: Old Testament and Hebrew Bible as Scripture · 3

1. Why Learn about the Old Testament? · 3
2. Scripture and Canon · 4
   - Sidebar 1.1. BCE and CE · 4
   - Table 1. Diverging Canons · 5
3. The Jewish Canon of the Hebrew Bible · 7
   - Fig. 1. Aleppo Codex · 8
4. The Christian Canon of the Old Testament · 9
   - Fig. 2. Codex Sinaiticus · 10
   - Sidebar 1.2. Chapter and Verse · 11
5. Catholic, Orthodox, and Protestant Canons · 12
   - Sidebar 1.3. The Quran · 13
6. Establishing the Earliest Text · 14

Further Reading · 15

Contents

Chapter 2: Geography, History, and Religion	17
1. Geography	17
(a) Israel's Homeland	17
Map 1. Fertile Crescent	18
(b) Physical Regions	19
Map 2. Physical Regions of Palestine	20
Map 3. Important Urban Centers	22
(c) Climate and Agriculture	23
Sidebar 2.1. The Gezer Calendar	23
Fig. 3. Gezer Calendar	24
(d) Neighboring Peoples	25
2. History of the Pre-Exilic Period	26
(a) Pre-Monarchic Period (about 1200 to 1000 BCE)	26
Fig. 4. Merneptah Stele	27
(b) Monarchic Period (about 1000 to 586 BCE)	28
3. Religion	28
(a) Yahweh and the Gods	29
Sidebar 2.2. Asherah	30
(b) The Name Yahweh	30
(c) Holy Places	31
Further Reading	32

PART II: TORAH

Chapter 3: Investigating the Pentateuch	35
1. The Documentary Hypothesis	35
(a) Irregularities and Inconsistencies	35
(b) Documents Combined into the Torah Story	37
(c) Yahwist and Elohist	37

Contents

Sidebar 3.1. Angels	38
(d) The Priestly Writing	39
Sidebar 3.2. Covenant	39
(e) The Flood according to J and P	41
2. Form Criticism	42
(a) Narrative Genres in Genesis	43
Further Reading	44
Chapter 4: Creation: Genesis 1–3	**45**
1. Understanding Myth	45
Sidebar 4.1. *Enuma Elish*	46
2. Creation according to the Priestly Writer—Genesis 1:1–2:4a	47
Sidebar 4.2. The Image of God	49
3. The Yahwist's Perspective on Creation—Genesis 2:4b–3:24	50
(a) Etiology	50
(b) Creating the World of Eden	51
(c) Temptation and Tragedy	52
4. Interpreting the Eden Story	53
(a) Women and Men	54
Further Reading	55
Chapter 5: Origins: Genesis 4:1–11:9	**57**
1. Rivalry and Vengeance—Genesis 4	57
2. Before the Flood—Genesis 5:1–6:4	58
Sidebar 5.1. Generations before the Flood	59
Sidebar 5.2. Divine Beings	60
3. The Great Flood—Genesis 6:5–9:17	61
Sidebar 5.3. Mesopotamian Flood Stories	61

Fig. 5. Gilgamesh Epic	62
4. After the Flood—Genesis 9:18–10:32	63
5. The City and Its Tower—Genesis 11:1-9	64
Further Reading	65
Chapter 6: Abraham and His Descendants	67
1. A Family Story	67
Table 2. The Family of Abraham	68
2. Abraham and Isaac—Genesis 12–23	69
(a) Promise and Covenant	69
Sidebar 6.1. Circumcision	70
(b) Faith and Unbelief	71
Sidebar 6.2. The Matriarch in Danger	71
(c) Testing Abraham—Genesis 22	73
Sidebar 6.3. Hagar and Ishmael	73
3. Isaac and Jacob—Genesis 24–36	74
4. Tamar and Judah—Genesis 38	75
5. The Story of Joseph—Genesis 37, 39–50	76
Sidebar 6.4. Israel and Hebrew	77
Further Reading	78
Chapter 7: Exodus	79
1. Exodus and Identity	79
(a) Let My People Go—Exodus 1–11	79
Sidebar 7.1. Miriam	80
(b) The First Passover—Exodus 12–13	81
(c) Deliverance at the Sea—Exodus 14–15	82
2. Life in the Wilderness	83

(a) Manna—Exodus 16	83
(b) The Gold Bull Calf—Exodus 32	83
Fig. 6. Bull Stele	84
3. Torah and Covenant at Sinai	85
(a) Apodictic and Casuistic Instruction	85
(b) Ten Commandments—Exodus 19–20	85
(c) The Book of the Covenant—Exodus 20:22–23:19	86
(d) Another Decalogue—Exodus 34:10-26	87
4. The Tabernacle—Exodus 25–31, 35–40	88
Further Reading	88
Chapter 8: Leviticus and Numbers	89
1. Leviticus	89
(a) The Priestly Worldview	89
Sidebar 8.1. Urim and Thummim	90
(b) Clean versus Unclean	91
(c) Common versus Holy	91
(d) Sacrifice	92
(e) Day of Atonement—Leviticus 16	94
(f) The Holiness Code—Leviticus 17–26	94
2. Numbers	95
(a) Census and Encampment	96
(b) Law and Ritual	97
Fig. 7. Ketef Hinnom Amulet	97
Sidebar 8.2. Samaria Ostraca	98
(c) Rebellion and Controversy	99
Sidebar 8.3. Female Images for God	99
(d) Journey and Warfare	101
(e) Balaam	102
Sidebar 8.4. Deir ʿAlla Inscription	102

Further Reading ... 102

Chapter 9: Deuteronomy ... 103

1. The Origin of Deuteronomy ... 103
2. The Shape of Deuteronomy ... 104
    Sidebar 9.1. Numbering the Commandments ... 105
3. Centralization of Sacrifice—Deuteronomy 12 ... 106
4. Covenant and Treaty ... 107
    Sidebar 9.2. Assyrian Treaty Curses ... 108
5. Motivated Instruction ... 109
    Sidebar 9.3. An Eye for an Eye ... 110
6. Instructions That Create Community ... 110
    Sidebar 9.4. Remember the Sabbath ... 111
7. The Death of Moses—Deuteronomy 32–34 ... 112

Further Reading ... 113

PART III: FORMER PROPHETS

Chapter 10: Joshua ... 117

1. Joshua and the Deuteronomistic History ... 117
2. The Conquest of Canaan ... 118
    Fig. 8. Baal Stele ... 119
    (a) Yahweh as Divine Warrior ... 119
        Sidebar 10.1. Divine Warrior ... 120
    (b) *Herem*—Devoting to Destruction ... 120
3. Crossing the Jordan—Joshua 1–5 ... 121
4. Conquest—Joshua 6–12 ... 122

    (a) Jericho—Joshua 6   122
    (b) Achan and Ai—Joshua 7–8   122
    (c) Victories in the South and North—Joshua 9–11   123

5\. Allotment of the Land—Joshua 13–21   124

    Sidebar 10.2. Twelve Tribes   124

6\. Warnings—Joshua 22–24   126

7\. Interpreting Joshua   126

    Sidebar 10.3. Archaeological Periods   127

Further Reading   128

Chapter 11: Judges   129

1\. Shape and Composition   129

2\. Incomplete Conquest—Judges 1:1–2:5   130

3\. The Cycle of Major Judges   131

4\. Ehud and Shamgar—Judges 3:12-31   132

5\. Deborah and Barak—Judges 4–5   132

6\. Gideon and Abimelech—Judges 6–9   134

    (a) Gideon   134
    (b) The Rise and Fall of Abimelech   135

    Sidebar 11.1. Shechem   136

7\. Jephthah—Judges 10:6–12:7   136

8\. Samson—Judges 13–16   137

    Fig. 9. Philistine Captives   138

9\. There Was No King—Judges 17–21   138

    Sidebar 11.2. Images and Idols   139

Further Reading   140

Chapter 12: 1 and 2 Samuel — 141

  1. The Narrative Shape of Samuel — 141
  2. Sources Used in Samuel — 142
     (a) The Ark Story—1 Samuel 4–6, 2 Samuel 6 — 142
     (b) The Rise of David—1 Samuel 16:14–2 Samuel 5:12 — 142
     (c) The Court History—2 Samuel 9–20 (1 Kings 1–2) — 143
  3. The Story of Samuel — 143
  4. The Story of Saul — 144
  5. The Story of David — 145
     (a) Who Will Inherit David's Throne? — 146
  6. Women in Samuel — 147
     (a) Hannah — 147
     (b) Michal — 148
     (c) Abigail — 148
     (d) The Woman Who Communicated with Ghosts — 148
     (e) Bathsheba — 149
     (f) Princess Tamar — 149
  7. The Book of Samuel and History — 150
  Further Reading — 150

Chapter 13: The Book of Kings and the Story of Solomon — 151

  1. The Book of Kings — 151
     (a) The Scope of Kings — 152
     (b) Sources Used by Kings — 153
     (c) Organization and Chronology — 154
       Table 3. Kings of Israel and Judah — 155
     (d) The Theology of Kings — 156
       Sidebar 13.1. Women in Kings — 157
  2. The Story of Solomon — 158

– xii –

(a) Solomon in All His Glory—1 Kings 1–11	158
(b) Solomon's Temple	159
Fig. 10. Dome of the Rock	160
Sidebar 13.2. Temples	161
(c) Solomon and Yahweh	162
Further Reading	162
Chapter 14: 1 and 2 Kings and the History of Israel and Judah	**163**
1. Jeroboam (Israel) and Rehoboam (Judah)—1 Kings 12–14	163
2. Omri and Ahab (Israel)—1 Kings 16:21–22:40	165
(a) Ahab and Jezebel	165
(b) Yahweh versus Baal	166
(c) The Battle of Qarqar (853)	166
Table 4. Significant Assyrian Rulers	167
(d) The Death of Ahab	167
Fig. 11. Mesha Stele	168
Sidebar 14.1. The Mesha Inscription	168
3. Jehu (Israel) and Athaliah (Judah)—2 Kings 9–11	169
(a) The Rebellion of Jehu	169
(b) Jehu and History	170
Fig. 12. King Jehu	170
(c) Queen Athaliah	171
4. The Last Days of Israel—2 Kings 14–17	171
(a) Menahem and Pekah (Israel)	171
(b) Ahaz (Judah)	172
(c) The Fall of Israel	172
5. Hezekiah and Manasseh (Judah)—2 Kings 18–21	173
(a) Hezekiah	173
Sidebar 14.2. Hezekiah's Tunnel	173

Fig. 13. Conquest of Lachish	175
Sidebar 14.3. Hezekiah and Sennacherib in 701 BCE	175
(b) Manasseh	176
6. Josiah—2 Kings 22:1–23:30	176
Table 5. Significant Neo-Babylonian Rulers	178
7. The Last Days of Judah—2 Kings 23:31–25:30	178
Further Reading	179

PART IV: LATTER PROPHETS

Chapter 15: Prophets and Prophecy	183
1. The Prophetic Books	183
2. The Prophetic Office	184
3. Prophetic Speech	185
4. Prophets and the Future	188
Further Reading	188
Chapter 16: The Isaiah Scroll	189
1. Three Collections of Prophetic Material	189
2. Isaiah Son of Amoz—Isaiah 1–39	190
(a) Isaiah and History	190
(b) A Message of Judgment	191
(c) A Remnant Will Survive	192
(d) Yahweh's Choice of Jerusalem	193
Sidebar 16.1. Isaiah 7:14	193
(e) Yahweh's Promise to David	194
3. Second Isaiah—Isaiah 40–55	195
(a) Look Homeward	195
(b) The Beginning and Conclusion of Second Isaiah	196

(c) "I Am Yahweh; There Is No Other"	196
(d) Four Servant Songs	197
4. Third Isaiah—Isaiah 56–66	198
5. The Isaiah Apocalypse—Isaiah 24–27	200
Further Reading	200

Chapter 17: Catastrophe and Exile: Jeremiah and Ezekiel — 201

1. The Book of Jeremiah	201
(a) Three Types of Literary Material	202
(b) Five Periods of Jeremiah's Career	203
(c) Jeremiah as an Individual	204
2. The Book of Ezekiel	205
(a) Call and Vision—Ezekiel 1–3	206
(b) A Message of Judgment—Ezekiel 4–32	207
(c) Israel's History of Sin	208
(d) A Message of Hope—Ezekiel 33–39	209
(e) Utopian Vision—Ezekiel 40–48	210
Further Reading	210

Chapter 18: Prophets of Social Justice: Amos, Hosea, and Micah — 211

1. Amos	211
Fig. 14. Jeroboam II	212
(a) A Society under Judgment	212
(b) Empty Religion	213
Sidebar 18.1. The Day of Yahweh	214
(c) Five Visions of Doom	214
(d) Hope on the Other Side of Judgment	215
2. Hosea	215
(a) Historical and Social Background	216
(b) Hosea and Gomer—Hosea 1–3	216
(c) Judgment Oracles	218

(d) The Problem with Religion	218
(e) Yet Yahweh Still Loves Israel	219

3. Micah — 220

- (a) Background and Structure — 220
- (b) God Demands Justice — 221
- (c) A Ruler from Bethlehem — 222

Further Reading — 222

Chapter 19: Judah in the Orbit of Assyria, Babylon, and Persia — 223

1. Zephaniah — 223

2. Nahum — 224

3. Habakkuk — 225

4. Obadiah — 226

5. Haggai — 226

Table 6. Significant Persian Rulers — 227

6. Zechariah — 228

- (a) First Zechariah—Zechariah 1–8 — 228
- (b) Zechariah 9–11 and 12–14 — 229

7. Malachi — 230

8. Joel — 231

9. Jonah — 231

- (a) The Story — 232
- (b) The Lesson of Jonah — 233

Further Reading — 233

PART V: WRITINGS

Chapter 20: Psalms — 237

1. Shape and Composition — 237

2. Psalms as Poetry	239
3. Laments and Thanksgiving Psalms	240
Fig. 15. Horned Altar	241
4. Hymns	242
5. Enthronement Psalms	242
6. Royal Psalms	243
Sidebar 20.1. Messiah	243
7. Zion Songs	244
8. Songs of Trust	245
9. Wisdom and Torah Psalms	245
Further Reading	245
Chapter 21: Optimistic and Pessimistic Wisdom: Proverbs and Job	247
1. Wisdom	247
2. Proverbs	247
3. Job	250
(a) Background and Composition	250
Sidebar 21.1. Satan	251
(b) The Narrative Frame	252
(c) The Dialogues	252
Sidebar 21.2. Honoring the Dead	252
(d) Creation in Job	255
Further Reading	256
Chapter 22: The Five Scrolls	257
1. The Five Scrolls	257
2. Song of Songs	257

3. Ruth	259
(a) Naomi's Problems and Ruth's Loyalty—Ruth 1	259
(b) Hope on the Horizon—Ruth 2	260
(c) A Solution, Almost—Ruth 3	260
(d) A Happy Ending—Ruth 4	261
(e) The Theology of Ruth	262
4. Lamentations	262
5. Ecclesiastes	264
6. Esther	265
Sidebar 22.1. Purim	266
(a) The Plot of Esther	266
(b) Additions to Esther	268
Further Reading	268
Chapter 23: Ezra–Nehemiah and 1 and 2 Chronicles	**269**
1. Ezra–Nehemiah	269
Sidebar 23.1. Cyrus Cylinder	269
Fig. 16. Cyrus Cylinder	270
(a) Ezra–Nehemiah as History	271
(b) Rebuilding the Temple—Ezra 1–6	272
(c) Ezra Proclaims the Law—Ezra 7–10, Nehemiah 8–10	272
(d) Nehemiah Rebuilds the Wall—Nehemiah 1–7 and 11–13	273
(e) Later Developments in the Persian Period	274
Fig. 17. Elephantine Papyri	275
Sidebar 23.2. Elephantine Papyri	275
2. 1 and 2 Chronicles	276
(a) Sources and Audience	276
(b) Organization	277
(c) The Theology of Chronicles	278

Further Reading . . . 279

Chapter 24: Daniel . . . 281

1. Alexander the Great and His Successors . . . 281
2. Shape and Date . . . 282
   - Table 7. Seleucid Rulers in the Maccabean Period . . . 283
   - Sidebar 24.1. Noah, Dan(i)el, Job . . . 284
3. Tales of Encouragement—Daniel 1–6 . . . 285
   - Sidebar 24.2. Writing on the Wall . . . 286
4. Apocalyptic Visions—Daniel 7–12 . . . 286
   - (a) Judgment on the Beasts—Daniel 7 . . . 287
   - (b) A Ram and a Goat—Daniel 8 . . . 288
   - (c) Daniel's Final Vision—Daniel 10–12 . . . 289
   - Sidebar 24.3. Persian Religion . . . 289
   - (d) Timetables . . . 290
5. Additions to Daniel . . . 290

Further Reading . . . 291

PART VI: APOCRYPHAL / DEUTEROCANONICAL BOOKS

Chapter 25: Spellbinding Tales and Profound Wisdom . . . 295

1. Tobit . . . 295
   - (a) Cultural Background . . . 295
   - (b) Tobit as Literature . . . 296
   - (c) The Narrative Structure of Tobit . . . 296
2. Judith . . . 298
   - (a) The Story . . . 298
3. Wisdom of Solomon . . . 300
   - (a) Structure . . . 300

(b) Themes 301
 4. Sirach 302
  (a) Advice and Wise Teaching 303
  (b) In Praise of Wisdom 304
  (c) Let Us Praise the Famous 304
 5. Baruch 305
 Further Reading 306

Chapter 26: 1 and 2 Maccabees 307
 1. 1 Maccabees 307
  (a) Persecution by Antiochus IV Epiphanes 308
  Table 8. The Maccabee Family in 1 and 2 Maccabees .. 309
  (b) Judas the Maccabee 310
  (c) Jonathan, Simon, and John Hyrcanus I 310
   Fig. 18. John Hyrcanus I 310
   Sidebar 26.1. Samaria 311
 2. 2 Maccabees 312
  (a) 2 Maccabees as History 312
   Sidebar 26.2. Hanukkah 313
  (b) The Succession of High Priests 313
  (c) God Defends the Temple 314
  (d) Heroic Martyrdom 315
 3. Later Jewish Religious Works 315
 Further Reading 316

Chronology of Significant Events 317

Vocabulary 319

PREFACE

This book is intended to help students and other readers encounter the Old Testament as a *canon* of books understood against their *historical* background and as *literary* works. After a coverage of introductory matters (part 1), books are discussed in the canonical order of the Hebrew Bible (parts 2–5), followed by the deuterocanonical books of Christian canonical tradition (part 6). Historical considerations lead to two exceptions to the canonical sequence of organization. The Minor Prophets (that is, the book of the Twelve) are treated in approximate chronological order, and Daniel is discussed as the last component of the Writings section. Books are described against the background of the history that prompted their composition. Literary issues such as structure, theme, and narrative shape receive attention when this is helpful for achieving a fuller understanding.

This organizational scheme has advantages for both student and teacher. For example, experience shows that it is difficult to motivate students actually to read the Old Testament itself, rather than limiting themselves to the textbook. Linking textbook chapters directly to biblical books is intended to facilitate this practice. Moreover, academic study of the Bible at the university or theology-school level usually focuses more directly on the literature itself rather than on the details of ancient history. The Hebrew Bible/Old Testament is usually explored in the context of world literature, religion, or theology. A book-by-book approach that recognizes the importance of canon is appropriate for pursuing these topics. Finally, this approach recognizes and respects the reality that different configurations of this literature continue to function as canonical scripture for Judaism and the three major divisions of Christianity.

All dates cited are BCE (Before the Common Era) unless otherwise noted. Scripture is quoted from the Common English Bible (CEB) except as indicated. Chapter and verse designations follow those of the English Bible. References to ancient texts are abbreviated as:

ANET   *Ancient Near Eastern Texts Relating to the Old Testament.* Ed. James B. Pritchard. 3rd ed. Princeton University Press, 1969.

COS   *Context of Scripture.* Ed. W. W. Hallo and K. L. Younger. 3 vols. Brill, 1997–2002.

Part I
LAYING THE GROUNDWORK

Chapter 1
OLD TESTAMENT AND HEBREW BIBLE AS SCRIPTURE

Why Learn about the Old Testament?

The Old Testament is part of humanity's cultural heritage. Even people who have never read parts of it will be able to recognize a huge wooden boat with paired animal heads poking out of its windows as Noah's Ark, or a bearded man holding two stone slabs as Moses. Eve and Adam appear regularly in cartoons. The Old Testament may be appreciated as an example of ancient literary art with a religious theme like the *Iliad or Bhagavad-Gita*. Western art and music history would be unintelligible without familiarity with the stories and themes of the Old Testament. Popular language is peppered with allusions to the Old Testament: "forbidden fruit" (Gen 3:3), "the skin of my teeth" (Job 19:20), "writing on the wall" (Dan 5:5).

As part of the world's literary or cultural canon, the Old Testament provides insights about the human condition. It explores topics such as political leadership, gender relationships, power disparities, personal strengths and weaknesses, as well as social and political ethics. As a source for the academic study of religion, the Old Testament provides insight into one example of religion over a thousand-year period as it was believed and practiced by one people. Many today, both inside and outside organized faith communities, find comfort in Psalms, challenge and hope in the Prophets, and ethical guidance in the Ten Commandments. As revered scripture, the Old Testament or Hebrew Bible has been a significant factor in shaping Judaism and Christianity, and its stories and characters have strong connections to Islam as well.

Chapter 1

Scripture and Canon

The faith communities of Judaism and Christianity recognize similar collections of religiously themed writings as authoritative. Christians designate the first section of their Bible as the *Old Testament*. Jewish scripture is often called the *Hebrew Bible*, among other names. Although today bound as a single volume, *Bibles* (from *biblia*, meaning *books* in Greek) are made up of what were originally individual documents written on separate scrolls. Thus the Old Testament and Hebrew Bible are really anthologies, collecting together various sorts of ancient literary compositions from different historical periods. These individual works were produced over the course of almost a thousand years by a people who knew themselves first as Israel and later as Jews.

The earliest biblical materials appear to be from the tenth century BCE. These are the legal document called the Covenant Code in Exodus 20:22–23:19 and the poetic Song of Deborah that makes up Judges 5. The latest book in the Hebrew Bible is Daniel (composed in 164), and certain books in the Old Testament of the Roman Catholic and Orthodox churches were composed somewhat later.

1.1. BCE AND CE

The calendar used almost universally today counts years in two eras, divided by what was once thought to be the year in which Jesus was born. This calculation was made in the sixth century CE, but the determination of the year of Jesus's birth (as year 1) was off by several years. Years in the present era are traditionally designated as AD (*Anno Domini*, "in the year of the Lord"), placed before the year number. Years before AD 1 are labeled with BC (before Christ), which comes after the year number. AD 1 comes immediately after 1 BC. There is no year zero. Because BC and AD have unambiguously Christian implications, modern historical and biblical scholarship commonly uses CE (for Common Era) instead of AD and BCE (before the Common Era) instead of BC. Keep in mind that dates in the BCE period count downward as time moves forward, so that 586 BCE is eleven years *after* 597 BCE. The eighth century BCE ran from 800 to 701 BCE. All dates in this book are BCE unless noted otherwise.

A recognized list of revered and authoritative religious books is called a *canon*. *Canon* derives from the Greek word meaning "reed used for measuring" and thus

– 4 –

"standard" or "norm." A scriptural canon is brought together over time by the needs and practices of a faith community. In the case of the Jewish people, a variety of literary works proved to be especially meaningful and useful to the community over the centuries. Books inherited from past generations were understood to speak words of challenge, comfort, and identity to Jews confronted by new situations and dangers. Those highly valued scrolls were reread, recopied, and sometimes expanded. Other, less popular works were not recopied so often, and many of these simply vanished. Books seen as most beneficial were increasingly drawn on as authoritative sources for teaching, ethics, self-identity, and worship life. Eventually and by degrees, these cherished books evolved into the canon of Judaism.

Christianity, at first a dissident movement within Judaism, used the evolving Jewish canon as scripture. Christians discovered material in those books that supported and gave expression to their belief that Jesus was the promised messiah and that the end of the present age was about to occur. However, because opinions and practices about certain books were still in flux among different groups of Jews in different parts of the world, the canons of Judaism and Christianity developed in different directions after the two religions diverged.

Table 1. Diverging Canons

JUDAISM	CATHOLIC/ ORTHODOX CHRISTIANITY*	PROTESTANT CHRISTIANITY
Torah (Law)	Pentateuch	Pentateuch
Genesis	Genesis	Genesis
Exodus	Exodus	Exodus
Leviticus	Leviticus	Leviticus
Numbers	Numbers	Numbers
Deuteronomy	Deuteronomy	Deuteronomy
Nebiim (Prophets)	History	History
Former Prophets		
Joshua	Joshua	Joshua
Judges	Judges	Judges
	Ruth	Ruth
Samuel (1 and 2)	1 and 2 Samuel	1 and 2 Samuel
Kings (1 and 2)	1 and 2 Kings	1 and 2 Kings
Latter Prophets	1 and 2 Chronicles	1 and 2 Chronicles
Isaiah	Ezra	Ezra
Jeremiah	Nehemiah	Nehemiah

Chapter 1

JUDAISM	CATHOLIC/ORTHODOX CHRISTIANITY*	PROTESTANT CHRISTIANITY
Ezekiel	Tobit	
The Twelve	Judith	
Hosea	Esther (with additions)	Esther
Joel	1 and 2 Maccabees	
Amos	**Poetry and Wisdom**	**Poetry and Wisdom**
Obadiah	Job	Job
Jonah	Psalms	Psalms
Micah	Proverbs	Proverbs
Nahum	Ecclesiastes	Ecclesiastes
Habakkuk	Song of Solomon	Song of Solomon
Zephaniah	Wisdom of Solomon	
Haggai	Sirach (Ecclesiasticus)	
Zechariah	**Prophets**	**Prophets**
Malachi	Isaiah	Isaiah
Kethuvim (Writings)	Jeremiah	Jeremiah
Psalms	Lamentations	Lamentations
Proverbs	Baruch	
Job	Ezekiel	Ezekiel
Five Scrolls	Daniel (with additions)	Daniel
Song of Songs	Hosea	Hosea
Ruth	Joel	Joel
Lamentations	Amos	Amos
Ecclesiastes (Qoheleth)	Obadiah	Obadiah
Esther	Jonah	Jonah
Daniel	Micah	Micah
Ezra–Nehemiah	Nahum	Nahum
Chronicles (1 and 2)	Habakkuk	Habakkuk
	Zephaniah	Zephaniah
	Haggai	Haggai
	Zechariah	Zechariah
	Malachi	Malachi

*Orthodox and Roman Catholic canons exhibit minor differences in order and naming. The Eastern Orthodox canon also includes 1 Esdras, 3 Maccabees, Psalm 151, and Prayer of Manasseh, with 4 Maccabees as an appendix. Chapter 6 of Baruch is treated separately as the Letter of Jeremiah. Slavonic Bibles (Russian and other Orthodox churches) include 3 Esdras.

The Jewish Canon of the Hebrew Bible

The biblical canon of Judaism consists of twenty-four books divided into three groups. These books are written in Hebrew, with parts of Daniel and Ezra composed in the related language of Aramaic. The *Torah* (Law or Teaching), consisting of five books, is assigned the highest level of sanctity. Authorship of these books was traditionally attributed to Moses. The *Nebiim* (Prophets) section incorporates four books recounting history (designated as Former Prophets) and four books conveying the words and actions of prophets (the Latter Prophets). In the Former Prophets section, Samuel and Kings are treated as single books. The Latter Prophets consist of Isaiah, Jeremiah, Ezekiel, and the book of the Twelve, which is made up of twelve shorter compositions grouped together. The eleven books of the final *Kethuvim* (Writings) subdivision are more diverse in content, incorporating poetry, wisdom, stories, and history. Ezra–Nehemiah and Chronicles are each reckoned as single books. The acronym *Tanak*, utilizing the first consonants of the three canonical divisions (*T*orah, *N*ebiim, *K*ethuvim), is a common designation for the canon of the Jewish Bible.

The historical path that led to these particular books being considered, first as respected and useful, and eventually as the only books in a closed and fixed canon, is obscure. The evidence is fragmentary and ambiguous. Pointers to this ongoing process do appear in the Hebrew Bible, however. Second Kings 23:1-3 reports that King Josiah of Judah had a newly rediscovered *covenant scroll* (or *Instruction scroll* according to 22:8, 11) read publicly, and then he proceeded to reform national religious life in accordance with it. The nature of his reforms indicate that this scroll was an early form of the book of Deuteronomy. According to Ezra 7:25-26, the priest Ezra was commissioned by the Persian imperial government to promulgate and enforce *the laws of your God*. Nehemiah 8:1-3 then recounts that Ezra read out the *Book of the Law of Moses* (or *Instruction scroll from Moses*, CEB) to the assembled nation. This document was almost certainly related in some way to portions of the present Torah section of the Jewish canon.

The division of the Hebrew Bible into three categories is historically significant. Because the Writings section is a relatively diverse collection of books mostly composed at a comparatively late date, scholars generally agree that the Torah and Prophets were together recognized as authoritative (or canonical) before the Writings. This conclusion is borne out by references to scripture in later texts. The book of Sirach (composed about 180) praises a catalogue of biblical heroes in chapters 44–49 that corresponds to the content and order of the Torah and Prophets, but does not mention any luminaries in the Writings section except for Nehemiah. The prologue to the Greek translation of Sirach (about 132) refers to *the Law, the Prophets, and the other ancestral scrolls* (vv. 8-10, similarly vv. 1-2 and 24-25). In Luke 24:44 (about 80–90 CE), Jesus expounds on *the Law of Moses, the Prophets, and the Psalms*.

The general outline of the Hebrew Bible canonization process may be expressed as follows. Two clusters of books that would come to be known as Torah and Prophets came together in the consciousness of the community as particularly authoritative. This development took place for the two collections in a parallel fashion, but perhaps the process finished first for the Torah. The connected narrative of Genesis through Numbers and then Deuteronomy constituted the Torah. At the conclusion of the Torah section, the appointment of Joshua by Moses in Deuteronomy linked directly forward to the continuous account of the books Joshua through Kings, and to this were added other books featuring prophets (Isaiah, Jeremiah, Ezekiel, and the Twelve). This Prophets collection was considered to be closed at some point, possibly as early as 350. Because of this, other valued materials such as Psalms could not be slotted into the Torah and Prophets collection and were labeled Writings. It is significant that the order of the books in the Writings section was never completely finalized in Jewish tradition. Several different sequences are represented in manuscripts and later printed versions.

Fig. 1. Aleppo Codex. This tenth-century CE Hebrew manuscript is the earliest example of the contribution of the Masoretes to the preservation of the text of the Hebrew Bible.

The canonical situation remained fluid up to the last part of the first century CE, in part because Judaism remained a diverse religion encompassing competing factions and movements. For example, the Dead Sea Scrolls produced or used by a dissident community at Qumran included copies of every book of the final form of the Jewish canon except Esther. However, that group also produced and collected a library of other works that supported their own particular interests and practices. Moreover, neither the content nor the order of the book of Psalms was stabilized in the Qumran community. In a similar way, quotations and allusions in the New Testament show that early Christianity, as a movement within Judaism, valued all the books of the Jewish canon that would later be fixed, but also several others.

It is impossible to fix a sharp date for closing the Jewish canon as an authoritatively fixed and settled list. The final delineation of the canon was triggered by two crises. First, the destruction of the Jerusalem temple in 70 CE required a recentering of Jewish religious life into other directions. Second, the expanding Christian movement challenged Jewish faith and identity. As a result, the wide variety of factions and trajectories within Judaism were replaced by the dominant Pharisee movement, which represented the future of Judaism. Rabbinic literature shows that by the second century CE, the extent and shape of the normative Jewish canon was fixed, and that for all practical purposes this process was completed by the end of the first century CE.

The Christian Canon of the Old Testament

The development of the Christian Old Testament canon diverged from that of Judaism after the two faith communities separated. This process began in the first century CE. Quotations and allusions in the New Testament show that the Christian movement adopted both the Jewish concept of authoritative scripture and the books of the evolving Jewish canon. Passages from those books were treated as sources for the proclamation of the Christian message and the understanding that Jesus was the promised messiah. Individual scriptural quotations were gathered into documents called *Testimonia* in order to provide background for events in the Jesus story, keys to an explanation of his mission, and apocalyptic teachings about the impending end of the world. The books most often quoted explicitly by the New Testament are Genesis, Deuteronomy, Isaiah, the twelve prophets, and Psalms.

Most Christians, however, utilized those books in Greek translation. Beginning around 250 BCE, Jews in Egypt had begun a process of translating the Hebrew Bible into Greek in order to meet the needs of Jewish communities in the Greek-speaking Mediterranean world. This translation process began with the five books of the Torah and then extended to other books. This compendium of translations was eventually called the *Septuagint* (related to the Latin word for "seventy") because of a legend that it had been produced simultaneously by seventy translators. The Septuagint is commonly designated by the Roman numeral LXX.

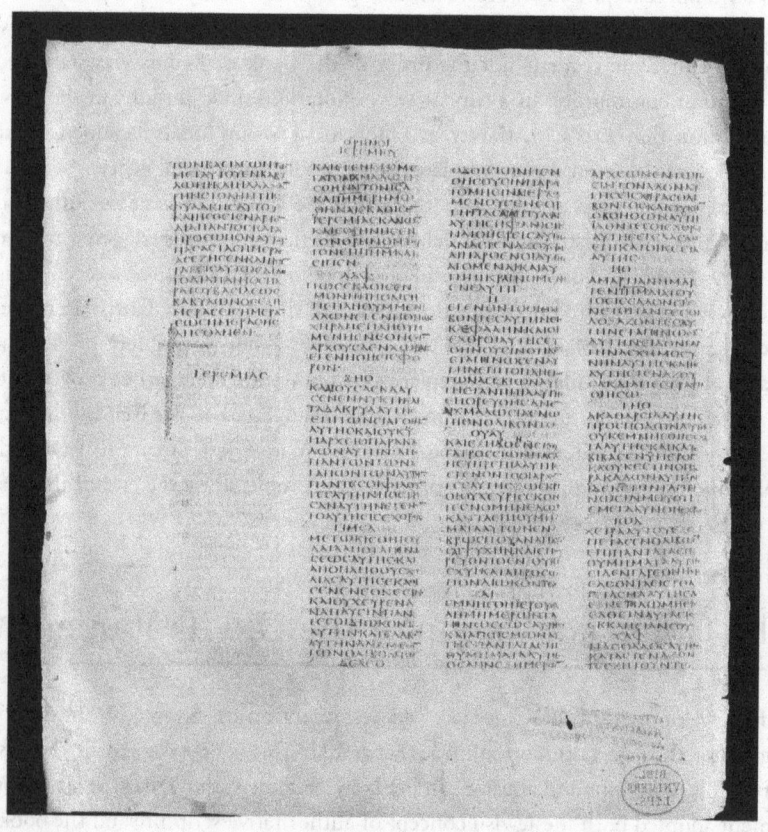

Fig. 2. Codex Sinaiticus. Produced in the fourth century CE, this is one of the most significant manuscripts of the Greek Septuagint.

The practice of treating scrolls accessible in Greek as scripture, combined with the circumstance that the concept of a fixed and closed canon had not yet completely taken hold in the first century CE, led Christians to value a wider roster of books than the twenty-four that eventually constituted the canon of Judaism. As a result, as the Christian Old Testament became fixed, most Christians ended up treating Tobit, Judith, 1 and 2 Maccabees, Wisdom of Solomon, Sirach, and Baruch as canonical scripture. Although several of these books had originally been written in Hebrew or Aramaic, their Greek translations were part of the Septuagint translation stream embraced by the Christian movement. To complicate matters further, the Greek versions of Esther and Daniel contained more material that the original Hebrew versions of those books.

Moreover, the order of books in the Christian canon is based on a different principle that that of the Jewish canon. Instead of a three-part division of Law, Prophets, and Writings, the Christian sequence follows the first five books (Pentateuch, Greek for *five volumes*) with books recounting history in chronological order. Judges is followed by Ruth. This historical sequence includes Tobit and Judith and ends with 1 Maccabees and 2 Maccabees. Books of a poetical and wisdom nature follow, with Job coming first, including Wisdom of Solomon and Sirach. The Christian canon sequence ends with the prophets, to which category Daniel is added. Works treated as single books in the Jewish canon are divided in the Christian canon: 1 and 2 Samuel, 1 and 2 Kings (actually 1–4 Reigns in the Septuagint), 1 and 2 Chronicles, and Ezra and Nehemiah. The twelve Minor Prophets appear as twelve individual books.

Thus, the Christian canon puts the prophets at end of the sequence and treats the apocalyptic book of Daniel as a prophetic book. This format may reflect early Christianity's strong interest in final judgment and the end of the world. The Christian Old Testament concludes with Malachi's promise of a future return of Elijah as messenger (Mal 3:1; 4:5), a theme that is picked up in the New Testament Gospels (for example, Matt 11:10). Most versions of the Hebrew Bible conclude instead with a reference to a return to Jerusalem (2 Chr 36:23). Consequently, the conclusion of the Hebrew Bible points to Jerusalem; the end of the Christian Old Testament points to the story of Jesus.

Christianity gradually abandoned the earlier scroll form for biblical books and produced its Bible in the codex format. This process culminated in the production of large codex Bibles in the fourth century CE. A codex consists of pages written on both sides and stitched together into a volume like a modern book. A codex was easier to consult than a scroll and could hold more text since each page had two sides for writing. The codex format meant that the notion of canon as an abstract list of separate works received a unitary physical form. Individual scrolls kept together in a basket or on a shelf were replaced by a single bound volume: the Bible. Judaism adopted the codex form for some manuscripts in the early eighth century CE.

1.2. CHAPTER AND VERSE

Modern Bibles are divided into chapters, which are further divided into numbered verses. The verse divisions of the Hebrew Bible go back to at least the early tenth century CE when punctuation marks indicating full stops were inserted into the text, although these were not numbered. This punctuation system was the contribution of the Masoretes. These were early medieval Jewish scholars who sought to achieve and transmit an accurate text of the Hebrew Bible. Numbered chapter divisions only came later, in the thirteenth century. This was a Christian innovation that appeared first in manuscripts of the Latin Bible. Printed Hebrew Bibles picked up this practice in the fifteenth century. This complex history sometimes resulted in discrepancies in chapter and verse numbering between the Hebrew Bible and versions based on Christian Bibles. For example, 1 Chronicles 5:27-41 in the Hebrew Bible is equivalent to 1 Chronicles 6:1-15 in most English-language Bibles. Deuteronomy 13:2 in the Hebrew Bible is Deuteronomy 13:1 in English versions. Such differences are usually noted in the footnotes of the CEB, NRSV, and other modern translations. This book uses the chapter and verse designations of the English Bible.

Differences between the Septuagint translation of the Old Testament consulted by Christians and the original Hebrew text used by Judaism became a source of controversy between the two rival faith communities. As the Christian church became culturally and politically dominant, it often used Septuagint renderings as a polemical weapon against Jews. In part as a reaction to a long and tragic history of persecution and misunderstanding, today some people object to calling the first part of the Christian canon the *Old* Testament in comparison with the New Testament. They argue that "old" implies a supersession of the Jewish scriptures as obsolete and inferior and their replacement by something new and better. They suggest replacement terms such as "First Testament" and "Second Testament" instead. In contrast, others point out that "old" does not necessarily imply any criticism and can refer merely to a difference in chronology. Certainly the New Testament itself values the Old Testament highly and treats it as scripture. In any case, the term *Old Testament* with reference to canon first appears in Christian writing at the end of the second century CE.

Catholic, Orthodox, and Protestant Canons

Developments in Christian history led to further complications. Western Christianity (centered at Rome) and Eastern Christianity developed various differences in theology and practice. The resulting alienation of the Latin Catholic West from the

Greek Orthodox East led to slight differences in their respective canons. Orthodox churches recognize a few more books as canonical than Catholic Christianity does. While the Eastern Church continued to use the Greek Septuagint as its Old Testament (along with translations based on it), Christians in the West began to utilize scripture in a Latin translation known as the Vulgate. This translation was made from the original Hebrew by Jerome at the end of the fourth and beginning of the fifth century CE.

Following the view of some earlier church leaders, Jerome advanced the opinion that books not found in the Hebrew Bible should not be considered canonical. He used the term *apocrypha* (hidden) for these books. Although Jerome's position was not adopted, a minority of Catholic theological thinkers continued to share his view. However, in the sixteenth century the emerging Protestant movement marginalized those books not found in the Hebrew Bible, sometimes explicitly denied their canonicity, and printed them as an isolated separate section in their Bibles as *Apocrypha*. For the books they retained as canon, Protestants continued to use the traditional sequence found in the Septuagint and Vulgate. In reaction, the Roman Catholic Church definitely affirmed the canonicity of seven disputed books at the Council of Trent (1546). These books are referred to as *deuterocanonical*. Until the nineteenth century, most Protestant Bibles continued to print the Apocrypha (with some variation as to what books were included) in a separate section. Today many study Bibles and ecumenical Bibles include the seven deuterocanonical books, along with other books valued by the Orthodox tradition.

As a result of this prolonged and complex process of evaluation, acceptance, and rejection, the Jewish canon and the Christian canons are characterized by diversity rather than uniformity. The Hebrew Bible and the Old Testament embrace different types of literature, display diverse ideologies and theologies, and reflect a wide range of historical periods. Because the Old Testament and Hebrew Bible are so pluralistic, they have been able to continue to function as scripture for their respective faith communities even as circumstances have radically changed over the centuries. In addition, the internal pluralism that characterizes the Bible means that some parts of the canon have been able to serve as alternative and corrective voices. These alternative voices can modify or push against other parts of the biblical text that may now be seen as inappropriate or morally problematic. The impact of the biblical canon on Judaism and Christianity has been and continues to be a dynamic process.

1.3. THE QURAN

Many Old Testament events and figures appear in the Quran, and the sacred text of Islam has its own perspective on these. Often biblical personages are mentioned only in passing.

In other cases more extensive particulars are recounted and expounded on. The creation of Adam and Eve (*Hawa*) and the first murder involving their sons receives attention. The Quran focuses on Noah's role as a messenger who warned people to turn from their sinful ways and was ignored. Abraham struggles against his father's idolatry. Ishmael, Abraham's son by Hagar, is a prophet and helps his father build the Kaaba in Mecca. The experiences of Joseph (*Yousuf*) as a model of virtue are recounted at length. Moses (*Musa*) is a prophet, along with his brother Aaron (*Harun*). The stories of the birth of Moses and the protective role of his (unnamed) sister, his killing the Egyptian, his encounters with Pharaoh, and the golden calf incident are recounted or touched on. The story of Jonah (*Yunus*) is told in some detail. The Queen of Sheba comes to Solomon at his command, is able to recognize her throne, which had been transferred to Solomon's place and disguised, and submits to the true God.

Establishing the Earliest Text

Any literature that has been transmitted from ancient times through a process of repeated hand copying will inevitably accumulate textual errors and uncertainties. The Old Testament is no exception, and the various paths through which it has come down to us give evidence of alterations and errors in copying that have crept into its text. The disciplined attempt to achieve an earlier and more correct text is called *text criticism*.

Such errors and variants originated in various ways. Letters were misread for other letters that looked similar. Words or lines were accidently left out, often because a scribe's eyes jumped over words or phrases that ended in a similar way. Sometimes words or lines were inadvertently repeated. Occasionally an explanatory or pious note that had been written into the margin of a manuscript would be mistakenly incorporated in the biblical text itself when it was recopied. Sometimes scribes thought that a word or passage was incorrect, offensive, or inappropriate and simply "corrected" it.

Evidence for making corrective judgments about the text comes from various sources. The work of the Jewish Masoretes, who guarded and transmitted the traditional Hebrew text in the early medieval period, preserves important information. The Samaritan religious group treasured their own version of the Torah (Samaritan

Pentateuch), which is sometimes different from the text handed down within Judaism. The Greek Septuagint translation reveals the wording of the Hebrew manuscripts that were used by its translators from about 250 BCE on. Manuscripts found among the Dead Sea Scrolls from Qumran show that competing texts of biblical books co-existed in the second and first century BCE.

Most modern Bibles use footnotes to indicate places where errors or alterations in the traditional Hebrew text have been corrected. However, for religious or cultural reasons, some Jewish and Christian faith communities continue to utilize only the traditional, standardized Hebrew text.

Further Reading

James C. Paget and Joachim Schaper, eds. *The New Cambridge History of the Bible.* Vol. 1, *From the Beginnings to 600.* New York: Cambridge University Press, 2013.

Lee Martin McDonald. *The Formation of the Biblical Canon: The Old Testament, Its Authority and Canonicity.* Vol. 1. New York: Bloomsbury T & T Clark, 2017.

Chapter 2
GEOGRAPHY, HISTORY, AND RELIGION

Geography

Israel's Homeland

Up until the late sixth century, the world of the Old Testament and its people consisted of a narrow strip of land between the Mediterranean Sea and desert lands to the east. This region is bounded on the south by the Sinai Desert and to the north by the Lebanon and Anti-Lebanon mountain ranges. It is naturally oriented north and south by its central mountain ridge and the valley of the Jordan River. An ancient name for the part of this region west of the Jordan was *Canaan*, a term that also incorporated lands farther to the north (today Lebanon). The Greeks and Romans termed this region *Palestine* after the Philistine people who lived on its southern coastlands. The name Palestine has become politically contentious in recent decades, but remains the most common designation for this territory in biblical studies. The Old Testament sometimes uses the phrase *from Dan to Beer-sheba* (for example, Judg 20:1) to designate the extent of the Israelite homeland. Israelites inhabited areas to the east of the Jordan River as well, and *Transjordan* is sometimes employed to refer to that region. Although the slopes down to the Jordan Valley are steep, the Jordan River itself could be crossed by fords at several points. Deserted, dry terrain surrounded Israel's homeland to the south and to the east.

Palestine forms the southern part of a region conventionally described as the Fertile Crescent. This arc of arable land stretches northward from Palestine and Syria and then eastward and southward down through Mesopotamia to the Persian Gulf. The eastern arm of this crescent is watered by the Euphrates and Tigris rivers and

Chapter 2

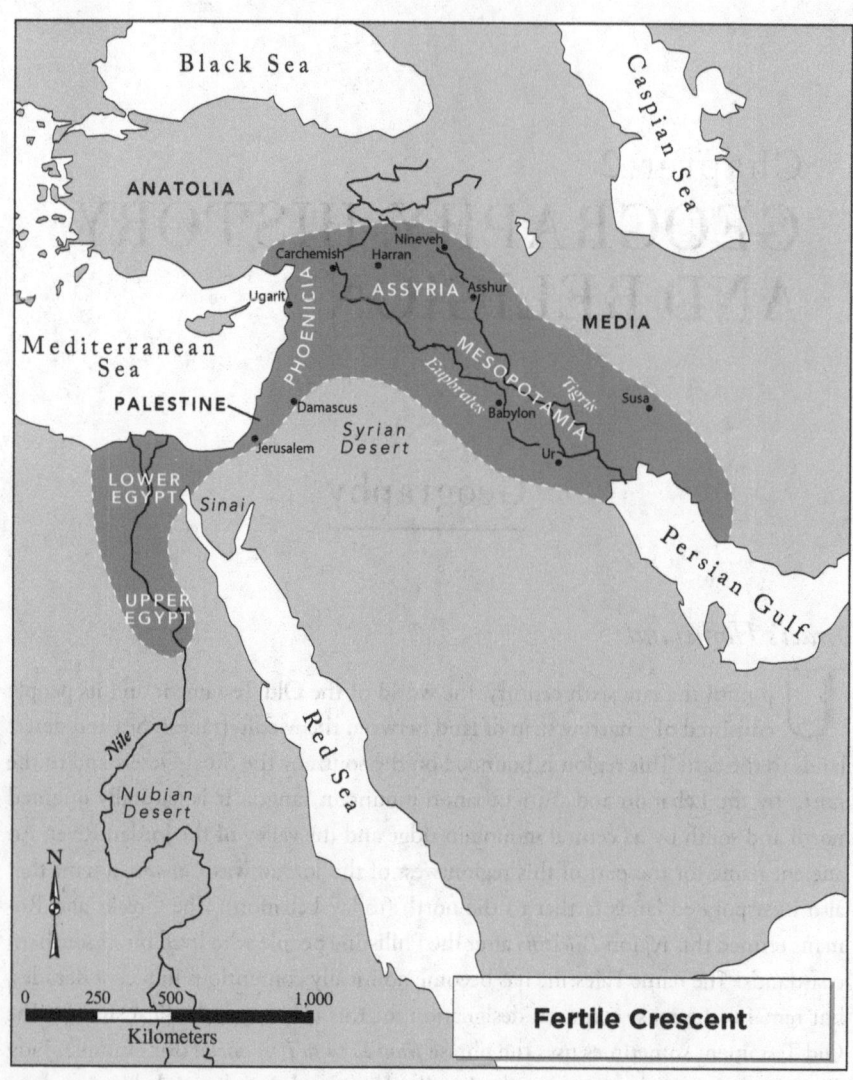

Map 1. Fertile Crescent

their tributaries. The western arm (Palestine and Syria) receives enough rain to make agriculture possible. The Fertile Crescent is bounded on the north and east by high mountain ranges. Within the southern concave hollow of its arc lies desert.

Israel's homeland formed a land bridge between the great power centers of the ancient world. Egypt lies to the south of this bridge, and Asia Minor and Mesopotamia are to the north. This fateful location meant that Palestine, especially its northern portion, was open to trade and outside influences. Foreign armies marched through Palestine on a regular basis. When both Egypt and Mesopotamia were robust and expansionistic, Palestine was an arena of conflict between them. When either Egypt or the empires to the north were dominant, the small nations of Syria and Palestine were subjugated. Only when both Egypt and the Mesopotamian states were weak or preoccupied with internal affairs could small states like Israel and Judah flourish. This, for the most part, was the geopolitical situation from about 1200 to about 745 BCE. Relative freedom from outside interference allowed Israel to develop as a people in the pre-monarchic period and then prosper for some centuries as two parallel kingdoms.

Physical Regions

The terrain of Palestine is rugged. There are no rivers helpful for agriculture and few good ports. The region is characterized by a rapid transition in topography and climate from west to east. A low coastal plain, poorly drained in ancient times, runs along the Mediterranean shoreline, growing narrower as one moves north. Much of the coastal plain between Joppa and Mount Carmel, called *Sharon*, was marshy and forested in ancient times. South of the Sharon are broken foothills, the *Shephelah* (lowland). Eastward from the coastal plain, the terrain rises to a region of central highlands and then drops off abruptly into the rift of the Jordan Valley. On the east side of the Jordan, the land rises again to an elevated plateau.

The north part of the central highlands (the *hill country* NRSV) of Ephraim was the heartland of the northern kingdom of Israel. After Assyria conquered this territory and incorporated it into its empire, it bore the name *Samaria*. The most important city in this region was Shechem, which guarded the strategic pass between the two mountains of Gerizim and Ebal. Judah's highlands (or *hill country*) lay to the south, with Jerusalem as the principal city. Several valleys run up to Judah's highlands from the coastal plain through the Shephelah, providing routes by which invading armies could threaten Jerusalem. Shechem and Jerusalem had each dominated their respective highland regions from at least the fourteenth century, long before the emergence of Israel. Consequently, the division of Israel's homeland into the two kingdoms of Judah in the south and Israel to the north seems to have been a fundamental administrative reality caused by economic and topographic differences.

Chapter 2

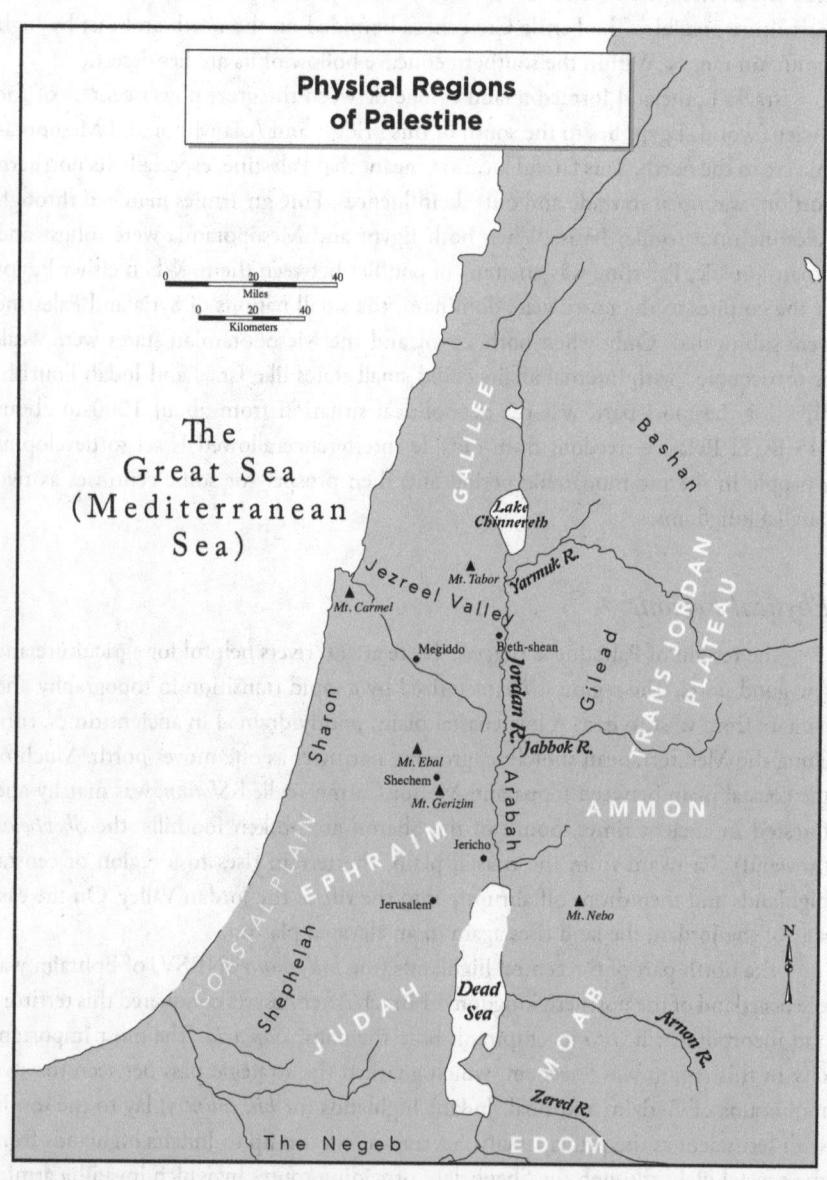

Map 2. Physical Regions of Palestine

The wide and fertile *Jezreel Valley* (or Esdraelon) runs west to east. It divides the northern part of the central highlands from the region of Galilee to the north. The Jezreel Valley was (and is) a rich agricultural region. It provided an easy pathway for both international trade and invading armies. The port city of Acco was situated at its northwest terminus. The route through the valley was dominated by the cities of Megiddo to the west and Beth-shean to the east, where the Jezreel Valley meets the Jordan Valley.

Lower (southern) *Galilee* features fertile valleys. Upper (northern) Galilee is more rugged and reaches higher elevations. In ancient times, much of both Galilee and the central highlands was forested.

East of the central highlands, the Jordan River runs through *Lake Chinnereth* (New Testament: Sea of Galilee). It then descends through a deep valley (the *Arabah*). The northern portion of this valley is mostly fertile, but farther south the Arabah becomes desert. The existence of the very ancient city of Jericho there was made possible by a plentiful perennial spring. Ravines go up westward from Jericho, one of which leads directly to Jerusalem. The Dead Sea marks the lowest elevation on earth, and because it has no outlet, it has a high concentration of salt and other dissolved minerals. The Arabah continues southward to the Gulf of Aqaba, an arm of the Red Sea.

To the east of the Jordan Valley and Dead Sea rises a plateau, where rain dropped by prevailing west winds makes cultivation and stock raising possible. Farther east lies desert. Four waterways cut up the area east of the Jordan. The *Yarmuk* River runs into the Jordan just south of the Sea of Galilee and divides *Bashan* to the north from *Gilead* to the south. Bashan and Gilead were part of the Israelite homeland. Farther south, about halfway down the Jordan, the *Jabbok* drains Gilead. The *Arnon* runs into the Dead Sea at about its midpoint. The *Zered* enters the Dead Sea at its south end.

The region's most important travel route ran northward from Egypt along the Mediterranean coast, keeping a few miles inland in order avoid sandy and marshy ground. As it headed north, the route was forced inland by Mount Carmel and proceeded to Megiddo, where it divided. One branch went north by heading back westward to the seacoast at Acco and on to Phoenicia through Tyre and Sidon. The other branch went eastward along the Jezreel Valley and then turned north along the west side of Lake Chinnereth to Damascus. East of the Jordan River, a second international trade route ran northward along the plateau from the Gulf of Aqaba to Damascus. Numbers 20:17 calls this Transjordan route the King's Highway. A road of regional importance ran along the central spine of the central highlands linking Beer-sheba, Hebron, Jerusalem, Bethel, and Shechem.

Map 3. Important Urban Centers

Climate and Agriculture

Prevailing winds blow from northwest to southeast across Palestine. This means that there is more rainfall in northern areas, making the northern kingdom of Israel generally more fertile and prosperous than Judah to the south. Moving south, the territory of Judah becomes increasingly dry until the Negeb desert begins around Beer-sheba.

Israelite farmers practiced a mixed, subsistence economy, which provided greater food security than a focus on only a few crops. Palestine has two seasons, a hot, dry summer and a cooler and wetter winter. October *early rains* soften the ground for plowing, followed by sowing and planting. The *late rains* of April and early May conclude the growing season. The grain harvest took place in May and June, beginning with barley followed by wheat. The harvest of grapes and summer fruits such as dates and figs took place July through August, followed by olives in October and November. In biblical times, the staple foodstuffs were barley and wheat bread, olive oil, and wine. Dates, figs, chickpeas, and lentils supplemented the diet. Sheep and goats provided textiles, milk, meat, and manure for fertilizer. Oxen served to pull plows and threshing sledges.

> ### 2.1. THE GEZER CALENDAR
>
> An inscription from the tenth century coordinates the lunar months with Palestine's agricultural cycle. This Gezer Calendar sheds light on Israel's agricultural life and its religious calendar. The inscription seems to negotiate the interaction between the experience of farmers, whose lives were scheduled by natural cycles, and centralized authorities who scheduled tax collections and impositions of forced labor on the basis of the twelve-month lunar calendar. One plausible way to interpret this ancient agricultural "to do list" is:
>
> Two months of [olive] harvest (October, November)
>
> Two months of planting (December, January)
>
> Two months of late sowing (February, March)
>
> A month of cutting flax (April)
>
> A month of harvesting grain (May)
>
> A month of harvesting and measuring grain (June)

> Two months of harvesting grapes (July, August)
>
> A month of gathering summer fruit (September)

The Gezer Calendar begins in the fall, as does the calendar used in Judaism today, although biblical Israel usually counted months starting in spring. Israel's three pilgrimage festivals marked successive stages of harvest: barley (Passover/Unleavened Bread), wheat (Feast of Weeks), and summer fruits like olives, grapes, and figs (Feast of Booths). (*ANET* 320; *COS* 2.85:222)

Fig. 3. The Gezer Calendar is written in Canaanite or paleo-Hebrew script and is dated to the tenth century on that basis. It was discovered in 1908.

Palestine's broken landscape restricted trade. Only olive oil and wine, which have a high value-to-weight ratio, could be trafficked beyond a limited area. Rugged topography tended to divide the population into different ways of life. Fortified, major cities were located in the coastal lowlands, the Jezreel Valley, and the upper Jordan Valley. Each urban area was surrounded and sustained by its own agricultural land and dependent rural villages. These major cities predated the emergence of Israel and included Gezer, Megiddo, Taanach, Beth-shean, and Hazor. Before the establishment of the kingdoms of Israel and Judah, these cities were controlled by local kings and supported an elite class of professional warriors capable of fielding chariots. In contrast, the population of the central highlands and southern Galilee lived in small, unwalled villages. They kept flocks and herds and raised a variety of crops, but only for local consumption.

Neighboring Peoples

The *Philistines* play a role in many Old Testament narratives. Originating from the Aegean region or the southern coast of Asia Minor, they had moved into the southern coastal area of Palestine in the first part of the twelfth century. These colonists formed a military elite who came to dominate the indigenous population and created a hybrid culture. According to the Bible, Philistia was composed of five city-states: Gaza, Ashkelon, Gath, Ashdod, and Ekron.

The term *Canaanites* had been used earlier by Egyptians and others to refer to the inhabitants of Phoenicia and of Palestine west of the Jordan River. The Old Testament uses Canaanite to designate non-Israelites whose land had been wrested away by Israel. In reality, Israel and those described as Canaanites shared essentially the same language and many elements of culture and religious practice. Today it is thought that Israel and Canaan represented not so much different ethnic groups as rival cultures and economic systems inhabiting the same territory. Palestine's urban population in the twelfth and eleventh centuries was culturally Canaanite, and its rural, highland population was emerging as a new political, cultural, and religious entity that can be identified as Israel. In spite of (or because of) these numerous close similarities, the Old Testament consistently condemns Canaanite religion and civilization as something negative and dangerous.

Canaanite language and culture stretched northward along the coast of present-day Lebanon. At the time of Israel's emergence, about 1200, the city of Ugarit on the Mediterranean coast was a center of Canaanite culture. Documents from Ugarit shed light on many aspects of the religion, language, literary traditions, and legal practices reflected in the Old Testament. Later, the cities of Tyre and Sidon emerged as centers of Phoenician civilization. In the eighth century, mass emigration from Phoenicia colonized locations in the Mediterranean (Cyprus, Sicily, Sardinia), North

Africa (most notably Carthage), and Spain. The language and civilization of this later migration is termed Punic.

Three kingdoms developed in areas east of the Jordan River (*Moab* and *Ammon*) and south of the Dead Sea (*Edom*). These nations were culturally and linguistically similar to the kingdoms of Israel and Judah. Moab's undisputed territory lay between the Arnon and Zered watercourses. In the ninth century, Moab and Israel fought over contested territory north of the Arnon River. Ammon consisted of territory surrounding its capital Rabbath-ammon (today Amman, the capital of Jordan). Edom occupied territory south of the Zered and the Dead Sea. These kingdoms collapsed under the onslaught of Neo-Babylonian imperialism about the same time as Judah did.

By the early to mid-tenth century, several states founded by Aramaic-speaking groups (*Arameans*) had emerged in what is today Syria. Most significant for the biblical story was the kingdom centered on Damascus, designated as *Aram* (or Syria) in the Old Testament. Other Aramean kingdoms were *Geshur* and *Maacah*, east and north of the Sea of Galilee, and *Zobah*, north of Damascus in what is today Lebanon.

History of the Pre-Exilic Period

Pre-Monarchic Period (about 1200 to 1000 BCE)

Israel emerged in the context of a period of great social and economic upheaval. The transition from the archaeological period of the Late Bronze Age (about 1550–1200) to the Iron Age I (about 1200–1000) was a time of profound change, involving the collapse of the Hittite Empire in Asia Minor and the weakening of Assyria. Large-scale movements of displaced or aggressive peoples took place. Egypt was endangered by migrating peoples from the Aegean and Asia Minor, including the Peleset (that is, the Philistines). The umbrella term *Sea Peoples* is used to refer to these invaders and migrants. Egypt's control of Canaan weakened after about 1200 BCE and came to an end around the mid-twelfth century. This power vacuum in the region allowed for new political and social arrangements to develop, including the emergence of Israel.

The first mention of the existence of a people in Palestine named Israel was by Pharaoh Merneptah in a propagandistic inscription from about 1208 BCE. A few years earlier Merneptah had campaigned in Canaan in order to shore up deteriorating Egyptian control there. Looking back to this campaign in his inscription, Merneptah celebrated victories over a people called Israel, as well as over three cities. He proclaimed,

Fig. 4. The Merneptah Stele memorializes that Pharaoh's victories and contains the first extra-biblical mention of Israel. A stele is an upright stone slab.

"Israel is wasted, its seed is not" (*COS* 2.6:40). It is apparent that this Israel group was a significant foe, important enough to serve the inscription's purpose of honoring the king. However, it remains uncertain exactly how the Israel mentioned by Merneptah relates to biblical Israel. Probably the inscription refers to only one of several population elements that eventually coalesced into Israel. During the pre-monarchic era, Israel was characterized by tribal structures and rule by local strong men. It had not yet developed into a nation state.

Chapter 2

Monarchic Period (about 1000 to 586 BCE)

The tenth century ushered in a pattern of centralized state organization, with which the figures of Saul, David, and Solomon are traditionally associated. Beginning about 930, the political situation evolved into two complementary and sometimes rival kingdoms: Israel and Judah. The inhabitants of these two kingdoms shared much the same culture, spoke the same language, and venerated Yahweh as their national God.

The northern kingdom of Israel experienced numerous upheavals and was ruled by several royal dynasties in turn. The most significant of these dynasties were those founded by Omri (four kings from about 880 to a little before 840) and Jehu (five kings from a little before 840 to about 745). After a period of intense internal conflict in response to increasing pressure from the growing empire of Assyria, Israel lost a large expanse of territory to Assyria in 732. The kingdom of Israel survived in much reduced form until about 720, when it was completely conquered by the Assyrians and incorporated into their empire. Assyria engaged in a policy of forced resettlement, moving elements of the population of Israel into other parts of their empire and importing elements of other conquered peoples to replace them.

Judah was less powerful and internationally significant than Israel, but at the same time more internally unified and stable. In contrast to the multiplicity of dynasties that governed Israel, only one royal family, "the house of David," reigned over Judah. Its capital Jerusalem was an ancient and well-fortified power center and featured a temple to Yahweh that became more and more important. Judah persisted more than a century longer than Israel, retaining its independence until the early sixth century. Before this, however, Judah and Jerusalem had barely survived an Assyrian invasion in 701 and had lost a strip of territory to the west. Judah eventually fell to the Neo-Babylonian Empire, which had superseded Assyria. King Nebuchadnezzar overcame Jerusalem twice, first in 597, and then decisively in 586. Leaving most ordinary people behind, the Babylonians deported the upper classes and ruling elements of Judah into agricultural resettlement projects in Mesopotamia.

Religion

Devotion to Israel's national God, Yahweh, was apparently not indigenous to Canaan. For example, hardly any place names in Canaan incorporate Yahweh as an element, in contrast to locations such as Bethel and Peniel (the god El) or Anathoth (the goddess Anat). Yahweh seems to have been a cultural import from further south, as indicated by traditional poetry that describes Yahweh's passage as a warrior deity from Sinai and other southern regions (Deut 33:2; Judg 5:4-5; Hab 3:3). (See 10.1, DIVINE WARRIOR).

In the early period, the practices of Israel's religion did not differ much from those of its neighbors. Of course, what is conventionally called "Canaanite religion" was polytheistic, while the gradually developing ideal in Israel was loyalty to a single national deity, Yahweh. However, both Israel's practice of animal sacrifice and the names of its various sacrifices correspond to what is known of Canaanite religion from extra-biblical texts.

Yahweh and the Gods

El (as incorporated into the name Isra*el* or Beth*el*) was the proper name of a deity well-known from texts originating from outside Israel. El appears with various titles in the Old Testament, especially in the Genesis narratives. Over time, Israelite worshippers apparently simply treated El as the equivalent of Yahweh. The relatively colorless El, who is represented in extra-biblical texts as distant from human concerns, presumably presented no particular threat to the position of Yahweh. Thus, the identification of El with Yahweh was straightforward and unproblematic. Sometimes the name El was expanded with further designations. For example, *El Shaddai*, conventionally translated as *God Almighty*, is associated with Abraham (Gen 17:1) and with Jacob at Bethel (Gen 35:11; 48:3). Exodus 6:3 explicitly identifies El Shaddai with Yahweh. *El ʿOlam* is conventionally translated *Everlasting God*. Genesis 21:33 locates this name at Beer-sheba and identifies this deity with Yahweh. In Genesis 33:20, Jacob builds an altar at Shechem and names it *El Elohe Israel* (*El, God of Israel*). Jacob also erects an altar for Yahweh at Bethel and names the holy place *El-bethel* (Gen 35:7). Genesis 14 uses the title *El ʿElyon* (*God Most High*) for the deity of Jerusalem (Salem). Various lines of evidence suggest that El ʿElyon was the preeminent god of Jerusalem in pre-Israelite times. Jerusalem did not become part of the Israelite realm until the time of David (about 1000). Several psalms use poetic parallelism to equate Yahweh and Elyon (for example, Pss 18:13; 21:7). Apparently, the worship of Yahweh at Jerusalem adopted this name from the religion of the city's pre-Israelite inhabitants.

Baal is a title meaning "lord" or "owner." In texts from Ugarit, Baal is a god of storm and fertility. The proper name of this cosmic Baal was Hadad. The Old Testament makes it clear that Baal was popular with Israelites, who were naturally concerned with the fertility of their fields and domestic animals. Israel worshipped Baal at numerous local shrines. Many people did not see any contradiction in simultaneously worshipping Yahweh as a national war god and Baal as their benefactor in the realm of fertility. At times, devotion to Baal was promoted by kings, most infamously by Ahab of Israel and Jezebel his foreign queen.

2.2. ASHERAH

Israel's religious life was a more complicated affair than the reader of the final form of the Old Testament would be likely to assume. The controversial topic of the role of the *asherah* is a striking example of this complexity. In the period before the emergence of Israel, Asherah (as a proper name) is featured in Ugaritic texts as a mother goddess and consort of the high god El. Although Asherah does appear a few times as the name of a deity in Old Testament texts, the word is nearly always a common noun. As such it denotes a sacred pole or tree associated with a worship site. It seems likely that asherah poles were venerated as icons of a numinous power able to promote the fertility of a person's crops, animals, and family. There is disagreement, however, regarding to what degree the asherah was conceptualized as a concrete personification of the power of fertility (that is to say, a goddess) and whether it (or she) was sometimes treated as Yahweh's wife or consort.

Two sets of inscriptions provide background, but have not settled the controversy. Kuntillet 'Ajrud, a mid-ninth to mid-eighth-century site located on a trade route in Judah, preserved inscriptions and pictorial representations of figures that seem to be deities. These inscriptions mention Baal and El, but their most striking elements are wishes for blessing by "Yahweh and his asherah." The reference to asherah could relate to an associated drawing of a female figure. At Khirbet el Qom, also in Judah, a tomb from the late eighth century revealed an inscription that appears to indicate that Yahweh had saved someone named Uriyahu from his enemies "by his asherah." The grammar of these inscriptions point to asherah being considered as a common noun (*his* asherah) and not a personal name. Most likely this refers to a power for fertility associated with the wooden asherah pole and not to a full-fledged goddess. (*COS* 2.47A–D:171–73; *COS* 2.52:179).

The Name Yahweh

The specific name for the God of the Old Testament is *Yahweh*. This is God's proper name, comparable to Venus or Mars. In a polytheistic environment like that of the earlier portions of the Old Testament, deities needed to have proper names so they could be invoked and spoken about without ambiguity. As suggested by the narrative of Moses's encounter with Yahweh at the burning bush (Exod 3:14–15), the name Yahweh is related to the third person singular of the Hebrew verb "to be," which is to say, *the One who is*. Converted into the first person when God speaks, the name becomes, *I Am* or *I Am Who I Am*. Other possible interpretations of the verbal impact of the name Yahweh are *the One who will be* or *the One who causes to be*. The divine name appears in Hebrew manuscripts as the four consonants YHWH, called the Tetragrammaton (Greek: "four letters"). This was almost certainly pronounced Yahweh. Over time, it was thought inappropriate to pronounce God's name, in part from a desire to obey the commandment prohibiting the empty use of Yahweh's name (Exod 20:7). One effect of this development was a reediting of some biblical texts in order to change the name *Yahweh* to the title *Lord*. This process can be observed by comparing Psalm 14 with Psalm 53.

In some manuscripts the consonants YHWH were provided with vowels directing readers to say *my Lord* (*'adonay*) instead of pronouncing the name. A medieval misunderstanding of this convention led some Christians to use the hybrid form *Jehovah*. The Septuagint replaced Yahweh with the Greek word for *Lord* (*kyrios*). Most modern translations follow this practice and represent Yahweh with *Lord* written in small capitals (LORD).

The generic or non-specific designation for Israel's deity is *Elohim*, translated as God. *Elohim* is plural in form. When *Elohim* is used as a name or proper noun, it is grammatically singular. When it is used as a common noun to denote gods and goddesses in general, it operates grammatically as a plural noun.

Holy Places

Israelites and their neighbors considered distinctive natural features, such as mountains (Exod 3:12; Josh 8:30-31), trees (Gen 13:18; 21:33; Josh 24:26; Hos 4:13), and water sources (Gen 16:7; 26:24-25), to be holy places where interaction with divine power could be expected. Traditions of an appearance by God or a divine messenger to an ancestor or hero would authorize such places as sites for worship (Gen 18:1; 26:23-25; 35:1). Recounting stories that connected a sanctuary to an ancestor such as Abraham or Jacob was a way of claiming it as a worship location for Israel, even if it had formerly been used by another people to honor a different god. Examples of this divine appearance or *theophany* tradition involving Jacob are Genesis 28:11-22 and 35:1-7 (Bethel), 32:24-32 (Penuel), and 33:18-20 (Shechem). Similar traditions connected Abraham to holy sites at Shechem, Bethel, and Beer-sheba (Gen 12:6-8; 13:3-4; 21:33). The Oaks of Mamre site was associated with Abraham and Sarah (Gen 18:1-15; 13:18). Abraham offered sacrificial gifts at

Jerusalem (Salem; Gen 14:17-20). The divine messenger from Yahweh appeared at Jerusalem to stop a plague, and David built an altar at that spot (2 Sam 24:16, 25).

An open-air holy place was called a *high place* (Hebrew: *bamah*; CEB: *shrine*). In contrast to a temple building, high places were outdoor installations, sometimes located on a prominent hill or a built-up platform. The high place presided over by Samuel had a banquet hall for eating the sacrifices offered there (1 Sam 9:22). A shrine would have an earthen or stone altar for sacrifice. The primary purpose of an altar was to serve as a platform for the fire that consumed the offering. Altars were also places where blood from an animal sacrifice was applied or disposed of and beside which offerings to God could be set (Deut 26:4). Altars were focal points for religious processions (Ps 26:6). In the early period, sacrifice was carried out by ordinary individuals, usually the head of the household. Priests emerged later as a special class of ritual specialists.

In the realm of private life, houses often contained domestic shrines with devotional figurines of women or horses with riders, along with equipment for pouring out drink offerings and burning incense. Women no doubt participated in (and presided at) those household rituals, but they also assisted with public worship in support roles (Exod 35:25-26; 38:8) and in the much-discussed position of *qedesha* (*consecrated woman*, CEB: *consecrated worker*). The function of these female religious specialists remains unresolved, although it is doubtful that they served as temple prostitutes (Hos 4:14; Gen 38:21-22; Deut 23:17-18). Women performed in worship as singers and dancers (Ps 68:24-25; perhaps Ezra 2:65). They attended pilgrimage festivals (Deut 12:12, 18; 16:11, 14) and public worship gatherings (Deut 29:10-11; 31:12; Ezra 10:1; Neh 12:43). Samuel's mother Hannah not only shared in the family sacrificial meal (1 Sam 1:4-5), but is paired with her husband in sponsoring sacrifice (1 Sam 1:24-25; 2:19-20).

Further Reading

Richard D. Nelson. *Historical Roots of the Old Testament (1200–63 BCE)*. Atlanta: SBL Press, 2014.

Patrick D. Miller. *Religion of Ancient Israel*. Louisville, KY: Westminster John Knox, 2007.

Part II

TORAH

Chapter 3
INVESTIGATING THE PENTATEUCH

The five books Genesis, Exodus, Leviticus, Numbers, and Deuteronomy make up the first section of the Hebrew Bible, called the Torah. They are also called the Pentateuch (Greek: "five books") or the books of Moses, reflecting the traditional view that he was their author. Torah is conventionally translated as *Law*, but a better rendering is *Instruction* (see CEB) or *Teaching*. The basic framework of the Torah is really an extensive narrative, which pauses now and then to incorporate legal material. The story begins with the creation of the cosmos and humanity and ends in Deuteronomy with Israel poised on the threshold of its new homeland.

The Documentary Hypothesis

Irregularities and Inconsistencies

The alert reader of the Pentateuch will discover irregularities and unevenness. Some of these issues were already recognized by early rabbis and church teachers. For example, some stories are told more than once. Different accounts of Abraham fearing that he was in danger and saying that his wife Sarah was his sister are told in Genesis 12 and 20. A similar story is told about Isaac and Rebekah in Genesis 26. Yahweh makes a promise to Abraham in Genesis 12 in terms of a blessing, and the same deity bearing the name God Almighty does much the same thing in terms of a covenant in Genesis 17. There are two parallel stories about God rescuing and providing water for Hagar and her son Ishmael, one in Genesis 16 and one in Genesis 21. Matching lists of forbidden foods occur in Leviticus 11 and Deuteronomy 14. Often sentences seem to be repeated unnecessarily, as in the case of Genesis 32:22 and 23. There are doublets of names: Abram and Abraham, Sarai and Sarah, Jacob and Israel. The mountain of divine revelation is usually called Sinai, but sometimes Horeb. The father-in-law of Moses is usually Jethro (Exod 3:1), but at other times Reuel (Exod 2:18).

According to Genesis 1:24-27, animals were created first, and then male and female human beings. According to Genesis 2:4-25, the male human was created first, then the animals were formed from the earth, and only after this was the female human created. In reading the flood story in Genesis 7, the reader may wonder how many pairs of ritually clean animals entered the ark. There are seven pairs in 7:2, but apparently only one pair in 7:15-16. Sometimes laws differ. According to Deuteronomy 12:13-14 there is to be one altar only, but Exodus 20:24-25 appears to envisage multiple altars.

One variation struck early modern biblical scholars as particularly significant. Some portions of the Torah consistently use the generic, non-specific designation for the deity, namely *Elohim* (that is, God). Other sections refer to the deity as *Yahweh*, using the specific or proper name for Israel's God. According to Genesis 4:26, people began invoking the name Yahweh soon after the creation of humanity. However, Exodus 6:2-3 reports that Yahweh revealed the special name for the first time to Moses and had interacted with Israel's ancestors under another name.

A careful reading of the story of Joseph and his brothers in Genesis 37 reveals a confusing situation. The brothers plot to kill Joseph and throw his body into a pit when they see him arriving, but Reuben rescues him by suggesting they simply put him in a pit with no water and let nature take its course. They do so, but Reuben plans to rescue him later (37:19-24). When Judah sees a caravan of Ishmaelites, he proposes that they not kill Joseph but sell him, as though they had not already decided to spare his life (37:25-27). Then some Midianites arrive in 37:28 and they pull Joseph out and they sell him to Ishmaelites. When Reuben comes to rescue Joseph, he is unaccountably surprised to find his brother gone (37:29-30). In the end it is Midianites (not Ishmaelites) who sell Joseph in Egypt (v. 36).

Such variations and irregularities can be explained in several ways. A single author or group of authors might have gathered material from a variety of sources. Different forms of the name for God might have been thought to be appropriate in different contexts. Until the last two centuries, almost all Jews and Christians assigned the authorship of the Torah to Moses as a single author and read its five books without these anomalies causing any particular concern. However, the issue is not really one of inconsistencies alone but of differences and variations that cluster together in the same sections in a consistent way. This circumstance points to elements from originally independent documents being used as building blocks to create the final whole. In some cases these building blocks were left relatively intact. In other case, independent versions of similar stories were woven together into a composite narrative. This is the case in the flood narrative and the Joseph story.

Documents Combined into the Torah Story

This explanatory model for the origin of the Torah is called the Documentary Hypothesis. Although questions about the authorship of Moses and suggestions of earlier sources emerged in the seventeenth and eighteenth centuries CE, the Documentary Hypothesis in its classic form developed in the last half of the nineteenth century. Elements of the Pentateuch were traced back to four originally independent hypothetical sources: the Yahwist (J, from German *Jahwe*), the Elohist (E), the Deuteronomist (D), and the Priestly Writing (P). (For the D source, mostly confined to the book of Deuteronomy, see chapter 9.) Differences in style and vocabulary, theology, and themes were found to cluster together into these four groups of texts. An important criterion for assigning material to the J, E, D, or P documents was how those four sources dealt with the name for Israel's God. According to the J source, people invoked the name Yahweh from very early times (Gen 4:26). The verbal basis of the sacred name is revealed to Moses in Exodus 3:13-14, according to E. In the Priestly Writing (P), Yahweh does not reveal his name until Exodus 6:2-3.

Yahwist and Elohist

In sections in which the name Yahweh is used (that is the Yahwist source, J), the previous inhabitants of the region are named Canaanites, the mountain of lawgiving is called Sinai, and the deity is presented in a distinctly anthropomorphic way. In these narratives, the God named Yahweh is closely involved in human matters and often speaks directly to people. Yahweh walks about in Eden and gets angry. Yahweh is a "hands-on" deity who shapes humans out of dust and a rib, who makes clothes for the first humans, and who closes up the ark (Gen 2:7, 22; 3:21; 7:16). Yahweh smells the pleasing fragrance of sacrifice (Gen 8:21). In material from the Yahwist, Abraham is able to negotiate with Yahweh over the fate of Sodom (Genesis 18). At one point the Yahwist even reports that Yahweh tried to kill Moses (Exod 4:24). If one isolates all the passages typically assigned to J, one can trace a fairly well-connected storyline. A pattern of promise and anticipated fulfillment runs through this narrative (for example, Gen 12:2-3; 13:14-17; 18:18-19). The Yahwist is usually dated to the monarchy period and thought to have originated in Judah.

Likewise, a number of passages using the generic name for God (the Elohist source, E) designate the inhabitants of the land as Amorites and the mountain of divine revelation as Horeb. In those sections, God communicates indirectly, in dreams (Gen 20:3; 28:12) or by means of a divine messenger (Gen 21:17; 22:11; Exod 3:2). The Elohist displays an interest in the prophetic office and designates Abraham as a prophet (Gen 20:7). Only fragments of E material exist, and E may not have been a continuous written document like the Yahwist. E passages do not appear until

Genesis 20. It is not always possible to separate J and E in a convincing manner. However, the contrast between the two seems clear when comparing the double narratives about Abraham and his sister/wife Sarah (J: Gen 12:10-20; E: 20:1-18), Hagar and Ishmael (J: 16:4-14; E: 21:8-21), or Beer-sheba (J: 26:26-33; E: 21:22-34). The Elohist embodies the traditions and geographical interests of the northern kingdom.

3.1. ANGELS

From both Hebrew and Greek, the word translated *angel* (which is a cognate from the Greek *angelos*) in many translations can also be translated *messenger*. Angels are understood to be messengers from the divine realm. In Genesis 28:12, the messengers from God are portrayed as going up and down a stairway (or ladder) and in this way serving as a communication link between heaven and earth. These messengers belonged to a broader class of transcendent beings who attended Yahweh in heaven and performed the divine will. (See 5.2, DIVINE BEINGS.) As a specific entity, the *angel of Yahweh* (CEB: *the Lord's messenger*) appears to humans such as Hagar, Moses, or Gideon in order to communicate commissions or promises. This discrete figure is directly associated with Yahweh. In places the Lord's messenger is in effect the form or disguise in which Yahweh appears to humans. In Judges 6, for example, Gideon first encounters the Lord's messenger (6:11-12), but this figure quickly transforms into Yahweh in 6:14 and 16. The Lord's messenger performs divine actions such as inflicting a plague or slaughtering enemy troops (2 Sam 24:16-17; 2 Kgs 19:35).

Later on, divine messengers became more prominent and acquired specialized duties and personal names. Zechariah, for example, experiences visions in which messengers are conspicuous participants. A messenger explains visionary matters to him (Zechariah 1–6) and to Daniel (Dan 8:15-16). Tobit's companion angel takes human form, but only pretends to eat and drink (Tob 12:19). Three messengers are given names in the Old Testament: Gabriel and Michael in Daniel and Raphael in Tobit. In later Jewish literature, such as 1 Enoch and materials from Qumran, the number and roles of angels are greatly elaborated. The term *angelology* is used to describe this growing body of tradition and thought. The New Testament reflects many of these developments.

The Priestly Writing

The Priestly Writing is the easiest of the sources to recognize. In P, religious instruction outweighs narrative. Whole blocks of text demonstrate a concern for matters of interest to priests, such as calendar, chronology, sacrifice, and law. The Priestly Writing includes many genealogies. The P creation story that begins Genesis conceives of Sabbath as foundational to the created order, because God rested on that day and made it holy. P's interest in dietary prohibitions starts with Noah (Gen 9:4-6), and its concern with the rite of circumcision begins with Abraham (Gen 17:9-14). In the Priestly narrative, no one offers sacrifices in the ancestral period until the priest Aaron appears to perform them legitimately.

The deity in the Priestly Writing is more distant than in J or E and does not make direct contact with humans. The language of P is repetitive, formulaic, and stately. P organizes the evolving relationship between God and humanity in terms of three successive covenants or agreements. The first covenant is with Noah (Gen 9:12-17), the second with Abraham (Gen 17:11), and the third with Israel (Exod 31:12-17). The information about the construction of the tabernacle in Exodus 25–31 and 35–40 is Priestly material, as is the main portion of Leviticus with its concern for ritual and festivals. The Priestly Writing was composed in the Neo-Babylonian or the early Persian period, but preserves the lore and traditions of Israel's priests from earlier times.

3.2. COVENANT

There are significant similarities between the various expressions of covenant in the Old Testament and the structure and content of ancient treaties. Such parallels can be traced back to Hittite examples from 1500 to 1200 and to Assyrian treaties from the seventh century. Those international agreements are called *suzerainty treaties* because they were imposed by a superior ruler (suzerain) upon inferior vassal kings. The most striking parallels involve (1) evoking the history of the suzerain's gracious dealings with his vassal, (2) detailing obligations of loyal behavior required of the vassal, and (3) pronouncing statements of blessing and curse contingent on the vassal's obedience or disobedience. These parallels suggested to an earlier generation of scholars that the notion of covenant went back to Israel's pre-monarchic past. More recently it has been recognized that covenant language in the Old Testament first emerged around the time of the prophet Hosea in the eighth century. In the century following Hosea, covenant developed as a dominant theological concept in Deuteronomy and Jeremiah.

The Hebrew word for covenant is *berith*. The covenant with Abraham (Genesis 17) involved the obligation of circumcision, and the word *berith* (*bris*) is used in Judaism to refer to that practice. Genesis 15 describes a covenant-making ceremony in which animals are cut in two and laid out in rows. A common Hebrew expression for making a covenant is to *cut a covenant*, which seems to reflect this practice. A repeated formula expressing Yahweh's commitment to the covenant relationship between God and people is often termed the *covenant formulary*. One example of this is Exodus 6:7: *I'll take you as my people, and I'll be your God.* Variations on this formula appear throughout the Old Testament (Hos 2:23; Jer 7:23; 11:4; 24:7; 30:22; 31:1, 33; 32:38; Ezek 36:28; Deut 29:13).

In Genesis and Exodus, P is structured by a repeated heading: "these are the descendants of" (Hebrew: *toledoth*). Different English versions translate *toledoth* in a variety of ways depending on context, such as "account," "story," "record of descendants," "lines," and "descendants."

The first of these expressions is Genesis 2:4a: "the *toledoth* of the heavens and the earth when they were created." Because all other *toledoth* formulas point forward to the material they introduce, this phrase seems to serve as an overture to the J creation story that follows in Genesis 2:4b-25.

Genesis 5:1, "the book of the *toledoth* of the descendants of Adam," is the heading for the genealogies recorded in chapter 5.

Genesis 6:9, "the *toledoth* of Noah," serves as a heading for the flood.

Genesis 10:1, "the *toledoth* of Shem, Ham, and Japheth" heralds the Table of Nations and the Tower of Babel story (chapters 10 and 11).

Three *toledoth* formulas in Genesis 11:10 (Shem), 25:12 (Ishmael), and 36:1, 9 (Esau) introduce relatively short genealogies.

In contrast, Genesis 11:27, the *toledoth* formula for Abraham's father, Terah, introduces the long story of Abraham (11:27–25:11).

Genesis 25:19 (Isaac) introduces the story of Jacob as far as Genesis 35:29.

Genesis 37:2 (Jacob) prefaces the Joseph story as far as the end of Genesis.

After a long gap, the formula recurs for a final time in Numbers 3:1: "these are the *toledoth* of Aaron and Moses."

The Flood according to J and P

Persuasive evidence for the Documentary Hypothesis can be found in the flood story of Genesis 6–9. The narrative shows that it was constructed by alternating blocks of J and P sections. The J narrative consists of Genesis 6:5-8; 7:1-5, 16b-23; 8:6-12, 20-22. Yahweh is distraught over humanity's evil and determines to wipe them off the face of the ground. But Yahweh does approve of Noah. Yahweh commands Noah to take seven pairs of each clean animal and of birds and only one pair of each unclean animal. Yahweh closes up the ark. The flood waters remain for forty days, and every living things is wiped off the face of the ground. After forty days, Noah sends out birds and discovers that the water has subsided. Noah builds an altar and sacrifices some of the ritually clean animals and birds. A strikingly anthropomorphic Yahweh smells the pleasing fragrance of the sacrificial smoke and determines never to curse the land or destroy all living things.

The originally independent P narrative consists of Genesis 6:9-22; 7:6-16a; 7:24–8:5, 13-19; 9:1-19. It begins with a characteristic *toledoth* formula. God sees that the earth is full of violence. God tells Noah that he will destroy the earth and all creatures. God commands Noah to build an ark and gives detailed instructions for its design. God promises to make a covenant with Noah. Noah is to bring one pair of every living thing, each according to its kind, and gather food for them. The flood lasts 150 days. Noah's family and the animals leave the ark. Animals and humans are to be fruitful and multiply. It is significant that the P flood story utilizes distinctive language that also appears in the first chapter of Genesis, which is also from the Priestly Writer. One example of this *is according to its kind* (Gen 1:11-12, 21, 25; 6:20; 7:14; this consistency is obscured in many translations). The vocabulary of *male and female* in Genesis 6:19; 7:16 is the same as that found in 1:27. In contrast, J uses a different expression for the gender of the animals in 7:2, and these are the same words that J uses for humans in its creation story (2:23).

Chapter 3

In recent decades the classic form of the Documentary Hypothesis has been sharply criticized. This critique centers on the comparative dating of the sources, on whether the fragmentary pieces of E could ever have existed as a connected source document, and especially on the understanding of the process by which source materials were combined. The Pentateuch is a complex document and it is unlikely that anything like full agreement will ever be achieved on these matters. Nevertheless, the Documentary Hypothesis does explain a great deal and still dominates modern scholarship. As a working principle, this book assumes that the Pentateuch does encompass distinct written sources and that these can often be identified and untangled. It also takes the view that the Yahwist is the earliest source and can be separated with little difficulty from P material, that the Yahwist exhibits a continuous storyline, and that fragments of the Elohist can sometimes be recognized.

Form Criticism

Traditional materials of various sorts have been combined to form the books of the Torah. Recognizing the diverse forms of literature that lie behind the present Old Testament is the task of the discipline of form criticism. *Criticism* has unfortunate negative connotations in English, so the term "genre history" is sometimes used as a less ambiguous label for this approach. Basically, form criticism studies the social history of biblical literature. It centers on how different types of literature relate to various social situations and social purposes. Form criticism recognizes that much of what lies behind the Old Testament circulated originally as oral tradition, that is, as stories and poems that were recited, performed, and remembered. These oral forms were only later written down and shaped into written texts.

Human communications, whether oral or written, naturally fall into a limited number of forms or genres. Anyone who lives within a given culture can recognize its standard genres. We have little or no trouble distinguishing among jokes, love letters, advertisements, or instructions for tax filing. The most important insight of form criticism is that literary forms connect to recurring situations in the life of a culture and that they serve specific purposes within those life settings. Jokes are told in certain situations and not others and have the function of entertaining and reducing social tensions. Love letters emerge from romances and seek to influence the emotions and decisions of the recipient. Ads seek to motivate purchasing behavior, and instructions guide people to complete tasks in a competent manner. The recurring social setting out of which a traditional genre arises and in which it is preserved is known by the German phrase *Sitz im Leben* ("setting in life"). Another important insight of form criticism is that in oral and written literature "form follows function." That is to say, the shape and language of a given genre is largely molded by its purpose. Jokes have punch lines, and instructions break down complex tasks into a sequence of individual steps. When practicing form criticism, biblical scholars look primarily for three things: setting in the life of a given culture, intention connected to that setting, and the shapes or forms used to accomplish that purpose. Ultimately, traditional oral genres may be borrowed and reused in the production of written literature, and this is what has happened in many places in the Torah. In Genesis the most important narrative genres are traditional legends and sagas, along with the short story or novella about Joseph that concludes the book.

Narrative Genres in Genesis

The category of *legend* is somewhat misleading because in common usage the word implies falsehood and fiction. In form-critical terms, a legend is a story about virtuous people, holy places, or ceremonies, told to inculcate wonder or awe and uplift or improve the hearer. The term *legend* originates from the medieval practice of reading the uplifting tales (*legenda*) of the saints in monastic communities. In Genesis, a legend may speak of the origin of a holy site and ceremonies practiced there. Such sanctuary legends recounted the origin of sacred sites where sacrifices were offered and would have been retold at those locations. They were intended to legitimate the holy place as an appropriate location for sacrifice to Yahweh. A common feature of a sanctuary legend was a revelation or appearance by God or a divine messenger (a *theophany*). By relating the involvement of a patriarchal ancestor with a holy place, Israel was able to claim it, even if worship of a god other than Yahweh had previously taken place there.

Somewhat confusingly, in common speech *saga* denotes a long and heroic epic tale. In Old Testament form criticism, however, a saga is a brief story about heroes or ethnic ancestors, usually with an etiological (explanatory) intent. Sometimes the label *family story* is used instead. A saga's original purpose was to build ethnic or family identity. Sagas are short and feature a limited number of characters. The relationships in a saga are familial. Genesis contains ethnological sagas that portray the basis for the origin and interrelationships of ethnic groups. The often antagonistic relationship between Edom and Israel, for example, is communicated in terms of sibling rivalry on the part of their respective ancestors Esau and Jacob. The origin and national character of the Ishmaelites is explored by stories about family rivalry between Sarah the mother of Isaac and Hagar the mother of Ishmael. An insulting narrative recounting the incestuous birth of Ammon and Moab participates in the universal human penchant for strengthening one's own ethnic identity by disparaging foreigners (Gen 19:30-38). Israel enjoyed hearing that their ancestor Jacob easily outsmarted Esau. As an indication of their patriarchal worldview, sagas proudly celebrate Israel's women ancestors for their beauty (Gen 12:11, 14; 24:16; 26:7).

A *short story* (sometimes called a *novella*) is a longer narrative told as a series of incidents or episodes and exhibiting characterization and plot. The plots of short stories are driven by problems that need to be resolved and end with a climax that results in the resolution of those problems. The Joseph story in Genesis 37, 39–50 is a prime example of a short story. It unfolds in several episodes and in the end resolves the overlapping narrative problems of Joseph's relationship with his brothers, his imprisonment, famine in Egypt, and his family's survival. Ruth, Jonah, and Judith are also short stories.

Further Reading

Jean-Louis Ska. *Introduction to Reading the Pentateuch*. Winona Lake, IN: Eisenbrauns, 2006.

Marvin A. Sweeney and Ehud Ben Zvi, eds. *The Changing Face of Form Criticism for the Twenty-First Century*. Grand Rapids: Eerdmans, 2003.

Chapter 4
CREATION: GENESIS 1–3

Understanding Myth

Like us, ancient people sought explanations for the way things are and how natural and human systems work. They needed a structure to conceptualize reality. Accordingly, Israel's neighbors developed and retold myths about primeval origins in order to explain their world. A *myth* may be defined as a narrative about gods or transcendent beings and their struggles, which led to the way things are today. In myth, gods interact with each other through intrigue, battle, and sexuality. Pairs of male and female gods may give birth to other deities. This way of describing the origin of a multitude of gods through divine genealogy is called *theogony*. Myths are set into a time long past, an eon of primordial origins radically different from our present age.

Like other peoples, Israel told its own mythic stories to explain origins, and the narratives of Genesis 1–11 are examples of these. How did the orderly universe, with its round of days and months and seasons come to be? Why are plants and animals so prolifically fertile and why do they produce new generations of their own unique kind and no other? Why are men and women so alike and so different and so intensely attracted to each other? Why are there weeds in the fields and why is birthing so difficult? How did human violence originate? Why are there a multitude of mutually incomprehensible languages? In regard to the social order, why do men dominate women, and why are some nations subjugated to others?

These narratives about first origins in Genesis are not really full-blown myths because Israel's myth-like stories could not be about *gods* in the plural and their dealings with each other. Of course, earlier writers such as the Yahwist assumed the existence of other gods associated with other nations. However, the only deity with real divine power and any claim to Israel's loyalty was Yahweh. In the Old Testament as it stands today, Yahweh does not struggle and does not engage in sexuality. For this reason, the expression *broken myths* is often applied to the narratives preserved in the early chapters of Genesis. Like the myths of other ancient peoples, these broken myths seek to explain the origins of things, but do so from the perspective that only one God is the decisive actor. *God began to create* (Gen 1:1) and *Yahweh God formed the human* (2:7). Moreover, Genesis 1–11 actually undercuts the divine claims of rival, so-called gods.

4.1. *ENUMA ELISH*

Enuma Elish is informally known as the Babylonian creation story. It recounts how Marduk, the chief god of Babylon, created the world and in the process became the king of the gods. In the beginning, things were not the way they are now:

> When on high no name was given to heaven
> Nor below was the netherworld called by name.

Apsu, representative of the fresh water of rivers, and Tiamat, embodying the salt water of marsh and ocean, joined together. From their union successive generations of gods were born. This multitude of lower-status gods proved to be noisy, and they disturbed Apsu, so that he could not sleep. Apsu determined to destroy them, but it was Tiamat who took up the lethal mission. Marduk the storm god rose to the occasion in order to protect the divine order, but demanded that if he were to defeat Tiamat, he would be made king of the gods.

> If indeed I am to champion you
> Subdue Tiamat and save your lives . . .
> nominate me for supreme destiny!

The gods acclaimed Marduk as king. With net, arrow, and storm winds, he killed Tiamat and split her body in half. He put up one half to fashion the sky and restrained her waters so they could not escape. He made celestial bodies to regulate the calendar. Parts of Tiamat's body became earth's physical features. Her breasts formed mountains, and from her eyes flowed the Tigris and Euphrates. Humans were formed from the blood of the god Qingu, Tiamat's slain confederate, so that they could

Creation: Genesis 1–3

serve the gods. (*ANET* 60–72, 501–3; *COS* 1.111:390–402, from which the quotations are taken.)

The myth-like stories of Genesis begin in primordial time, when things were different than now, and present-day systems and realties were not yet in effect.

The earth was without shape or form. (1:1)

There was still no human being to farm the fertile land. (2:5)

A helper . . . was nowhere to be found. (2:20)

The two of them were naked . . . but they weren't embarrassed. (2:25)

All people . . . had one language. (11:1)

When these stories finish, the realities of our world are in force.

The heavens and the earth and all who live in them were completed. (2:1)

Yahweh made the man and his wife leather clothes. (3:21)

Yahweh sent him out . . . to farm the fertile land. (3:23)

They won't understand each other's language. (11:7)

Creation according to the Priestly Writer— Genesis 1:1–2:4a

The concerns and language of Genesis 1:1–2:4a show that it is a product of the Priestly Writer. This solemn, almost poetic account of the total universe, as it was understood by pre-modern people, presents the cosmos in uniformly positive terms. From start to finish everything is assessed as *good* in God's judgment. The first week of creation connects to present time through God's institution of a weekly Sabbath on the seventh day.

The P creation story is a stately, rhythmic narrative. Perhaps surprisingly to modern readers, the narrative does not begin with a situation of absolute nothingness. A shapeless earth, darkness, and a watery deep are already in existence. At the start of the creative process, God structures and tames those preexisting entities into an orderly creation. Creation means putting limits on the waters to hold them up and hold them back in order to expose the land underneath (1:6, 9). God names and thus controls preexistent darkness as *Night* and the preexistent waters as *Seas* (vv. 5, 10). Creation also means separating and categorizing realities into their proper and orderly domains. So God separates light and darkness, a dome separates waters above and below the earth, and sun and moon separate day and night (vv. 4, 7, 14).

A tight and repetitive structure unifies the account. Eight creative episodes are spread out over a work week of six days. Consequently there are two creative results rather than just one on day three (earth and sea followed by vegetation) and on day six (land animals and then humans). This circumstance suggests that the author has squeezed an earlier source list of eight items into the all-important six-day pattern. Moreover, there are correspondences between paired days. Day four (sun, moon, and stars) corresponds to day one in that both explore the topic of light. The generalized light of the first day is regulated and ruled by the heavenly bodies on the fourth day. In the same way, day two coordinates with day five. The sky dome and waters created on the second day are populated on the fifth day by water animals and birds that fly in the sky dome. Finally, days three and six correspond. The two outcomes of day three are the dry land called earth and then plants. On day six, the earth brings forth animals and then humans, and the plants are given to them for food. The summation statement *it happened* (NRSV: *and it was so*) marks off six of the eight creative acts: v. 7 (day two), vv. 9 and 11 (day three), v. 15 (day four), and vv. 24 and 30 (day six).

The scene begins in total darkness. The primordial waters are swept by *God's wind* (CEB; other versions translate as *a mighty wind* or *the spirit of God*). An inclusive bracket holds the literary unit together: *God created* (1:1, CEB footnote) and *which God created to do* (2:3, CEB footnote). Each of the eight creative episodes begins with a verbal command (*let there be light*, and so forth). But the pattern of creation by divine word is not the whole story, because God follows up with other, more direct action verbs. God *made* the sky dome, the heavenly bodies and land animals, and God proposed *let us make humanity* (1:26). God *created* the sea creatures and birds and then human beings as two genders in the divine image (vv. 21, 27). God *named* in order to categorize and control. Darkness is tamed when God names it Night and appoints the smaller light (the moon) to rule it (vv. 3, 16). God commands unruly waters to gather together, they obey, and then God names them Seas (vv. 9-10).

God also blesses and evaluates. God blesses the fertility of water animals and birds, and then blesses humans with the same words: *be fertile and multiply* (vv. 22, 28). P will restate this command after the flood (9:1, 7). God repeatedly performs a quality check on the creation project. Seven times God *saw* and assessed what was created as *good* (vv. 4, 10, 12, 18, 21, 25; *supremely good* in v. 31).

Creation itself plays a role in creating. The sky dome exists to separate the heavenly waters (explaining why the sky is blue) from the water below (vv. 6-7). Heavenly bodies separate day and night on an ongoing basis and regulate the calendar (vv. 14, 18). Waters obediently gather into their place so the dry land can *appear* in the newly created light of day. Moreover, creation is designed so that it can continue on its own without constant divine effort. Water produces living things, and the earth generates vegetation and produces every kind of animal on its own (vv. 11, 20, 24). Plants have seed, so that vegetation can continue automatically, and animals and humans proliferate on their own accord (vv. 12, 22, 28).

Everything narrows down to the creation of humans in the last part of the last day. God speaks to others in the first person plural: *let us make . . . in our image* (v. 26). These words are addressed to semi-divine beings that were thought to make up the royal council of God as ruler and perform God's will. (See 5.2, DIVINE BEINGS.) Genesis 1:27 is a balanced poetic expression that emphasizes both God's image and human gender. The expression *God created* is used three times and the noun *image* is used twice. God blesses humanity as female and male and gives them a task: *be fertile and multiply*. In matters of diet, peace reigns, because all living, breathing creatures are vegetarians. This will change after the flood.

4.2. THE IMAGE OF GOD

Genesis 1:26 quotes God:

> Let us make humanity in our image to resemble us
> so that they may take charge.

In its most concrete sense, possession of the divine image means that men and women were thought to have a shape similar to that of divine beings and even God. Whenever God is visualized as having a physical form (Ezek 1:26, for example), the figure of God is described as elusively human. According to Genesis 9:6, possession of the divine image means that human life is sacrosanct and murder must be repaid by the death penalty. In the context of Genesis 1, image also means that humans have an administrative role over the earth and sea: *that they may take charge* (NRSV: *let them have dominion*). Humans are to *master* the earth (1:28). This verb has an aggressive connotation, and the traditional translation is *subdue*. However, a careful reading shows that men and women are to master the earth responsibly, in accordance with the administrative role entrusted to them.

On the seventh day creation is complete, so God stops creating (2:2-3). God can rest (that is to say, *cease activity*) and appreciate a well-done, quality job. Everything is *supremely good* (1:31; the word also means *beautiful*). The connection between Sabbath rest and creation rest is highlighted in the Exodus version of the Ten Commandments (Exod 20:11).

By asserting that God alone is creator, the Priestly Writing downgrades other things that neighboring, polytheistic nations thought of as gods. Such entities do not have divine status and power but are completely under God's control. Sun, moon, and stars are merely fabricated lamps set into the sky dome. They have their purposes, but they are only created things. The sun is not the fundamental source of light, for it did not come into being until the fourth day. Sea is not a godlike power but something named and tamed by God. Its waters obeyed God's command without a fight and stay in their place. Sea monsters (1:21; CEB: *great sea animals*) are simply created beings, just like tiny swarming ocean creatures. God did not need to struggle or battle with other divinities to establish the universe. God simply spoke, separated, made, named, and created. The universe is now an ongoing, self-generating system.

The Yahwist's Perspective on Creation— Genesis 2:4b–3:24

In Genesis 2:4b–3:24, a second creation story follows the six-day creation account. It is told from a perspective more limited than the cosmic viewpoint of Genesis 1 and focuses more directly on the concerns of human existence. Comparison with other parts of the Pentateuch establishes that this narrative was part of the Yahwist document (J). This Eden narrative differs from Genesis 1 in significant ways. The creating deity is named Yahweh God (translated Lord *God*) rather than God (*Elohim*). The male human is fashioned first, then the animals and birds are formed, and finally Yahweh fashions the first woman. In a sense, Genesis 2 backtracks to the state of affairs described in Genesis 1:27-28, when humans are created, in order to focus more closely on the human story.

Etiology

The Eden story is an *etiology*. Etiologies seeks to set forth the original causes that lie behind our present world. Etiological narratives recount how things got started and why things are the way they are. Etiologies answer the sorts of questions children love to ask: Why? How? How did the earth become fertile and productive? Where did language come from (2:19-20)? Why is humanity at war with snakes (3:15)? How did clothing originate (3:7, 21)? Where did agricultural life and the diet based on it come from, and why is the life of the farmer so harsh and uncertain (3:17-19)? Why are we buried in soil and why do we decompose back into it (2:7; 3:19)? And most fundamentally, what has gone wrong with human existence?

As a story of origins, Genesis 2–3 follows a plot line of "once there was not, but now there is." It focuses on agriculture and human sexuality. Once there were no *wild plants* or *field crops* and no human being *to farm the fertile land* (2:5), but at the end of the story there are crops and someone *to farm the fertile land* (3:18, 23). The situation of a lone and lonely human individual was *not good* (2:18) so animals emerged (2:19). When this solution proved inadequate in that *a helper perfect for* the human was not found, Yahweh God fashioned Woman (2:20-22).

The origins of human sexuality and marriage are of central interest. Why are women and men sexually attracted to each other? It is because Yahweh God fashioned one from the body of the other.

Creating the World of Eden

Yahweh formed the first human from dirt (2:7), and a play on words in Hebrew illustrates this. *Adam* (human) is taken from the *adamah* (NRSV: *ground*; CEB: *fertile land*). One might approximate this pun in English with "human from the humus" or "earthling from the earth." This intimate relationship between the ground and humanity stands at the center of story. At first, the fertile land (*adamah*) cannot produce, because there is no human being (*adam*) to farm it (2:5). In the end, humans spend their lives tilling the fertile land (3:17, 23), and in death return to it (3:19).

Yahweh God formed animals from the ground, but none were able to solve the problem that the human was alone. The human needed *a helper that is perfect for him*, which is to say, a colleague, associate, ally, and collaborator (2:18). There is nothing automatically subservient about being in the role of *helper*, for the Old Testament often calls God the helper of humanity (Pss 33:20; 70:5; 115:10-11; 146:5). So Yahweh God builds up Woman from the first human's rib (or side), perhaps hinting at the side-by-side existence of a married couple. The first human greets her as a wonderful addition—*finally*—and as a person corresponding to him as his very *bone* and *flesh* (Gen 2:23). This reality is indicated by the distinctive method by which she was created from a bone of his body. *Bone* and *flesh* points to close kinship and relationship (Gen 29:14; Judg 9:2; 2 Sam 5:1; 19:13). The special affiliation of marriage transcends one's family of origin or biological kinship and results in the *one flesh* of a child (2:24). Of course in the biblical world, a husband did not leave his parents' home to live with his wife. Rather, v. 24 refers to turning away from one's emotional focus on one's parents in order to establish a new focus on one's spouse. For now, being naked is a neutral thing and not socially embarrassing. Yet before the story is over, the delight (compare *embraces* in 2:24) and innocence (2:25) of the original marriage union will be marred by patriarchy and pain (3:16).

In 2:25, Hebrew wordplay again supports the narrative. The human who has been giving names invents words to express this most intimate of relationships: woman (*ishshah*) is taken out of man (*ish*). Up until this point in the story, the word *adam* has denoted a human one, without regard to gender, but now the representation of all humanity also becomes the male in the story. Nevertheless, what is said to Man in 3:18-19 applies to both men and women. In 3:22-24, Woman as a distinct character drops out and *adam* as the single human being is the only character on stage. By the time Genesis 4:1 is reached, the common noun *adam* has segued into a proper name, Adam.

Temptation and Tragedy

Eden is a place of ambiguity. Yahweh has complicated matters by planting beautiful trees and creating a crafty, articulate snake. In addition to *the tree of life*, Yahweh God planted a *tree of the knowledge of good and evil* (2:9). Many food options are available for choice (2:16), but that one tree is off limits and deadly. This prohibition is stated without explanation or justification. In the far distant special time of origins, the snake can talk and is *intelligent* (3:1; NRSV: *crafty*). The tree of the knowledge of good and evil takes center stage in 3:5. In the Old Testament, knowing good and evil implies the ability to discern between what is beneficial and what is detrimental and harmful. This is a capacity that adults have and children still lack (Deut 1:39; Isa 7:15-16; 2 Sam 14:17; 19:35; 1 Kgs 3:9). The metaphor of being able to *see clearly* explains what is meant (Gen 3:5, 7; the Hebrew speaks in terms of "opened eyes"). Ironically, humanity's initial lack of this capacity for discernment in regard to the dangers and benefits of eating from the tree is what leads to tragedy.

The snake's initial question in 3:1, *Did God really say that you shouldn't eat from any tree*, is confusing. Does this prohibition mean that you are not to eat from any and all of the trees? Or does it mean, is there any particular tree from which you may not eat? This ambiguity induces Woman to clarify the prohibition for the snake (vv. 2-3) and even strengthen it for herself (*don't touch it*). In 3:4-5, the snake raises doubts about what the consequences of eating would really be. *You won't die* (true at least in the sense that they will not die immediately; compare 2:17). The snake's next words are undoubtedly true, but misleading: *you will see clearly and you will be like God* (compare 3:7, 22). But the snake's most dangerous insinuation is one that questions God's motives. The snake implies that the prohibition is actually intended to protect God's divine prerogatives (v. 5). Based on her perception of the tree's beauty, deliciousness, and potential for wisdom, Woman eats and shares with Man.

Eating from the tree leads to mixed consequences. Woman has correctly perceived that *the tree would provide wisdom* (3:6). The Old Testament values wisdom highly, because it leads to success and the mastery of human existence. Knowing the difference between good and evil does not seem like an entirely bad thing either. However, the humans' new capacity to know good and evil also results in shame and fear. They cover their bodies and hide from God (3:7, 10).

In 3:9-13, Yahweh God interrogates Man and Woman but not the snake. God treats them as responsible people who are capable of speaking for themselves and who deserve a hearing. Man lets slip the momentous truth that he knows he is naked. Yahweh's follow-up questions spring the trap: *Who told you? Did you eat?* Man does not simply confess, but defends himself, seeking to duck responsibility. Sure I ate, but *you* gave me Woman and *she* gave me the fruit, so my responsibility is diminished. Woman's defense shows that she has reflected further on the snake's words and now perceives them as trickery.

Some interpreters understand 3:14-19 as punishments caused directly by God. Others see these verses as a more neutral disclosure of the inevitable consequences of disobedience. The snake is cursed, but the humans are not. Instead, it is the ground that is cursed as regards human agriculture. There is now pain in childbirth, and there is also pain in farming (vv. 16, 17). The consequences in vv. 17b-19 obviously apply to both sexes, not just to males. Men and women both die, and agriculture was the task of both sexes in the ancient world. *Bread* (v. 19) points to agricultural life; fruit is no longer at the center of the human diet. The full circle of "from dust . . . to dust" (CEB: *soil*), from creation to burial, will now be traveled by every human.

Yahweh God addresses the members of the divine council in 3:22 (*like one of us*). Having achieved a new level of perception and knowledge, humans have become in some limited ways like God and the subordinate heavenly beings. For this reason, open-ended life without any termination in view must be denied them. The tree of life that would make immortality possible is made permanently unattainable, and the way back to Eden is blocked by several *winged creatures* (Hebrew: *cherubim*) and a flaming sword. Yet, these first humans do carry on with some resiliency. Man names Woman "Eve," meaning Life, mother of all humans. The feisty pair perseveres in producing a new generation (4:1-2, 25), and life's story goes on.

Interpreting the Eden Story

The interpretation of the Eden story has taken several directions over the centuries. In evaluating these, one should note that Genesis 2–3 mentions neither sin nor Satan. The snake only became identified with the devil or Satan much later on.

Chapter 4

The topic of sin only first appears in Genesis 4:7 in the story of Cain. The Eden story does not say explicitly that humanity was originally intended to be immortal, but concludes by making unavailable the resource that made ongoing life possible. In Genesis 3:19, death seems to be a natural and expected consequence of having been formed from dust.

Paul in the New Testament provided the foundation for the interpretation of Eden most common in Christian thought (Rom 5:12-21). Woman and man disobeyed a clear divine command and in so doing brought sin and death into the world. However, some early church fathers saw the Eden story as teaching good behavior: avoid gluttony, shun temptation, and marry only once. For others, it demonstrated that people are not bound by the dictates of impersonal fate, but have free will in deciding what to do. The first humans were tempted and tricked, but no uncontrollable force compelled them to eat from the tree.

When read as a folktale against the background of universal human concerns, Genesis 2–3 can also be seen as a timeless story of how human beings grew up from primordial childhood to maturity, into a sadder-but-wiser adulthood. It is about what happened when humans started making independent judgments and autonomous choices. They lost their childlike innocence when their eyes were opened to perceive the harsh realities of adult life. According to this perspective, in the first part of the story the first humans have not yet grown up. Man is developing his language skills like a child (2:19-20, 23). Like children, the pair are not disturbed about being naked and cannot tell the difference between what is good and helpful and what is bad and harmful. They do not yet face the adult burden of pregnancy and frustrating toil.

Women and Men

The comparative status of women and men is another area where the Eden story has provoked centuries of controversy. Does the circumstance that Woman was created after Man and created from him mean that she is inferior in some way? However, the sequence and method of creation in Genesis 2 actually allows the origin of Woman to be just as unique as that of Man. Each gender had its own special origin, and Yahweh God invested a hands-on effort to form and fashion each. Does Woman's acceptance of the snake's blandishments mean that women are more open to temptation? The careful reader will note that Man was actually silently present during the conversation with the snake (3:6, *who was with her*). Given the patriarchal culture of Israel, if Man had eaten first and then given the forbidden fruit to his wife, would eating really have been a free choice for her? Could she be held equally accountable? Man receives his own full share of blame for listening to a voice other than the divine command (3:17).

The Eden story presents Woman as an equal partner and her role as critically important. Things are *not good* with the initial male-only situation (2:18), and a proper state of affairs is achieved only when God fashions Woman as counterpart. Woman is capable of sophisticated thought and makes independent choices (3:2-3, 6). She speaks on behalf of her husband and herself (*we*, 3:2) and is addressed individually by God (3:16). No conclusions are drawn about the respective status of the sexes until Yahweh God outlines the consequences of eating (3:16). After Eden, the original relationship is deformed, and women are ruled over by their husbands.

Further Reading

Bill T. Arnold. *Genesis*. New York: Cambridge University Press, 2009.

Othmar Keel and Silvia Schroer. *Creation: Biblical Theologies in the Context of the Ancient Near East*. Winona Lake, IN: Eisenbrauns, 2015.

Chapter 5
ORIGINS: GENESIS 4:1–11:9

Rivalry and Vengeance—Genesis 4

The J narrative of origins continues in Genesis 4. The breakdown in human relationships continues, first within the family (Cain) and then in society at large (Lamech). Again the writer explores and explains the origins of various present-day realities. Why do siblings fight? How did murder and retribution originate? What was the starting point for farming and shepherding, the two chief and often competing ways of making a living in the Old Testament world? Where did cities, cattle herding, music, and metal-working come from (4:17, 20-22)? What was the basis for the lifestyle of nomadic peoples (4:12, 14)? When was the name Yahweh first known and invoked (4:26)?

The basic structure of Genesis 4 is that of a genealogy or family line. The story of Cain is set into the context of a seven-generation genealogy from his own birth to the birth of Lamech's children. The genealogy begins in 4:1-2. The first six generations (down to 4:17-18) make up a direct line from father to son, with side references to various cultural advances. Lamech is father of the seventh generation, at which point the linear genealogy breaks out into a tree that presents Lamech's two wives and four children (4:19-22). Then 4:25-26 starts the genealogy over from the beginning, tracing a second line from Adam and Eve through a third son, Seth. Seth and Enosh make up a two-generation genealogy, and there is another advance in human culture, this time having to do with religion. Parallel wording in 4:1 and 4:25 encloses and unifies chapter 4. At the beginning and the end of the chapter, Adam has intercourse with his wife, and Eve gives birth. Her son is named, and the name is explained in terms of God's action.

Abel means "ephemeral vapor," and he is basically an empty shell who does nothing. Abel is described as Cain's brother seven times, but Cain is never described as Abel's brother. Cain is the center of attention—as son, murderer, father and city builder, and finally as the reference point of Lamech's song (4:24). The story does not explain why Yahweh accepted Abel and his sacrifice of meat but not the agricultural produce of Cain. One possible explanation is that Abel's sacrifice was from the *oldest* offspring of his flocks, that is the first and the best. Abel's animal sacrifice was of the sort that Yahweh enjoyed, the fragrant smoke of fat and meat (Gen 8:20-21). The narrative also fails to explain how Cain found out that his sacrifice had been disregarded. Reticence about incidental matters is common in Old Testament narratives. What is important here is not Yahweh's action but Cain's *reaction*.

Cain's internal anger shows up in his sullen face (4:5). Yahweh's forewarning (4:6-7) indicates that Cain still has the opportunity to do the right thing and is capable of controlling the situation. Sin (mentioned here for the first time) is like a dangerous, lurking animal ready to pounce. Cain does not answer Yahweh, but speaks instead to his brother (4:8). *Brother* is repeated six times in vv. 8-11, perhaps to hammer home the broken relationship. The two stand in *the field*, out in the open country, where there can be no witnesses. Verse 9 is well-known: *am I my brother's guardian?* (NRSV: keeper). This line is usually read as a denial of fraternal solidarity, but could also be understood as a sarcastic riposte. Am I supposed to know where my brother is at every moment? Aren't you, Yahweh, supposed to be everyone's guardian? Abel's blood voices the desperate cry of the victims of violence who appeal to Yahweh for justice (4:10; *to me*). Cain is cursed with respect to the ground and driven from it (4:11-12, 14). Early readers would understand that this means that Cain (Hebrew: *qayin*) was the ancestor of his namesakes, the nomadic Kenite people (*qeni*), who had no settled home.

Verse 15 comes as a surprise. Ancient readers would have viewed the execution of an intentional murderer as a laudable civic or family duty. (The J narrative here tacitly assumes there are other people in the world, as it does in v. 17 when Cain acquires a wife.) But Yahweh, in an unexplained act of favor, prevents this by marking Cain and protecting him by the threat of seven-fold divine retribution. Lamech is the last in Cain's line. His violent nature reiterates and even exceeds that of his murderous ancestor and points forward to the conditions that will make the flood necessary (Gen 6:5, 11).

Before the Flood—Genesis 5:1–6:4

Genesis 5:1-32 is a contribution of the Priestly Writer. It traces generations from Seth, Adam's third son, down to Noah and his three sons. This chapter parallels the Yahwist's genealogy in 4:17-24 describing the generations stemming from Cain. The names in each list overlap to a degree. In the P source, the order of names is somewhat different from that of J.

In Genesis 4:17, Enoch is the son of Cain and has the world's first city named for him. Genesis 5:18 mentions an Enoch who is the son of Jared.

The Yahwist's Lamech is the author of unrestricted vengeance (4:23-24). In P there is a Lamech who is the father of Noah (5:28-29).

Other parallels are Cain and Kenan (Hebrew: *qayin* and *qeynan*), Irad and Jared, and Methushael and Methuselah.

J and P clearly had access to different versions of an older tradition. The great ages attained by the ancestors, in chapter 5, call attention to how different the pre-flood era was from our own.

5.1. GENERATIONS BEFORE THE FLOOD

Genesis 5 portrays the generations between Adam and the flood in a fashion similar to Mesopotamian literary tradition. For example, the Sumerian Kings List catalogues a sequence of kings who reigned before the flood. These worthies supposedly enjoyed immensely long reigns of tens of thousands of years. After the flood, royal reigns become shorter, but continued to be phenomenal for generations (*ANET* 265–66). In Genesis 5, the lifetimes involved are limited to several centuries, and a much shorter time is covered overall because generations overlap. The most well-known figure in the list is Methuselah, who lived 969 years, which means that he died in the year of the flood.

Enoch became a significant figure. He marks the seventh generation and lived 365 years, the number of days in a solar year. Unlike the other pre-flood worthies, the formula *died* is not used for him. Instead, he *walked with God and disappeared* (Hebrew: *and he was no more*) *because God took him* (5:24). To have *walked with God* means that Enoch was righteous, as would be the case with Noah (6:9). Enoch would later be cited as an example of repentance (Sir 44:16) and faith (Heb 11:5). As biblical tradition developed, Enoch was celebrated as someone who did not die but was translated directly into the heavenly realm (Sir 49:14; Wis 4:10), similar to Elijah (2 Kgs 2:11; Sir 48:9; 1 Macc 2:58). Because of his special, otherworldly experience, Enoch was presumed to be someone able to reveal cosmic secrets and apocalyptic truths. Consequently, a good deal of later Jewish and Christian apocalyptic literature was attributed to Enoch.

Genesis 6:1-4 leads up to the flood and gives a partial explanation for it. Here the Yahwist recounts a seemingly bizarre incident involving a violation of the proper boundary between humanity and the *divine beings* whom Yahweh had addressed in 1:26 and 3:22. Those low-ranking divinities *married* (Hebrew: *took for themselves*) attractive women. Yahweh responded by limiting the human lifespan to a maximum of 120 years. Human life is a function of Yahweh's *breath* or spirit (6:3). The offspring of these improper unions were *ancient heroes*, who would have been known to early readers from songs and folktales about the distant past. They must have been similar to the partly human, partly divine Gilgamesh of Babylonian myth. They are called *Nephilim* in 6:4 (NRSV; CEB: *giants*). In Hebrew this means "fallen ones," apparently in the sense of being ancient heroes who have fallen dead. These beings also lived after the flood (*and also afterward*) and will reappear later to terrify Israel when they invade Canaan (Num 13:33). This fragmentary story has an etiological flavor. Why was the flood necessary? How did the warrior heroes of epic songs and stories come into being? Why do even righteous people live so much shorter lives than those who lived before the flood?

5.2. DIVINE BEINGS

The heavenly ones who violate the boundary between the human and the divine in Genesis 6:1-4 are called the "sons of God" in Hebrew. The idiom *sons of* designates the member of a group. Thus, the "sons of the prophet" were members of a prophetic group (1 Kgs 20:35) and in poetry a "son of the bow" was an arrow (the Hebrew wording in Job 41:28). These were conceived of as gods of a lower rank who made up a heavenly council or cabinet, ready to do God's bidding. Yahweh's divine council is portrayed in 1 Kings 22:19-22 and Isaiah 6:1-8. In Job this group assembles before Yahweh (1:6; 2:1) and is said to have reacted in joy to the creation of the earth (38:7). In Psalm 82, God stands up for justice in the divine council and addresses that assembly with an inclusive *us* (as in Gen 1:26; 3:22; 11:7). The deuterocanonical books refer to the episode of Genesis 6:1-4 (Wis 14:6; Sir 16:7; Bar 3:26). Later texts would describe these divine beings as rebellious, fallen angels, and the notion of rebellious angels was picked up in the New Testament (2 Pet 2:4; Jude 6).

Origins: Genesis 4:1–11:9

The Great Flood—Genesis 6:5–9:17

Like many other ancient cultures, Israel told of a universal flood that divided the primeval world from the present world. Perhaps Israel's story was influenced by Mesopotamian myths, but an important difference in approach resulted from Israel's commitment to a single God. Mesopotamian versions recounted rivalry among the gods resulting in one god sending the flood and another god warning the human protagonist about it. Yahweh performs both functions in the Genesis narrative. Yahweh, who now regrets making humanity, vows to wipe out the human race (6:6-7). At the same time Yahweh approves of Noah and warns him (6:8, 13).

5.3. MESOPOTAMIAN FLOOD STORIES

Flood accounts occur in the *Epic of Atrahasis* and in a scene in the *Gilgamesh Epic*. In *Atrahasis* a subordinate class of worker gods has the chore of digging and repairing the irrigation canals on which agriculture depends. They go on strike, so the god Enlil orders a mother goddess to make humans to take over these tasks and relieve the gods of onerous labor. She fashions seven men and seven women from clay and the blood of a slain god. However, a problem soon emerges. The humans reproduce too successfully, and soon there are so many that their noise disturbs the gods. Successive attempts are made to exterminate them, leading to disease, drought, and famine. Finally Enlil decides to send a destructive flood. Atrahasis, however, is warned by the god Enki, who instructs him how to construct a boat with a roof and caulk it with pitch. Atrahasis loads his livestock and family on board and survives a seven-day flood. Because sacrifices have been curtailed, the gods are hungry and thirsty. They need humanity, but to keep the human population in check, birth control measures are established. Some women are to be barren, some babies will die at birth, and special priestly classes of women are forbidden to have children.

In the *Epic of Gilgamesh*, Gilgamesh visits Utnapishtim, the man who survived the flood, in order to learn the secret of his immortality. Utnapishtim tells how he was warned by a god and instructed to build a boat. He describes the measurements and construction details of his boat and how he loaded up his possessions, his kinfolk, and the animals. After the flood, the boat grounds on a mountain. In a close parallel to Genesis 8:6-12, he sends out three birds one by one to see if the waters have receded. A dove and a swallow come right back, but the third bird, a raven, does not. Disembarking, Utnapishtim offers sacrifice, and by now the gods, who depend on human offerings, are famished:

> The gods smelled the savor
> The gods smelled the sweet savor
> The gods crowded around the sacrificer like flies. (COS 1.132:460)

The similarity to Genesis 8:20-21 is striking. (For *Atrahasis*, see *ANET* 104–5, 512–14; *COS* 1.130:450–52; for *Gilgamesh*, *ANET* 72–99; *COS* 1.132:458–60.)

Fig. 5. Tablet XI of the Babylonian version of the Gilgamesh Epic, from the fifteenth century.

As outlined above in chapter 3, both a J version and a P version of the basic flood story are preserved. Characteristically, J presents Yahweh in anthropomorphic terms. Yahweh experiences regret, closes up the ark, and smells the good scent of Noah's sacrifice (6:6-7; 7:16b; 8:21). J favors the storyteller's stock numbers of seven and forty

(7:2-4, 10; 8:10, 12 and 7:4, 12, 17; 8:6). In the end, the flood makes no difference in humanity's fundamental inclination to evil (6:5; 8:21).

The version of the Priestly Writer describes the flood as God's response to humanity's proclivity for *violence* (6:11, 13). The flood is a reversal of creation as portrayed in Genesis 1. Genesis 7:11 undoes 1:6-7 as chaotic waters gush upward and pour downward and refers to the primordial *deep sea* of 1:2. Professional priestly concerns appear in a carefully constructed calendar of events (7:11; 8:4-5, 13-14) and in the absence of any sacrifice by the non-priestly Noah. For P the flood means a new start for humanity. God's blessing at creation and command to produce offspring are reiterated (8:17 and 9:1 allude to 1:28). The vegetarian dietary guidelines of 1:29-30 are relaxed to allow humans to eat animals, but not their lifeblood (9:3-4). Humanity's divine image remains in force (9:6). The Priestly Writing expresses God's promises for the future in terms of a covenant (6:18; 9:8-17) made with the entire human race. This covenant involves a promise (9:11), stipulations about human behavior (9:4-6), and a sign (CEB: *symbol*) in the form of God's war bow reappearing as a rainbow (9:12-17). The Priestly Writing's conception of God's covenant with an associated sign will appear again in regard to Abraham (Genesis 17, circumcision) and the people of Israel (Exod 31:13, 16-17, Sabbath).

After the Flood—Genesis 9:18–10:32

Genesis 9:18-29 is from the J source and recounts a story about Noah and his sons exhibiting clear etiological interests. Who first practiced growing grape vines and discovered the intoxicating properties of wine? What was the origin of the slavery that was a feature of the Old Testament world? The narrative also justifies Israel's conquest of Canaan and repression of its Canaanite neighbors. It validates Israel's ethnic identity as offspring of the favored Shem. The narrative probably also served as a cautionary tale to teach the importance of honoring parents. Ham shamed and dishonored Noah by allowing himself to view his father's drunken, uncovered state. In contrast Shem and Japheth honored Noah by carefully avoiding the sight of his disgrace and by covering him up. So Noah blessed Shem and Japheth, but cursed Ham's son Canaan with slavery. This was a matter of balanced retribution. Noah was dishonored as father by the actions of his son. So in return, Ham was to be dishonored as father by the enslavement and humiliation of his son, Canaan. The narrative of Noah's curse on Canaan has proved dangerous. In the nineteenth century it was used to justify black African slavery.

Genesis 10 is termed the Table of Nations. It describes the international political scene known to Israel in terms of Noah's three sons. Israel's awareness of geography stretched from the Greek Aegean world to northwestern Iran and to southern Arabia. This verbal map combines J material (10:8-19, 21, 24-30) and P material (10:1-7, 20, 22-23, 31-32). Its tripartite division of Japheth, Ham, and Shem was based on political affiliation, cultural similarity, and approximate geography. *Japheth* represents Mediterranean islands and Asia Minor as far west as the Aegean Sea, but also the Medes (*Madai*, 10:2) in northwestern Iran. The *Ashkenaz* (10:3) are Scythians, wild horsemen from north of the Black Sea. *Javan* (10:4) relates to the Ionian Greeks. *Ham* corresponds to Egypt and Africa to the south and west. Nations under Egypt's political or cultural influence are also assigned to Ham. Thus, *Canaan* is a son of Ham because it had long been under Egyptian control. *Shem* represents tribally organized nomads and semi-nomads in Mesopotamia, Syria, and the Arabian Peninsula. *Eber* represents the eponymous ancestor of the Hebrews (10:25; 11:16-17). A fragmentary legend about the hero *Nimrod* in 10:8-12 provides an etiology for the foundation of the great cities of Assyria and Babylon.

The City and Its Tower—Genesis 11:1-9

The story of the Tower of Babel has etiological roots. It explains our inability to understand the languages of other peoples, in spite of our common descent from Noah's sons. It also provides an explanation for the name of the city of Babylon. In context, the Babel story (from the Yahwist writer) should be read against God's command to populate the earth (Gen 1:28; 9:1, both P). The citizens of Babel do not want to be scattered across the earth (11:4). They want to achieve fame (a *name*) by building an extraordinary city and tower. New technology makes this project possible, because with baked brick and bitumen, they can build a city and even a tower, in a land without stone. However, Yahweh delights in diversity and human difference and thus perceives that this concentration of population into a single city will lead to problematic consequences, so Yahweh responds by confusing human language and scattering the people. As a result humans are dispersed *over all the earth* (11:8, 9), which was precisely the outcome they were trying to avoid (11:4). They do get a name, but it turns out to be Babel, asserted to derive from a Hebrew word meaning confusion (11:9). Babel is the ordinary Hebrew designation for Babylon.

Details are worth noting. Three parallel speeches that begin *come let's* coordinate the two halves of the plot. In 11:3 and 4, humans use this phrase to encourage each other in their plans. Then in 11:7, Yahweh uses it to address the minor deities of the divine council. The tower is the most well-known part of the story and is typically interpreted as an arrogant human assault on heaven. Early readers would have been familiar with the temple towers of Babylon called ziggurats. However, they would also know that every major city would have featured a defensive tower. In fact, the tower is not really the center of attention. After 11:4-5, it drops out of the story, and the city alone is the focus. That its top was planned to be *in the sky* is a way of saying that it would be "sky-high." From Yahweh's perspective, in fact, the tower is puny, and Yahweh must come down to investigate it (11:5).

If one looks at Genesis 1–11 as a whole, a theme of progressive alienation emerges. This begins with estrangement between humans and God and between wife and husband. Then hostility explodes between the first two brothers and continues in Lamech's threat of vengeance. In the story of Noah's sons, there is a breakdown between parent and child. In Genesis 11, an inability to understand one another's speech alienates the speakers of one language from another.

The remainder of Genesis 11 is a ten-generation genealogy of Shem that stretches down to Terah and then branches out to include Abram (Abraham), his wife Sarai (Sarah), and nephew Lot. The stage is set for Yahweh's challenge to Abram in Genesis 12.

Further Reading

Andrew George, trans. *The Epic of Gilgamesh*. New York: Penguin, 2003.

Mark S. Smith. *The Early History of God: Yahweh and the Other Deities in Ancient Israel*. 2nd ed. Grand Rapids: Eerdmans, 2002.

Chapter 6
ABRAHAM AND HIS DESCENDANTS

A Family Story

Genesis 12–50 traces the story of Abraham and his family down through four generations. The book climaxes with the twelve eponymous ancestors of the tribes of Israel settled in Egypt, in position for the next great episode of the national epic, the exodus. Genealogy structures the backbone of the story. The links from Abraham to Isaac to Jacob to the sons and grandsons of Jacob unfold through traditional narratives fashioned into various narrative genres. Along the way, the origins of related peoples are explored. Moab and Ammon are sons of Abraham's nephew Lot (19:29-38). The Ishmaelites (Arabs) descend from Abraham's son by Hagar (25:12-18). Isaac's son Esau is the ancestor of Edom (Genesis 36). These other groups related to and descended from Abraham are sidetracked as the line of divine promise narrows down to the sons of Jacob alone.

Three women ancestors play roles alongside the patriarchs. Sarah reacts with laughter to God's promise (18:9-15). She endures danger (12:10-20; 20:1-18) and fiercely protects the birthright of her son Isaac (21:8-21). Rebekah becomes the wife of Isaac because of her admirable hospitality (chapter 24). She conspires to advance the cause of her favorite son, Jacob, over that of his twin, Esau (chapter 27). Jacob's favored wife, Rachel, competes aggressively with her sister, Leah, and together they supply Jacob with twelve sons, with the help of two surrogate mothers. Rachel steals to preserve her family inheritance (31:19, 34-35). God's favor causes each of these three women ancestors to conceive: Sarah (17:16; 21:1-2), Rebekah (25:21), Leah (29:31), and Rachel (30:22). Rebekah receives a divine revelation (25:23). The marriages that lead from Abraham to Joseph are kept within the larger family through the practice of endogamy. Rebekah is a daughter of one of Abraham's nephews (Bethuel son of his brother Nahor), and Rachel and Leah are daughters of Rebekah's brother Laban.

Chapter 6

Table 2. The Family of Abraham

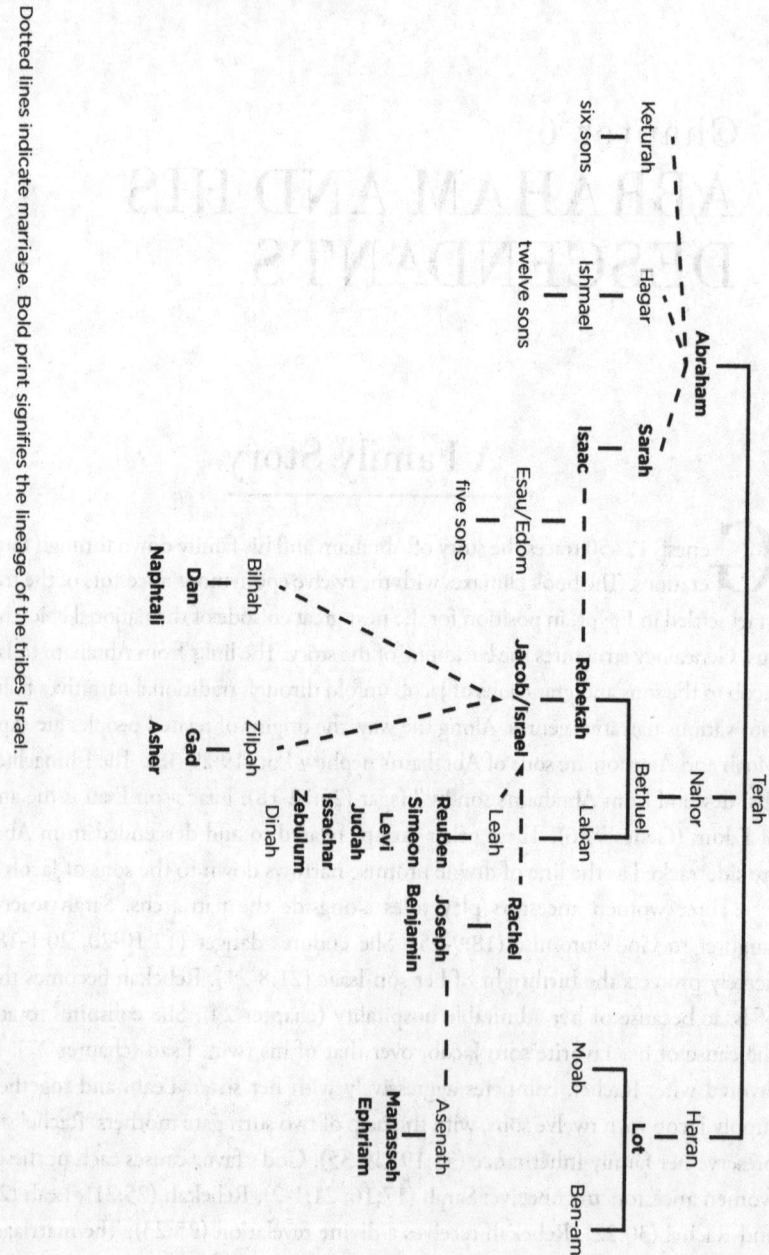

Dotted lines indicate marriage. Bold print signifies the lineage of the tribes Israel.

– 68 –

Abraham and Isaac—Genesis 12–23

Promise and Covenant

Genesis 12–36 tells a story of divine promise and blessing and human response. God promises Abraham and Sarah that they will engender a renowned and blessed people. Abraham and Sarah, Isaac and Rebekah, and Jacob and Rachel take actions that sometimes advance and sometimes seem to hinder the fulfillment of God's promise. For Abraham especially the decisive issue is his faith in God's declaration that competes with his fearful disbelief. In Genesis 12:1-9, Yahweh challenges Abram, whose name will be changed to Abraham in Genesis 17, to emigrate to the land of Canaan. Yahweh blesses him and promises to make him famous as the founder of *a great nation* (12:2).

> I will bless those who bless you,
> those who curse you I will curse;
> all the families of the earth
> will be blessed because of you. (12:3)

God restates forms of this promise to Abraham several times (13:14-17; 15:5; 22:17-18), and reiterates it to Isaac (26:2-5) and Jacob (28:13-15).

In Genesis 15 and 17, God's relationship with Abraham and his descendants is enacted into a formal covenant. In Genesis 15, Abraham expresses doubts concerning the promise of offspring, because he is still childless (15:1-3) and is unsure about his possession of the land (15:7-8). God restates the promise and Abraham believes it (15:4-6). A striking covenant-making ceremony guarantees a positive outcome, although a long interval of slavery and exodus will intervene before Abraham's descendants will return to the land of promise (15:13-16, 18-21). The covenant ceremony itself involves splitting animal carcasses in half and passing between the pieces. God ratifies the covenant by being present in symbolic form as smoke and fire. This procedure for affirming oaths and covenants was practiced among Israel's neighbors and is alluded to in Jeremiah 34:18-21.

Genesis 17 describes God's covenant with Abraham from the perspective of the P source and encompasses several distinctive features.

> Abram's name is changed to Abraham and Sarai's name to Sarah (17:5, 15). In this way two different traditions about Israel's ancestors could be harmonized.
>
> Circumcision of sons and other males within the households of Abraham and his descendants is the sign by which the covenant will be observed.
>
> This is an *enduring covenant* (17:7, 13, 19).

Sarah is explicitly included in God's promise of blessing and a son. God's words to her and to Abraham are comparable (17:6 and 16).

Abraham responds with disbelieving laughter (17:17).

Sarah will give birth to Isaac (meaning "he laughs"). The covenant will continue through Isaac and not through Ishmael, the son of Hagar and Abraham.

6.1. CIRCUMCISION

God commands Abraham to circumcise all the males of his household (Gen 17:10-14). In biblical times, removing the prepuce (foreskin) of a male baby or boy was a common practice in ancient West Asia and Egypt (Jer 9:25-26). Parallels from cultural anthropology indicate that this custom began as a rite of passage at puberty. Old Testament stories evidence a conceptual link between circumcision and readiness for marriage (for example, Gen 34:14-17). As a religious ceremony, Israel practiced circumcision when an infant boy was eight days old (Lev 12:3). The great age of this custom is indicated by its association with flint knives (Exod 4:25; Josh 5:2-3).

The Philistines, with whom Israel had a hostile relationship, did not practice circumcision and are labeled antagonistically as *the uncircumcised* (for example, Judg 14:3). Probably it was first in opposition to the Philistines that circumcision become a decisive ethnic marker for Israel. Because the Babylonians (and later Greeks) were also uncircumcised, circumcision received even stronger emphasis in the diaspora as a hallmark of Jewish identity (1 Macc 1:15, 60-61; 2:46). In Joshua 5:2-9, Yahweh requires that all the men who enter the land of promise to conquer it be circumcised.

As a sort of "unblocking," circumcision of the heart became a metaphor for openness to God's ways (Deut 10:16; 30:6; Jer 4:4). Similarly Moses has trouble speaking because his lips are uncircumcised (Exod 6:12, 30; obscured in many translations; CEB: *not a very good speaker*).

Abraham and His Descendants

Faith and Unbelief

For God's promise to be realized, Abraham and Sarah must have a son, but this prospect is hindered by their great age and by Abraham's alternation between belief and unbelief in God's promise. In Genesis 12:10-20 (J) and 20:1-18 (E) Abraham endangers Sarah and her capacity to bear his heir out of fear. In chapter 16, Sarah and Abraham seek to provide an heir through Sarah's slave woman Hagar. Hagar bears Ishmael for Abraham, but this plan fails to work out. Both Abraham and Sarah laugh in disbelief (17:17; 18:12) at the prospect of finally becoming parents.

6.2. THE MATRIARCH IN DANGER

Genesis contains three stories with similar plots: 12:10-20, 20:1-18, and 26:1-11. Each involves a threat of improper sexual relations affecting a patriarch's wife (Sarah or Rebekah) and a foreign ruler (Pharaoh or Abimelech of Gerar). In each narrative this danger arises because of a claim that the matriarch is the sister of the patriarch, intended to protect the patriarch because she is so dangerously beautiful. The ruler discovers this danger and is offended. The threat to the family line is averted, and the patriarch ends up with great riches. From a form-critical perspective, these three texts are different versions of the same tale, told with different characters and from different perspectives.

Genesis 12:10-20 stems from the J document. Abram and Sarai go to Egypt. The information that this beautiful woman is the man's sister leads Pharaoh to take her into his house, where she implicitly becomes part of his harem. In return, Pharaoh showers Abraham with riches. Great plagues ensue, but no explanation is given for how Pharaoh discovers the true situation. He is distressed and expels the couple along with the wealth he has given them.

In Genesis 20:1-18, usually assigned to E, Abimelech king of Gerar hears about the sibling relationship from both Abraham and Sarah. This version is very careful to safeguard Sarah's reputation. Even though she becomes part of the king's domestic establishment, God prevents any sex from taking place (20:4, 6). Moreover, it turns out that Sarah really is Abraham's half-sister, so technically no lie has been told (20:12). Discovery of the situation comes through a dream in which God speaks to Abimelech. Abimelech gives riches to Abraham in order to underscore Sarah's complete vindication (20:16). Even though Abimelech's act was unintentional, the resultant infertility of his harem can only be undone through intercession by Abraham in his role as prophet (20:7, 17-18).

In Genesis 26:1-11 (J), the danger to Rebekah is only potential (26:10) and can only be understood on the basis of the other two narratives. She is not taken into the king's harem. Abimelech discovers the couple's marital relationship by observing their intimate behavior. Riches come to Isaac from Yahweh after the episode is over.

Genesis 18–19 ties together Yahweh's pledge of a son to Abraham and Sarah (18:1-15), Abraham's negotiations with Yahweh over the doom of Sodom (18:16-33), and the escape of Abraham's nephew Lot from Sodom (19:1-29). In Genesis 18, Yahweh's promise to Abraham is overheard by Sarah, who reacts with understandable laughter (18:10-15). The promise is made within a traditional narrative that legitimated the sacred site of the oaks of Mamre (near Hebron) as a place for the worship of Yahweh. Yahweh appears in human form in the context of three visitors, two of whom turn out to be divine messengers on their way to destroy Sodom (19:1). Abraham shows them outstanding hospitality, something that was an expected civic virtue in the ancient world: *He ran . . . to greet them and bowed deeply. . . . Abraham ran to the cattle . . . and stood under the tree near them as they ate* (18:2, 7-8).

At another level, however, the festive banquet he hosts (18:6-8) is a prefiguring of the sacrificial banquets that the worshippers of Yahweh would share at that site, marked by the holy tree under which the three heavenly visitors had dined.

Abraham accompanies his guests as they leave, and Yahweh reveals the grave misdeeds of Sodom. The two angels head down to Sodom, but Abraham intercedes for Sodom's fate. This episode is meant to reveal the great moral courage of Israel's patriarch, the intimate relationship Yahweh had established with him (as expressed in 18:19), and Yahweh's commitment to balanced justice (18:25). Step by step Abraham haggles with Yahweh, so that Yahweh eventually agrees that the existence of no more than ten righteous persons would save Sodom from destruction (18:23-32). It was not to be.

Like the stories that surround it, the focus of Genesis 19 is Abraham's family. The Sodom story is included in order to convey that Lot was alerted by the two men (angels) and escaped with divine help. The history of its interpretation shows that the story of Sodom and Gomorrah has been misunderstood as though it were a general diatribe against same-sex orientation. This can happen if cultural differences between the ancient and modern world are overlooked. Because the concept of innate sexual orientation did not exist in Israel, early readers would have understood the attempt at homosexual gang rape by the men of Sodom as the most outrageous possible violation of proper behavior toward strangers. In the ancient cultural context, same-sex rape was an assertion of power, with the intent of feminizing and thus dishonoring one's adversary. Lot's virtue (as understood by ancient moral standards) is emphasized by his attempt to protect his guests even at an appalling personal cost (19:7-8). Modern readers are likely to be revolted by his decision to give greater weight to the obligation of hospitality to his male guests than to the duty he owes to his own daughters. The incident of Lot's wife turning into a pillar of salt (19:26) explained the origin of a distinctive landmark in the region.

Testing Abraham—Genesis 22

The theme of belief and unbelief concludes in chapter 22 (from the E source) when Abraham passes the test of faith by his willingness to sacrifice Isaac at God's command. Many present-day readers have difficulty with this narrative, with its echoes of what may sound like child abuse and religious fanaticism. Earlier readers must have interpreted Abraham's willingness to destroy the son, on whom all God's promises rested, in a positive light. Child sacrifice was not unheard of the Israelite world (Judg 11:39; 2 Kgs 3:27). Genesis 22 emphasizes the emotional connection between father and son: *your only son whom you love* (22:2), *the two of them walked on together* (22:6, repeated in v. 8), and the reciprocal interchange of *my father* and *my son . . . my son* (22:7-8). Abraham's prediction that God would *see to* (NRSV: *provide*) the entirely burned offering (22:8) might be read as his attempt to hide the grim truth from Isaac or as evidence of a desperate faith, but it does come true at the last minute. At an earlier stage in its history, this narrative functioned as a sanctuary legend. It provided an explanation of why child sacrifice was not to be practiced in the worship of Yahweh and validated the holiness of Mount Moriah (that is, Jerusalem; see 2 Chr 3:1).

6.3. HAGAR AND ISHMAEL

Genesis contains two stories of Hagar's journey into wilderness and divine promise to her. Genesis 16:1-16 is a combination of J and P material, and 21:8-21 is considered to be E. The first narrative recounts the prelude to Ishmael's birth; the second takes place after Isaac has been born. In the first the narrative problem is Hagar's contempt for Sarah, while in the second the issue is Sarah's fear that Hagar's son will inherit along with Isaac. In both, Hagar leaves or is sent off into wilderness and receives a divine promise that her son will have notable offspring. Both texts specify one or more distinctive characteristics for Ishmael and feature a divine messenger (angel) and a well. They each provide etiological explanations for the origin and character of the Ishmaelites. Ishmael is circumcised along with Abraham (chapter 17) and joins Isaac in burying their father (25:9). Twelve tribal groups descend from Ishmael (25:12-17), and many of these names appear in ancient West Asian sources as groups in northern Arabia. In Islam it is not Isaac but Ishmael the firstborn who is the focal point of God's choice. According to the Quran, Ishmael joined his father Abraham in founding the sacred Kaaba in Mecca.

Isaac and Jacob—Genesis 24–36

Only a few stories are recounted about Isaac as an adult. These are the delightful romance of his marriage to Rebekah, recounted in Genesis 24, his interactions with Abimelech of Gerar connected with disputed wells (Gen 26), and the struggle between Jacob and Esau to receive their father's blessing (Gen 27).

Most of the narratives about Jacob are tightly organized into a cycle of stories (25:19–33:17). This material is structured so that the troubled relationship between Jacob and Esau surrounds the similarly fraught interactions between Jacob and his uncle Laban. Two sanctuary legends detailing Jacob's foundation of the holy places of Bethel and Penuel provide transitions between Jacob's dealings first with Esau, then with Laban, and then with Esau again:

Esau (25:19–28:9)

   Bethel (Jacob flees Esau and encounters Yahweh; 28:10-22)

      Laban (29:1–31:55)

   Penuel (Jacob returns to Esau and encounters a numinous being; 32:22-32)

Esau (preparations: 32:1-21; face-to-face encounter: 33:1-17)

Jacob is celebrated as a clever trickster who gets the better of his twin brother (sometimes with his mother Rebekah's assistance) and then of his father-in-law Laban, who was himself a master of deception (29:23, 25; 31:7). Modern readers tend to view cunning and craftiness as negative moral qualities, but early Israelites enjoyed retelling stories of Jacob's successful trickery in order to build up ethnic pride. The implication is that the descendants of Jacob (Israel) are shrewder than the progeny of Esau (Edomites) or Laban (Aramean groups).

Competition in successful motherhood plays out between Jacob's wives, Rachel and Leah, in 29:31–30:24. Their machinations results in him fathering the twelve sons who are the eponymous ancestors of Israel's twelve tribes. Rachel gives birth to Joseph (whose two sons become the tribes of Ephraim and Manasseh) and Benjamin. Her sister Leah is mother to six tribes. Four other tribes were said to descend from the sisters' two female servants, who function as surrogate mothers. Rachel's second son, Benjamin, is born last (35:16-20).

Tamar and Judah—Genesis 38

The story of Joseph (see the next section) is interrupted by a narrative about the unfolding family line of his brother Judah. Both the Joseph story and the Tamar story feature the motifs of recognition by personal items (Joseph's robe in 37:32-33 and the garment seized by Potiphar's wife in 39:12-18) and non-recognition (42:8). Tamar joins the matriarchs Rebekah and Rachel as a woman willing to take decisive action and even engage in subterfuge to advance the cause of family. Tamar seems to be a foreigner because Judah is living apart from his kinfolk, but the narrative makes nothing of this situation.

The cultural background for this narrative is the custom of levirate marriage. This practice obligated the brother of a married man who died without offspring to marry the dead man's widow. He was to provide her with a son to carry on the family line of the deceased (Deut 25:5-10; Ruth). The narrative problem arises when Tamar's husband Er dies childless (*Yahweh put him to death*, 38:7). Although Judah properly directs the second son Onan to do his duty for his deceased older brother, Onan selfishly refuses to do so, even though he does engage in sex with Tamar. As a result, Yahweh also kills Onan. Judah then betrays Tamar (and Er) by refusing to marry her to his remaining son, Shelah, and forcing her to live as a widow within her father's household. Judah's excuse for this eventually proves to be dishonest. Realizing this, Tamar takes action and demonstrates her commitment to the obligation she owes to her dead husband Er. She proves willing to transgress taboo and engage in a cunning deception in order to maneuver Judah into doing his family duty. Tamar changes her clothing, puts on a veil, and sits by the roadside. Judah perceives her as a soliciting prostitute and initiates negotiations. She cleverly steers the conversation so that she ends up with hallmarks of his personal identity. These tokens give her the upper hand when her pregnancy is discovered.

When Judah tries to send the promised baby goat as payment, his friend does not inquire about a commercial prostitute, but asks instead about a female religious functionary (38:21-22; CEB: *consecrated worker* or *holy woman*; Hebrew: *qedesha*). Apparently the idea is that this approach would make his errand seem more respectable. It may be that bringing an animal to a *qedesha* could be explained as donating a sacrificial victim. (The NRSV translation of this word as *temple prostitute* and then simply *prostitute* in 38:21-22 is unjustified and confusing.) At the climactic moment of revelation in 38:25-26, Judah confesses the undeniable conclusion: *She's more righteous than I am.* Tamar was faithful to her duty. Judah was not and had to be tricked into doing it. As the narrative wraps up, Judah's twin sons by Tamar are born. Perez and Zerah are the eponymous ancestors of two clans belonging to the tribe of Judah. The episode explains how it happened that Perez became the more important of the two, in that King David would stem from him (Ruth 4:18-22).

The Story of Joseph—Genesis 37, 39–50

Genesis 37, 39–48, 50 presents the Joseph story. This is a short story of betrayal, revenge, and reconciliation, told with narrative artistry. The plot is held together by unifying themes, although there are irregularities caused by the combination of sources. One of these unifying themes is *clothing*. Jacob makes his favorite son a special *long robe* (37:3; LXX: *many-colored*). After they have ambushed him, Joseph's jealous brothers dip that robe into the blood of a goat and present it to Jacob as evidence that Joseph was killed by a wild animal (37:31-33). While Joseph serves as a slave in Egypt, the seductive wife of his master uses a garment he has left behind as evidence of her claim of sexual assault (39:12-18). When Pharaoh elevates Joseph to high office, he clothes him in fine linen (41:42).

A second unifying theme centers on *dreams*. Dreams appear three times and do so in pairs. First Joseph experiences a pair of dreams that foreshadow his dominance over his brothers (37:5-11). When he is in the Egyptian prison, two of his fellow inmates recount dreams to him, and he is able to decipher these accurately (chapter 40). After some delay, Pharaoh is told about this accomplishment and gives Joseph the task of interpreting the two dreams Pharaoh has had about cows and ears of grain (41:1-36). Joseph does so, and this leads to him being appointed to prepare for the impending famine foreshadowed by these dreams.

The initial narrative problem of bad relationships between brothers is compounded by other developments (sub-plots) in the shape of Joseph's enslavement, Potiphar's wife, Joseph's imprisonment, the cupbearer's initial forgetfulness about Joseph (40:23), and famine. Even though Joseph overcomes these obstacles one by one and becomes successful in Egypt, the original problem of family dysfunction continues to lurk in the background. In fact, it is exacerbated by Joseph's desire for revenge against his brothers for their betrayal. Only in chapter 45 does the plot finally reach its climax, when Joseph reveals his true identity to his brothers.

> I'm your brother Joseph! The one you sold to Egypt. Now, don't be upset and don't be angry with yourselves that you sold me here. Actually, God sent me before you to save lives. (45:4-5)

The family of Jacob is saved from famine and installed in Egypt. When Jacob dies, Joseph assures the brothers that all is forgiven (50:15-21). The scene is set for the start of the book of Exodus.

6.4. ISRAEL AND HEBREW

The name Israel designated the people among whom the Old Testament developed from the earliest reference to them in the Merneptah Inscription (see chapter 2, Pre-Monarchic Period). In the very old Song of Deborah (Judges 5), the society called Israel and the deity Yahweh go hand in hand. Israel is styled *Yahweh's people* (5:11, 13) and Yahweh is termed *the God of Israel* (5:3, 5). However, Isra-*el* actually incorporates the name of the god El. Although the folk etymology in Genesis 32:28 traces its meaning back to a "struggle with God," Israel actually means something like "El fights" or "El rules." Israel is an eponymous name in the sense that it appears as the alternate name for Jacob (35:10). The name Israel was used in various ways, depending on context. It designated the northern kingdom of Israel, but also Yahweh's people as a whole including the population of Judah and their descendants.

In contrast, Potiphar's wife and Pharaoh's cupbearer identify Joseph as a *Hebrew* (39:14, 17; 41:12). The designation *Hebrew* is much less common in the Old Testament. Outsiders use it to refer to Israelites, or it is employed when interaction with foreigners is taking place (for example, Exod 1:15; 2:6).

Chapter 6

> Jonah introduces himself to his foreign shipmates, saying *I'm a Hebrew* (Jonah 1:9). The term *Hebrew* also served as a label for a certain class of slaves (Exod 21:2; Deut 15:12). Early extrabiblical documents designate groups of marginalized groups who operated outside the control of established rulers as *'apiru or habiru*. At one time it was thought that the designation "Hebrew" might have been connected in some way with those disruptive social elements, but this suggestion has been largely abandoned.

Further Reading

Tammi J. Schneider. *Sarah: Mother of Nations*. New York: Continuum, 2004.

Roland J. Faley. *Bonding with God: A Reflective Study of Biblical Covenant*. New York: Paulist, 1997.

Chapter 7
EXODUS

Exodus and Identity

The distinctiveness of Israel's God is expressed in Yahweh's repeated self-identification: *I am Yahweh your God who brought you out of the land of Egypt* (for example, Exod 20:2). Likewise, Israel articulated its identity as a specially elected people in the same terms: *Yahweh brought us out of Egypt with great power* (13:16). Thus a core element of Israel's self-understanding involved a story narrating their enslavement in Egypt, a miraculous escape, a journey to the homeland, and their acquisition of it. The story of the exodus is recounted in Exodus 1–15. It forms a dramatic plot consisting of the problem (slavery; chapter 1), providing and equipping a liberator (chapters 2–4), failed attempts to leave Egypt (chapters 5–10), and the climactic solution (freedom; chapters 11–15).

Let My People Go—Exodus 1–11

An important theological theme in these chapters revolves around Yahweh's goal to be recognized as God in the face of the counterclaims of Pharaoh. Who is really God? Is it Pharaoh, who was understood to be a divinity in human form? The issue of Yahweh's identity as undisputed God is raised by Pharaoh's first reaction to the mission of Moses: *Who is this Yahweh whom I'm supposed to obey? . . . I don't know this Yahweh* (5:2). In contrast, in the death of the firstborn, Yahweh declares judgment on the gods of Egypt, who prove powerless to protect their devotees (12:12).

Yahweh's motives in the contest with Pharaoh are unambiguous. On the one hand, Yahweh overhears the complaint of enslaved Israel, recognizes earlier promises made to the patriarchs, and feels empathy (2:23-25). Yet Yahweh also repeatedly reveals a desire to be acknowledged as God—by Israel (6:7), Pharaoh (7:17; 8:22;

9:14, 29), the Egyptians (7:5; 14:4, 18), Israel's future generations (10:2), and the whole earth (9:16). Yahweh's goal of receiving proper recognition as God causes the plagues to stretch out, seemingly unnecessarily, into a prolonged process (9:14-16). Whenever Pharaoh seems ready to relent, Yahweh makes him *stubborn* so that the plagues continue (7:3; 9:12; 10:1, 20, 27; 11:10; Pharaoh makes himself stubborn in 8:15, 32; 9:34). It is the reason that Yahweh lures Pharaoh and his army into a fatal trap at the Red Sea (14:1-4, 18).

Exodus 1 outlines the narrative problem. A new Pharaoh, who does not recognize an earlier relationship with Joseph, fears the presence of a foreign immigrant community with a high birth rate (1:7). He seeks to control and weaken them by enslaving them (1:11). However, this step only causes Israel to multiply faster, so the Egyptians make their servitude harsher (1:13-14). A second royal plan calls for the two midwives who serve Israel to kill all boy babies at birth, but these women outwit Pharaoh with a clever excuse (1:15-19). Pharaoh then orders that all newborn boys be put in the Nile River to drown (1:22).

7.1. MIRIAM

> According to Micah 6:4, Miriam was one of three, along with Moses and Aaron, whom God sent to Israel in the context of the exodus. In Exodus 15:20-21, she is called a prophet and as such leads the celebrating women and sings a victory song after Israel is rescued from Egypt's army. The sister of Moses who watched what happened to his basket in the river and arranged for Moses's own mother to nurse him is not named in Exodus 2:4, 7, but she is traditionally identified with Miriam. Miriam died before Israel entered the land of promise and was buried at Kadesh (Num 20:1).

In Exodus 2, women continue to take action. The mother of Moses obeys Pharaoh, but in her own fashion. She places her baby in the Nile in a waterproof *basket* or "ark" (the same word is used for Noah's boat). The sister of Moses stations herself where she can watch. The Egyptian princess feels sympathy for baby Moses and cancels out her father's program of death. Moses's sister proposes that his mother be paid to nurse her own child (2:7-9). Although the name Moses appears to be Egyptian, Exodus 2:10 gives the name a Hebrew meaning connected with how his adoptive mother acquired him: *"I pulled him out."*

In Exodus 3 and 4, as is typical in stories about heroes, Moses is summoned to his task in an extraordinary way and provided with what he will need to succeed.

These resources include God's presence and a sign to build Moses's confidence (3:12). Moses is given knowledge of God's own personal name, Yahweh (3:13-15). He is provided with a wonder-working shepherd's rod and Aaron as a spokesperson (4:2-5, 14-17). As is typical in Old Testament stories reporting a divine call, Moses objects at various points to God's mandates and plans. Who am I to do such a thing (3:11)? What is this God's name (3:13)? What if Israel does not believe me (4:1)? I am not a good public speaker (4:10).

The account of ten plagues inflicted on Egypt intermingles elements from the J and P sources, although there is controversy over exactly how these should be divided. Of the first nine plagues, J is responsible for *insects* (perhaps horseflies), cattle disease, *hail*, *locusts*, and *darkness* (8:20-32; 9:1-7, 13-35; 10:1-20, 21-26). P contributed *lice* (perhaps gnats or mosquitoes) and *skin sores* (or boils; 8:16-19; 9:8-12). Both sources contained the first two plagues, the Nile converted into *blood* and *frogs* (7:14-25; 8:1-15). Aaron is a more prominent character in the P version, and P features Egyptian magicians (CEB: *religious experts*) as well. They also turn the Nile to blood and produce frogs. But in 8:18-19, they fail to reproduce lice and so recognize God's supremacy. Finally, in 9:11 they themselves suffer from the plague of skin sores.

The decisive plague is the death of *the firstborn* (NRSV) of every social class and even of domestic animals. *Firstborn* in this context would seem to refer to any male person or male animal that was the first offspring of his mother (see 13:12, 15). However, some interpreters point out that the description of who lives and who dies on Passover night makes no explicit distinction between males and females, and the CEB favors the translation *oldest child*.

The First Passover—Exodus 12–13

The core of the exodus tradition centers on the Passover ritual, which must have served as the recurring setting in life (German: *Sitz im Leben*) for recounting the exodus story. Passover became basic to Israel's identity. Renewals of Israel's self-understanding were marked by special celebrations of Passover, as when entering the land (Josh 5:10-12), reforming worship life (2 Kgs 23:21-23), and rededicating the temple (Ezra 6:19-22).

The description of the first Passover on the night of the plague of death gives an etiology and rationale for the festival. It also provides guidance for how Passover is to be celebrated. For every generation, Passover is to be a time for *intent watching* (12:42, NRSV: *a night of vigil*) and for remembering the departure from Egypt and liberation (13:3). The name Passover is linked to Yahweh's passing over or skipping over the Israelite dwellings marked by the blood of sacrificial lambs (12:13, 23, 27).

It is generally accepted that Passover began as a ritual marking the transfer of flocks to springtime pasturage. The sacrifice was intended to protect newly born lambs and baby goats. A second observance, Unleavened Bread, also took place in spring. This involved a taboo against eating bread that had been leavened with dough from last year's harvest. Not eating leavened bread thus established a sharp break between the grain of the new harvest and what remained from the previous year. In Exodus, the two celebrations are coordinated by eating unleavened bread as part of the sacrificial meal (12:8) and by pointing to haste as a reason for not waiting for that bread to rise (12:33-34, 39). Smearing blood around doors (12:7, 13, 22-23) was a feature only of the night of exodus and not part of later Passover celebrations.

In Exodus the victim was slaughtered by the head of the household (12:21) and eaten by a family-oriented gathering of participants (12:4, 8, 10). In later times, this domestic Passover centered on the household developed into a festival celebrated exclusively in Jerusalem. The sacrificial animals were killed by priests in the temple area and taken away to be eaten by groups. This shift in practice is reflected in Deuteronomy 16 and 2 Kings 23:21-23. This remained the pattern throughout the Second Temple period (Ezra 6:19-22; and for the New Testament). When the destruction of the temple in 70 CE made sacrifice impossible, Passover reverted to a family-oriented celebration.

Deliverance at the Sea—Exodus 14–15

It is usually thought that the narrative of Israel's escape through the sea represents a combination of the source documents J (with a few verses of E) and P. Under influence from the Greek Septuagint, it is traditional to translate the location of this event as *Red Sea* (NRSV; 13:18; 15:4), but some versions such as CEB opt for *Reed Sea*. Reed Sea points to the marshy, reed-filled lakes adjacent to Egypt. The J version treats the event as a victory of Yahweh the Divine Warrior (*Yahweh will fight for you*, 14:14). A wall of clouds separates Israel from the Egyptian army as an east wind blows back the water and turns the sea into dry land (14:19b-21). As morning draws near, Yahweh causes the Egyptians to panic when they recognize that Yahweh is fighting against them (14:24-25). They flee, and Yahweh throws them into the sea. Israel witnesses their dead bodies on the seashore (14:27, 30-31). In contrast, the interwoven P version pictures the water as divided like walls on either side of escaping Israel and then dramatically returning upon the pursuing chariots (14:15-18, 22-23, 26, 28-29).

Exodus 15:1-18 parallels the prose description of chapter 14 with a celebratory hymn of praise led by Moses. The victory of Yahweh as Divine Warrior (15:3: *Yahweh is a warrior*) results in Israel's victorious progress to the land of promise. This song does not mention Israel crossing the sea. Instead, Yahweh uses the sea to destroy the enemy and causes them to sink into it. In 15:20-21, Miriam, functioning as prophet, leads the women in a victory dance and sings the hymn's first line, probably to indicate that they performed the whole song.

Life in the Wilderness

The remainder of Exodus follows three themes: life in the wilderness, torah and covenant, and God's dwelling (KJV: *tabernacle*). Stories about Israel's time in the wilderness are recounted in Exodus and Numbers. They emphasize God's care and provision for Israel, but contrast this with Israel's tendency to rebel, disobey, and complain. This pattern is first established in 15:22-26. Yahweh solves the problem of undrinkable, bitter water at Marah (*bitter*), but only after the people complain to Moses and he appeals to Yahweh.

Manna—Exodus 16

The manna story in Exodus 16 is a classic example of the wilderness tradition. Israel begins to complain that Moses and Aaron have led them into the desert in order to kill them. They remember slavery as a time of plentiful food. Moses insists that they are really rebelling against Yahweh, not just their human leaders. Yahweh promises that bread will rain from the sky and meat will appear in the form of quail. Manna (named for the question in 16:15, *What is it?*) appears regularly on schedule *every morning* (16:21). It is versatile and delicious (16:23, 31). Everyone who goes out to gather it gets precisely the right amount for their household's daily needs. However, manna is also a test of Israel's obedience. If one is too late to collect it, it melts away. It cannot be accumulated or stored up for another day. The manna schedule forces Sabbath to be a day of rest in that a double portion arrives on Friday and none appears on Saturday. Interpreters sometimes connect manna with the natural occurrence of sugary, scale-like deposits produced by certain desert insects. Such naturalistic explanations are alien to the purpose of the biblical texts, which sought to celebrate Yahweh's benevolence and amazing power. Exodus 17:1-7 (water from the rock) is another story about rebellion, punishment, and deliverance.

The Gold Bull Calf—Exodus 32

The gold calf incident is recounted in Exodus 32. While Moses is away on Mount Sinai, the anxious people induce Aaron to make an image in the form of a *bull calf*, cast from donated gold earrings. The people proclaim, somewhat ambiguously, *These are your gods, Israel, who brought you up out of the land of Egypt*, yet Aaron announces

Chapter 7

a festival for Yahweh (32:4-5). Yahweh informs Moses of this outrage and threatens to wipe out Israel. However, Moses argues that this would ruin Yahweh's reputation with the Egyptians and break the promise Yahweh made to Israel's ancestors (32:12-13). In anger, Moses breaks the law tablets he has received. He then orchestrates a ritual to remove the danger caused by the image (32:19-20). In the end, Moses's attempt to intercede with Yahweh has only partial success (32:30-35).

Fig. 6. Bull images representing power and fertility were associated with powerful male deities such as Baal (Hadad) or Yahweh. This eighth-century stele portrays a stylized bull with crescent horns and armed with a sword. It was discovered at Bethsaida, the capital of the Aramean kingdom of Geshur. It may represent Hadad or a moon god.

The gold calf story was told and retold for polemical purposes. The royal sanctuaries of Bethel and Dan in the northern kingdom featured bull images representing Yahweh (1 Kgs 12:26-30; Hos 13:2). Aaron is also a target of this polemic. He submits to the peoples' request and then on his own builds an altar and institutes a festival. When questioned, he shifts blame onto the people and tells an incredible falsehood about how the image came to be (32:22-24). In contrast to this criticism directed against the priestly family descended from Aaron, the account praises the Levites, who display selfless zeal in liquidating the guilty parties (32:26-29). There was a long-standing rivalry between the priests of the Aaronic family and the lower-status group of religious specialists called Levites.

Exodus

Torah and Covenant at Sinai

Exodus 19–24 and Exodus 34 concern the instructions or teachings promulgated by Yahweh and Yahweh's relationship with Israel understood in terms of covenant. The Ten Commandments given on Mount Sinai (Exodus 19–20) have been joined to an old collection of laws called the Book of the Covenant (20:22–23:19). Israel's encounter with Yahweh at Sinai is set in the context of covenant (19:3-6), and a covenant-making ceremony is described in Exodus 24. In Exodus 34, Moses ascends Mount Sinai again in order to replace the tablets that he broke during the gold calf fiasco. A list of commandments concerning worship and ritual is connected to this episode (34:10-26), and these become the stipulations of a covenant made by Yahweh (34:10, 27-28).

Apodictic and Casuistic Instruction

Old Testament instruction appears in two forms or genres. *Apodictic* sayings are flat statements of what is prohibited or required: *Don't say a curse against God* (Exod 22:28) or *Observe the Festival of Unleavened Bread* (23:15). Apodictic instructions communicate and motivate appropriate behavior. They sometimes appear in lists suitable for teaching situations and formal proclamation, such as the Ten Commandments or the twelve-item list (in a curse format) in Deuteronomy 27:15-26. In contrast, *casuistic* statements have an "if . . . then" format. The first clause describes a situation, sometimes with sub-clauses exploring variations of that situation. This is followed by a consequence or punishment. Casuistic instructions are useful in actual legal situations in which judgments have to be made about the nature of an alleged offense and an appropriate penalty or recompense needs to be assigned. Exodus 22:6 is a characteristic example. The situation is a fire that destroys grain, wherever it may be. The consequence is that the person who started the fire must fully repay the owners. Exodus 22:10-13 governs a more complex case outlining several possibilities.

Ten Commandments—Exodus 19–20

Both Jewish and Christian tradition consider this list of *ten words* (Exod 34:28) an expression of the core ideals of correct behavior. Yahweh comes down to Mount Sinai in thunder, lightning, cloud, and smoke to speak instructions to Moses. This is the poetic language of *theophany*, describing the appearance of God (or God's representative) to humans in conjunction with manifestations of glory and power. Chapter 19 sets the stage for this event in a complex way. Moses moves up and down the mountain several times, indicating the existence of multiple sources. Although later

Christians and Jews have interpreted the Ten Commandments to relate to their own situations, the commandments originally applied to Israel's ancient social system. They are addressed to elite male property owners in an agrarian economy, who own livestock, live in houses with neighbors, and have slaves.

In 19:3-6, Yahweh's self-identification as their liberator encourages Israel to exclusive loyalty. No other gods *before me* (that is, in preference to me) may also mean *besides me* (instead of me). A ban on the worship of divine images extends Yahweh's demand for absolute fidelity. Punishment could extend to the three or four generations of a family that would be alive at any given time, but in contrast, Yahweh also promises to be loyal and gracious to the thousandth generation of the obedient.

Exodus 20:7 prohibits employing the power of God's personal name Yahweh for a worthless purpose, such as making false solemn pledges or performing harmful magic. Verses 8-11 make it clear that the enjoyment of Sabbath rest applies to all: children, slaves, non-Israelite immigrants who are part of one's household, and even domestic animals. Exodus 20:12 is directed primarily to adult children, many still living in multigenerational family units under the authority of aged parents. *Do not kill* (20:13) is not a ban on all killing. Israel practiced capital punishment, fought wars, and sacrificed animals. The commandment originally outlawed outright murder, causing death by carelessness, and killing someone in unlawful reprisal. *Do not commit adultery* (20:14) focuses on offenses against the betrayed husband. In ancient Israel's patriarchal culture, adultery was limited to what a man or woman might do to violate the marriage rights of that woman's husband or of the man to whom she was betrothed. Exodus 20:16 is a prohibition not on lying in general but on false witness in legal proceedings. Israel's legal system depended almost entirely on truthful witnesses (Num 35:30; Deut 17:6; 19:15). The final prohibitions in 20:17 seem to move beyond outward behavior to prohibit even envious thoughts. However, some believe that the verb usually translated *covet* implies actually taking action to possess the object of desire. Thus, the CEB translates this verb both as *desire* and *desire and try to take*.

The Book of the Covenant—Exodus 20:22–23:19

Exodus 20:22–23:19 is a collection of legal instructions positioned between the Ten Commandments and the covenant ceremony of chapter 24. Sometimes called the Covenant Code (CEB: *covenant scroll*, see 24:7), it represents the oldest collection of laws in the Old Testament and is usually dated to the early monarchy period. These instructions reflect the situation of settled agricultural communities governed by local elders. Topics include offenses against persons and property, religious behavior, and duties toward slaves, the poor, and the marginalized. There is no hint of urban life and, with exception of a ruler mentioned in 22:28, no effective centralized authority. In Exodus 20:23–22:17, statements are cast into a casuistic, "if . . . then" format. The instructions in 22:18–23:19 are primarily apodictic. The collection begins with a teaching about altar construction (20:24-26) and concludes with a religious calendar concerning Sabbath and the three major festivals (23:12-19).

The Book of the Covenant is the basis for a covenant ceremony in Exodus 24. In 24:3-8, blood from a sacrifice (the *blood of the covenant*) is sprinkled both on an altar (representing God) and on the people. This ritual action ratifies a covenant between the two parties, the stipulations for which are contained in the scroll that Moses reads aloud (24:7). In 24:9-11, Moses and other leaders go up the mountain, where they see God, although the text is careful to describe only the floor on which God's feet rest. They share in a ceremonial meal that also ratifies the covenant.

Another Decalogue—Exodus 34:10-26

A third collection of instructions in Exodus is often called the Ritual Decalogue. This list of instructions appears in the middle of material about God's dwelling place (tabernacle) in Exodus 25–31 and 35–40 and just after the gold calf episode. Moses reascends the mountain and is provided with a replacement set of instruction tablets. Strikingly, however, these *ten words* (34:28) appear to be different from the rules for life in Exodus 20 and regulate ritual matters. As in Exodus 20, idols and work on the Sabbath are prohibited, but in different language (34:17, 21). Worshippers are commanded to appear at a local sanctuary to observe three festivals (34:18, 22-23, 25-26; compare 23:14-17). Improper worship is linked to the religious practices of the Canaanites (34:11-16). Exodus 34:26b (paralleled in 23:19) is the origin of the prohibition in Judaism of serving dairy and meat products together. This proscription of boiling a baby goat in its own mother's milk may reflect a feeling that such a practice would pervert the life-giving nature of the maternal relationship.

As part of this revelation to Moses, Yahweh appears to him and proclaims a creed-like definition of Yahweh's character. Yahweh self-identifies as

> a God who is compassionate and merciful,
>> very patient,
>> full of great loyalty and faithfulness,
>> showing great loyalty to a thousand generations,
>> forgiving every kind of sin and rebellion,
>> yet by no means clearing the guilty,
>> punishing for their parents' sins
>> their children and their grandchildren,
>> as well as the third and the fourth generation. (Exod 34:6-7)

Similar words are repeated in Numbers 14:18; Nehemiah 9:17; Jeremiah 32:18; Joel 2:13; Jonah 4:2; Nahum 1:3; and three times in the Psalms.

Chapter 7

The Tabernacle—Exodus 25–31, 35–40

In Exodus 25–31 Moses sets out Yahweh's instructions for constructing the tabernacle and its associated accessories. Chapters 35–40 describe how those plans were carried out. The word traditionally translated as *tabernacle* (KJV, NRSV; CEB: *the dwelling*) means "a place where one lives." The tabernacle is conceived of as a sanctuary appropriate for Israel's wandering desert existence and is depicted as a portable tent version of the Jerusalem temple. It replicates the temple's courtyard, altars, and furnishings. Woven curtains hung on a wood framework form a courtyard. In the western part of this is situated an enclosed space or tent (the tabernacle proper) containing an incense altar, a table for displaying sacrificial bread, and a lampstand. The ark (CEB: *chest*) representing God's presence is sheltered in an interior space in the back of the tabernacle area. The eastern part of the courtyard contains an altar for sacrifice. The vestments of Aaron and of other attending priests are described in Exodus 28 and 39, and the ceremony of their priestly ordination in chapter 29.

An alternative designation for the tabernacle is the *meeting tent* (KJV, NRSV: *tent of meeting*), because the divine presence interacted there with the people or their representatives. This phrase seems to derive from an early tradition which spoke of a tent of revelation located outside Israel's encampment, where God would appear from time to time in order to interact with Moses and others (for example, Exod 33:7-11).

Further Reading

Thomas B. Dozeman. *Commentary on Exodus*. Eerdmans Critical Commentary. Grand Rapids: Eerdmans, 2009.

Patrick D. Miller. *The Ten Commandments*. Louisville, KY: Westminster John Knox, 2009.

Chapter 8
LEVITICUS AND NUMBERS

Leviticus

Leviticus is an expression of the lore and ritual traditions of the priests of Judah. As part of the Priestly Writing, the book is a product of priests who had been forced to migrate to Babylon after the defeat of Judah and the demolition of the temple. Most scholars place the composition of Leviticus into the exilic period, that is, between those deportations (597 and 586) and the reconstruction of the Jerusalem temple (beginning in 520). Without a temple, the all-important practices of sacrifice and temple ritual were brought to an abrupt end, and knowledge about these matters could no longer be transmitted as living traditions. Priestly lore had to be written down in order to preserve priestly and Jewish identity in the alien environment of Babylonian culture. The main themes of Leviticus are legitimacy, orderliness, proper procedure, and purity.

Leviticus begins as Moses is summoned by Yahweh to receive divine instruction about sacrifices (chapters 1–7), the inauguration of the priesthood and tabernacle liturgy (chapters 8–10), purity laws (chapters 11–15), and an annual Day of Atonement (CEB: *Day of Reconciliation*) intended to remove ritual impurity from the tabernacle and people (chapter 16). A constant repetition of the refrain *Yahweh said to Moses* (4:1; 5:14, and so forth) structures these instructions.

The Priestly Worldview

Priests served as a special class of ritual specialists who saw themselves as descendants of Aaron. Leviticus 8–9 describes the priestly ordination ceremony in terms of its first performance for Aaron and his sons. Like Israel's kings, priests were anointed with olive oil in order to bring about their special status (8:12). Only priests were allowed to approach the holy altar to offer sacrifices and deal with holy things (for example, 9:7-8). Aaron was entrusted with the Urim and Thummim, a sacred lot that could reveal the divine will (8:8). Chapter 10 recounts a polemic and cautionary story that explains why the priesthood was limited to the descendants of only two of Aaron's four sons, namely to Eleazar and Ithamar.

8.1. URIM AND THUMMIM

Priests were thought to be able to discover unknown information or determine Yahweh's will through the use of these two objects. In the Priestly Writing, they are set into the *chest piece* of the vestments of Aaron and the high priests who succeeded him (Exod 28:30; Lev 8:8; Num 27:21). According to Deuteronomy 33:8, using the Urim and Thummim was a special prerogative of the tribe of Levi. Although the exact nature of this oracle and how it was operated remain unclear, it seems that Urim and Thummim were two stones that provided answers to specific questions by indicating either *yes* or *no*. Perhaps these were engraved with symbols or letters to that effect. They may have been shaken together in a container until either the yes or no stone came out. Or it may be that each of the two stones had both yes and no sides, so that when thrown out like dice, a match of yes-yes or no-no would give a decisive answer. The absence of a match would then represent *no answer*, which appears to be the situation experienced by Saul in 1 Samuel 28:6. More complex information could be ascertained by a series of ever-narrowing questions and yes-or-no pronouncements. Saul's quest to discover the wrongdoer in his army in 1 Samuel 14:36-42 describes such a procedure. Joshua 7:16-18 also portrays the identification of individuals by a process of successive elimination, although Urim and Thummim are not explicitly mentioned. Centuries later, when many Jews returned from their forced exile in Babylon, there seems no longer to have been a priest capable or authorized to use the Urim and Thummim oracle (Ezra 2:63). However, Sirach 45:10 indicates that the high priest in the second century still wore Urim and Thummim.

To appreciate the ritual instructions in Leviticus, one must understand two pairs of cultural categories. The first of these category pairs distinguished that which was *holy* over against that which was *common*. The second pair distinguished what was considered in a *clean* state as opposed to what was in an *unclean* state. Leviticus 10:10 expresses the fundamental priestly worldview about these categories:

> So that you can distinguish between the holy and the common, and between the unclean and the clean, and so that you can teach the Israelites.

These two oppositions dealt with separate issues, but were also conceptually interrelated.

Clean versus Unclean

The categories of *clean* (ceremonially pure) and *unclean* (ceremonially impure) had nothing to do with hygiene or good health. Persons, objects, and foods could be regarded as clean or unclean. Leviticus 11 sets forth regulations for animals that are clean or unclean for food purposes. The ordinary domestic animals raised by Israel (sheep, goats, cattle) provide the standard, so that animals that do not have a divided hoof and do not re-chew their food are unclean for food purposes (11:3-4; for example, pigs, v. 7). Although people normally existed in a state of being clean, some situations (mostly involving corpses, sex, blood, and skin disease) could bring about uncleanness, and this impurity could be of varied degrees of seriousness and duration. To be in an unclean state meant that one could not participate in worship and sacrifice. Some sorts of impurity were contagious. Simply bathing and washing one's clothes were routine procedures for removing everyday impurity. Other more serious cases required a special ceremony.

In daily life, women were more affected by purity rules than men. Leviticus 12 provides instructions for uncleanness resulting from childbirth. Male and female genital discharges are covered in chapter 15, and one can see that uncleanness resulting from menstruation would have a major impact on a woman's life (15:19-24). Various sorts of *skin disease* are lumped together under the category commonly and misleadingly translated as "leprosy" (Leviticus 13–14; NRSV: *leprous disease*). Persons (and even objects and houses) with these conditions were regarded as intensely unclean and suffered devastating social consequences. Because of a need to be in a clean state in order to deal with holy things, priests and their family members had particularly strict regulations about impurity (21:1–22:16).

Common versus Holy

Most things and people were ordinarily thought of as being in the *common* condition. The usual translation for *to make common* is *to profane* (as NRSV), which has unfortunate negative connotations. (CEB translates this verb as *make impure* or *defile*, which confuses the states of being unclean and being common.) In most situations, to be in the common or profane state was simply to be ordinary and normal. In contrast, things and persons were considered to be *holy* (and not common or profane) if they were closely associated with Yahweh. Thus, priests and everything to do with the altar and sacrifices were holy. Priests were required to retain their holy state in order to perform their duties (21:6-8). Serious problems were thought to arise if something or someone in the unclean state was brought into relationship with what had to remain holy for the sake of Israel's relationship to Yahweh. An unclean person or thing had the potential to desecrate or degrade something holy into something common. The teachings contained in Leviticus sought most of all to prevent Israel from making the sanctuary common or profane (20:3; 21:12) or doing the same thing to Yahweh's holy name (18:21; 21:6; 22:2, 32). Making common or profaning Yahweh's name would mean catastrophically undermining the holiness of Yahweh.

Sacrifice

Sacrifice involved offering an animal or something like grain or incense to God in order to bring about or strengthen one's relationship to God. Transfer to the world of the divine could be achieved by turning all or part of the offering into smoke through burning it, lifting it up, or pouring it out. Yahweh was said to enjoy the smoke of a sacrifice as a pleasing odor (1:9, 13; 2:2, 9; 3:5, 16; 26:31). The primary purpose of an altar was to serve as a platform for the fire that consumed the offering. An altar also served as a place to apply or dispose of blood from the sacrifice (for example, 1:5 and 4:7). A sacrificial animal had to be whole and without physical imperfection.

The animal victim would be killed in the near vicinity of the altar (1:11; 3:2) and therefore in the presence of (that is, before) Yahweh (1:5; 4:4, 24). Obviously slaughtering the sacrificed animal was a necessary first step in its being burned or eaten. Death decisively transferred the living animal out of the realm of the ordinary and meant that it was no longer in the possession of the one who contributed it as a sacrificial victim. Persons offering an animal identified it as their own by placing a hand on it. The donor was responsible for killing the animal, as well as skinning and washing it (compare the division of duties in 1:2-9; 3:1-16; 4:24). Women could sponsor and present sacrifices on their own (12:6-7; 15:28-30).

Sacrifice was largely about building relationships. A sacrifice was a gift to God and, just as is the case with human gift-giving, it was thought to establish or maintain a relationship between the human giver and the divine recipient. Many if not most animal sacrifices involved the worshippers eating portions of the sacrificial victim. Sacrifice understood as meal was seen as a way to strengthen both the vertical divine-human relationship and the horizontal social relationships of the worshippers. A portion of the meal was set aside for God by burning. In 1 Samuel (composed at an earlier date than Leviticus), one reads that the company of human diners would consist of family (1 Sam 1:3-5) and a circle of invited guests (1 Sam 9:12-13; 16:3-5). The portions for human consumption were boiled in a pot (1 Sam 2:14) or roasted (1 Sam 2:15).

The practice of animal sacrifice had other benefits, not so obviously religious. The distribution of animal protein to the general populace was facilitated and regulated by sacrificial practice. Festive sacrificial meals served as social support for the disadvantaged. Sacrifice probably had positive ecological benefits by encouraging the slaughter of flocks and herds and thus reducing overgrazing. Leviticus describes several types of sacrifice. The word translated as *sacrifice* (noun and verb) derives from the verb *to slaughter*. It describes the offering of an animal that resulted in a communal meal eaten by the human participants after designated fatty portions were burned and the blood disposed of (CEB: *communal sacrifice*). The fuller expression *communal sacrifice of well-being* indicates that the purpose of the offering was to generate goodwill and solidarity as the victim was apportioned out as a shared meal (7:15-21). Certain sacrifices were individual and situational. Through these the worshipper could express thanksgiving, fulfill a vow made to God (CEB: *solemn promise*), or present God with a voluntary gift. These sacrifices may be grouped together as appreciative responses to God's benevolence (for example, 7:12-16; 22:18-23).

In contrast to sacrifices resulting in a meal shared by the human participants, a *burnt offering* (CEB: *entirely burned offering*) transferred the entire slaughtered animal into the divine realm by burning it up completely. In a *gift offering* (CEB: *grain offering*), grain, flour, or cakes were burned, with portions handed over for the priests to eat. By offering *tithes* (CEB: *tenth-part gift*), *first fruits* of agricultural produce, and *firstlings* of newborn domestic animals, Israel recognized God's rights as their ruler and as the one who had given them their homeland. Offerings also involved incense burned on special altars and in censers (16:12) and libations of wine (23:13). Loaves of bread were set out periodically on a table in the sanctuary as a display offering before Yahweh (24:5-9).

Blood produced by sacrificial slaughter was considered to be highly charged with power. Equating blood and life, Leviticus 17:10-14 connects the taboo against eating blood with its powerful ritual use at the altar to bring about reconciliation. Sacrificial blood was smeared on the horns of the altar to purify the altar (8:15) or thrown against its side. It was sprinkled before the sanctuary curtain (4:6), or applied to the earlobes, thumbs, and toes in the ordination of priests and to reintegrate persons healed from skin diseases (8:23; 14:14).

Leviticus evidences a particular concern for sacrifices that dealt with sin and guilt. This focus on the problem of transgression grew stronger after the conquest of

Judah by Babylon and the resulting forced deportations, because those catastrophes were interpreted as divine punishment for the nation's infidelity and disobedience. The priestly sacrificial system adjusted to put greater emphasis on sacrifice as a way to block the effects of sin. Sacrifices designated as *sin offerings* (CEB: *purification offerings*) and *guilt offerings* (CEB: *compensation offerings*) were intended to negate the negative effects of wrongdoing, whether intentional or unintentional. Sin and guilt were considered to be objective matters, so that even inadvertent errors had negative consequences. Leviticus 4–5 outlines sacrificial procedures for removing sin and guilt acquired by unintentional violations. Deliberate misdeeds are dealt with in 6:1-7.

Day of Atonement—Leviticus 16

Sacrifice was thought to *make atonement* (CEB: *make reconciliation*). Some interpreters emphasize that in the Hebrew text of Leviticus, *atonement* implies the purging or removal (or deactivation) of sin or guilt by wiping it off or covering it over. Other interpreters emphasize that the Hebrew term meant removing a barrier or an obstacle that hindered a relationship with God. The sixteenth-century English word from Tyndale's translation is a construct—"at-one-ment"—which entered the KJV vocabulary. Whether by purging guilt or by reconciling with God, sacrificial slaughter and sacrificial blood could erase or hide the impurity and sin that obstructed the proper relationship between Israel and God.

Leviticus 16 describes an annual Day of Atonement (Hebrew: *Yom Kippur*; CEB: *Day of Reconciliation*) ceremony. This ritual involved the sacrifice of a young bull and one of two goats. Every year, Aaron (and the high priest who was his successor) was to apply the sacrificial blood to purify and make atonement for the sacred things of the sanctuary. To do this, he entered the holiest part of the sanctuary, something otherwise completely forbidden. A second goat was invested with the offenses and sins of the people (16:21) and then driven out into the wilderness to Azazel, apparently some sort of demonic being (16:8, 10). This second goat (traditionally identified in English as the *scapegoat*) was thought to carry the sins of the nation out to an isolated place where they could do no damage (16:22; birds are used in a similar way in 14:7, 53).

The Holiness Code—Leviticus 17–26

Leviticus 17–26 is a special collection of instructions related to, but yet somewhat different from, the other teaching material of the Priestly Writing. These chapters represent a distinct, self-contained document, which is called the Holiness Code (with the symbol H). This designation stems from its recurrent demand that Israel must be holy because Yahweh is holy. This mandate is repeated in Leviticus 19:2;

20:7, 26; 21:8. It remains unclear whether H is older than or later than P. The Holiness Code extends the demand for holiness beyond priestly personnel and the objects of Israel's worship life to include the entire nation and the homeland itself. Holiness is to be achieved through the people's obedience in regard to social safeguards, justice, avoiding incest, and observing Sabbath rest and the festival calendar. Holiness, therefore, is a matter not only of ritual propriety and avoidance of impurity, but also of ethics and obedience in ordinary life. Lack of holiness on Israel's part would endanger their relationship to Yahweh by degrading or undermining the holiness of Yahweh (19:12; 22:2, 32). Leviticus 26 motivates Israel's obedience by a series of blessings and extensive curses.

Leviticus 25 decrees a radical expansion of an older teaching concerning the sabbatical year. The earlier Book of the Covenant required that farmland remain fallow every seventh year (Exod 23:10-11; Lev 25:3-7). The Holiness Code adds to this by mandating that after seven of these sabbatical year cycles (totaling 49 years), the fiftieth year was to be a *Jubilee year*. In the Jubilee year, farmland was to lie unsown for a second year. A trumpet (*yobel*) was to be blown, and there would be a universal forgiveness of all obligations of debt, a return of land ownership to the families from which it had been alienated, and an end to all terms of servitude. The words of Leviticus 25:10 (KJV) are inscribed on the Liberty Bell in Philadelphia and give it its name: *proclaim liberty throughout all the land unto all the inhabitants thereof*. It is generally believed that these Jubilee year requirements were utopian and never actually implemented.

Numbers

The book of Numbers features an interplay of divine instruction and narrative action set into a journey framework. The book recounts Israel's journey from their encampment at Mount Sinai (Num 10:11-12) to the edge of the land of promise on the plains of Moab (22:1). The usual name Numbers reflects the two military censuses taken, first at Sinai in chapters 1 and 3–4, and then in chapter 26 at the plains of Moab. That second census is taken after forty years have passed and the earlier generation has died off and been replaced by a new one. The name of the book in the Hebrew Bible is identical to its opening words, "in the wilderness," which is also an appropriate description of its contents. Israel has not moved in its journey since Exodus 19:1-2, when they arrived at their camp in the Sinai desert. Yahweh had commanded them to leave Sinai in Exodus 33:1-3, but their journey remained stalled while Moses received and obeyed further instructions from God throughout Exodus 35–40 and Leviticus.

Chapter 8

Numbers falls into three parts.

The first part, 1:1–10:10, takes place in the Sinai desert. God continues to instruct Moses, using the same repeated refrain found in Leviticus: *Yahweh spoke to Moses* (Num 1:1; 2:1, and so forth). A description of the first census and the layout of the wilderness encampment in chapters 1–4 is followed by instructions about ceremonial matters in 5:1–10:10.

The second part of the book, Numbers 10:11–21:35, recounts Israel's desert experiences. The march forward finally gets underway in 10:11-12 after Israel has been at Sinai for eleven months and nineteen days (Exod 19:1; Num 10:11).

The third division of the book begins when the people reach the plains of Moab in Numbers 22:1.

Because Numbers is loosely structured and contains many different kinds of materials, it is best to review its contents thematically.

Census and Encampment

In Numbers 1–4, Yahweh decrees a census of the men of military age, and the results are reported tribe by tribe. The resulting statistics (over 600,000) are unrealistically huge, but are intended to bolster later Israel's identity as heirs to a magnificent past. A second, parallel census of the new generation who will enter the land of promise is reported in chapter 26.

Wilderness Israel is portrayed idealistically as a vast military camp, organized so that the various tribes surround the tabernacle situated in its center. The priests encamp close by the tent shrine on its eastern side in order to guard its sanctity. The rest of the tribe of Levi, the families of Gershon, Kohath, and Merari, protect the west, south, and north sides respectively. Each of these groups is assigned its own duties in the service of the tabernacle. The twelve "secular" tribes (counting Ephraim and Manasseh) encircle this inner ring of priests and Levites. Three tribes encamp on each of the four sides. This utopian arrangement communicates the holiness of the sanctuary, the special vocation of priests and Levites, and the unity of Israel as a people sharing a single kinship.

The description of the census reveals the basic social and kinship structure of Israel. Individual family units—each termed a *father's house* (NRSV: *ancestral house*; CEB: *household*)—consisted of several generations living together and headed by a patriarch. These family units combined to form kinship associations called *clans*. Clans consisted of several father's houses linked together by geography (as a region or a single village) and intermarriage.

Clans in turn were associated with other clans into *tribes* connected to specific territories. Clans and tribes understood themselves as being descended from and named for a common, eponymous (name-bearing) ancestor. In the case of the tribes, their eponymous figures were considered to be the sons (or in the case of Ephraim and Manasseh, the grandsons) of Jacob (Israel).

Law and Ritual

Numbers contains material similar to the instructions found in Leviticus. Numbers 5:11-31 prescribes a process for determining the guilt or innocence of a woman suspected of adultery. Because there are no witnesses to the alleged act, truth can only be determined by divine judgment. She undergoes a test in which she takes a self-cursing oath, which is written down and dissolved in water mixed with dust from the tabernacle floor. She drinks this. If guilty she will not be able to bear children. If she is innocent, nothing will happen.

Fig. 7. Ketef Hinnom Amulet. This is one of two silver amulets from the seventh or early sixth century that were discovered in a tomb near Jerusalem. Originally rolled up like a small scroll, it contains a form of the Aaronic Blessing close to the text of Numbers 6:24–26. Apparently a string was threaded through the center of the scroll so that it could be hung around the neck.

Leviticus 19 provides a procedure for purifying those who have become unclean through touching a human corpse. A red-colored cow is slaughtered and burned in a location away from the encampment. Its ashes are used to create a cleansing liquid. This *water of purification* (19:9) allows the affected person to rejoin the worship assembly.

The special inheritance laws set out in 27:1-11 and 36:1-12 are of particular interest. The situation of the five daughters of Zelophehad presents a dilemma. Inheritance was normally from father to sons, but a problem arises if a man dies without sons. Yahweh directs that in such a case, daughters may inherit. They are to marry within their father's tribe so that the ancestral property will remain with the tribe. At least three of these daughters' names designate clans within Manasseh, so that these women were understood to be the eponymous ancestors of those kinship groups.

8.2. SAMARIA OSTRACA

An *ostracon* (plural *ostraca*) is an inscribed piece of broken pottery. These served as the common writing material for notes and records. The Samaria Ostraca come from the reigns of Joash and Jeroboam II, kings of Israel, which is to say from the first half of the eighth century BCE. Found in what seems to have been an administrative building, these appear to be delivery memoranda for wine and oil sent to the royal capital from surrounding estates. Some of the personal names involved incorporate the divine name Yahweh, while others incorporate the designation Baal. Israelite names in the Bible follow the same pattern. The Samaria Ostraca provide information about place names in the tribal area of Manasseh around the city of Samaria. These towns correspond to clan names for Manasseh, represented in the Old Testament as his male and female descendants. The "female" clans mentioned are Noah and Hoglah, who appear in Numbers 27:1-11 and 36:1-12 as two of the five daughters of Zelophehad. (*ANET* 321)

Numbers 35 provides for six cities of asylum or refuge, where a person accused of murder could find temporary shelter until the matter of culpability could be determined. In ancient Israel, intentional murder was resolved by vengeance taken upon the perpetrator by a near male relative called the *avenger of blood* (CEB: *close relative responsible for the blood*). This relative was tasked with hunting down and killing the culprit. Other ritual matters are covered in chapters 15 (offerings), 18 (priests and Levites), 28–29 (scheduled offerings), and 30 (vows made by women).

Rebellion and Controversy

Numbers recounts several traditions reflecting the theme of wilderness rebellion. These narratives display a repeated pattern consisting of misdeed, Yahweh's resulting anger, punishment, and successful intercession by Moses. This pattern first emerges when Israel begins to complain as soon as they leave Sinai (11:1-2). Complaints about manna follow in 11:4-6, resulting in Yahweh's anger (11:10). Moses confronts Yahweh about his intolerable leadership situation (11:11-15). He uses striking feminine imagery (conception, birth, and nursing) to describe his leadership burdens, implying that they were roles for which Yahweh should take responsibility. Chapter 11 concludes with a return to complaint and craving, and Yahweh's anger gives rise to a plague (11:31-34).

> ### 8.3. FEMALE IMAGES FOR GOD
>
> In Numbers 11:12, Moses refuses to accept his onerous leadership role. He compares it to the experience of a woman bearing and nursing children and implies that this is properly God's responsibility.
>
> > Did I conceive all these people? Did I give birth to them that you would say to me, "Carry them at the breast, as a nurse carries an unweaned child"?
>
> In the ancient world, deities were either male or female, although one must be careful about anachronistic assumptions about gender roles. Some female gods such as Anat and Astarte were violent and fought as warriors. Grammatically and as a character in biblical narrative, Yahweh is presented as a male divinity. However, as Israelite religion moved more and more to an unquestioned monotheism, Yahweh's gender and potential for sexuality lost any real meaning. Social interaction in the heavenly realm no longer could take place when Yahweh was seen as one who could announce, *I myself, I'm the one; there are no other gods with me* (Deut 32:39; compare Deut 4:35; Isa 45:5). The concept of Yahweh's maleness no longer functioned in any practical way.
>
> Old Testament prophets and poets used images for God taken from the domain of the female. Isaiah 42:14 describes Yahweh as a mother giving birth: *Like a woman in labor I will moan; I will pant, I will gasp*. According to the poetry of

Deuteronomy 32:18, God gave birth to Israel. Yahweh is said to be like a mother who cannot forget her nursing child (Isa 49:14-15) and who comforts her children (Isa 66:13). God is described as performing tasks and roles that are often culturally determined as female. God is a midwife, who pulls a baby from the womb and places it on its mother's breast (Ps 22:9-10; compare Job 38:8-9). God cuts the umbilical cord according to one translation of Psalm 71:6 (CEB: *you cut the cord when I came from my mother's womb*). God self-identifies as a parent who teaches a child, picks up a baby to nuzzle it, and bends down to feed it (Hos 11:3-4). Interaction between servants of each gender and their respective master and mistress provides a simile for how the faithful look to Yahweh (Ps 123:2). Animal images for God are sometimes explicitly female or at least potentially so: a bird protecting its young (Deut 32:11; Ps 17:8; Isa 31:5) or an angry mother bear (Hos 13:8).

Numbers 16 explores rivalries between priests, who claimed descent from Aaron, and Levites, who traced their lineage to other families of the tribe of Levi. The Levite Korah tries to offer incense, for all intents and purposes claiming priestly status (16:10). The editors of Numbers associated the Korah story with a second narrative concerning Dathan and Abiram from the tribe of Reuben. These two also reject Moses's leadership. The insertion of Dathan and Abiram into the Korah story results in a fairly confusing narrative, but in the end those to be punished are swallowed up into the earth and descend directly to Sheol, the world of the dead (16:32-33). The preeminence of Aaron and the tribe of Levi in ritual affairs is also asserted by the episode of Aaron's blooming staff recounted in Numbers 17.

Numbers 20:2-13 connects the place name Meribah (*quarrel*) with a story of quarreling about a lack of water. At Yahweh's direction, Moses hits a rock with his staff to produce water. In doing this, however, Moses commits a misdeed of some sort. Apparently by striking the rock rather than speaking to it (contrast v. 8 with v. 11) Moses fails to show compete trust, so neither he nor Aaron can enter the land of promise (20:12, 24; 27:13-14).

In Numbers 21:4-9 the people complain about an unrelieved diet of manna. Yahweh sends poisonous snakes with fiery venom. Moses intercedes and is instructed to make and display a replica bronze snake, and the sight of this heals those bitten. This story served as an etiological (explanatory) account for the origin of the image of a bronze snake that was kept in the Jerusalem temple until eliminated by Hezekiah (2 Kgs 18:4).

Numbers 25 recounts a final rebellion story just as the people are ready to invade the homeland. Verses 1-5 (thought to be J) recount how the men engaged in sex with Moabite women, and so became involved in worship of the deity Baal at Peor. A second version of the story in 25:6-18 describes the sexual misbehavior of a single Israelite man in the context of a punishing plague. Yahweh rewards the zeal of Phinehas, Aaron's grandson, with a covenant guaranteeing the perpetual continuation of Aaron's priestly line.

Journey and Warfare

Israel moves as an army in a pre-determined order of march, accompanied by the cloud that hovered over the tabernacle and the ark (CEB: *chest*). This cloud embodies the presence of Yahweh as strategic commander (9:17-19). An ancient battle cry preserved in 10:35-36 addresses Yahweh as Divine Warrior: *Arise, Yahweh, let your enemies scatter, and those who hate you flee. . . . Return, Yahweh of the ten thousand thousands of Israel.*

Israel treks in the wilderness for thirty-eight years (from Num 1:1 to 33:38). This allows for the generation that experienced the exodus to die off as punishment for an initial invasion that failed because of their skepticism and folly (Numbers 13–14). Israel had been poised to invade Canaan through the southern desert. Twelve spies returned with a mixed message: the land is fruitful but its defenses are formidable (13:25-33). The people complained against Moses, Aaron, and Yahweh (14:1-4). The rebellious generation had to perish before the homeland could be conquered (14:20-23, 26-35). Israel then compounded its offense with a failed assault launched without Yahweh's sanction or the presence of the ark (14:40-45).

After the exodus generation has passed from the scene (except for Joshua and Caleb), Israel's path turns again toward Canaan. The attack will strike westward across the Jordan from Moab. Edom refuses Israel permission to pass through on the main road (20:14-21), so Israel circles around Edom (21:4). The account of the journey toward Moab, beginning in 21:10, preserves old poetic materials:

Numbers 21:14-15 establishes the Arnon River as the northern boundary of Moab and is quoted from a source called the *Scroll of Yahweh's Wars.*

Numbers 21:17-18 celebrates a well visited on the way.

Numbers 21:27-30 recalls a past defeat of Moab at the hands of the Amorite king Sihon.

Before marching toward the plains of Moab in Numbers 22, Israel begins its acquisition of territory by defeating Sihon and seizing the region north of the Arnon. Then by defeating King Og, Israel takes possession of Bashan. In Numbers 32, these territories east of the Jordan are assigned to Reuben, Gad, and elements of Manasseh.

Balaam

Israel threatens Moab's security once they reach the plains of Moab. Numbers incorporates a folktale at this point that involves a talking donkey and delicious irony. King Balak of Moab has commissioned a professional prophet and diviner named Balaam to lay a curse on Israel. In chapter 22, on his way to curse Israel, Balaam confronts God's anger in the shape of a divine messenger blocking his path. Ironically Balaam's donkey can see this messenger, but the supposed seer cannot. The donkey stops in its tracks and finally speaks up to complain about being beaten. At this point, Yahweh reveals the truth to Balaam, and it turns out that the donkey has saved his life. After appropriate ritual preparations, Balaam delivers four oracles (23:7-10, 18-24; 24:3-9, 15-24). However, instead of the curses Balaam is supposed to produce, his oracles consist of blessings. His climactic fourth oracle foresees Israel's ascendancy over Moab and Edom and the rise of the Israelite monarchy:

> A star comes from Jacob;
> a scepter arises from Israel. (24:17)

8.4. DEIR ʿALLA INSCRIPTION

Balaam son of Beor appears in a fragmentary literary text that was discovered at Deir ʿAlla, a site in the Jordan Valley east of the river. It combines features of Aramaic and early Hebrew (or Canaanite) and is commonly dated to about 800. The inscription was written on plaster walls in black with red subject headings. Balaam is described as a seer (or prophet) who experiences a nighttime vision and is warned by the gods of a coming disaster. The god El is the ultimate source of this message, and a council of the gods is mentioned. Balaam takes action to avert the catastrophe. The inscription reveals that the figure of Balaam was well known as a prophetic visionary.

Further Reading

Jacob Milgrom. *Leviticus*. Continental Commentaries. Minneapolis: Augsburg Fortress, 2009.

W. H. Bellinger. *Leviticus and Numbers*. New International Biblical Commentary. Peabody, MA: Hendrickson, 2001.

Chapter 9
DEUTERONOMY

The Origin of Deuteronomy

Deuteronomy takes the form of a final address by Moses to Israel in the land of Moab, just before they are to cross the Jordan into the land of promise. They have defeated the Amorite kings Sihon and Og, as reported in Numbers 21. Moses reiterates and reaffirms the instruction that has been set forth in Exodus, Leviticus, and Numbers, but also modifies those teaching materials and stresses characteristic themes. The name Deuteronomy derives from the Greek tradition and appropriately means "second law" or "restated law."

Priests produced and preserved the narrative, legal, and ceremonial materials of the Priestly Writing in the first four books of the Torah, but the authors of Deuteronomy represented another set of social and religious groups. The language, content, and rhetorical skill displayed in Deuteronomy suggest that prophets, scribes, wisdom teachers, and Levites (as opposed to priests) all contributed to its composition. Although Deuteronomy was written to influence the people of Judah, the book incorporates many traditions characteristic of the northern kingdom of Israel. For example, Deuteronomy exhibits close theological similarities to the northern prophet Hosea.

It is generally believed that Deuteronomy emerged from the political and religious crises faced by Judah during the seventh-century reigns of Hezekiah, Manasseh, and Josiah. Second Kings 18–23 describes the seventh century as a dangerous period for Judah's fidelity to Yahweh and continued existence as a nation. After conquering the kingdom of Israel (about 720), the Assyrian Empire had strengthened its control over Judah and threatened to destroy it. The popularity of Assyrian culture led some to adopt Assyrian religious practices. This was particularly true during the long reign of Manasseh (697–642), who followed a policy of compliance and cooperation with the Assyrians. Some Judahites continued to engage in devotion to Baal and other indigenous gods of Canaan. Yahweh was worshipped at numerous shrines for sacrifice (NRSV: *high places*). These popular local sanctuaries and their altars had been used for generations, but were thought by the authors of Deuteronomy to involve dangerous practices and to promote problematic ideas. Deuteronomy developed as a call for religious and political reform.

Another facet of the crisis in seventh-century Judah was economic and social. For some time the economy had been shifting from an agriculturally based system of barter to a money economy that used uncoined silver as the medium of exchange. This development meant that wealth could be accumulated and loaned out at interest. As a result, independent farmers who could not pay their debts were losing their ancestral fields to creditors and were increasingly being reduced to the status of day laborers. Sometimes the inability to pay debts led to enslavement (Deut 15:12-18). Social change also caused a breakdown in family solidarity (21:18-21). The judicial system was corrupted by bribery and favoritism (16:18-20). To meet this social crisis, the authors of Deuteronomy restated and revised older material, particularly instructions found in the older Covenant Code (Exod 20:22–23:19).

Second Kings 22–23 recounts that a torah scroll was found in the Jerusalem temple in the time of King Josiah (the discovery was made in 622/621). This teaching document motivated Josiah to engage in a radical reform of Judah's worship life. He closed down all places of sacrifice throughout the country, whether to Yahweh or to other gods, and centralized all sacrifice at the Jerusalem temple. He celebrated a centralized Passover in Jerusalem. These actions demonstrate that the newly discovered legal scroll was some portion of the present book of Deuteronomy.

The Shape of Deuteronomy

Five headings introduce the major sections of Deuteronomy and give structure to the book as a series of speeches by Moses. These headings are:

These are the words that Moses spoke (1:1)

Now this is the Instruction that Moses set (4:44)

These are the regulations and the case laws (12:1)

These are the words of the covenant (29:1)

This is the blessing that Moses . . . gave (33:1)

The basic laws of Deuteronomy 12–26 are enclosed by a motivational framework formed by chapters 5–11 and a statement of blessings and curses in chapter

28. This material represents the central core of Deuteronomy. Other elements were added later. Chapters 1–3 and 4 serve as an introduction giving the background for the speech of Moses. Two poems appear at the end of the book as the Song of Moses (chapter 32) and the Blessing of Moses (chapter 33). Chapter 34 recounts the death of Moses.

Moses begins his speech by reviewing in chapters 1–3 what has happened from the time Israel left Mount Horeb (Deuteronomy's name for Sinai) until their arrival in Moab, east of the Jordan River. These events cover much of same ground as Numbers 11–31, but rely on somewhat different traditions. Chapter 4 exhorts the people to keep the instruction that Moses is about to teach and especially to steer clear of images and the worship of other gods. A version of the Ten Commandments, slightly different from Exodus 20, follows in chapter 5. In chapters 6–11, Moses delivers a motivational sermon to encourage the people to obey the instruction. In chapters 12–26 Moses moves into the main part of his speech and proclaims the law that Israel is to follow in the land. After this, Moses tells Israel about the special relationship (covenant) that God is now making with them in the land of Moab. However, he also warns them of future punishment if they should disobey the instruction (chapters 27–30). Deuteronomy ends as Moses recites two poems (chapters 32 and 33). The change of leadership from Moses to Joshua and the death of Moses (chapters 31 and 34) prepare for the conquest of Canaan that will be recounted in the following book of Joshua.

9.1. NUMBERING THE COMMANDMENTS

There is no one way to number the Ten Commandments. Exodus 34:28 calls them *ten words* rather than commandments, so they may not necessarily consist of ten imperatives. Moreover, the Decalogue (Greek: "ten sayings") appears in slightly different forms in Exodus 20 and Deuteronomy 5. For these reasons, it is not certain how the ten statements are to be divided and enumerated. Jews count Exodus 20:2 (*I am Yahweh your God . . .*) as the first word, as God's self-identification, and then count nine further words. Verses 3-6 (*no other gods . . . do not make an idol*) make up the second word. All of 20:17 (*Do not desire . . . Do not desire*) is considered to be the tenth. Roman Catholics and Lutherans count all of 20:2-6 as the first commandment, and treat the sentences about improper desire in 20:17 as two commandments, numbers nine and ten. Thus they regard the prohibition against idolatry to be part of the ban on worshipping other gods. The remainder of the Protestant world (and the Eastern Orthodox Church) considers Exodus 20:3 as the first commandment and the idol prohibition (20:4-6) as the second commandment, and treat all of 20:17 about desire as the last and tenth commandment.

Centralization of Sacrifice— Deuteronomy 12

The most revolutionary demand of Deuteronomy is its insistence that all sacrificial worship be centralized at a single place (chapter 12). Up until the application of this mandate by Josiah (2 Kgs 23:4-20), people were accustomed to sacrificing at local sanctuaries. These were within convenient walking distance so that animal sacrifices could be taken to them easily and festivals celebrated there. Fugitives could run to those local shrines for asylum. Deuteronomy demands that Israel destroy these venerable sanctuaries because they are the places where the nations that Israel replaced worshipped their gods (12:2-4). In contrast, Israel is to worship Yahweh only at the single place chosen by Yahweh (12:5-14). The older Covenant Code regulation about altars (Exod 20:24-25) implied that altars could be erected in multiple locations (*in every place*), but Deuteronomy 12:13-14 rewrote this to allow for one altar only, at the place chosen by Yahweh.

Deuteronomy never names this single place, but its original readers, including King Josiah, naturally understood it to be Jerusalem. The principle of centralization required many changes in traditional lifestyle and worship, and numerous ritual instructions in Deuteronomy deal with its effects. For example, animals could be slaughtered for food in a non-religious way and did not automatically have to be taken to the central sanctuary to be treated as sacrifices (12:15-22; see also 15:19-23). If the distance to the central sanctuary was too great, tithes could be converted into money and spent there to provide a celebratory meal (14:22-26). Passover and other festivals were to be celebrated at the central place and not locally (16:1-17). Because local shrines could no longer serve as havens of refuge for those accused of murder, asylum cities were to be set up around the country (19:1-13). Deuteronomy calls for worship to be a matter of joy and community solidarity. Festive worship is to include everybody, regardless of social class, age, or gender (12:12; 16:11, 14) and is to serve as social support for the less fortunate (14:29).

Covenant and Treaty

A characteristic feature of Deuteronomy is its use of the concept of covenant to express the relationship that Yahweh has established with Israel and the obedience that Yahweh expects from them. This covenant theology is also characteristic of the northern-kingdom prophet Hosea (active between about 750 and 725). This suggests that the notion of a covenant between Yahweh and Israel developed in the last part of the eighth century. Deuteronomy 29 describes the contents of Deuteronomy as a new covenant made at Moab, one based on God's promises to the ancestors. This covenant is also being made with future generations, including the audience of the book of Deuteronomy (29:14-15). In Deuteronomy 29:13, Moses employs a balanced formula that expresses the covenant relationship established by Yahweh: *Yahweh will make you his own people right now—he will be your God.*

Similar reciprocal language asserting Yahweh's commitment to the interrelationship between God and God's people reappears throughout the Old Testament (Exod 6:7; Hos 2:23; Jer 7:23; 11:4; 24:7; 30:22; 31:1, 33; 32:38; Ezek 36:28). This turn of phrase is often called the *covenant formulary*. Deuteronomy 26:16-19 employs the concept of reciprocal covenant commitment to emphasize Israel's duty to obey God's commands.

Some interpreters suggest that Deuteronomy uses the format and vocabulary of international suzerainty treaties in order to express its theology and claims. Its authors may have been familiar with the language of Assyrian treaties, because both Israel and Judah had submitted to Assyria as vassal kingdoms. For example, Deuteronomy uses the vocabulary of *love* between overlord and vassal that was often used in treaties to describe the proper relationship between God and Israel. Yahweh has expressed love by choosing Israel as a special people and freeing them from Egypt (7:7-8, 13; 10:15). Israel is to love God in return and show their love by obeying God's law (6:5; 7:9; 10:12; 11:1, 13; 13:3; 30:6). (See 3.2, COVENANT.)

Ancient treaties were guaranteed by divine witnesses. This concept lies behind Moses's call for heaven and earth to serve as witnesses to Israel's commitments (4:26; 30:19; 31:28). The laws of Deuteronomy parallel the stipulations that treaties imposed upon submissive vassals. In fact, the radically loyal behaviors enjoined on Israel in chapter 13 closely match the requirements of known Assyrian treaty documents. Deuteronomy also follows the treaty practice of concluding with blessings and curses laid upon the participants. Chapter 28 cements God's demand for compliance with the law by laying out blessings that will follow on obedience (28:1-14), followed by a much longer catalogue of horrifying curses that will afflict the people if they disobey (28:15-68). Assyrian treaties favored curses over blessings as a motivational tool, and in fact some of the curses in Deuteronomy 28 are remarkably similar to those known

Chapter 9

to us from a treaty that the Assyrian king Esarhaddon imposed on his vassals in 672. It is highly likely that Judah's king Manasseh submitted to that very treaty and that its wording would have been known to the literate population of Judah.

9.2. ASSYRIAN TREATY CURSES

Esarhaddon imposed treaties on his vassal kings in 672 in order to ensure the peaceful succession of his son Assurbanipal to the throne. Subject kings swore to these Vassal Treaties of Esarhaddon (VTE; also known as his Succession Treaty) as loyalty oaths (*ANET* 534–41). Most likely King Manasseh of Judah, who was an impeccably loyal Assyrian vassal, would have been one of those. The VTE had a direct effect on the composition of Deuteronomy. Deuteronomy 13 concerns three possible cases of rebellion against Yahweh: by a prophet, by family members, and by an entire city, and words of the perpetrators are quoted. A section of the VTE is very similar to this. A person's relative and a prophet appear as potential instigators and their words are overheard. Deuteronomy 13 and the VTE mandate the same extreme level of ruthlessness in response to such rebellion.

Deuteronomy 28 involves a long catalogue of curses that will fall on those who disobey the covenant. Again, there are striking correspondences between the curse language of VTE and Deuteronomy 28. For example, the sequence of curses in Deuteronomy 28:26-33 is strikingly similar to a section of VTE, and the thematic order of 28:20-44 as a whole tracks that of another part of VTE. Deuteronomy 28:23-24 has the same combination of motifs as lines from VTE:

> The sky over your head will be as hard as bronze;
> the earth under your feet will be like iron.
> Yahweh will turn the rain on your land into dust.
> Only dirt will fall down on you from the sky
> until you are completely wiped out. (Deuteronomy)

> May all the gods that are named in this treaty
> reduce your soil in size to be as narrow as a brick,
> turn your soil into iron, so that no one may cut a furrow in it.
> Just as rain does not fall from a copper sky,

> so may there come neither rain nor dew upon your fields and meadows, but let it rain burning coals in your land instead of dew.
>
> (VTE, lines 63-64; *ANET* 539)

Motivated Instruction

Deuteronomy has been characterized as "preached law" (others would say, "instruction") because it seeks to motivate obedience. Motivation is the central theme of chapters 6–11, chapters that encourage obedience to the laws set forth in chapters 12–26. If Israel fails to obey, the covenant curses will strike them and Yahweh's anger will destroy them (6:13-15; 11:28). However, fear is not the principal reason to follow the instruction. Rather Israel is to obey out of love for God and neighbor (10:12-13, 19). Israel should conform to God's will because God freed them from slavery in Egypt (24:17-18, 22).

Deuteronomy's concern to encourage obedience is evident in the short exhortations found in 6:10–9:6. Each of these statements begins with a characteristic situation in which readers might find themselves and then draws a cautionary application to readers' lives:

> Now once Yahweh your God has brought you into the land . . . Don't forget Yahweh. (6:10, 12)
>
> Now once Yahweh your God . . . drives out numerous nations before you. . . . Don't make any covenants with them. (7:1-2)
>
> When you eat, get full, build nice houses, and settle down . . . don't become arrogant, forgetting Yahweh your God. (8:12, 14)

In Deuteronomy 9:7–10:11, Moses reminds his hearers of the gold calf episode in order to convince them to change their hearts and rely on divine forgiveness. Likewise, 10:12–11:32 presents additional positive and negative incentives to obedience, such as Yahweh's just and loving character (10:17-19), the history of God's gracious acts (11:1-7), and the fertility of the homeland (11:8-12)

As Moses proclaims various requirements in chapters 12–26, he carefully adds motivational clauses to encourage compliance. Treat slaves properly and provide justice for immigrants and orphans because you were once slaves in Egypt (15:15; 24:18). *Don't detest Egyptians because you were immigrants in their land* (23:7). Provide a charitable tithe to feed the unfortunate so that God may bless you (14:28-29). Do not use dishonest weights so that you may enjoy long life in the land (25:15). Every Israelite is your *brother* (CEB: *fellow Israelite*; NRSV: *neighbor*), so return his lost animals and do not charge your fellow Israelite interest or degrade an Israelite when inflicting physical punishment (22:1; 23:20; 25:3).

Deuteronomy offers a choice to everyone who reads it. This choice is between disobedience leading to death and faithful obedience leading to life (30:15-20; see also 11:26-28). Deuteronomy urges its audience: *Choose life* (30:19).

9.3. AN EYE FOR AN EYE

The phrase "an eye for an eye" is used in common parlance to express heartless, harsh, and thoughtlessly equalized punishment. It has become a catchphrase for retribution, retaliation, and revenge. It appears in Exodus 21:23-25, Leviticus 24:19-20, and Deuteronomy 19:21. This principle is sometimes referred to using the Latin phrase *lex talionis*, the "law of the claw." However, the formula was actually intended to limit the scope of retribution to what was balanced and fitting. The eye-for-an-eye principle prevented people from exacting unlimited vengeance beyond the scope of the original crime. Lamech in Genesis 4:19-24 provides the classic example of this ruthless mindset, aspiring to be avenged seventy-seven times on his foes and announcing, *I killed a man for wounding me, a boy for striking me* (4:23). Deuteronomy 25:11-12, brutal and peculiar by modern standards, is the only law actually exacting punishment by means of bodily mutilation in the Old Testament.

Instructions That Create Community

In Deuteronomy 5, Moses prefaces his restatement of divine instruction with the Ten Commandments. Unlike the better-known version in Exodus 20, which provides the reason for Sabbath as God's rest on the seventh day of creation (Exod 20:11), Deuteronomy motivates Sabbath rest with a reminder of Israel's slavery (Deut 5:15). Sabbath means that lower-class groups, male and female slaves and immigrants, can enjoy some leisure. Deuteronomy stresses the inclusion of animals by adding *your oxen or donkeys* to the simple livestock of Exodus 20:10. In the commandment(s) about coveting, Deuteronomy forbids the coveting of one's neighbor's wife first, thus separating her from the household items with which the Exodus version classifies her.

This appears to be evidence of Deuteronomy's increased concern for women and their rights as members of the covenant community.

9.4. REMEMBER THE SABBATH

Both versions of the Ten Commandments decree that a day of rest, a Sabbath, must be observed after six days of work (Exod 20:8-10; Deut 5:12-14). Sabbath rest is also commanded in the Covenant Code (Exod 23:12), in a list of teachings often called the Ritual Decalogue (Exod 34:21), and elsewhere. For Amos, keeping Sabbath was a hallmark of ethical business practice (Amos 8:4-6). Jeremiah proclaimed that Judah's continued existence depended upon observing it (Jer 17:20-27). In the New-Babylonian and Persian periods, abstaining from work on the Sabbath increasingly marked off Jews in the diaspora from their neighbors and served, along with circumcision and dietary restrictions, as a strong marker of religious identity (Neh 13:15-22).

Sabbath is the last day of a seven-day week (Saturday) and in Judaism begins at sundown on the evening before. The practice of refraining from work according to a seven-day calendar cycle cannot be found in any surrounding contemporary cultures and seems to have been an exclusively Israelite development. Celebration of the resurrection of Jesus on Sunday as the first day of the week ("the Lord's Day") became the norm in the Christian movement by the end of the first century CE (Acts 20:7; 1 Cor 16:2; Rev 1:10), although observance of Saturday as a day of rest continued in some Christian circles for a few centuries. The notion of Sunday as a day of rest from labor entered civil society with a decree of the first Christian Roman emperor, Constantine, in 321 CE. Some forms of Protestantism advocate observing Sunday as a Sabbath day of rest or consider Saturday to be the day decreed for weekly worship.

Deuteronomy revised and updated a number of laws from the older Covenant Code (Exod 20:22–23:19). For example, that older instruction prescribed letting the land lie fallow every seven years (Exod 23:10-11). Deuteronomy 15:1-11 elaborated this into a general remission of all debts. In this way, Deuteronomy sought to turn the predatory practice of lending to desperate people into a form of social benevolence. Deuteronomy 15:12-18 modified the law on Hebrew slaves as found in Exodus 21:2-11 by requiring that the owner make a generous provision for the released slave. Deuteronomy also makes it clear that female slaves are included in the law's provisions. Exodus 23:4-5 demanded returning and rescuing domestic animals belonging to an enemy. Deuteronomy 22:1-4 redefined that enemy as any *fellow Israelite*, even if that Israelite should live at a great distance, and expanded the principle of return to lost property of every kind. The practice of taking collateral for a debt was controlled by Exodus 22:25-27, but this is more strictly regulated by Deuteronomy 24:10-13 in order to preserve the dignity of the debtor and prevent undue hardship.

Deuteronomy's laws were intended to be socially beneficial, although they also protected the privileges of higher-status groups. They promoted concern for the poor and underprivileged, including slaves. Deuteronomy repeatedly urges a social safety net for three economically marginalized groups, namely resident aliens, the fatherless, and widows (CEB: *immigrants, orphans, widows*). This ideal is repeated over and over. Deuteronomy 16:18–17:20 offers a sort of "constitutional proposal" that envisions judges, priests, and the king working together to ensure social fairness and faithfulness to God. Fair justice must be everyone's right (16:18-20). Definite limits are put on royal wealth and power in the so-called "law of the king" in 17:14-20. Instead of accumulating horses, wives, and riches, the king is to study the law and live according to it. The authors of Deuteronomy appear to be criticizing the practices of contemporary kings of Judah.

Deuteronomy includes instruction that gave women some small increases in protection and status in society. Female war captives have some minimal protections (21:10-14). The inheritance of the sons of disliked wives is safeguarded (21:15-17). Sexually assaulted women and brides whose reputations have been slandered are protected to some degree (22:13-19, 25-29). Newly married men are not to be drafted for a year (24:5). Deuteronomy was also concerned with the welfare of the Levites (for example 12:12; 14:27, 29). Apparently many of those religious specialists would have been unemployed by the centralization of worship and experienced a loss of status over against the priests functioning in Jerusalem.

The Death of Moses—Deuteronomy 32–34

Two poems close Deuteronomy and connect its message forward into the future. In Deuteronomy 32 (the Song of Moses), Moses recounts the ups and downs of Israel's relationship with God. God has been faithful, a Rock who has given them birth (32:18). In contrast, Israel has been faithless and perverse in its worship of other gods, and so will be punished by invasion and defeat. In the end, however, God's purposes will win out, and Israel will be vindicated (32:43). Deuteronomy 33 (the Blessing of Moses) incorporates a collection of aphorisms about the tribes (33:6-25) as the core of a poem celebrating the victories of Yahweh as Divine Warrior.

In chapter 34, Moses enjoys a panoramic view of the land from a mountaintop, but he is not to enter it. He dies in Moab at age 120 and is buried in an unknown location. Moses is celebrated as a prophet who had the closest possible relationship of communication with God and through whom God worked wonders (34:10-12).

Further Reading

Mark E. Biddle. *Deuteronomy*. Smyth & Helwys Bible Commentary. Macon, GA: Smyth & Helwys, 2003.

Walter Brueggemann. *Deuteronomy*. Abingdon Old Testament Commentaries. Nashville: Abingdon, 2001.

Part III
FORMER PROPHETS

Chapter 10
JOSHUA

Joshua and the Deuteronomistic History

Joshua connects back to Deuteronomy by means of a transition of leadership from Moses to Joshua (from Deut 31:7-8; 34:1-6 to Josh 1:1-9). Joshua connects forward to Judges through the death of Joshua and the dismissal of the national assembly he convened (from Josh 24:1, 29-31 to Judg 1:1; 2:6-10). Joshua, Judges, Samuel, and Kings tell a single, connected story recounting Israel's national traditions about its origins and history. Beginning with narratives of conquest (Joshua), the story moves through disorder in the period before the establishment of monarchy (Judges), and then describes how David's kingship emerged (1 and 2 Samuel). First and Second Kings conclude the account with a theological and moralizing history reporting the deeds of the kings of Israel and Judah, prophets who interacted with them, and the catastrophic collapse of each kingdom in turn.

At one stage of their development, Joshua and the other books of the Former Prophets made up what is referred to as the Deuteronomistic History (DH). This work of history was introduced by Deuteronomy 1–3 and 31. DH viewed Israel's history in the land of promise from a unified theological perspective derived from Deuteronomy. The most important examples of Deuteronomistic theological commentary appear in speeches or editorials that mark important transitions in Israel's history. In Joshua 1:1-9, Yahweh encourages and instructs Joshua as Israel is about to invade the land. In Joshua 23, Joshua in turn exhorts and warns the people when he is on the point of death and a transition in leadership is about to take place. Other examples of transitional passages in DH are Deuteronomy 1–3 (Moses reviews history), 1 Samuel 12 (Samuel at the start of the monarchy), 2 Samuel 7 (announcing God's covenant with David's successors), 1 Kings 8 (Solomon dedicating the temple), and 2 Kings 17 (the fall of the kingdom of Israel).

The involvement of DH is very apparent in Joshua 8:30-35, which ties Joshua directly back to Deuteronomy. By engaging in a ceremony of covenant renewal at Mount Ebal, Joshua carries out the command given to Moses in Deuteronomy 27:2-13. He erects an altar, offers sacrifice, inscribes the law (CEB: *instruction*) of Moses on stones, and engages the people in blessing and cursing. Joshua 8:31 quotes Deuteronomy 27:5. In agreement with Deuteronomy 31:10-12, Joshua then reads the instruction to an all-inclusive assembly. In Joshua, Deuteronomistic influence is absent from chapters 13–21, which describe the allotment of the land, leading to the conclusion that these chapters were added to Joshua after it had become an independent book detached from DH.

Joshua begins with the death of Moses *servant of Yahweh* and the handover of leadership to Joshua (1:1-2). It ends in a parallel way with the death of Joshua, who is designated *servant of Yahweh*, and a changeover to a new generation (24:29-31). The story falls into four acts: preparations and crossing the Jordan (chapters 1–5), conquest (chapters 6–12), allocation of the land to the tribes (chapters 13–21), and warnings about the future in a story about intertribal conflict and two farewell speeches by Joshua (chapters 22 and 23–24).

The Conquest of Canaan

Joshua 2–11 was composed from individual narratives, many of which were connected to places that were part of the landscape of the region. In part, Israel retold these stories to provide explanations or etiologies for city ruins, commemorative markers, and topographic features. Israel could see that its land had been inhabited for a very long time. Then as now the terrain was dotted with mounds (*tels*) formed by the ruins of cities inhabited in former times. Israel's current towns and cities were situated on top of these mounds, and stones from ancient walls and buildings had been reused to build them. Israel attributed those remnants and ruins to a successful conquest by their forebears. An example of this is the story of the conquest of Ai (Joshua 8). The very name Ai means *the ruin*, and 8:28 points out that it still existed as a *permanently deserted mound*. Similar narratives accounted for how other great and venerable cities such as Jericho (chapter 6) or Hazor (11:1-11) became part of Israel's heritage. Other explanatory, etiological narratives may have been recounted at commemorative markers such as the standing stones at Gilgal (4:9, 20) or grave monuments (7:26; 8:29). Stories also explained landscape features such as the strikingly named Foreskins Hill (5:3) or piles of huge stones (10:27). Other narratives explained why certain non-Israelite groups co-existed with Israel within the homeland.

Rahab's descendants benefitted from her sharp-witted cooperation (chapter 2), and the Gibeonites were devious (chapter 9).

Fig. 8. This thirteenth-century stele from Ugarit represents Baal as a storm and warrior god, brandishing a battle mace in his right hand and wielding a lightning bolt in his left.

Yahweh as Divine Warrior

Israel considered that its homeland was Yahweh's gift, and conquest stories attributed victory to Yahweh in terms of Divine Warrior theology. At Beth-horon, for example, Yahweh insists that Israel have no fear, throws the foe into a panic so they flee, drops great stones on them, and arranges an astronomical phenomenon to facilitate victory (10:8-14). The sun stands still to provide time for a more complete victory. At Ai, Yahweh forbids fear and promises success, then directs the course of the battle (8:1, 7-8, 18). The capture of Jericho is also presented as a victory of the Divine Warrior (see 6:2, 20). Joshua 10:14 and 42 sum up the Divine Warrior principle: *Yahweh fought for Israel*. The overarching theme of the conquest is that the enemy kings react (usually in fear) when they hear about Israel's success (2:9; 5:1; 9:1-2; 10:1-2; 11:1-4).

Chapter 10

10.1. DIVINE WARRIOR

The Old Testament often conceptualizes Yahweh as a warrior god who fights for Israel. Scholars refer to Yahweh's warlike aspect using the term *Divine Warrior*. As Divine Warrior, Yahweh marches forth to do battle from southern mountain regions (Judg 5:4-5; Deut 33:2-3; Ps 68:7-8, 17; Hab 3:3-7). The title *Yahweh of heavenly forces* (CEB; NRSV: *the Lord of hosts*) signifies that Yahweh deploys a supernatural army (2 Sam 5:22-25; 2 Kgs 6:15-17; Zech 14:5). An old poem, Numbers 10:35-36, centers the Divine Warrior's action in battle on the ark of the covenant, from which Yahweh sets off and to which Yahweh returns. As warrior, Yahweh uses natural forces as weapons: wind (Exod 14:21; Ps 48:7), hailstones (Josh 10:11), storm and lightning (2 Sam 22:15; Ps 77:17-18; Hab 3:11). Yahweh may attack at dawn (Exod 14:24). The most characteristic weapon of the Divine Warrior is a divinely induced panic that demoralizes the enemy (for example, Exod 23:27-28; Deut 2:25; Josh 10:10; 1 Sam 7:10). Yahweh prevails in Judges 4 and 5 by means of panic (Judg 4:15) and the participation of supernatural combatants and natural forces (stars and a flooding river, 5:20-21). The classic example of divinely induced panic is Gideon's victory over the Midianites in Judges 7:19-23. Psalms 46, 48, and 76 celebrate Yahweh's defense of Jerusalem in Divine Warrior terms. Though the city is surrounded by enemy kings (48:4) and chaos (46:2-3), Yahweh defends it at dawn (46:5) by means of cosmic power (46:6; 76:3) and enemy terror (48:5-6; 76:5-6).

Ḥerem—Devoting to Destruction

A striking and disconcerting feature of the conquest stories is Yahweh's demand to slaughter entire enemy populations—not only adult male warriors but women and children too (Josh 6:21; 10:28, 35, 37, 40; 11:11, 14). At Jericho this mandate goes further and extends to killing a city's domestic animals and an injunction against taking any valuables as plunder. The rationale behind this demand was that whatever was captured in war—people, animals, or costly booty—properly belonged to Yahweh alone as the true victor. Whoever and whatever belonged to Yahweh in this way fell into a category termed *ḥerem*. *Ḥerem* may be translated as *a devoted thing* or *devoted to destruction* (NRSV) or as *something reserved for God* (CEB).

It was common in the ancient world to enslave enemy populations, so *ḥerem* meant that captured people were to be killed in order to prevent humans from profiting from their slave labor. For the same reason, cattle and other booty might also be considered as *ḥerem* and made unavailable for human use. Unlike people, however, animals and material wealth were not always treated in this way (8:2, 26-27; 11:14). Joshua's reports of *ḥerem* destruction are making a theological point: credit for conquest victory belonged exclusively to Yahweh.

Crossing the Jordan—Joshua 1–5

Joshua 1:10-18 prepares for invasion. Supplies are organized, and the Transjordanian tribes are enlisted to join in the campaign. Before leading Israel westward across the Jordan, Joshua sends out two spies or scouts (Joshua 2). Spying was a common feature of conquest stories (Numbers 13; Josh 7:2-3; Judg 18:2-10). However, Rahab outsmarts both the spies and the king of Jericho and rescues her family from impending catastrophe. She is a prostitute and possesses her own house (2:1), which means that she is a legally independent woman. Presumably, no one would question the presence of male strangers at her house. The location of Rahab's house within the city wall (2:15) does not fit well with the collapse of Jericho's wall reported in chapter 6 or the report that she sheltered her family there (2:18; 6:22-23). *Inside the wall* suggests she lived in a casemate wall, one that featured internal chambers used for storage or housing. Rahab is able to arrange protection for her extended family (2:13-14). She is able to negotiate an advantageous agreement with the spies because they are trapped. Pursuers block the way back to the Jordan and the city gate has been shut (2:7). Even after the spies have been lowered outside the city wall, Rahab still remains in charge of the situation. She directs them westward into the hills so they can avoid the pursuers she has sent eastward to the Jordan (2:7, 16, 22). Rahab's story is picked up again in 6:22-25.

Israel's passage across the Jordan to the staging point of Gilgal is described in terms of a liturgical procession and echoes Israel's exodus escape though the Red Sea (Joshua 3–4). In Joshua 5, Israel's irreversible move out of the wilderness and into the new land is signaled by the circumcision of the new generation of males born on the journey, a celebration of Passover, and the cessation of the manna that is no longer needed.

Chapter 10

Conquest—Joshua 6–12

The geography of the invasion is set forth in campaigns against three sets of foes: the central cities of Jericho and Ai (Joshua 6–8), an alliance of southern cities (Joshua 9–10), and a northern coalition led by Hazor (Joshua 11). A list of conquered kings in chapter 12 emphasizes the extent of Israel's triumph. Yahweh as Divine Warrior is the true victor, who gave the foe into Israel's *hand* (CEB: *power*; 10:30, 32; 11:8).

Jericho—Joshua 6

Because walled cities like Jericho were almost impossible to conquer, especially by a group unskilled in siege warfare, Israel required the help of Yahweh the Divine Warrior. The order of march is a mixture of liturgical procession and military maneuver: *armed soldiers*, *seven priests* blowing trumpets, the ark (CEB: *chest*), and a *rear guard* (6:7-9). Yahweh, who was sometimes associated with earthquakes (Judg 5:5; 1 Sam 14:15), collapses the city wall so that encircling Israel can make a frontal assault from all sides simultaneously (6:20). Joshua blocks any reconstruction and resettlement of Jericho with a curse (6:26). First Kings 16:34 reports the rebuilding of Jericho and fulfillment of this curse. Israel is warned (6:18) that booty from Jericho will be contagious in the sense that to *take some of the things reserved* (*ḥerem*) would place Israel itself into the deadly category of *ḥerem* (*doomed to be utterly wiped out*).

Achan and Ai—Joshua 7–8

In chapters 7 and 8, the conquest of Ai is entangled with Achan's violation of the *ḥerem* decree of 6:17-18. Much of the Old Testament operates on a principle of corporate responsibility in which an entire family or community might be punished or rewarded for the actions of an individual. Even though Achan acted alone, his misconduct means that all *the Israelites broke faith* (NRSV; CEB: *did a disrespectful thing*), and *Yahweh is furious with* the entire nation (7:1, 11). Consequently, Israel's first attack on Ai is repulsed.

The story starts positively. Again spies are sent (7:2). Their report forecasts easy victory, but the expected situation is reversed. Israel experiences the fear that their enemies were supposed to feel in campaigns directed by the Divine Warrior (7:5). Joshua intercedes for the people. He seeks to motivate Yahweh to act by citing the danger to Israel and the likelihood that Yahweh's reputation (*name*) will suffer (7:7-9; see Exod 32:12; Num 14:13-14). Yahweh responds that Achan's crime has violated the *covenant* (7:11, 15). The booty that should have been devoted to God has had a contagious effect, and Israel itself has moved into the *ḥerem* state (CEB: *a doomed thing reserved for me*), so Yahweh can no longer be with Israel (7:12).

Achan is identified (probably by the sacred lot; SEE 8.1, URIM AND THUMMIM). The process of elimination follows the three concentric realms of Israel's system of personal identity: tribe, clan, and household (7:16-19). The principle of corporate responsibility comes into play in that Achan's children (and even domestic animals) must perish with him (7:24-25). The cautionary story of Achan and his dramatic execution was probably recounted at a stone cairn in the *Valley of Achor* (7:25-26). Achor means *calamity*.

The subsequent conquest of Ai is a victory of Yahweh the Divine Warrior. The battle is described in a confusing manner, but the general outlines are clear. Ai's forces are lured from the city's fortifications by Israel's feigned retreat. Once Ai is emptied of its defenders, the hidden Israelite ambush captures Ai and burns it. The rising smoke demoralizes the soldiers of Ai and serves as the signal for the retreating Israelites to turn around and attack (8:20-21). When the Israelite ambush party comes out of Ai to attack the enemy from the rear, Israel's victory is complete (8:22). Joshua obeys the directive concerning hanging bodies found in Deuteronomy 21:22-23. Finally, the reader is reminded that the imposing ruins of Ai and the great pile of stones at its gate could still be seen (8:29). This stylistic device also appears in 4:9; 5:9; 6:25; and 9:27.

Victories in the South and North—Joshua 9–11

Chapter 9 raises another difficulty. When the news about Israel's victories is reported, enemy kings join together to resist (9:2). However in contrast, the inhabitants of Gibeon come up with a clever plan: they pretend to be from a distant country, ask for a treaty, and support their falsehood with appropriate costumes and props (9:4, 6, 9). If true, their claim would exempt them from the destruction demanded by Deuteronomy 20:16-18. Israel does not ask Yahweh for directions, but blunders ahead to conclude a treaty with them (violating Deut 7:2; 20:10-18). Although the truth is soon revealed, Israel must still respect the treaty because it has been guaranteed by a *solemn pledge* to Yahweh (Josh 9:18). The result is that Gibeonites living in four towns to the northwest of Jerusalem are allowed to live as a subordinate class within Israel's territory, and some of these will become support staff for the sanctuary that Yahweh will someday designate. The reliability of the narrative is confirmed by a statement that this situation still obtained in the time of the earliest readers (9:27).

Chapters 10 and 11 continue to report victories. In chapter 10, a coalition of kings from the southern part of Canaan and headed by the king of Jerusalem threatens the Gibeonites, to whom Israel now owes protection because of the treaty. Victory is won through the direct intervention of Yahweh (10:8-14). Five allied kings are captured and executed (10:16-27). Cities in the south are destroyed (10:28-39) and the principle of *ḥerem* is applied (10:28, 40). Joshua 11 recounts victory over a coalition headed by Jabin king of Hazor in far northern Galilee. In Judges 4, Deborah and Barak also defeat a king of Hazor named Jabin, so perhaps Jabin was a dynastic name for the royal family of Hazor. Chariots were the most sophisticated and powerful weapons system of the period and buttressed the military superiority of the Canaanite cities At Yahweh's command, Joshua makes captured chariot horses unfit for battle and burns the chariots (11:6, 9). Israel would have lacked the ability to maintain and use them. Joshua 10:40-42 and 11:16-23 summarize Israel's victories, and chapter 12 totals up the kings defeated by Moses and Joshua respectively.

Allotment of the Land—Joshua 13–21

The tribes of Reuben, Gad, and part of Manasseh had already received their allocations from Moses, as described in Deuteronomy 3. Joshua now apportions Canaan (14:1), that is, the land on the west side of the Jordan, to the remaining tribes. He does so in two phases. In Joshua 14–17, the prominent tribes of Judah, Ephraim, and Manasseh receive their land. Then in chapters 18–19, a survey of the remaining territory is conducted in the context of a national assembly at Shiloh. Seven appropriate portions are determined on the basis of this survey, and these are assigned to the remaining tribes by lot. Chapters 20 and 21 cover the interrelated topics of cities of asylum to which those accused of murder could flee and cities for the members of the tribe of Levi, which does not receive any allotted territory.

Tribal territories are described using two types of geographic material. Boundary descriptions trace borders. City lists supplement the boundary descriptions (only a city list is present for Simeon). These city lists appear to have been derived from administrative sources from the monarchy period. This is particularly clear for 15:20-62 (Judah) and 18:21-28 (Benjamin), which taken together preserve a stage in the district organization of the kingdom of Judah, probably in the seventh century.

> ### 10.2. TWELVE TRIBES
>
> The twelve-tribe system mixes some historical reality with considerable later idealism. Israel understood its tribal structure to be the result of descent from eponymous ancestors (such as Judah or Ephraim). However, the Song of Deborah (Judges 5), the earliest witness to Israel's tribal structure, shows that the tribal roster was in flux before the traditional twelve-tribe system became fixed. The distinctive number twelve came

to express Israel's national unity. However, an inherent tension existed between the twelve sons of Jacob (who included Levi) and the concept of twelve designated territories (which excluded Levi as a tribe without territory). As a result, some tribal rosters include Joseph's sons Ephraim and Manasseh and exclude Levi (Numbers 1). Others list Levi and count Joseph as a single tribe only (Genesis 49, Deuteronomy 27, and Ezekiel 48). Deuteronomy 33 eliminates Simeon (which was absorbed into Judah at an early period) and includes Levi, Ephraim, and Manasseh.

Some tribal names were originally geographical designations, suggesting that they came into being when already settled in that locality. Thus, Ephraim inhabited the south part of a larger "highlands of Ephraim." Issachar (perhaps "hired man") seems to relate to that group's subservient situation in an area dominated by Canaanite cities (Gen 49:15). The name Benjamin, meaning "son of the south" or "southerner," reflects that tribe's location to the south of the heartland of Ephraim and Manasseh. The tribe of Judah was associated with various previously distinct groups in the south part of Palestine, such as Caleb, Jerahmeel, Othniel, Kenaz, and Kenites. Levi was an affiliation of religious specialists scattered in various places.

Genesis 29–30, 35 portray intertribal relationships in genealogical terms. Benjamin, Manasseh, and Ephraim are considered to be the son and grandsons of Rachel, something that reflects their close association as the *house of Joseph* (Amos 5:6). Certain tribes are designated as the sons of Jacob's secondary wives rather than as the natural children of his wives Leah and Rachel. Zilpah bears Asher and Gad, and Bilhah is the mother of Dan and Naphtali. This seems to point to a more marginal status for these tribes in the tribal association. Genesis 49 and Deuteronomy 33 preserve two collections of sayings or blessings that describe tribal interactions, prosperity, temperament, assertiveness, and circumstances.

Chapter 10

Warnings—Joshua 22–24

Chapter 22 recounts a story of tribal conflict over an altar built by the tribes living to the east of the Jordan. The narrative promotes national unity and Deuteronomy's call for a single place of sacrifice.

Two final speeches to Israel by Joshua appear one after the other in chapters 23 and 24. In chapter 23, Joshua explains the meaning of the conquest and calls for obedience. In Joshua 24, which takes place at Shechem, he recounts to the assembled Israelites the saga of God's election of Israel. In so doing, he refers to events in the books of Genesis, Exodus, and Numbers. In each of these two final speeches, Joshua warns that the future threatens great danger if Israel proves to be disobedient (23:15-16; 24:19-20).

Interpreting Joshua

Joshua's celebration of Israel's tradition that it had invaded Canaan and annihilated the land's indigenous inhabitants at the behest of God cannot be read today without raising awkward ethical issues. One dare not excuse or gloss over the dangers implicit in glorifying genocidal conquest within the biblical canons of Christianity and Judaism. Two points need to be made, however.

First, there is a general consensus among historians that hardly any of the material preserved and retold in Joshua is of the sort that can be used to reconstruct an authentic history of invasion and conquest. These are folktales used to make a theological point, not historical reports. Archaeological reconstructions of the history of Israel's emergence in Palestine during the Iron I period do not support the traditional narrative of outside invasion and violent conquest. Some cities important to Joshua's conquest tradition were not occupied as urban centers in the period in question (Jericho, Ai). Some cities were wiped out (for example, Bethel, Lachish, Hazor), but there are several possible candidates for who might have been responsible. Finally, many important cities were never destroyed in this period. Most archaeologists and historians now connect the first emergence of Israel with indigenous groups living in small, unfortified villages in the central highlands of the region. These settlements appeared during the early Iron Age in areas not under the economic or political control of the large urban centers. The village population of the highlands (that is, Israel) gradually dominated the urban centers ruled by local kings. No doubt violence was an element in this process, but political and economic factors seem to have been more important. Understanding that early

Israel was mostly indigenous to the region does not exclude the possibility that some elements of what became Israel did enter the land from the outside and had experienced Egyptian oppression.

> ## 10.3. ARCHAEOLOGICAL PERIODS
> During Roman rule, the region was named Palestine. Archaeology divides the chronology of Palestine into eras. These periods are determined by characteristic changes in pottery style and other cultural remains, but are also coordinated with large-scale historical developments. Thus, the transition between the Late Bronze Age and the early Iron Age is indicated by changes in pottery, but also by transformations in culture, economics, and social organization about 1200. Archaeologists disagree as to how best to divide the Iron Age after about 1000.
>
> | | | | |
> |---|---|---|---|
> | Late Bronze Age II A | 1400–1300 | | |
> | Late Bronze Age II B | 1300–1200 | | |
> | Iron Age I | 1200–1000 | | |
> | Iron Age II A | 1000–900 | Iron Age II | 1000–720 |
> | Iron Age II B | 900–720 | *or* | |
> | Iron Age II C | 720–586 | Iron Age III | 720–586 |
> | Neo-Babylonian Period | 586–539 | | |
> | Persian Period | 539–333 | | |
> | Hellenistic Period | 332–63 | | |

Second, throughout its history Israel's possession of its land was endangered by outside attack or foreign domination. These enemies included the culturally and militarily superior cities of Canaan before they were absorbed into Israel and Judah, Midianite desert raiders, the Moabites, and the Aramean kingdom of Damascus. Telling conquest stories was a way for Israel to sustain its claim on its homeland in the face of these dangers. After the northern kingdom had been conquered by Assyria and then Judah by Babylon, these narratives supported the hope that someday Yahweh's people might return to reclaim their homeland and regain political independence.

Chapter 10

Further Reading

Brad Kelle and Brent Strawn, eds. *The Oxford Handbook to the Historical Books of the Hebrew Bible*. New York: Oxford University Press, 2019.

Thomas B. Dozeman. *Joshua 1–12: A New Translation with Introduction and Commentary*. New Haven, CT: Yale University Press, 2015.

Chapter 11
JUDGES

Shape and Composition

Judges continues the story of Israel in the land of promise that began with Joshua. In Judges 2:6-10, Joshua dismisses the national assembly at Shechem (Josh 24:29-31). Judges also links forward to 1 Samuel. The last judge, Samson, is only able to begin to deliver Israel from the Philistines (Judg 13:5; 15:20; 16:31) so that Philistine oppression continues into 1 Samuel 4:1–7:2. Topically and structurally, Judges divides into three parts. These are 1:1–2:5 (an incomplete conquest), 2:6–16:31 (narratives about deliverers or judges organized into a cyclical pattern), and chapters 17–21 (anarchy in the absence of a king).

Most scholars consider the core of Judges (2:6–16:31) to be the product of DH (the Deuteronomistic Historian). That writer gathered originally independent narratives about six local military heroes into an account of leaders of national significance who followed one after the other. DH provided those heroes with a chronology and created a unifying, cyclical structure of recurring disobedience. When Judges was detached from DH into a separate book, 1:1–2:5 was added at the beginning to set up the problematic situation in which Israel found itself. Two story cycles in Judges 17–21 were appended to explore the problem of anarchy caused by the lack of central authority in the pre-monarchic period.

Telling heroic stories about successful military leaders gave the clans and tribes of Israel a sense of pride and identity. The tales recounted in Judges are also simply entertaining. They exhibit narrative tension and suspense and feature attention-grabbing characters. How will Ehud be able to commit murder and then escape (chapter 3)? How will Sisera die by the hand of a woman (chapter 4)? What will be the fate of Jephthah's daughter (chapter 11)? Both Gideon and Samson are complex personalities. Gideon doubts and believes. He is a superlative war leader, but personally vengeful. Samson is strong and impulsive and has a weakness for women. As is the case with most biblical folktales, these stories touch on matters of etiology. They explain topographic names (2:5; 10:4; 15:17, 19; 18:12) and describe the origin of customs and holy places (6:24; 11:39-40; 21:4). Judges 18 recounts the origin of the northern kingdom sanctuary at Dan and its priesthood.

Documents from neighboring cultures show that the term *judge* (or *leader* CEB) could be applied to civil rulers and administrative officials. This is the way the verb *judge* is used in the list of what are usually termed *minor judges/leaders* (10:1-5; 12:7-15). These are Tola, Jair, Jephthah, Ibzan, Elon, and Abdon. These figures stand in contrast to the belligerent heroes (the *major judges/leaders*). The list of minor judges was an earlier source document incorporated by the author of Judges. This catalogue was divided in two so that it brackets the story of Jephthah. Jephthah is unique in having a dual role as both hero (or major) judge and member of the minor judges list. Rather than being military leaders who appeared only when circumstances required, the minor judges are portrayed as administrative officials who succeeded each other without interruption and occupied their office for a varied number of years. Each of them judged Israel, died, and was buried.

The presence of Jephthah both as a minor judge and as a renowned deliverer was probably the source for the idea that Israel's renowned military deliverers could also be termed *judges* (CEB: *leaders*; 2:16-19) and that they *judged Israel* (CEB: *led Israel*; 3:10; 15:20; 16:31) in succession without overlapping one another. The terms of service for the minor judges are given precisely: 23, 22, 6, 7, 10, and 8 years. This timetable served as the nucleus for the overall chronology of Judges. In contrast, the periods of activity assigned to the major judges except Jephthah are round numbers such as 20, 40, and 80 years. These round figures have the appearance of being artificial contributions by the author. All the chronological information in Judges, including the various periods of oppression that precede the activity of the major judges (3:8, 14; 4:3; 6:1; 10:8; 13:1) and the tenure of Abimelech (9:22), works together as part of a chronological system of 480 years. This system is a contribution of DH and extends from the exodus to the construction of Solomon's temple (1 Kgs 6:1).

Incomplete Conquest—Judges 1:1–2:5

Judges begins with the death of Joshua, reported twice (1:1; 2:8). The initial notice of his death introduces efforts to complete the conquest of the land. The first stage of this campaign is led by Judah and is largely successful (1:1-21). A second stage involves the northern tribes and combines success in the capture of Bethel with repeated failures to drive out the Canaanites (1:22-36). Judges 1 was made up from material taken from various places in Joshua 13–17 and 19, along with other traditions. The incident at Bochim (meaning *those who weep*; Judg 2:1-5) sets a negative tone for the rest of the book. Israel's failure to obey Yahweh's command to stay aloof from the inhabitants of the land and to destroy the altars of their religion means that God will no longer grant Israel victory over them. Different explanations for their survival are given: they remain as punishment (2:20-21), as a test (2:22-23; 3:1), or to train Israel for war (3:2).

The Cycle of Major Judges

A second notice of Joshua's death in 2:6-10 leads into the main action (Judg 3:7–16:31). These verses are repeated in slightly different order in Joshua 24:28-31, where they conclude the national assembly at Shechem.

The six major judges are Othniel, Ehud, Deborah, Gideon, Jephthah, and Samson. Their careers are organized by a repeated cycle, which narrates Israel's apostasy, oppression by an enemy, Israel's cry to Yahweh, and provision of a deliverer. When the exploits of each deliverer have been recounted, the cycle returns to its starting point. This pattern is partially summarized in 2:6-19; however, that summary is somewhat at odds with the structure of disobedience and repentance actually described in Judges 3–16.

The colorless paragraph about the first deliverer, Othniel (3:7-11), contains little narrative detail, but does serve to illustrate the structural pattern. To what was outlined in 2:6-19, the Othniel paragraph adds several further items that are carried through for other judges. There are six items that appear for most or all of the major judges.

Israel did evil in Yahweh's judgment (3:7, 12; 4:1; 6:1; 10:6; 13:1)

Yahweh sold or gave them into an enemy's power (3:8 [3:12 in different language]; 4:2; 6:1; 10:7; 13:1)

The years of enemy domination are stated (3:8, 14; 4:3; 6:1; 10:8; 13:1)

Israel cried out to Yahweh (3:9, 15; 4:3; 6:6; 10:10)

The enemy was defeated or subdued (CEB: *brought down*) (3:10, 30; 4:23; 8:28; 11:33)

The land had rest (CEB: *was peaceful*) for a stated number of years (3:11, 30; 5:31; 8:28)

Samson is largely ineffective and does not complete the cycle, so his narrative lacks the last three items. Other shared items appear less regularly. Yahweh's anger is mentioned for Othniel and Jephthah (3:8; 10:7). Yahweh's spirit empowers Othniel,

Gideon, Jephthah, and Samson. The task of deliverance is applied to Othniel, Ehud, Gideon, and Samson. Othniel, Jephthah, and Samson *judged* (CEB: *led*) Israel in the sense of military leadership. (Deborah judged Israel as well, but as one who decided legal matters; 4:4-5). The deaths of Othniel, Ehud, Gideon, and Samson are highlighted as narrative turning points (3:11; 4:1; 8:32-33; 16:30).

This repeated pattern permeates Judges with a feeling of Israel being stuck, drifting along without progress or improvement. Events seem to be trapped in a repeated sequence of disobedience and only temporary repentance. If anything, there seems to be an overall decline in the leadership quality of the judges. Othniel and Ehud are completely successful, and Deborah proves to be an effective leader and accurate prophet. In contrast, ambiguity appears with Barak, who declines to take the lead without Deborah. Gideon has doubts and engages in personal vengeance. Jephthah sacrifices his daughter. And Samson has issues in his relationships with women. His personal and leadership failings leave the Philistine crisis unresolved.

Ehud and Shamgar—Judges 3:12-31

Ehud is a wily hero from Benjamin who defeats the Moabites and their allies. The core of the Ehud story is a trickster tale in which the underdog national hero outsmarts the enemy king and his dull-witted retainers. (A trickster is a wily folktale hero who uses devious means to achieve goals.) Being left-handed helps Ehud slip the short sword into the king's presence. He persuades King Eglon to meet him in private by claiming to have a secret message, supposedly from God. The king rises to receive it, so that Ehud can pierce him in the stomach with a double-edged blade, just right for the job. Ehud escapes and assembles Israel for a stunning victory over Moab. Victory is credited to Yahweh with what is called the "conveyance formula": *Yahweh has handed over your enemies*. This formula also appears in Judges 4:9, 14; 7:7, 9, 15; 20:28. Following Ehud is a short notice about Shamgar, who delivered Israel as a result of his astounding exploit of slaying hundreds of Philistines with an ordinary farm implement. It is not clear if Shamgar is even an Israelite, and he is not part of the book's chronological system. Yet his inclusion does fill out the number of protagonists so that there are twelve.

Deborah and Barak—Judges 4–5

The section celebrating Deborah, Barak, and Jael is incorporated into the larger story of Judges by the cyclical framework (4:1-3, 23; 5:31b). The narrative is distinctive in that it tells of more than one protagonist, two of whom are women. Furthermore, the story of victory and assassination is told twice, once in prose (chapter 4) and once in poetry (chapter 5). Israel's enemies are King Jabin of the great northern metropolis of Hazor and his general Sisera. Their *iron chariots* (4:3; actually wood with iron fittings) signal overwhelming superiority. Yahweh is the decisive victor. Through the prophet Deborah, Yahweh commands strategy and promises success, then goes out ahead of Israel and induces panic in the enemy (4:6-7, 14-15). As Divine Warrior, Yahweh advances to the scene of conflict, triggering natural phenomena along the way (5:4-5), and Canaan's kings are defeated by stars and flooding waters (5:20-21). The enemy general Sisera meets his death at the hands of a resourceful woman (4:17-21; 5:24-27). The military engagement begins at Mount Tabor (4:12, 14), which was a holy place shared by the tribes of Issachar, Zebulun, and Naphtali (4:6, 10; 5:18; see Deut 33:18-19; Josh 19:12, 22, 34). It is likely that this traditional story and song were preserved and recited there.

Under Deborah's prophetic command, Barak leads Israel's troops. His response to the assignment she gives him is to insist that she accompany him (4:8). Some think this response was intended by the author to indicate faintheartedness; others feel that it makes good sense and shows faith in Deborah's prophetic authority. The result, in any case, is Deborah's announcement that Barak will be robbed of fame. Yahweh will hand Sisera over to a (yet unnamed) woman. Her prediction builds interest and tension for the reader. Who will this woman be? Deborah herself? Barak musters the tribal troops at Tabor and leads them down to attack. But after battle is joined, he can only pursue the escaping Sisera and then witness his dead body (4:22).

The exploit of Jael demonstrates that Yahweh has the power (and perhaps a tendency) to deliver Israel by unexpected means and by an unusual person. Fleeing Sisera seeks shelter with Jael because her husband's clan is at peace with the king of Hazor. On the surface, Jael shows him the hospitality that was expected in ancient culture (milk instead of the water he requests, a cover as he rests). Yet the ancient reader would also have perceived that she is violating proper social norms by inviting a man to be alone with her in her tent—and letting him sleep there as well! He trusts her to keep watch, but she hammers a tent peg into his skull, in a grisly echo of a routine task for nomadic women.

The war ballad of chapter 5 is called the Song of Deborah. It is probably the oldest piece of literature in the Old Testament, perhaps dating from the late pre-monarchic period. Its language is obscure and is not well-understood, so that translations vary widely. One of the poem's most striking features is its roster of only ten tribes. This does not match the traditional twelve-tribe list found in later texts and appears to reflect an earlier stage in Israel's tribal organization. For example, Gilead and Machir appear in place of Gad and Manasseh. The tribes who engage in battle are Ephraim, Benjamin, Machir, Zebulun, Issachar, and Naphtali. Four other tribes are mocked and reprimanded for remaining aloof from the conflict: Reuben, Gilead, Dan, and Asher. The southern tribes of Judah and Simeon are not mentioned at all.

The staging of the assassination scene, as Sisera falls to the ground in 5:26-27, sounds somewhat different from that of 4:21. Is Sisera lying down or more upright when he is killed? This apparent disparity may be due to poetic technique. In 5:27, humiliating sexual overtones are suggested in the tent peg that penetrates Sisera and in his position between Jael's feet. The final scene of chapter 5 is powerful and deeply ironic. Sisera's mother waits for him in vain. She imagines that he must be committing battlefield rape upon captured Israelite women, but will soon arrive with sumptuous booty.

Gideon and Abimelech—Judges 6–9

Gideon

Gideon confronted the Midianites, who were camel-riding raiders from the east. The Gideon story is complex, made up of numerous episodes. With Gideon the deterioration of the judges' leadership qualities becomes evident. He is successful from a military point of view, but repeatedly seeks reassurance about his appointment as leader and about God's assurance of victory. He confuses his duty to deliver Israel with his own desires for personal vengeance against Israelite cities and enemy leaders (8:4-9, 13-17, 18-21). Near the end of his career, Gideon steers the nation into an improper worship practice (8:24-27).

Gideon's hesitations and doubts are highlighted in the narrative of his call, in his seeking a confirming sign, and in the story of the dream he overhears. In 6:11-18, the messenger from Yahweh (really a manifestation of Yahweh; see 6:16) commissions Gideon as one who will deliver Israel. It is typical in such call narratives that the one chosen as leader or prophet will object, and Gideon does so on the basis of his youth and low status. He requests a sign, and a sign is given him in a wondrous acceptance of his sacrifice (6:19-24). Yet that confirming sign is not enough, and after mustering an army, Gideon seeks further reassurance from God by putting out a wool fleece on two successive nights (6:36-40). On the first morning the fleece absorbed the dew, but the ground around it was dry, which would not be a particularly surprising result. So Gideon requests a reversed situation on the second night, and God responds with the unexpected phenomenon of a dry fleece on a dewy morning. Yet the question of Gideon's hesitation is raised one more time in 7:10-14. Yahweh sends him down into the Midianite camp, where he overhears a dream that portends Israel's victory and is emboldened to launch his attack.

The tradition of Gideon's extraordinary victory over Midian (7:19-25) was so significant that the prophet Isaiah cited it centuries later as a classic example of Yahweh's deliverance (Isa 9:4: *the day of Midian*). The story is told in a way that strongly emphasizes that it was unquestionably Yahweh who won the day. Through a two-step process outlined in Judges 7:2-7, Yahweh insists that Gideon's army be reduced to a mere handful. A larger force would allow Israel to claim credit for Yahweh's achievement (7:2). Those who are afraid are told to go home (compare Deut 20:8). Then a somewhat perplexing test involving how the soldiers drink results in a final force of only 300 to face the vast horde of Midianites, who are *like a swarm of locusts* (7:12). Israel occupies the heights above the enemy encampment in the valley. By surrounding the Midianites, Israel appears to them to be a vast force. Gideon's troops act in the middle of the night. They make a great commotion with hundreds of blaring trumpets, smashing jars, and suddenly exposed torches. Panic is always the most characteristic weapon of the Divine Warrior, and terror engulfs the Midianite camp. Yahweh causes them to attack each other, and they are hunted down as they flee. Gideon's story concludes with a reminder that it was undeniably Yahweh who rescued Israel from all their enemies (8:34).

The Rise and Fall of Abimelech

The story in chapter 9 about Gideon's overambitious son, Abimelech, lies outside the cyclical framing structure for Gideon (6:1-6; 8:28), but does cover three years of the book's timetable (9:22). The idea that monarchy was an inappropriate choice for Israel appears in a number of places in the Old Testament (for example, 1 Sam 8:6-7; 10:19). Gideon himself had rejected the attempt to make him king (Judg 8:23). This anti-monarchical attitude is reflected in the fable told by Jotham, the only survivor of Abimelech's massacre of Gideon's other sons (9:8-15). A fable is an instructive story in which animals or plants are the dramatic characters. One after the other, four candidates are offered the opportunity to become king over the trees. The olive tree, fig tree, and the grape vine each refuse, explaining that the fruit they produce is delicious, useful, and provides enjoyment. The last offer goes to the worthless thornbush, who accepts. It can only offer shade that is scant and prickly and threatens destructive fire that would endanger even the cedars of Lebanon, the tallest and noblest of trees. The point of Jotham's fable may be that monarchy is a chancy option because only the useless and inadequate will occupy the kingly office. It could also be an attack on those who are so focused on their own concerns that they permit an incompetent candidate to become a leader. Abimelech's destructive career as king of Shechem is ended when a woman drops an upper millstone on his head. Such a death was considered to be a shameful one (9:53-54).

11.1. SHECHEM

Shechem was an important city in Israel's pre-monarchic and early monarchic period. It was strategically located in the pass that runs east to west between Mount Ebal to the north and Mount Gerizim to the south. Shechem was at a crossroads, where a regionally important road running up the central spine of the country intersected routes to the north and to the west. For several centuries before Israel's emergence, Shechem ruled over the central highlands. The assertive policies of its king Lab'ayu are known from the fourteenth-century Amarna Letters. For a while, Shechem served as the capital of the northern kingdom of Israel until King Omri replaced it with the newly built capital of Samaria.

Shechem was also an iconic religious center. Tradition connected a sacred site there to Jacob (Gen 33:18-20; 35:4). The story about Dinah in Genesis 34 recounts a tradition of how the area came to be part of Israel's sphere of control. The tomb of Joseph was believed to be at Shechem, as well as a sacred stone erected by Joshua (Josh 24:25-27, 32). Deuteronomy climaxes with a covenant made at Shechem involving its two mountains. Judges 9 locates a temple to El- (or Baal-)berith ("El of the covenant") at Shechem. Much later, nearby Mount Gerizim became the location for a temple used by Samaritan Yahweh worshippers. This was destroyed by the Hasmonean ruler John Hyrcanus in the late second century BCE. Nevertheless, Mount Gerizim continues to serve as the center of worship for the surviving Samaritan community. The ruins of biblical Shechem are located near the West Bank city of Nablus.

Jephthah—Judges 10:6–12:7

The tradition about Jephthah names the Ammonites as Israel's oppressors. This kingdom was located east of Israel's Transjordanian territory, and the conflict focuses on southern Gilead. Israel justified their claim on this territory in that it was the former realm of Sihon, from whom they had wrested it (as Jephthah explains in

11:19-21, 26). He first engages in some fruitless diplomacy with the Ammonites, who stake their own claim based on ancestral rights (11:12-28). In the end, Jephthah is victorious, but he is infamous for a reckless and dangerously open-ended pledge made to Yahweh before battle is joined. Jephthah pledges to sacrifice as an entirely burned offering whoever or whatever comes out of his house to meet him when he returns victorious (11:31; the Hebrew allows for him to mean either a person or an animal). Will this be one of the sheep or goats sheltered in his house? But it was usually women who greeted returning heroes (Exod 15:20-21; 1 Sam 18:6-7; Jer 31:4), so this was an exceedingly rash and foolish pledge. Tragically, it is Jephthah's daughter, his only child, who greets him. Both she and Jephthah agree that his words must be respected, but she asks for time to come to terms with the dreadful fate of dying while still unmarried and not yet a mother (11:35-38). This story may have originally been recounted to explain an otherwise unknown custom of a four-day event marking the transition of young women into the stage of marriageability, what anthropologists call a rite of passage.

Samson—Judges 13–16

Samson rounds off the parade of judges with a career marred by an ineffective leadership style. Israel's enemies are the Philistines, who lived along the Mediterranean to the west of Judah and Dan's original territory. He kills many Philistines in his adventures, but over his twenty-year career, he only *begins* to liberate Israel (13:5). His birth story (chapter 13) indicates he was chosen by Yahweh. This point is underscored by his status as a nazirite, a special class of people who did not cut their hair and lived by other restrictions on their lifestyle (13:4-5; 16:17). Samson is celebrated as a solitary, mighty hero, who kills a lion with his bare hands, bursts bonds apart, slays a thousand opponents with a donkey's jawbone, and causes a great temple to come crashing down. However, he also displays a weakness for relationships with inappropriate women. He first marries a Philistine woman, and a contest of riddles at the wedding leads him to kill thirty Philistines and terminates his marriage (chapter 14). Samson's frustrated attempt to recover his wife leads to retaliation against her people and a murderous rampage (chapter 15). The famous story of his love for Delilah and her betrayal of him to the Philistines (chapter 16) has been often revisited in literature and film. Shorn of his great strength, blinded, and humiliated, Samson nevertheless has one last comeback and in the end kills more Philistines in his last exploit than he had during his whole previous life (16:30).

Fig. 9. This relief from Medinet Habu in Egypt shows Philistines who have been captured in battle by Pharaoh Rameses III in about 1175. They wear distinctive headdresses that set them off from other ethnic groups that made up the invading Sea Peoples.

There Was No King—Judges 17–21

A self-contained epilogue concludes the book of Judges and creates a break before the story of Philistine oppression is taken up again in the initial chapters of 1 Samuel. It consists of two story units. Judges 17–18 recounts how the tribe of Dan migrated to a new home in the far northern city of Dan and established a sanctuary for Yahweh there. Judges 19–21 describe the cause and outcome of a civil war fought between the tribe of Benjamin and the rest of Israel. In these final chapters, Judges shifts away from the problem of Israel's repeated religious disloyalty and the oppression of foreign enemies to focus on the emergence of chaos in the absence of the strong central authority of a king. In these five chapters, one reads of theft, problematic religious practices, rape and murder, civil war, application of *ḥerem* slaughter against fellow Israelites, and irregular marriage arrangements. An explanatory formula is repeated at the beginning and the end of the epilogue: *there was no king in Israel; each person did what they thought to be right* (17:6; 21:25). The reader is reminded about the absence of a king at two other points as well (18:1; 19:1). This emphasis points forward to the establishment of kingship in Israel in the persons of Saul and David, as recounted in 1 and 2 Samuel.

11.2. IMAGES AND IDOLS

Judges indicates that the sanctuary at Dan contained a silver image connected to the worship of Yahweh (Judg 17:3-4; 18:30-31). Even though the Ten Commandments prohibit the production and veneration of images (Exod 20:4-5), Old Testament texts make it clear that some elements within Israel had a lively tradition of relating to Yahweh (and other gods) by means of sculpted or cast images. This was particularly true in pre-monarchic and early monarchic times. Other examples are the two bull-calf images venerated at the royal sanctuaries at Dan and Bethel (1 Kgs 12:28-30; Hos 13:2). The bronze serpent of Moses was initially an acceptable religious object in the Jerusalem temple until it was eliminated (Num 21:9; 2 Kgs 18:4). In the ancient world, divine images were understood as a means of focusing a god's attention and presence onto a visible object, rather than as an actual god. Worshippers could be assured that prayers and offerings made before the image would receive the god's full consideration. Because an image was susceptible to human control, the gods of a nation's enemies could be coopted by capturing their statues.

Over time, attitudes changed. Voices were raised in opposition to images (pejoratively construed as *idols* in English translations) by Israel's prophets (Jer 10:3-5, 14-15) and legal codes (Exod 20:23; 34:17; Lev 19:4; 26:1). The Deuteronomistic movement opposed images as a dangerous sacrilege (Deuteronomy 4). King Ahaz of Judah removed bull images from the temple courtyard that had been installed by Solomon (1 Kgs 7:23, 25; 2 Kgs 16:17). King Josiah eliminated horse images connected with solar worship (2 Kgs 23:11). Pictorial representations almost completely disappeared from seals used to authorize documents from the seventh century onward. By the Neo-Babylonian and Persian periods, Judaism had evolved into an aggressively aniconic (imageless) religion. The denunciation of images and comedy at the expense of those who venerate them became standard features of prophetic texts (Isa 42:17; 44:9-20; 45:16; Ezek 20:7-8; Hab 2:18-19). Opposition to images is a defining feature of both Judaism and Islam, and has played a complicated role in the history of Christianity.

Further Reading

Mark E. Biddle. *Reading Judges: A Literary and Theological Commentary*. Macon, GA: Smyth & Helwys, 2012.

Susan Niditch. *Judges*. Old Testament Library. Louisville, KY: Westminster John Knox, 2008.

Chapter 12
1 AND 2 SAMUEL

The Narrative Shape of Samuel

The textual tradition of the Hebrew Bible considers Samuel to be a single book, recognizing that the narrative moves without interruption from the end of 1 Samuel to the start of 2 Samuel. The Greek Septuagint divided Samuel at the death of Saul, but also treated Samuel and Kings together, designating the whole as 1–4 Reigns. The books of Samuel trace the beginning of kingship in Israel, focusing on three protagonists: the prophet Samuel; Saul, who proves to be a failure; and David, Yahweh's choice to be the founder of a permanent dynasty. The storyline of Samuel links back to that of Judges. Harassment by the Philistines, left uncorrected by Samson, is only resolved when Israel abandons its worship of other gods (1 Sam 7:3-4). Then Samuel wins a military victory with the help of Yahweh, and the Philistines are subdued (7:7-14).

Samuel presents many thought-provoking narrative episodes. For the most part, the story is told in chronological sequence from the birth of Samuel to the conclusion of a final rebellion against David (2 Samuel 20). However, chronological order breaks down with 2 Samuel 21–24. These last four chapters break into the continuation of David's career recounted in 1 Kings 1 and flashback to events and other materials from earlier in David's reign. Poetry creates a bracket around 1 and 2 Samuel. The Song of Hannah, the mother of Samuel, appears near the beginning of the book (1 Samuel 2), and two poetic pieces attributed to David come almost at the end (2 Sam 22:2-51 and 23:1-7).

Speeches of historical review in 1 Samuel 12 and 2 Samuel 7 demonstrate that Samuel was once part of the larger DH. Samuel's farewell speech in 1 Samuel 12 looks back over Israel's history from the exodus through the judges (12:6-11) and looks forward to the new era of kingship in order to warn of dangers and urge obedience (12:12-25). In 2 Samuel 7, the prophet Nathan speaks for Yahweh and revisits

Chapter 12

Israel's past wilderness experience when there was no permanent temple. Yahweh announces that David's offspring will form a permanent line of kings who will enjoy Yahweh's favor. These two themes of temple and Davidic dynasty are carried forward in the book of Kings.

Sources Used in Samuel

The Ark Story—1 Samuel 4–6, 2 Samuel 6

It is generally agreed that several earlier written sources were used to compose Samuel. For example, an earlier, self-contained *Covenant Chest* (KJV: *Ark*) *Story* was split up to become 1 Samuel 4–6 and 2 Samuel 6. This narrative describes the itinerary of the covenant chest from its capture by the Philistines to its permanent installation in Jerusalem. The covenant chest causes trouble in each Philistine city to which it is moved. The chest insults the Philistine god Dagon, brings about disease, and instigates panic. The Philistines come up with a plan intended to allow the chest to decide for itself where it wishes to go (1 Sam 6:7-9). The chest (hauled along by protesting cows) goes straight to the Israelite town of Beth-shemesh, where it continues to create problems. Later the chest remains quietly at Kiriath-jearim for twenty years. When David first tries to take it to Jerusalem, more complications ensue (2 Sam 6:6-11), until David slowly and carefully transports it to Jerusalem, which the narrative implies is its proper home.

The Rise of David—1 Samuel 16:14–2 Samuel 5:12

Another source narrative, the *Rise of David*, presents interlocking stories about David and Saul in order to affirm that David was God's authentic choice (1 Sam 16:14–2 Sam 5:12). As Saul collapses because Yahweh has withdrawn favor from him (1 Sam 16:14), David ascends to kingship because Yahweh is with him (16:18; 18:12). Yahweh removes the divine spirit from Saul, and the king is tormented instead by a spirit of depression and distrust. In contrast, David succeeds at every turn. He arrives at the royal court as a therapeutic musician (16:15-23) or, in another story, as a young hero who slays the giant Goliath (17:55-58). He is praised by the people and dearly loved even by Saul's son and daughter. When David escapes the royal household, Saul becomes desperate and jealous. His behavior is erratic and outrageous. He slaughters an entire priestly family. He attempts to learn the future by calling up Samuel's ghost. In contrast, David wins victories, eludes Saul's attempts to capture him, and acquires riches and wives. David benefits from the deaths of Saul and Jonathan, then of Saul's son and heir Ishbosheth (Ishbaal), and finally of Saul's general Abner. In the end, David, who began as a lowly shepherd boy (1 Sam 16:19) rises to become shepherd king (2 Sam 5:2). The *Rise of David* narrative seems to have been intended to defend David against potential charges that he was merely an opportunistic usurper.

The Court History—2 Samuel 9–20 (1 Kings 1–2)

There is less agreement about what is usually labeled the *Court History of David*. This work appears to consist of 2 Samuel 9–20 (along with 1 Kings 1–2). The Court History describes palace intrigues within David's family and concludes with Solomon's succession to the throne. As a work of literature, it skillfully portrays characterization, psychology, and family dynamics. Some believe that the author's main concern was to document how Solomon came to inherit David's throne. Others have concluded that the work focuses instead on exploring the family dysfunction and political tensions that blemished David's kingship. In any case, the Court History is not very positive about David. He commits adultery with the wife of a loyal officer and then arranges to have him die in battle. He unthinkingly sends his daughter Tamar to Amnon, who rapes her, but David fails to punish this outrage. He forgives another son Absalom for killing Amnon, and when Absalom rebels, is overly solicitous about Absalom's death. The Court History portrays Yahweh as a God who hides behind the scenes, and Yahweh's actions are revealed only by the comments of the narrator. Displeased by David's adultery and act of murder (2 Sam 11:27), Yahweh raises evil against David from within his own family (12:11), but loves Solomon from the day of his birth (12:24). Yahweh causes bad advice to sound like wisdom (17:14).

The Story of Samuel

The book of Samuel presents the overlapping stories of three leaders: Samuel, Saul, and David. Samuel is the sole protagonist in 1 Samuel 1–8. Samuel overlaps with Saul in 1 Samuel 9–15. Saul and David overlap in 1 Samuel 16–2 Samuel 1, and David stands alone as the central character in 2 Samuel 2–24. The career of each leader begins with Yahweh choosing and calling him (1 Samuel 3, 9, and 16).

Samuel begins his career as prophet and military leader in a situation of religious corruption and Philistine domination. He is called to be a prophet speaking Yahweh's word (1 Sam 3:20–4:1), but also acts like a judge, as indicated by the language used in 1 Sam 7:15. He leads Israel into repentance so that Yahweh can deliver them, and thus repeats the cyclical pattern established in Judges. Samuel also presides at sacrifices (7:9-10; 16:4-5), although he was not from the tribe of Levi (1:1; 1 Chr

6:26 adjusts this). This circumstance shows that the Samuel stories stem from an early period when sacrifice could be offered by persons other than Levitical priests.

The annunciation and birth stories of Samson and Samuel are similar and represent a familiar literary genre. Each begins with the same phrase (Judg 13:2; 1 Sam 1:1) and the typical problem of the future mother's infertility. Samuel also displays features of being a nazirite like Samson (Judg 13:4-5, 14; 1 Sam 1:11). Samuel wins his victory over the Philistines in concert with the actions of Yahweh the Divine Warrior and so completes what Samson had failed to achieve (7:10-11, 13).

The narratives about Samuel wrestle with the legitimacy of human kingship in Israel. A clash in viewpoints between Israel's older, non-monarchic and egalitarian social structure and the later centralized power of kingship is reflected several places in the Old Testament. Examples of the *antimonarchic* attitude are Jotham's Fable of the Trees (Judg 9:8-15) and the law about kings in Deuteronomy 17:14-20. Some places in 1 Samuel highlight the problematic and faithless aspects of monarchy (1 Sam 8:1-22; 10:17-27; 12:12-25). An old litany rehearsing the infringements of kingship on the personal freedoms and financial well-being of ordinary Israelites is reproduced in 8:11-17. To request a king like other nations have (8:5, 20) is to reject Yahweh (8:7; 10:19). Yet in 1 Samuel, such antimonarchic passages alternate with *pro-monarchic* passages that offer a positive perspective on kingship (9:1–10:16; 11:1-15). In the end, however, Yahweh proves willing to accept kingship as a flawed but tolerable institution (8:22; 10:1; 12:12-15, 20-25). One of the traditional roles for a prophet was to designate and anoint new kings, and Samuel performs this function first for Saul and then for David.

The Story of Saul

Three competing traditions describe how Saul was designated king. (1) According to 1 Sam 9:1–10:16, he is out searching fruitlessly for his father's lost donkeys and goes to consult with Samuel, who is renowned as a *seer* (another word for a prophet; 9:9). Samuel anoints Saul at Yahweh's direction and predicts three events to serve as confirming signs. (2) According to 10:17-27, Saul is chosen publically by a lot administered by Samuel. (3) In chapter 11, Saul demonstrates his capacity to lead when the Ammonite king demands humiliating surrender terms from an Israelite city in Gilead. Empowered by God's spirit, Saul calls out the militia with the signal of cut-up animals, probably reminding them that they are bound to their fellow Israelites by a covenant. Saul wins an overwhelming victory and the people make him king.

The Philistines, who have established garrisons in Israelite territory (1 Sam 10:5; chapters 13–14) and are technologically superior (13:19-22), prove to be a more serious adversary for Saul. To supplement Israel's unprofessional, part-time militia, Saul inaugurates a standing army (13:2; 14:52). In Saul's primitive monarchy, military leadership is a family affair. Saul's son Jonathan commands part of this professional force, and Saul's cousin Abner serves as general for the temporary militia.

Saul's promising start is undone by repeated acts of disobedience, as recounted in 1 Samuel 13 and 15. Yahweh regrets having chosen Saul to be king (15:11, 35). The ultimate cause for Saul's misfortune is the withdrawal of Yahweh's spirit from him (16:14). It its place he is tormented by a spirit of depression and suspicion.

Saul's tragedy climaxes with a devastating defeat by the Philistines at Mount Gilboa in the Jezreel Valley. To avoid a shameful death, he commits suicide (1 Sam 31:3-5). Jonathan and two other sons of Saul are also killed, and Saul's kingship passes to his son Ishbaal. (Ishbaal, meaning *man of Baal*, was later converted by scribes into a slur as Ishbosheth, *man of shame*). The epic defeat of Saul and Jonathan is memorialized in the Song of the Bow, which is quoted from a source called the Scroll of Jashar (2 Sam 1:18-27) and named for the bow of Jonathan (1:22). It mentions Jonathan's great love for David as surpassing the love of women (1:26; see also 1 Sam 18:1, 3; 20:17). Rather than implying a homoerotic attraction, which is not affirmed elsewhere in the Old Testament, this phrase is probably hyperbole that expresses the close friendship between the two men.

The Story of David

The story of David's kingship begins with a positive portrayal of its early successes in 2 Samuel 2–10. *David knew that Yahweh had established him as king over Israel* (5:12). David defeats the Philistines, unites Judah and Israel into a single kingdom, and captures Jerusalem as its capital. He wins victories over foreign enemies. The high points of this positive stage in David's story are his transfer of the covenant chest to Jerusalem and Yahweh's promise of an eternal dynasty (2 Sam 6–7). The tone changes into an ambiguous, even negative depiction of David in 2 Samuel 11–20. His adultery with Bathsheba and conspiracy to murder her husband leads into a decree of punishment communicated by the prophet Nathan in 12:10-11: *I am making trouble come against you from inside your own family*. One by one, three of David's sons are eliminated from the royal succession: Amnon the rapist, Absalom the rebel, and Adonijah the impetuous (in 1 Kings 1). The low point of this negative portrayal of David comes with his poignant but insensitive reaction to the death of his disloyal and most beloved son Absalom (2 Sam 18:33–19:7). After this, David's situation improves somewhat as he returns to Jerusalem and has a rebellion of northern dissent put down (chapters 19–20). The epilogue to the book (2 Sam 21–24) continues to stress the ambiguity of David's character.

Chapter 12

2 Samuel 7, labeled the *Nathan Oracle*, marks a major turning point in the history of Israel in the land as presented by DH. The transition from the leadership of judges to that of kings was dealt with by Samuel's farewell speech in 1 Samuel 12. Now, when David seeks to build a temple in his new capital city, Yahweh responds through the prophet Nathan. David is not to erect a temple (Hebrew: "house"); instead Yahweh will establish an enduring dynasty (Hebrew: "house") for him through one of his sons (2 Sam 7:5, 11).

> I will be a father to him, and he will be a son to me. . . .
> But I will never take my faithful love away from him. (vv. 14-15)

The theme of Yahweh's promise to David continues into the following book of Kings as the ups and downs experienced by the kings of Judah are explored.

Who Will Inherit David's Throne?

The question of who will be David's successor overshadows almost all of 2 Samuel. The most obvious candidate would have been a son of royal blood produced by his marriage to Saul's daughter, Michal. However, she remains childless (2 Sam 6:23). Amnon is David's oldest son, and David also fathered Absalom and Adonijah in the early days of his career, all three by different mothers (3:2-4). Solomon is born some time later, and the reader is told that Yahweh loves him (12:24-25). Second Samuel is mostly interested in the handsome (14:25) and decisive figure of Absalom. Absalom takes murderous revenge on Amnon for raping his sister Tamar. David exiles him for a spell, but then allows him to return. At first, he is banned from David's presence, but Absalom forces a reconciliation with his father as a result of an act of arson (14:30-31). He engages in a public relations campaign to pave his way to replace his father (15:1-6) and then gathers an army that proclaims him king. Civil war ensues, and Absalom is killed by David's general Joab, acting in direct violation of David's orders. Adonijah is next in line, and imitates Absalom in his own attempt to become king (1 Kgs 1:5). But he is forestalled by Nathan and Bathsheba, who successfully conspire to support Solomon.

There are several striking episodes in the account of the throne succession. Second Samuel 17 relates the conflicting advice given by Absalom's two counselors, Ahithophel and Hushai. At the height of his rebellion, Absalom is in control of Jerusalem and David has fled the capital. Ahithophel wisely advises Absalom to take quick action because David has not yet been able to organize resistance. Absalom should arrange for a "surgical strike" that will kill only David and gain Absalom popularity by avoiding many casualties. Hushai, who is actually an agent for David's interests, advises delay instead. This will allow Absalom to assemble an overwhelming force in order to crush David's followers. Hushai's speech is a psychological masterpiece. He plays on Absalom's fear of his father's military reputation and raises the specter of panic after a possible initial defeat. Absalom accepts Hushai's unwise recommendation, and the narrator asserts that it was Yahweh who brought about this outcome in order to bring down Absalom (17:14).

Women in Samuel

Although the various protagonists of Samuel are men in public leadership roles, the actions and decisions of important women move events along at critical points.

Hannah

The book begins with Samuel's mother Hannah. The Bible sometimes signals the introduction of a notable personage to the larger story by telling a special kind of narrative about their conception and birth. Examples of these stories are Genesis 16:7-14 (Hagar and Ishmael) and Judges 13 (Samson). The annunciation to Mary in Luke 1:26-38 is a New Testament instance. As was true of the mothers of Isaac, Jacob, and Samson, Hannah had been childless, but Yahweh reverses her misfortune (1 Sam 1:5, 19). Hannah takes the initiative by means of her prayer and solemn promise, and Eli announces the fulfillment of her request through his priestly ability to impart God's intentions (1:10-11, 17). Hannah gives Samuel to Yahweh at the Shiloh sanctuary (1:11, 24-28). Typically in such stories, the name of the child reveals some significant reality. In Hannah's case, this act of naming is slightly odd. In 1:20 she names him Samuel (*God has heard*), but in so doing references the Hebrew verb *to ask* (*sha'al*). But the verb *sha'al* really echoes the name Saul (*sha'ul*). It sounds as though Hannah's act of naming is providing a hidden reference to Samuel's future as the one who anoints Saul as king.

Hannah responds in joy with her song in 1 Samuel 2. This is a thanksgiving psalm that the author has taken up from another context and reused here. A connection to Hannah's situation is provided by 2:5: *The woman who was barren has birthed seven children*. Hannah testifies that Yahweh is acting decisively in Israel's history to implement reversal and transformation. Yahweh kills and gives life. Yahweh brings down but also exalts. The stories that follow in the book of Samuel illustrate this principle of topsy-turvy change. Hannah's infertility is overcome, and she becomes Samuel's mother. The ark is captured but goes on to defeat its enemies. Saul comes to royal power, but is brought down. David, the youngest of his father's sons, rises to kingship, only to be nearly undone by rebellion from within his own family.

Chapter 12

Michal

Saul's daughter Michal plays a role in David's rise to honor within Saul's court, in his flight to escape Saul's murderous anger, and in the complicated family dynamics of David's royal court. Saul uses the promise of marriage to her to try to bring about David's death, but David's military prowess allows him to wed her and gain an oblique claim to the throne as the king's son-in-law (1 Sam 18:17-27). Like her brother Jonathan, she loves David, so she urges him to flee her father and helps with his escape (18:28; 19:11-17). She becomes a political pawn when her father hands her over as wife to another man (1 Sam 25:44). Nevertheless after Saul's death, David demands her back (2 Sam 3:12-16). In the end, Michal despises David for his uninhibited behavior when he brings the covenant chest to Jerusalem and never bears him the son and heir who would have united the royal houses of Saul and David (2 Sam 6:14-16, 20-23).

Abigail

While David was on the run from Saul's fury, he commanded a band of malcontents and disenfranchised men. These outlaws hid out in isolated regions and lived by raiding (1 Sam 22:2; 23:5, 13-14; 27:8-12). According to 1 Samuel 25, at the time of a sheep-shearing celebration, David requests support from a rich sheep farmer named Nabal (Hebrew: *fool, miser*). David is polite and pointedly mentions that his men have protected and never mistreated Nabal's workers. Nabal refuses rudely and, given the reality that David commands six hundred experienced fighters, most unwisely. In contrast, Nabal's wife, Abigail, is wise, polite, and operates with good sense (25:3, 33). Even as David is on the march to avenge the insult, Abigail rushes to intercept him with polite and complimentary words, as well as a big consignment of provisions. Her speech is a model of wise rhetoric. She distances herself from her husband's stupidity and assures David that he is under Yahweh's protection. Someday he will rule and establish a sure dynastic house (25:25, 28-31). When Nabal soon dies, she agrees to become one of David's wives.

The Woman Who Communicated with Ghosts

As the Philistines gather against Saul for his final battle, Saul cannot determine God's will concerning the outcome. Yahweh has cut off all standard channels of communication (1 Sam 28:6). This predicament drives Saul to consult a medium or necromancer (CEB: *a woman who communicates with ghosts*), although he earlier banished them from his realm. Saul comes to her in disguise and at night and overcomes her initial resistance. As Samuel's ghost rises from the earth, she perceives that the man consulting her is Saul. She can see the dead prophet and describes him to Saul.

Saul hears an announcement of defeat, death, and the ultimate triumph of his rival David (28:16-20). The woman has taken a great risk for the king and goes to great lengths to provide Saul sustenance for the coming battle (28:9, 21-25).

Bathsheba

The watershed incident of David's adultery with Bathsheba and the arranged murder of her husband Uriah (2 Sam 11:2–12:25) is reported in the midst of recounting David's war with the Ammonites (2 Sam 10:1–11:1; 12:26-31). This narrative spares neither David, who abuses his powerful status to violate and then acquire a loyal subordinate's wife, nor his complicit general Joab. David first tries to pass off responsibility for Bathsheba's inconvenient pregnancy onto Uriah. In the end, David responds to the news that his plot to eliminate Uriah has succeeded with breathtaking cynicism (11:25). In contrast to its presentation of David, the narrative underscores Uriah's strength of character. Out of solidarity with his comrades who are besieging the enemy capital, Uriah twice refuses to sleep in his own house (11:8-13), perhaps because soldiers on active duty were not supposed to engage in sex (Deut 23:9-14; 1 Sam 21:5). Bathsheba's character remains opaque, however. Much daily life took place on the cool, flat rooftops of houses. Her bath after her menstrual period was a matter of following religious or cultural norms (11:4), but it also means that Uriah could not be the father of her baby. How voluntary was her escorted visit to the king's bed? She does speak out, but only once, with the message *I'm pregnant* (11:5). She grieves for her dead husband (11:26). David's deed triggers Yahweh's punishment of continuing violence within David's family, as announced by Nathan (12:7-12). The first son of her union with David dies (12:14-19). In contrast, Solomon, Bathsheba's second son by David, is beloved by Yahweh (12:24-25).

Bathsheba disappears from the narrative until 1 Kings 1. Now no longer silent and passive, she returns as a vigorous character. She conspires with the prophet Nathan to convince an aging David to put her own son Solomon on the throne instead of his older half-brother Adonijah. Solomon shows her great honor (1 Kgs 2:19-20). She intercedes with him for Adonijah when he asks to marry a woman from David's former household. Readers are likely to suspect that in so doing she is giving Solomon an excuse to liquidate his rival (2:22-25).

Princess Tamar

The competition among David's sons begins in earnest with 2 Samuel 13. One of David's sons, Amnon, develops a sexual craving for his beautiful half-sister Tamar, who is the full sister of Absalom, another son of David. Tamar is put into a dangerous situation by David, who has been manipulated by Amnon. Although she seeks with wise words to sidetrack his lust, Amnon rapes her, then repudiates her. In spite of her pleas, Amnon has her put out on the street, still wearing the special garment that identified her as a royal princess. She is not silent, but with ashes on her hair she shrieks out her grief publically until her brother Absalom muzzles her. Absalom bides his time, but two years later seizes a chance to avenge her disgrace by having Amnon murdered.

The Book of Samuel and History

The degree to which Samuel reports genuine history is a matter of dispute. Most of the source materials used by the author of Samuel are not of the sort that historians consider historically useful. The historical existence and leadership of Saul and David cannot be disproved. However, many of the stories told about them seem to derive from folktales and display later theological and political concerns.

Samuel hints that Saul and David were less like full-scale kings and more like what anthropologists sometimes term chiefs. Chiefs are leaders whose power depends not on governmental institutions or specialized offices but on their ability to provide status and wealth to their own family groups, who support and serve him. Saul was likely a historical person whose rule centered on the tribe of Benjamin. His historical existence is indicated by the tradition of his grave (2 Sam 21:12-14) and folk sayings concerning him (1 Sam 10:11-12; 18:7; 19:24; 21:11). The report of a two-year reign in 1 Samuel 13:1 seems too short to accommodate everything reported about him. There is also some evidence of David's historical authenticity. The kingdom of Judah was called *house of David* by outsiders in the late ninth century. (See chapter 14, Jehu and History.) The common designation of Jerusalem as *David's City* witnesses to the claim that it was he who captured the city, leading to it becoming the capital of Judah. Probably many heroic traditions became attached to David over time. For example, 2 Samuel 21:19 attributes the slaying of Goliath to one of David's champions named Elhanan instead of portraying it as an intrepid act of David.

Further Reading

A. Graeme Auld. *I & II Samuel: A Commentary*. Louisville, KY: Westminster John Knox, 2011.

Keith Bodner. *David Observed: A King in the Eyes of His Court*. Sheffield, UK: Sheffield Phoenix, 2005.

Chapter 13
THE BOOK OF KINGS AND THE STORY OF SOLOMON

The Book of Kings

First and Second Kings are considered to be a single book in the Hebrew canon. The division point between 1 and 2 Kings takes place at the phrase *after Ahab died* in 2 Kings 1:1 (the same transitional formula is used at Josh 1:1; Judg 1:1; and 2 Sam 1:1). This division is awkward given that it splits up the reign of King Ahaziah (1 Kgs 22:51-53 and 2 Kgs 1:2-18) and the career of the prophet Elijah.

The title *Kings* is appropriate because the kings of Israel and Judah are the central characters, and the fate of the two kingdoms is described as contingent on those monarchs' fidelity or infidelity to Yahweh. Royal reigns provide the core organizing principle. Most kings are treated briefly, with only a few sentences supplementing a bare-bones, standardized framework. However, a smaller number of significant kings are described more extensively. Stories of a number of prophets are also prominent. An extensive collection of traditional tales featuring the prophets Elijah and Elisha make up most of 1 Kings 17:1 to 2 Kings 8:15. The reigns of the northern kings Jeroboam and Ahab are illustrated by stories involving the prophet Ahijah (1 Kgs 11:29-39; 14:1-18), a prophet from Judah in connection with one from Bethel (1 Kings 13), and Micaiah son of Imlah (1 Kgs 22:1-28). A large portion of 2 Kings (2 Kgs 18:13–20:19) focuses on Isaiah. King and prophet are sometimes paired together. For Israel these pairings are Jeroboam with Ahijah, Ahab with Elijah, Jehoram with Elisha, and Jehu with an unnamed disciple of Elisha. For Judah, Hezekiah is paired with Isaiah and Josiah with Huldah.

Chapter 13

As part of the larger Deuteronomistic History, the presentation of history in Kings is pervaded by the theology of Deuteronomy. Two evaluative sections appear at important turning points, reviewing the past and pointing forward to future developments. The first of these is Solomon's address at the dedication of the Jerusalem temple (1 Kings 8). The second is an exposition concerning the persistent wrongdoing of the northern kingdom that led to its destruction (2 Kings 17). Solomon's dedication prayer is largely positive about the future, but 2 Kings 17 treats the fall of Israel as a warning sign of Judah's impending downfall.

Some scholars suggest that Kings (and the rest of DH) was the work of a writer working after the death of Judah's captive king Jehoiachin (2 Kgs 25:27-30). This author wanted to provide an explanation for the fall of Judah. Others postulate an optimistic pre-exilic historian writing before or just after the death of Judah's reforming King Josiah in order to support Josiah's reforming policies. According to this perspective, an originally optimistic portrayal of events was later revised into a pessimistic history of disobedience, one that blamed the destruction of Judah on the sinful policies of Josiah's grandfather Manasseh (2 Kgs 21:10-15; 23:26; 24:3-4). Another group of scholars propose DH as an exilic work subsequently overlaid by two later editorial expansions oriented toward prophecy and torah respectively.

The Scope of Kings

Kings traces the history of the kingdoms of Israel and Judah over almost four centuries, from Solomon's assumption of rule down to the defeat of King Zedekiah of Judah, the devastation of Jerusalem, and a forced deportation of Judah's leadership classes. (See Table 3, Kings of Israel and Judah.) The presentation falls into three parts. First Kings 1–11 deals with Solomon and concludes with a standardized formula that concludes his reign (1 Kgs 11:41-43).

The central part of the book (1 Kings 12–2 Kings 17) tells the parallel stories of Israel and Judah and concludes with Israel's crushing defeat by Assyria in about 720. Hostility between Israel and Judah unfolds in 1 Kings 12–14. First Kings 15–16 traces that enmity down to the accession of Israel's king Ahab. First Kings 17 to 2 Kings 10 focuses on the prophets Elijah and Elisha and their conflicts with the apostate northern kingdom kings of the Omri dynasty. This conflict culminates in a revolution by Jehu, who establishes a new dynasty. Briefer reports follow until 2 Kings 17, which explores the theological reasons for the fall of Israel.

The final section, 2 Kings 18–25, recounts the further history of Judah down to its destruction in 586 BCE. This presentation reflects a pattern of alternating righteous and wicked kings: Hezekiah (virtuous), Manasseh (evil), Josiah (virtuous), and Josiah's successors (evil). The religious reform of Josiah (chapters 22–23) is in some ways the climax of the entire book. Brief reports sketch out the wickedness and rebellions of Josiah's four successors and two successful attacks on Judah and Jerusalem by the Babylonians. Kings ends with an enigmatic report about King Jehoiachin, who dies as an honored captive in Babylon (2 Kgs 25:27-30). This concluding notice has been interpreted both positively as an optimistic sign of a potential future for the Davidic dynasty and negatively as the decisive last act in Judah's national tragedy.

Sources Used by Kings

Three earlier written sources are cited by name in Kings. The scroll containing the acts of Solomon (CEB: *the official records of Solomon*; NRSV: *the Book of the Acts of Solomon*) is described as reporting information on Solomon's deeds and his "wisdom" (1 Kgs 11:41). This work seems to have provided the author with administrative lists, along with narratives and notices illustrating Solomon's glory and wisdom.

The author of Kings gleaned information about the kings who followed Solomon from two other sources. These are cited as *the official records of Israel's kings* and *the official records of Judah's kings* (CEB; NRSV: *Book of the Annals of the Kings of Israel* and *Book of the Annals of the Kings of Judah*, 1 Kgs 14:19, 29, and so forth). These two documents provided information on wars, conspiracies, and building projects (as indicated by 1 Kgs 14:19, 29-30; 15:23, 31-32; 16:20; 22:39, 45; 2 Kgs 20:20). These citation formulas indicate that the two sources were accessible for readers to consult, which suggests that they were not actual royal annals but literary works based on inscriptions and other official sources. The editors of Kings used material from these sources to compose the formulaic summaries that conclude the reigns of most of the kings. A typical example of this is the concluding formula for Jeroboam, the first king of Israel: *the rest of Jeroboam's deeds—how he fought and how he ruled—are written in the official records of Israel's kings* (1 Kgs 14:19).

Kings may also have used an unnamed source document that reported on the assets of the Jerusalem temple. It is often suggested that such a source was the basis for what is said about Solomon's gold shields (1 Kgs 14:26) and raids on the temple treasury by Asa (15:18), Jehoash (2 Kgs 12:17-18), Ahaz (2 Kgs 16:8, 17-18), and so forth. Other material in Kings might go back to archival or inscriptional sources. For example, the report of the tribute paid by Menahem king of Israel to Assyria (2 Kgs 15:19-20) is confirmed by an Assyrian source. There is at least partial correspondence between 2 Kings 18:14 and Assyrian sources in regard to tribute paid by Hezekiah. In addition, an earlier collection of stories about the prophets Elijah and Elisha were incorporated to make up most of 1 Kings 17:1 to 2 Kings 8:15. This cycle of prophetic tales is held together by the transfer of Elijah's mantle to Elisha (2 Kgs 2:13-14) and the completion of Elijah's mission by Elisha and others (1 Kgs 19:15-17). The use of sources in the book of Kings indicates that it is of considerable historical value in places. However, unlike modern histories, historical causation in Kings is theological

Chapter 13

rather than political or economic. It is Yahweh's anger or favor that determines the course of events.

Organization and Chronology

Kings is organized by a system of opening and closing formulas that mark off sections reporting on the reigns of the individual kings of the two kingdoms. An opening formula synchronizes the year that each king comes to the throne with the year of reign for the ruler of the other kingdom, and then gives the total length of his reign. The opening formulas offer a judgment on each king's religious fidelity to Yahweh. Most of them, including every king of Israel, *did evil in Yahweh's eyes* (1 Kgs 15:26, 34, and so forth). Some kings of Judah *did the right things in Yahweh's eyes* (1 Kgs 15:11; 22:43, and so forth). At the conclusion of the section on each king, a closing formula refers the reader to the appropriate source document and reports on the king's death and his successor. These bracketing opening and concluding formulas give more information about the kings of Judah than for the kings of Israel: age at accession, mother's name, and a notice of burial. The introduction and conclusion formulas for Rehoboam of Judah provide a good example of the pattern (1 Kgs 14:21-22; 29-31).

Kings narrates the entire reign of a particular monarch and then backtracks to report on the king or kings of the other kingdom who came to the throne during the first king's rule. For example, in 1 Kings 15:9-10 the reign of King Asa from Judah is introduced with a stock phrase: *In the twentieth year of Israel's King Jeroboam, Asa became king of Judah. He ruled in Jerusalem for forty-one years.* Asa's reign is concluded with the formulaic language of 1 Kings 15:23-24: *The rest of Asa's deeds . . . aren't they written in the official records of Judah's kings? . . . He died and was buried. . . . His son Jehoshaphat succeeded him as king.* Then the presentation turns back in time to deal with five kings of Israel (Nadab, Baasha, Zimri, Omri, and Ahab), all of whom had succeeded to the kingship of Israel during the reign of King Asa in Judah. Then when Ahab's reign has been concluded, Kings goes back to introduce King Jehoshaphat in Judah, whose reign had begun in Ahab's fourth year (1 Kgs 22:41).

There are irregularities in the system. Concluding statements are missing for certain kings, such as the victims of Jehu's rebellious purge. Jehu himself lacks an introductory formula because of the special circumstances of how he came to be king. King Joash in Israel is inexplicably provided with two closing formulas (2 Kgs 13:12-13; 14:15-16). Some stories fall outside the frames, notably the transfer of authority from Elijah to Elisha (2 Kings 2) and the illegitimate reign of Queen Athaliah in Judah (2 Kings 11).

Another structural feature of Kings is a pattern of prophetic promise and fulfillment. The prophets are Yahweh's servants, announcing divine will and judgment (2 Kgs 17:13, 23; 21:10; 24:2). They correctly predict the breakup of Solomon's kingdom (1 Kgs 11:29-39 and 12:15), the fate of the royal family of Omri of Israel (1 Kgs 21:21-24; 2 Kgs 9:7-10; 10:17), the fall of Israel (1 Kgs 14:15-16; 2 Kgs 17:23), and the defeat of Judah (2 Kgs 21:10-15; 22:15-17; 24:2). The most striking example is the prophetic prediction of Josiah's reform (1 Kgs 13:1-10 and 2 Kgs 23:15-18).

A more subtle organizational pattern is revealed in analogies between paired narratives. Examples are stories of two mothers and their sons (1 Kgs 3:16-28 and 2 Kgs 6:26-31), violent death of a wicked queen (2 Kgs 9:30-37 and 11:13-16), and a king's wisdom and folly with visitors (1 Kgs 10:1-13 and 2 Kgs 20:12-19).

Kings presents a chronology for the history and rulers of Israel and Judah, but this information cannot simply be converted into dates for the reigns of the kings without a great deal of uncertainty. The chronological information in Kings connects back to what is reported about Saul and David (1 Sam 13:1; 2 Sam 5:4; 1 Kgs 2:11). Problems occur because the years of reign given for Israel's kings do not coordinate with those for Judah's kings. Moreover, the system of synchronisms (dating the year of a king's accession to the reign of the king of the sister kingdom) does not always match the reign lengths. There are also discrepancies with established dates known from available Mesopotamian records. In trying to untangle these problems, scholars postulate errors in textual transmission, different calendrical conventions for the two kingdoms at various times, and co-regencies in which a king and his designated successor reigned concurrently. As a result, many of the dates given for the kings of Israel and Judah given in textbooks and other introductory materials are not thoroughly consistent.

Table 3. Kings of Israel and Judah

ISRAEL	JUDAH
Jeroboam (22 years)	Rehoboam (17 years)
	Abijam (3 years)
	Asa (41 years)
Nadab (2 years)	
Baasha (24 years)	
Elah (2 years)	
Zimri (7 days)	
Tibni (overlaps with Omri)	
Omri (11 years)	
Ahab (15 years, was king in 853)	
	Jehoshaphat (25 years)

ISRAEL	JUDAH
Ahaziah (2 years)	
Joram (12 years)	
	Jehoram (8 years)
	Ahaziah (1 year)
Jehu (18 years, was king in 841)	Athaliah (7 years)
	Jehoash (40 years)
Jehoahaz (17 years)	
Joash (16 years)	
	Amaziah (29 years)
Jeroboam II (41 years)	
	Azariah/Uzziah (52 years)
Zechariah (6 months)	
Shallum (1 month)	
Menahem (10 years, was king in 740 and 738)	
Pekahiah (20 years is incorrect, perhaps 2 years)	
Pekah (4 years, was king in 734–732)	
	Jotham (16 years)
	Ahaz (16 years, was king in 734)
Hoshea (9 years, was king in 731)	
	Hezekiah 726–697 (29 years)
	Manasseh 697–642 (55 years)
	Amon 642–640 (2 years)
	Josiah 640–609 (31 years)
	Jehoahaz 609 (3 months)
	Jehoiakim 609–598 (11 years)
	Jehoiachin 598–597 (three months)
	Zedekiah 597–587/586 (11 years)

The Theology of Kings

The book of Kings critiques a failure to preserve the purity and unity of Yahweh worship on the part of both kingdoms. Its condemnations are based on the theology of Deuteronomy, so that the charges leveled against Rehoboam and Ahaz (1 Kgs 14:22-24; 2 Kgs 16:3-4), for example, closely reflect what is forbidden by Deuteronomy 12:2-3, 29-31.

Kings recounts that the worship of other gods was something that started with Solomon and was continued by some of the kings of both Israel and Judah. Kings sometimes calls the worship of gods other than Yahweh walking *in the ways of Israel's kings* (2 Kgs 8:18; 16:3) or *of Ahab's dynasty* (2 Kgs 8:27). Worship of Yahweh's rival god Baal is particularly condemned. According to Kings, Baal was sponsored in Israel by Ahab and Jezebel (1 Kgs 16:31-32), eliminated by Jehu (2 Kgs 10:18-28), but then revived again in Judah by Manasseh (2 Kgs 21:3).

The second focus of disapproval was sacrifice to Yahweh practiced outside Jerusalem. Kings condemns every one of the kings of Israel because they permitted and sponsored the royal sacrificial cult at the sanctuary of Bethel, said to have been instituted by Jeroboam, the founder of the northern kingdom. All of them participated by *walking in Jeroboam's ways* or *sins* (1 Kgs 15:34; 16:2, 19, 26, 31; and so forth). In Judah, non-central sacrifice was offered at holy places (NRSV: *high places*), which had served as traditional, local shrines for generations. Even otherwise faithful kings of Judah received only qualified approval because they failed to eliminate those shrines (1 Kgs 15:14; 22:43; and so forth). Only Hezekiah and Josiah receive total approval, because only they centralized sacrificial worship at the Jerusalem temple.

These two strands of evaluation are brought together in the reform of Judah's king Josiah, who both proscribed the worship of other gods (2 Kgs 23:4-5, 10-14) and removed the local shrines (23:8-9). He desecrated the shrine of Bethel and the shrines of Israel (23:15-20). Kings insists that the religious infidelity of Israel is what caused its destruction by the Assyrians (2 Kgs 17:7-18, 21-23). Similarly, Kings maintains that Judah eventually fell to Babylon as a result of similar offenses (2 Kgs 17:19-20), especially those sponsored by Manasseh (2 Kgs 21:10-15; 24:3-4).

Another important theological theme is the special favor shown by Yahweh to David and his descendants (1 Kgs 11:12-13). Yahweh promised an abiding Davidic dynasty reigning in Jerusalem (1 Kgs 11:36; 15:4-5; 2 Kgs 8:19). Kings regularly uses David's devotion as a model for measuring the fidelity of later kings (1 Kgs 3:3; 11:4, 6, 38; 15:3, 11; and so forth). Yahweh's special favor to David is given as the reason for the rescue of Jerusalem from attacking Assyrian armies in the time of Hezekiah's reign (2 Kgs 19:34; 20:5-6).

13.1. WOMEN IN KINGS

The book of Kings sometimes casts women as religious villains who endanger the people's fidelity to Yahweh. Solomon's many wives lead him into sponsoring the worship of other gods (1 Kgs 11:1-8). Ahab's foreign wife Jezebel sponsors Baal and Asherah, murders Yahweh's prophets, and undermines Ahab's integrity (1 Kings 18–19, 21). Athaliah murders the royal family to seize the throne of Judah (2 Kings 11). But women also serve as positive characters. Bathsheba helps plot the accession of Solomon her son (1 Kings 1). She and other royal mothers occupied the recognized public office of Queen Mother (1 Kgs 15:13; 2 Kgs 10:13). Two quarreling prostitutes and the Queen of Sheba enhance Solomon's reputation for wisdom (1 Kgs 3:16-28; 10:1-10). Women also play supporting roles in prophetic narratives (1 Kgs 14:1-18; 17:8-24; 2 Kgs 4:1-37; 8:1-6). The prophet Huldah interprets the significance of Josiah's policies (2 Kgs 22:14-20).

The Story of Solomon

Solomon in All His Glory—1 Kings 1–11

First Kings 1–11 recounts the career of Solomon. Solomon comes to the throne of David's kingdom through a very human and eventually violent process of palace intrigue orchestrated by the prophet Nathan, his mother Bathsheba, and the priest Zadok (chapters 1 and 2). The problem of David's great age is signaled by his failing sexual potency with the beautiful Abishag (1:3-4). His spoiled and handsome oldest surviving son, Adonijah, sponsors a sacrificial celebration, which the plotters Nathan and Bathsheba present to David as an attempt to seize the throne. They claim that David earlier swore to Bathsheba that Solomon would succeed him (1:13, 17, 30; no such solemn pledge is reported). David immediately arranges to have Solomon anointed as king, so that there is a co-regency of father and son ruling together until David's death. David's final advice to Solomon is Machiavellian (2:2-9): liquidate those who have proved untrustworthy, namely David's general Joab, who murdered Abner (2 Sam 3:22-30), and the Benjaminite Shimei, who was a supporter and relative of Saul (2 Sam 16:5-6; 19:16-23). Solomon arranges the death of those two, as well as of his rival Adonijah.

First Kings 3–10 celebrates the reign of Solomon as a gilded age of peace and prosperity, praising his wisdom, royal power, building programs, and piety. Admiring legends portray Solomon's wisdom. Following a common ancient practice of seeking communication with a deity (called incubation), Solomon sleeps at the sanctuary of Gibeon, because the Jerusalem temple has not yet been built. When Yahweh appears in a dream, Solomon asks not for the typical aspirations of monarchy (long life, wealth, death of his enemies) but for the wisdom a ruler needs to govern (1 Kgs 3:3-15; CEB: *a discerning mind . . . . a wise and understanding mind*). Solomon immediately displays his God-given wisdom in the well-known story of a child custody dispute, in which he discovers which of two competing women is the real mother of a baby boy (3:16-28). In another folktale, the queen of far-off Sheba (in the southwestern region of the Arabian peninsula) visits to test his wisdom and comes away breathlessly amazed at his great insight and wealth (10:1-10, 13). Solomon is said to have had unparalleled knowledge of plants and animals and to have composed thousands of proverbs and songs (4:29-34). This reputation led later tradition to assign to him authorship of the wisdom-oriented books of Proverbs, Ecclesiastes, and Wisdom of Solomon—as well as the erotic Song of Solomon.

Kings also celebrates Solomon's power and international influence. A list of court officials in 1 Kings 4:2-6 is reproduced in order to show the sophistication of his administration. First Kings 4:7-19 presents another (apparently authentic) roster of Solomon's officials. The list is treated as a description of twelve administrative districts in order to glorify his royal court and the huge quantity of supplies needed to support it (see 4:7, 22-23). The original list may have been a roster of representatives or agents who represented Solomon's interests in cities and tribal areas not actually under his direct control. It may be that Solomon's kingdom was actually limited to Judah and the city of Jerusalem.

Solomon's glory is emphasized by means of descriptions of his great territory, fabulous wealth, court furnishings, throne, and foreign trade (4:20-28; 9:26-28; 10:14-29). International trade was a source of income and provided the weaponry of horses and chariots that were the hallmark of any great military power (10:26-29). A notice admiring his prodigious harem of secondary wives (11:3) signals enormous wealth and international treaty relationships secured by an exchange of royal relatives and daughters. That one of these marriages involved an Egyptian princess may be an untrustworthy detail from folklore, since there are no other examples of Egyptian kings engaging in such a practice (3:1; 9:16, 24).

Solomon's Temple

Ancient kings characteristically demonstrated their grandeur through impressive building projects. Kings is most interested in Solomon's construction of the Jerusalem temple. Much effort is spent on describing construction techniques and materials (chapters 5–6) and the richness of its metal furnishings (7:13-51). There is every reason to suppose that this first temple was erected somewhere within the enclosed raised area that is today designated as the Haram esh-Sharif or Temple Mount. This would have been north of the original core city ("David's City"). The description of the temple in Kings may be based on the author's knowledge of its later appearance. As described in chapters 6–7, the temple structure proper was oriented longitudinally from east to west and incorporated three parts. An entryway *porch* flanked by two free-standing columns led into a *main hall* (NRSV: *nave*). To the west of the main hall was another room, the *most holy place* (NRSV: *inner sanctuary*). There the presence of Yahweh was concretized in the form of the ark (CEB: *chest*) of the covenant, which was conceived of as Yahweh's throne or footstool. The covenant chest was overshadowed by two large guardian winged creatures (Hebrew: *cherubim*) that were 15 feet high (a "cubit," an archaic English word used in many translations, is about eighteen inches).

Fig. 10. Dome of the Rock. The first Jerusalem temple was located north of the city, which at that time was limited to the ridge called the Ophel (or City of David). Its exact location within the present-day platform referred to as the Haram esh-Sharif or Temple Mount is uncertain. This enclosed area houses the shrine of the Dome of the Rock, originally completed in 691 CE. On the south side of the platform is the el-Aqsa mosque, the construction history of which also dates back to the seventh century CE.

The porch was fifteen feet deep, beyond which was the main structure with interior dimensions of 90 by 30 feet, with a height of 45 five feet (that is, 31.15 by 8.9 by 13.35 meters, taking a cubit at 44.5 cm). Of this ninety-foot length, the main hall took up 60 feet. Behind this, the inner sanctuary consisted of a cube measuring 30 feet on each side, the floor of which seems to have been higher than that of the main room. Around three sides of the exterior of the central building was a three-story outer structure with rooms for storage and other purposes. The temple's outdoor courtyard was the site of the sacrificial ritual, with an altar on which the sacrificial fires burned and a large round reservoir supported by twelve bull images that held water required for the sacrificial procedures. Group assembly took place outside in this courtyard, which was bounded by an enclosure. Eventually, there would also be a second, outer courtyard.

13.2. TEMPLES

Unlike a church or synagogue in which worshippers assemble, an ancient temple was conceived of as a house or palace for a god. The standard words used for *temple* in the Old Testament are the same as those denoting an ordinary human residence or king's mansion. Like a royal ruler, the deity was thought in some sense to reside in the temple or be present there in a manner especially accessible to human worshippers. Temples were set into areas of sacred space that were marked off from common use. Temples for Yahweh had existed in Israel before Solomon established the one in Jerusalem and continued to function alongside that temple for several centuries. The narratives about the priest Eli mention a temple associated with Yahweh in Shiloh (1 Sam 1:7, 24; 3:15; Judg 18:31). Judges 17:5 mentions a household temple (NRSV: *shrine*, CEB: *sanctuary*) for the use of well-to-do extended family. According to Judges 9 there was a temple at Shechem for the divinity Baal-berith.

The temple building proper was essentially a palace or house built for Yahweh. Just as in a human king's palace, Yahweh was attended to with domestic, ritual activities performed inside the building. There incense was burned on a special stand or altar, oil lamps were tended, and fresh bread was displayed on a weekly schedule, again as one might do in a royal palace (7:48-49). The main room seems to have been illuminated by clerestory windows and was decorated with symbolic carvings of palms and flowers, representing fertility, and winged creatures (Hebrew: *cherubim*), which served as guardian figures (6:29). The smaller dark inner room served as an analogy to the throne room of a human king. This first temple served the royal court and eventually the nation of Judah until it was razed by the Babylonians. Hence the period of the Judahite monarchy is often called the First Temple period.

First Kings 7:1-12, however, reveals that the temple was really only one element of a large royal administrative and residential quarter and was by no means its largest component. Solomon's palace complex took twice as long to build as the temple (6:38; 7:1; 9:10). Details are unclear, but there seem to have been five buildings surrounded by a wall that made it into a compound. Costly hewn stone and cedar wood were used throughout. Solomon built the House of the Forest of Lebanon (CEB: *Forest of*

Lebanon Palace), which at 100 by 50 by 30 cubits was much larger than the temple. Also described is a Hall of Pillars (the CEB treats this as a porch, 7:6), a Hall of the Throne for judgment, and separate palaces for Solomon and the daughter of Pharaoh.

Kings reports that Solomon built a wall for Jerusalem and strengthened various strategic cities (9:15-19). Similarities in the fortifications of Hazor, Gezer, and Megiddo have sometimes been adduced as evidence of Solomon's activities, but this conclusion remains controversial. Kings portrays Solomon as being powerful enough to employ the forced labor of Israelites and Canaanites to complete his building projects (5:13-18; 9:15, 20-22).

Solomon and Yahweh

Kings is somewhat paradoxical in its portrayal of Solomon's loyalty to Yahweh. Yahweh appears to him twice (3:5; 9:2). At the dedication of the temple, Solomon prays about its future importance to Israel's relationship to Yahweh (8:22-53). In his dedicatory prayer, Solomon asks that in situations of sin, drought, famine, and warfare, Yahweh would attentively listen to the prayers of the nation and respond. Even if sin should cause Israel to be defeated and sent into exile, he pleads that prayer toward the temple will result in forgiveness. The dedication ceremony concludes with Solomon sponsoring extraordinary sacrifices (8:62-66; see also 9:25).

However, there is a negative subtext to Solomon's accumulation of riches and many wives and horses. These royal activities are specifically forbidden by Deuteronomy 17:16-17. Solomon's career concludes on a negative note in 1 Kings 11. After quoting Deuteronomy 7:3-4, which forbids intermarriage with foreigners, the Deuteronomistic author asserts that the foreign women among Solomon's wives induced him to build sanctuaries for the worship of their gods, so that he was not completely loyal to Yahweh (1 Kgs 11:1-8). This infidelity results in divine anger, trouble for Solomon, and in the end a division of his realm into two kingdoms. Adversaries threaten his kingdom, including Edom, Damascus, and Jeroboam, whose rebellion will split up Solomon's glorious kingdom after his death (11:9-40).

Further Reading

Walter Dietrich. *The Early Monarchy in Israel: The Tenth Century BCE*. Atlanta, GA: SBL Press, 2007.

Walter Brueggemann. *Solomon: Israel's Ironic Icon of Human Achievement*. Columbia: University of South Carolina Press, 2005.

Chapter 14
1 AND 2 KINGS AND THE HISTORY OF ISRAEL AND JUDAH

Jeroboam (Israel) and Rehoboam (Judah)— 1 Kings 12–14

After its description of Solomon, Kings enters into the realm of verifiable history in the sense that many of the events reported can be coordinated with outside sources. Sometime around 930, Solomon's son *Rehoboam* became the first king of Judah, which was made up of tribal Judah, the city of Jerusalem, and a portion of the tribe of Benjamin. The northern part of Palestine and areas to the east of the Jordan, however, emerged as the kingdom of Israel with Jeroboam from Ephraim as its first king. Shechem was Israel's first capital. Yahweh was the national god of both kingdoms, worshipped at royal sanctuaries at Dan, Bethel, and Jerusalem, and at local shrines throughout the land. The populations of these two kingdom shared a common language and traditions. Kings describes this divided state of affairs as the result of a rebellion by Jeroboam against David's dynasty and the division of a previously unified state. This may have been the case, but the narrative recounted in 1 Kings 12:1-24 sounds more like a folktale featuring youthful folly and competing advisors than a historical report. Kings asserts that this development had been predicted by the prophet Ahijah and had been brought about by Yahweh (11:29-39; 12:15).

The northern state of Israel was the more populous and stronger of the two, with greater resources and geographically more open to contact with foreign nations. Judah remained more isolated. Israel suffered from dynastic instability in the beginning

Chapter 14

and concluding decades of its two-hundred-year history. In contrast, the political situation of Judah was stabilized by allegiance to a single royal line, the "house of David." The border between the two kingdoms remained in dispute for some time (1 Kgs 14:30; 15:7, 16, 22).

In the fifth year of his reign, Rehoboam was confronted by a military incursion by Pharaoh Shishak (Soshenq I, about 945–924). Shishak's own list of places involved (*ANET* 242–43, 263–64) seems to indicate that his real target was not so much Judah but the southern Negev desert and the northern parts of Israel.

Kings describes *Jeroboam* as the founder of two national sanctuaries, one near the northern border of his kingdom at Dan and the other near his southern boundary at Bethel (1 Kgs 12:25-33). Both of these locations had already been traditional holy sites (Gen 28:11-22; Judg 18:30-31). Yahweh was represented there in the form of a bull image (or perhaps thought of as invisibly standing on the bull statue as a pedestal). In light of the anti-image and pro-Jerusalem theology of the Deuteronomistic author of Kings, the report of Jeroboam's institution of these bull icons is totally critical. However, Jeroboam's actions seem to be in line with the opinions of his time and place.

Prophet stories in 1 Kings 13 strengthen the theme of condemnation. A prophet (the designation used is *man of God*) proclaims a judgment oracle against Jeroboam's Bethel altar. His prediction is strikingly detailed. Someday a scion of the family of David will desecrate this altar with human sacrifice. This word is fulfilled about 300 years later when King Josiah of Judah does just that (2 Kgs 23:15-18). A supplementary prophet story illustrates the importance of strictly obeying what Yahweh proclaims (1 Kgs 13:16-17, 20-22). In 1 Kings 14, a story featuring the prophet Ahijah dramatically announces Yahweh's judgment on Jeroboam and his potential successors. The obedience of David is used as the benchmark of royal behavior (14:8). The graphic language of 14:10-11 asserts that Jeroboam's religious actions will result in his dynasty being brought to an end. As the book unfolds, Jeroboam will be used as paradigm for the ongoing wickedness of Israel's kings (for example, 1 Kgs 15:30, 34; 16:19, 26).

Jeroboam is succeeded by his son *Nadab*, who is quickly killed in a coup by *Baasha* from the tribe of Issachar. Baasha then eliminates the rest of Jeroboam's royal house (15:27-30; v. 29 is a cross reference to Ahijah's threatening forecast). Baasha reigns for twenty-four years, but the pattern of rebellion continues. A prophet named Jehu predicts the downfall of his dynasty, repeating the words used earlier by Ahijah (14:11; 16:4), and Baasha's son and successor *Elah* is assassinated and his family wiped out by *Zimri*, one of his commanders (16:9-11). A week later Zimri is besieged in turn by another military leader named *Omri* and commits suicide (16:15-18).

Even so, Omri has to face down still another claimant to the throne before his kingship is assured (16:21-23). In contrast, the royal succession in Judah goes smoothly during this period, from Rehoboam to *Abijam* to *Asa*.

Omri and Ahab (Israel)— 1 Kings 16:21–22:40

Omri (1 Kgs 16:21-28) was in many ways the real founder of the kingdom of Israel, so much so that the Assyrians referred to it in later years as the "house of Omri." He built an impressive new capital at Samaria for his administration, replacing Tirzah (1 Kgs 16:23-24). The location of Samaria was more defensible than Tirzah and had better access to routes to the north and west. This site also suited Omri's interest in international contacts, as evidenced by the marriage of his son and heir Ahab to a Phoenician princess (1 Kgs 16:31). Omri's aim was to centralize his kingdom around Samaria, a magnificent capital built on a new site with no affiliation to older tribal structures. Excavation shows that most of the new city was devoted to public purposes. It featured impressive architecture incorporating expensive stonework and pilasters with handsome capitals. A large paved and elevated platform enclosed the royal buildings. In contrast to Jeroboam and Baasha, Omri was able to establish a stable dynasty that lasted for several generations. He was able to subdue Moab. However, Kings only dedicates eight verses to this important king, which demonstrates a historical perspective altogether different from that of modern historians. For Kings, Omri's religious disloyalty (16:25-26) is the really important matter.

Ahab and Jezebel

Omri's son *Ahab* (1 Kgs 16:29–22:40) receives a great deal of attention. Most of the material about him consists of prophetic stories and highly negative judgments. Kings cites him and his family as archetypal villains (for example, 1 Kgs 16:30, 33; 21:25; 2 Kgs 21:3, 13). Omri had arranged a diplomatic marriage between Ahab and the Phoenician princess Jezebel (1 Kgs 16:31). In prophetic sources, Jezebel as a foreign worshipper of the Baal of her homeland becomes the focus of much blame. A well-known example of this is the story of Naboth and his vineyard, recounted in 1 Kings 21. Ahab is portrayed as petulant and weak. He wants Naboth's vineyard because it is adjacent to his palace, but is frustrated by Naboth's refusal to part with his ancestral land. Jezebel, however, is impatient with her husband's scruples and sets Naboth up with false testimony, which results in his execution. Ahab gains a vineyard, but the prophet Elijah confronts him with an exceptionally colorful sentence of judgment against the males of his royal establishment (21:21-22; for this language, compare 1 Kgs 14:10 and 2 Kgs 9:8 CEB). Elijah also announces a particularly brutal punishment for Jezebel (21:23-24). Her dramatic end is recounted in 2 Kings 9:30-37.

Yahweh versus Baal

The Elijah narratives of 1 Kings 17–19 describe the reign of Ahab as a battleground in the rivalry between Yahweh and Baal. In 1 Kings 17:1, Elijah heralds the coming of a long drought. Because rain was thought to be Baal's special provenance, this was a direct challenge on the part of Yahweh to Baal's power and authority. This conflict is portrayed in a dramatic fashion in Elijah's contest with the prophets of Baal (1 Kgs 18:20-40). Baal's prophets in their hundreds prove unable to call down heavenly fire to ignite a sacrifice, even after herculean efforts. Yahweh's ability to do so at Elijah's request proves that it is Yahweh who is truly god (18:21, 24, 39). As a rule, the title Baal (meaning lord or owner) appears in the Old Testament as a designation for Hadad, a rainstorm and fertility deity indigenous to the region. However, the god sponsored by Ahab and Jezebel, and to which Ahab erected an altar and temple in Samaria (1 Kgs 16:31-32; 22:53), seems actually to have been the Phoenician god Baal Melqart. No doubt there was overlap in the minds of most Israelites between the Baal they had long worshipped at numerous local shrines and the Baal sponsored by the royal administration. Many Israelites venerated both Baal and Yahweh, sacrificing to Baal when fertility and agricultural prosperity were at issue and honoring Yahweh as their national god of war. In any event, Elijah (and the Deuteronomistic author of Kings) insisted instead on single-minded loyalty to Yahweh alone: *How long will you hobble back and forth between two opinions?* (1 Kgs 18:21). Elijah demands that the people chose unequivocally between Yahweh and Baal.

The Battle of Qarqar (853)

In contrast to attention on Ahab's religious policies, his most important international achievement receives no mention in Kings. Ahab was the first king of Israel directly to face the danger of Assyrian expansion. The Assyrian king Shalmaneser III (858–824) was engaging in military campaigns to the south and west on an almost annual basis. In 853, Ahab responded to this threat by confronting the Assyrians at Qarqar on the Orontes River as a significant part of a large allied force. Assyrian sources indicate that Ahab was able to field more chariots than any other coalition partner and provided the second most powerful total force to the effort (*COS* 2.113A–G: 261–70). This battle was enough of a success on the alliance's part to delay Assyrian incursions into Aram (Syria) and Israel for several years.

Table 4. Significant Assyrian Rulers

Shalmaneser III	858–824
Adad-nirari III	810–783
Tiglath-pileser III	744–727
Shalmaneser V	726–722
Sargon II	721–705
Sennacherib	704–681
Esar-haddon	680–669
Assurbanipal	668–about 627

The Death of Ahab

Other prophetic material in 1 Kings 20 and 22 reports that Ahab engaged in warfare with the kingdom of Aram (Damascus, Syria). More than likely, these Syrian wars actually took place later under a different king and were incorrectly assigned to the reign of Ahab. (This is also true of the wars with Aram attributed to Ahab's son, Joram, reported in 2 Kgs 6:8–7:20; 8:7-15). Ahab's death is recounted in the context of a prophetic story about Micaiah (1 Kings 22). As Israel and its ally Judah are about to attack Aram, the king of Judah proposes an inquiry about Yahweh's will concerning the outcome. The king of Israel (whom the author of Kings assumes to be Ahab) engages 400 prophets, who put on a dramatic performance promising victory. When the king of Judah requires a second opinion, Micaiah is summoned. He predicts defeat. He reports that he had a vision of Yahweh in the heavenly throne room discussing plans to entice Ahab into disaster. In the end a spirit volunteers to serve as a lying spirit who will inspire Ahab's prophets to proclaim a false message of victory. This story illustrates a basic dilemma about prophecy in ancient Israel. Because both false and true prophets could display the same prophetic behavior and claim to speak in the name of Yahweh, how was one to judge? The king of Israel decides to imprison Micaiah until the outcome of the battle has been decided. The king of Israel is defeated and killed.

Fig. 11. Mesha Stele. Mesha, king of Moab, erected this monument to commemorate his victories over Israel and the recapture of territory that had been taken by Omri four decades earlier. Mesha proclaims that this was achieved with the help of the Moabite national god Chemosh.

14.1. THE MESHA INSCRIPTION

Around 840 BCE, King Mesha of Moab erected an inscribed monument celebrating his building activities and military successes. This Mesha Inscription (or Moabite Stone) reports that, in the time of Mesha's father, King Omri of Israel had captured a swath of Moabite territory north of the Arnon River. Israel ruled this territory for forty years, during the reign of Omri and half the reign of his "son." Mesha probably did not mean Omri's actual son Ahab, who displayed great military power, but Omri's *grand*son Joram. 2 Kings 1:1 and 3:5 report that Moab rebelled after the death of Ahab. There are several ways to interpret the course of events described by Mesha, who did not necessarily report them in chronological order, and it is difficult to coordinate his account with events described in the Bible. Probably the battle with Mesha in 2 Kings 3 refers to a different event altogether.

Mesha refers to the tribe of Gad and names Yahweh as Israel's national deity. He says that the anger of Moab's national god Chemosh resulted in Moab being oppressed for those forty years (compare Judg 3:12; 13:1). But in Mesha's day, Chemosh ordered him to fight against enemy-held cities. Chemosh gave success to Mesha and drove the king of Israel away. Mesha wiped out the populations of captured cities, treating them as booty devoted to Chemosh and following the same procedure of annihilation mentioned in the Old Testament (*ḥerem*). (See chapter 10, *Ḥerem*—Devoting to Destruction). Mesha also captured some sacred objects for worshipping Yahweh and presented them to Chemosh. (*ANET* 320–21; *COS* 2.23:137–38)

Jehu (Israel) and Athaliah (Judah)—2 Kings 9–11

The Rebellion of Jehu

The dynasty of Omri and Ahab was brought to a violent end by the rebellion of *Jehu*. After being blocked at Qarqar in 853, Shalmaneser III returned to campaign in southern Syria in 849, 848, and 845. The anti-Assyrian alliance of which Ahab had been a member collapsed when the throne of Aram (Damascus) was usurped by one Hazael about 845, who was then weakened by a defeat by Shalmaneser III in 841. Ahab had pursued a policy of resistance to Assyria, and this would have been continued by Ahab's successors *Ahaziah* and the latter's brother *Joram*. However, the breakdown of Israel's alliance with Aram (Damascus) and ominous Assyrian successes made the resistance policy seem untenable to many and led to Jehu's successful revolt.

According to Kings, Jehu kills *Joram*, the last king of Israel in Ahab's line, at the town of Jezreel. Jehu also fatally wounds *Ahaziah*, the young king of Judah, who is visiting his relative Joram. Kings portrays the revolution of Jehu as a religious reform. He is anointed as king by a prophet under orders from Elisha and then acclaimed by the troops he is commanding (2 Kgs 9:1-13). Jezebel, who has sponsored Baal and murdered Yahweh's prophets, dies a gruesome death, her body eaten by dogs to fulfill a prophetic judgment oracle (9:36-37; see 9:10 and 1 Kgs 21:21-24). Jehu slaughters the worshippers of Baal and turns Baal's temple in Samaria into a latrine (2 Kgs 10:18-28).

Jehu and History

Kings reports that Jehu assassinated both King Joram of Israel and King Ahaziah of Judah. This version of events may not represent the whole truth, at least according to the evidence of the Tel Dan Inscription (*COS* 2.39:161–62). This inscription seems to have been erected at Dan by King Hazael of Aram (Damascus) or perhaps by his successor Ben-hadad. There are many difficulties in its interpretation, but it is commonly thought that the king of Aram is claiming personal responsibility for killing the two kings Joram and Ahaziah. Perhaps the king who sponsored the inscription dishonestly took credit for what Jehu had done. Or perhaps Jehu was conceived of as acting as an agent for the king of Aram in the matter.

Fig. 12. This panel of the Black Obelisk of Shalmaneser III shows King Jehu of Israel (or his envoy) bowing before the Assyrian king in the act of bringing tribute. Jehu first paid this vassal tribute in 841 and continued to do so at least until the date of this monument (828–827).

In Assyrian sources, Jehu emerges as Israel's king for the first time in 841, when he started to pay annual tribute to Shalmaneser III. He is famously pictured as an example of a loyal vassal on the Black Obelisk monument. Unfortunately, Jehu's policy of acquiescence to Assyria opened Israel up to successful attacks by the rulers of Damascus, Hazael and his son Ben-hadad, who were enemies of Assyria. These Aramean incursions continued through the reign of Jehu's son *Jehoahaz*. However, the next king of Israel, *Joash*, was able to defeat Aram and restore security to Israel's northern and western borders (2 Kgs 13:22-25).

Queen Athaliah

Ahaziah's mother was *Athaliah*, who seized control of the throne of Judah after her son's death. She was of the royal family of Israel, a granddaughter (or daughter) of Omri. As the story goes in 2 Kings 11, Athaliah eliminates all claimants to the throne, but overlooks one of her grandsons, *Jehoash*, who is hidden by his aunt in the temple complex. Eventually, when the young prince is seven years old, the priestly authorities bring him out of hiding and arrange for Athaliah to be ambushed in the temple and taken off to be assassinated. The boy king Jehoash engages in a program of temple restoration, as described in 2 Kings 12.

The Last Days of Israel—2 Kings 14–17

Because of Assyrian weakness, Israel and Judah enjoyed a period of prosperity and peace during the long, overlapping reigns of *Jeroboam II* of Israel and *Azariah* (or Uzziah) of Judah. Israel's era of security came to an end with the accession of the Assyrian king Tiglath-pileser III (744–727, called Pul in the Bible). Both Judah and Israel were targets of his imperial expansion, but Israel was eventually destroyed as a monarchy and reduced to the status of provinces within the Assyrian Empire. Judah survived as a tribute-paying satellite state.

Menahem and Pekah (Israel)

Increasing danger from Assyria meant that after the death of Jeroboam II, Israel fell into political instability. His son *Zechariah*, the last king of the Jehu dynasty, was murdered by *Shallum*, who in turn was overthrown by *Menahem*. Israel had two policy choices, either resistance to Assyria or compliance with Assyrian demands for tribute. Menahem advocated a compliance policy and paid tribute to Tiglath-pileser III at least twice (740 and 738). Details of the heavy taxation he required from the upper classes in order to pay this tribute are presented in 2 Kings 15:19-20. Not surprisingly, this huge financial burden increased political support for a resistance policy.

As a result, Menahem's son *Pekahiah* was quickly eliminated by *Pekah*, an advocate of resistance.

Pekah's reign was marked by disaster for Israel in the crisis of 734–732. In alliance with King Rezin of Aram (Damascus), Pekah chose to rebel against Tiglath-pileser III. As a result of this imprudent act, Tiglath-pileser moved against Damascus and Israel in 733 and 732. He defeated Rezin and reduced his kingdom to the status of a province of the Assyrian realm. He also devastated much of Israel, but apparently the timely assassination and replacement of Pekah by a new king, *Hoshea*, in 732 meant that the capital Samaria itself was spared. However, Israel did lose large expanses of its most fertile territory to Assyria. The territories of Jezreel and Galilee became an Assyrian province controlled from *Megiddo*, and another province was formed out of *Gilead* east of the Jordan. Only the core of the kingdom of Israel remained, reduced to the central highlands and portions of Benjamin. This rump state of Israel existed for only ten more years. Hoshea sent tribute to Tiglath-pileser, probably in 731.

Ahaz (Judah)

Ahaz was king of Judah during the critical events of 734–732 (apparently as a co-regent with his father *Jotham*). Kings describes the rebellion of Pekah and Rezin from the perspective of Judah, reporting that these two kings invaded Judah and besieged Ahaz (2 Kgs 16:5-6). For this reason, biblical scholars often term this affair the Syro-Ephraimite War (alluding to Damascus as Syria and Israel by the name of its most important tribe, Ephraim). Kings reports that a fearful and desperate Ahaz requested aid from Tiglath-pileser and sent him a tribute present to induce him to respond (16:7-10). It is entirely likely that the Assyrian king would have acted to attack Syria and Israel because of his own self-interest anyway. Isaiah 7:1-17 narrates the dilemma faced by Ahaz from a prophetic perspective and reports that the two attacking kings intended to replace Ahaz with a puppet king. This move would have neutralized Judah as a threat to their rebellion against Assyria. Assyrian sources indicate that Ahaz paid tribute to Tiglath-pileser sometime before 729.

The Fall of Israel

The final defeat of the kingdom of Israel by Assyria took place in either 722 or 720. This catastrophic defeat is described in 2 Kings 17:3-6 and 18:9-11. After several years of paying tribute as an Assyrian vassal, Israel's king Hoshea colluded with the Pharaoh of Egypt and withheld tribute to Shalmaneser V (727–722). This was an act of rebellion, and Hoshea was captured and imprisoned. After a three-year siege, Shalmaneser captured the city of Samaria and deported Israelites to locations in Mesopotamia and western Iran.

The testimony of the extra-biblical Assyrian records confuses the historical issue somewhat. In one source, Shalmaneser is credited with victory over Samaria. Since he died in 722, that would be the year of the final defeat of Israel. However, in other records his successor Sargon II (721–705) claims the victory over Samaria in the year 720. In any case, Israel was totally incorporated into the Assyrian Empire (as the province of Samaria), some Israelites were forcibly deported, and groups of foreign peoples were brought into the territory as replacement settlers. This practice of exchanging population elements was standard Assyrian policy and was intended to undermine national identity. Some refugees from the territory of Israel moved south, where they expanded the population of Jerusalem and brought with them distinctive northern traditions and religious ideas (as appear, for example, in Hosea and Deuteronomy).

Hezekiah and Manasseh (Judah)— 2 Kings 18–21

Judah was able to survive for over 130 years after the fall of Israel, during which time the Assyrian Empire collapsed and a new Babylonian Empire replaced it. King Hezekiah, his son Manasseh, his son Amon, his son Josiah, and then three of Josiah's sons and a grandson reigned during this period.

Hezekiah

Second Kings 18–20 describes the reign of *Hezekiah* (2 Kgs 18:13–20:19 is reproduced in Isaiah 36–39). Kings judges Hezekiah as a righteous king because of his religious reforms. Although there are chronological problems, he apparently reigned 726–697. Hezekiah at first followed a policy of accommodation with Assyria and its king Sargon II. Sargon was replaced by his son Sennacherib (704–681), who faced rebellions. Hezekiah reversed course and, along with other small states, also rebelled. Apparently to prepare for this momentous step, Hezekiah commissioned the Siloam tunnel as a major improvement to the security of Jerusalem's water supply.

> ### 14.2. HEZEKIAH'S TUNNEL
> Second Kings 20:20 reports on a memorable accomplishment of King Hezekiah: *how he made the pool and the channel and brought water inside the city*. Further information is provided by 2 Chronicles 32:30: *Hezekiah was the one who blocked the*

> *upper outlet of the waters of the Gihon Spring, channeling them down to the west side of David's City.* Remarkably, Hezekiah's water tunnel can still be visited today, and intrepid tourists can wade through it from end to end. This project was intended to protect the water supply of Jerusalem from Assyrian attackers. It shows that Hezekiah anticipated the likely outcome of his policy of resistance to Sennacherib and took action to strengthen the defenses of Jerusalem. The tunnel is over 1700 feet (500 m) long. It diverts the flow of Gihon Spring, located outside the city walls on the eastern slope of the Kidron Valley, to the Siloam Pool in the southwest portion of the city that was protected by fortifications.
>
> An inscription discovered on the wall of the tunnel reports on how workers started from opposite sides and met in the middle. The tunnel follows a serpentine course, and it seems that the diggers followed seepage through cracks in the rock. The inscription reports that once the two work parties drew close together, each team could listen for the sound of the other. Their picks broke through and the water flowed. Tool marks are still visible on the tunnel walls and roof. (*ANET* 321; *COS* 2.28:145–46)

In 701, Sennacherib moved against the allies of Hezekiah in Philistia and eliminated them as a threat. The prospect of aid from Egypt was blocked by a (claimed) victory over Pharaoh's forces at Eltekah. In Assyrian records, Sennacherib reports that he captured and looted fortresses and towns of Judah. His greatest achievement was the capture of the heavily fortified city of Lachish, which he commemorated in a series of palace reliefs.

Sennacherib then threatened Jerusalem itself, although biblical and non-biblical sources do not entirely agree on the order of events or on what took place. It is clear that in 701 the city of Jerusalem was besieged (or at least blockaded) but was not captured and that Hezekiah at some point paid tribute to Sennacherib. The biblical story, found in 2 Kings 19:35-36, recounts that Yahweh's messenger came at night and struck down 185,000 Assyrian troops and that Sennacherib returned home. The Assyrian evidence suggests that Sennacherib chose not to continue his attack on Jerusalem after Hezekiah submitted and paid him a substantial tribute. In any case, seemingly doomed Jerusalem survived untouched, and religious opinion credited this extraordinary development to Yahweh. Nevertheless, Hezekiah was forced to give up a slice of Judah's territory to the west and continued as an Assyrian vassal.

Fig. 13. Sennacherib commissioned wall panels for his palace at Nineveh to commemorate his successful siege of the Judahite fortified city Lachish. This detail shows Assyrian foot soldiers and archers scaling the walls of the city using mudbrick ramps. Other scenes show battering rams and the defeated population being put to death and going into exile as captives.

14.3. HEZEKIAH AND SENNACHERIB IN 701 BCE

Both the book of Kings and Assyrian sources report on Sennacherib's threat to Jerusalem during his successful invasion of Judah in 701. Neither version can be considered objective. Sennacherib's account seeks to increase the king's glory and prestige. It boasts that he besieged and captured forty-six fortified cities and other towns and appropriated their inhabitants and wealth. He locked up Hezekiah in Jerusalem "like a bird in a cage." He took land away from Judah and imposed higher annual tribute (*COS* 2.119B:302–303). In contrast, as a theological text, 2 Kings 18–19 seeks to intensify the wonder of Jerusalem's survival and so attributes it to Yahweh, who struck dead the enemy army. The biblical report also extols the accuracy of Isaiah's prophetic word. The Bible and Assyrian sources do agree on three things. Sennacherib captured fortified cities in Judah (2 Kgs 18:13), Hezekiah paid tribute to Sennacherib (18:14-16), and Jerusalem was not captured. The account in 2 Kings downplays the captured cities and tribute by placing this information *before* its story of what happened to Jerusalem, as though it referred to an earlier event. The material about the rescue of Jerusalem is of prophetic origin and consists of two somewhat parallel accounts: 18:17–19:9a together with 19:36-37, and 19:9b-35.

Manasseh

Hezekiah's son *Manasseh*, who came to the throne at age twelve (perhaps as a coregent), enjoyed an exceptionally long reign (about 697–642). Yet Kings insists that he did evil in Yahweh's opinion and catalogues numerous religious misdeeds. Assyrian records show that he served as a loyal vassal to the Assyrian kings Esarhaddon (680–669) and Assurbanipal (668–about 627). He provided forced labor for the erection of a palace in Nineveh and supported Assyrian military campaigns. No doubt, the catastrophe that resulted from Hezekiah's attempt at rebellion had taught Manasseh the value of complying with Assyrian demands. Some of his religious policies (particularly those reported in 2 Kgs 21:3, 5) may have resulted from a voluntary imitation of the dominant Assyrian culture. Archaeology shows that Jerusalem grew significantly in size during Manasseh's reign.

Josiah—2 Kings 22:1–23:30

The author of Kings lauds Hezekiah and *Josiah* (640–609) as incomparably righteous rulers (2 Kgs 18:5; 23:25). In Josiah's case, this judgment rests on a religious reform policy that, among other things, closed down the local shrines (high places) and reestablished the proper celebration of Passover. Josiah was made king by a conservative faction (*the people of the land*) in response to a palace rebellion that had resulted in the death of Josiah's father *Amon*. This coup and counter-coup is reported in 2 Kings 21:23-24. The political situation meant that Josiah came to the throne when he was only eight years old and was doubtless controlled for several years by advisors representing the faction that had made him king. There is every indication that Judah continued Manasseh's policy of loyal vassalage to Assyria. In Josiah's eighteenth year (622/621), Kings reports that Josiah instituted a temple renovation project (22:3-7). Next one reads that the leading priest Hilkiah reports that he has found the torah scroll (CEB: *Instruction scroll*) in the temple, although he does not explicitly connect his discovery with the restoration. Later this book is called more specifically the covenant scroll (23:2, 21) and connected to the figure of Moses (21:8; 23:25). It is almost universally supposed that this scroll was some earlier form of Deuteronomy.

Kings stresses that Josiah's reform reversed the actions of his predecessors. He cancelled out the errors of Solomon (2 Kgs 23:13; see 1 Kgs 11:7). His desecration of the Bethel altar nullified the "sin of Jeroboam" that had been the chief transgression of the kings of Israel (2 Kgs 23:15-20; compare v. 19 with 1 Kgs 13:32). Josiah's reform actions as described in 2 Kings 23:4-12 undid each of the misdeeds of Manasseh item by item (compare 21:3-7, 10-12).

Josiah's elimination of the shrines (23:8-9, 13, 15, 19-20) resolved the repeated criticism directed against most previous kings of Judah. Shutting down the shrines and sacrifice sites in Judah and in some areas of Israel meant that all sacrifice would have to take place at the single, central sanctuary of the Jerusalem temple. In doing this, Josiah followed the command of Deuteronomy 12, but he also created a situation in which royal supervision and control could be exercised over the economically important business of sacrifice. Centralized sacrifice also meant that the celebration of Passover was reformed so that it took place only in Jerusalem, as commanded by Deuteronomy 16:5-7.

The international situation during the last half of Josiah's reign was complex and fraught with both opportunity and danger for Judah. Egypt was enjoying a renaissance of power, but Assyrian influence was weakening. During the last part of Assurbanipal's reign, his twin sons struggled with each other for power, and he was forced to spend his final years in Harran until his death about 627. The challenges faced by Assyria were exacerbated when Nabopolassar (626–605) seized control of Babylon and engaged in open warfare with Assyrian forces. These developments permitted Josiah to follow a more independent policy and allowed him to take action against the northern shrines of Bethel and elsewhere in Samaria, even though it was nominally still a province of Assyria (2 Kgs 23:15-19).

The collapse of Assyria accelerated when Nabopolassar's allies the Medes captured the city of Assur in 614. Then the Babylonians and Medes together despoiled Nineveh in 612. The Assyrians' power base moved westward to Harran, but that city too was captured in 610, again by the Medes and Babylonians. In 609, the new king of Egypt, Neco II (610–595), moved northward up through the region in order to support the Assyrians at Harran and was met by Josiah at Megiddo.

Exactly what happened there is unclear and a matter of dispute. The Hebrew of 2 Kings 23:29 reports "Josiah went to meet him, and Neco killed him at Megiddo when he saw him." Based on the highly theological presentation of this scene is 2 Chronicles 35:20-25, it has usually been assumed that Josiah died in a battle while trying to block Neco's advance. Several modern translations assume that there was a battle in rendering this verse, the CEB among them. However, Kings actually mentions no battle, and it is quite likely that Neco had Josiah killed during negotiations of some sort. In any case, historical evidence makes it certain that Neco was marching northward in order to *support* Assyria, not to oppose Assyria. In spite of Egyptian intervention, Nabopolassar and his allies were able to capture Harran. At this point, Assur-uballit II, the last king of Assyria, disappears from history. Judah now faced a new dominant power, the Neo-Babylonian Empire, which was founded by Nabopolassar and inherited by his son Nebuchadnezzar (604–562).

Table 5. Significant Neo-Babylonian Rulers

Nabopolassar	626–605
Nebuchadnezzar II	604–562
Amel-Marduk (Evil-merodach)	561–560
Nabonidus	555–539
Bel-shar-usur (Belshazzar)	regent 549–543

The Last Days of Judah— 2 Kings 23:31–25:30

After Josiah's death in 609, a political faction called *the people of the land* enthroned his son *Jehoahaz* (2 Kgs 23:30; compare 21:24). In so doing, they bypassed the legitimate heir, Jehoiakim, who was an older son of Josiah. On his way back from Harran, Neco deposed Jehoahaz and replaced him with *Jehoiakim* (609–598), who was apparently viewed as more likely to support Egyptian aims. Jehoiakim collected the tribute he paid Neco from the very *people of the land* group who had bypassed him (2 Kgs 23:33-35)!

However, Egypt's power was soon replaced by that of Babylon when Nebuchadnezzar defeated the Egyptians and remnants of the Assyrian army at Carchemish in 605. At this point or perhaps a year or two later, Jehoiakim switched his loyalty from

Assyria to Babylon, but then shortly reversed course and rebelled against Babylon. Nebuchadnezzar had his local allies assail Judah at first (2 Kgs 24:1-2). Before the Babylonian armies arrived to besiege Jerusalem, Jehoiakim died and was replaced by his eighteen-year-old son, *Jehoiachin*. Unable to count on Egyptian help, Jehoiachin quickly surrendered. The Babylonians seized Jerusalem in March 597. Jehoiachin was taken prisoner and deported to Babylon with thousands of other citizens of Judah (24:10-16). The Babylonians replaced him with his uncle *Zedekiah* (597–586), another of Josiah's sons, but many Judahites still considered Jehoiachin to be the legitimate king. The Babylonians kept Jehoiachin under confinement, probably to serve as a backup king in case Zedekiah failed to cooperate.

Perhaps counting on help from Egypt, Zedekiah chose to rebel against Babylon after eleven years. This resulted in an eighteen-month-long siege of Jerusalem, during which food shortages caused great suffering within the city. Zedekiah attempted to flee the doomed city, but was captured, blinded, and deported. About a month later, the Babylonians burned the temple and other parts of Jerusalem and razed at least parts of its defensive wall. Once again, substantial elements of the population were deported. Because the evidence is open to more than one interpretation, some scholars assert that this second fall of Jerusalem took place in 587, although the summer of 586 is a more likely date. Jehoiachin himself remained imprisoned until 561 or 560, when he was released and lived under house arrest in the Babylonian royal household.

Further Reading

Volkmar Fritz. *1 & 2 Kings*. Continental Commentaries. Minneapolis: Augsburg Fortress, 2003.

Antoon Schoors. *The Kingdoms of Israel and Judah in the Eighth and Seventh Centuries BCE*. Atlanta: SBL Press, 2013.

Part IV

LATTER PROPHETS

Chapter 15
PROPHETS AND PROPHECY

The Prophetic Books

The Latter Prophets section of the Hebrew Bible consists of three books that preserve and interpret the words and actions of Isaiah (and his like-minded followers of a later period), Jeremiah, and Ezekiel. The fourth, called the Book of the Twelve, is itself a collection of shorter books associated with named prophets from a variety of historical periods (the Minor Prophets). At some point those twelve briefer books were collected and copied together as a single scroll that approximated the length of each of the three Major Prophets. Nevertheless, the distinct particularity of each book of the Twelve was protected by introductory headings. Unlike the Christian Old Testament, the Hebrew canon does not consider Daniel to be one of the prophetic books.

- Hosea, Amos, Isaiah son of Amoz, and Micah date to the eighth century, when Israel and Judah were threatened by Assyria.
- Zephaniah, Nahum, Jeremiah, and Ezekiel were active during the late seventh and early sixth century.
- Obadiah and Habakkuk reacted to events around the time of the Babylonian conquest in the early sixth century.
- Second Isaiah, an anonymous prophet whose words appear in Isaiah 40–55, responded to the situation of exile in Babylon.
- Haggai and Zechariah were active prophets in the period when religious and social life was restored in Judah and Jerusalem after the exile.

Third Isaiah (materials in Isaiah 56–66) and Malachi appear to stem from somewhat later in that post-exile period.

Joel may be from the late Persian period, and Jonah cannot be dated.

Although the words of the prophets themselves make up the core of the prophetic works (except for Jonah), those books are edited and reworked documents. Later disciples and supporters remembered and rethought whatever prophetic words seemed to apply to their own contemporary situations. Those disciples eventually collected, organized, and wrote down the words that were preserved. Because Yahweh was thought to be the true source of all prophetic words, transmitters and editors also sometimes felt it appropriate to add the words of other prophets to the developing scrolls. For example, the same oracle about Jerusalem's future appears in both Isaiah 2:2-4 and Micah 4:1-3, and there are many parallels between Isaiah 15–16 and Jeremiah 48.

The order of the first three books of the Latter Prophets is chronological. Isaiah was active in the late eighth century, Jeremiah served as prophet from 627 to about 580, and the words of Ezekiel are dated from 593 to 571. Chronological interest also plays some role in the ordering of the Twelve, in that the early prophet Hosea comes first and the later prophets Haggai, Zechariah, and Malachi close out the collection. At some point, most of the prophetic books were provided with similar headings or superscriptions that name the prophet and gives some personal background, characterizes his message, and specifies the kings during whose reigns he was active. Such superscriptions introduce Isaiah, Jeremiah, Hosea, Amos, Micah, and Zephaniah.

The Prophetic Office

Prophecy was a venerable institution among both Israel and its neighbors. Information about prophets from the ancient city of Mari and from Assyria has proved helpful in understanding biblical prophets, their role in society, and their relationship to the royal administration. Stories in the book of Kings about the ninth-century prophets Elijah and Elisha illustrate features of the prophetic vocation, especially as it was practiced in Israel's earlier period.

Rather than being lone actors, prophets worked as members of communities. Elisha lives in a house with other members of a support group termed *the sons of the prophets* (CEB: *the group of the prophets*), who share in a communal stew pot (2 Kgs 4:38-41; 6:1). In 2 Kings 2, this prophetic support group appears in the scene that describes Elijah's ascension to heaven and the transfer of his responsibilities (symbolized by his coat or mantle) to his disciple Elisha.

Prophets sometimes engaged in special behavior. Ecstasy or a trance-like state might accompany the reception and delivery of a divine communication. This is evident in the story of Saul's early career, when he or his envoys encounter bands of prophets and become caught up in their distinctive behavior of *prophetic frenzy* (1 Sam 10:5-6, 10-13; 19:19-24). Music plays a role in the first of these encounters. The prophets of Baal on Mount Carmel behave in a similarly remarkable fashion (1 Kgs 18:28-29). When Elisha is asked to provide an oracle in 2 Kings 3:15, he requests music in order to facilitate his prophetic performance. The power of Yahweh comes over him and he speaks for Yahweh. Elijah's characteristic clothing and idiosyncratic diet are examples of a different sort of unusual prophetic behavior (2 Kgs 1:8), and functioned to legitimate him as an authentic prophet.

Israel's early prophets had the reputation of being wonderworkers, who could perform deeds of power (2 Kgs 5:3; 8:4-5). The title *man of God* is used repeatedly of both Elijah and Elisha in relation to such phenomena (1 Kgs 17:24 and 2 Kgs 4:7, 9, for example). Such marvelous acts served as signs to validate a prophet's message. Elijah was famous for his habit of sudden disappearance and reappearance while being transported around by the spirit (1 Kgs 17:3; 18:10-12; 2 Kgs 2:16). The mere presence of a prophet was thought to bring blessing (2 Kgs 4:9-10) or danger (1 Kgs 17:18). Stories recounting the miraculous provision or restoration of food (1 Kgs 17:8-16; 2 Kgs 4:1-7, 38-44), healing (2 Kings 5), a floating ax head (2 Kgs 6:1-7), and even resuscitation (1 Kgs 17:17-23; 2 Kgs 4:32-37; 13:20-21) were retold in order to increase the reputations of prophets. It was a good idea to respect, even fear a prophet, lest one be killed by ravening bears (2 Kgs 2:23-24)! According to 2 Kings 2, Elijah was so extraordinarily intimate with Yahweh that he did not suffer death but was taken up by a windstorm directly to heaven.

Prophetic Speech

The role of a prophet in Israelite society was to be a messenger from Yahweh who delivered Yahweh's word. This is evidenced by the constant use of what is called the messenger formula, *thus says Yahweh*. This expression confirmed that the words being spoken originated with Yahweh (for example, 1 Kgs 17:14; 2 Kgs 3:16, 17; CEB: *this is what Yahweh says*). This same phrase was used by messengers sent in human situations (1 Kgs 20:2, 5).

Prophetic oracles sometimes promised deliverance and salvation (for example, 2 Kgs 2:21). More common, however, were admonitions coupled with threats of punishment and catastrophe (such as 1 Kgs 21:19). The typical prophetic oracle focused on both the present situation and the looming consequences of continued disobedience (consider the "because . . . therefore" structure of 1 Kgs 20:42; 2 Kgs 1:6, 16). Messengers were important conduits of communication in the ancient world. Genesis 32:2-5 illustrates the messenger situation on the purely human level. Jacob sends messengers to his estranged brother Esau and instructs them to deliver his message in the first person, prefacing it with the messenger formula "Thus says your servant Jacob" (CEB: *This is the message of your servant Jacob*). Genesis 45:9 is another example of the messenger situation. In a human setting, the messenger was expected to elaborate the bare bones of the basic message in ways appropriate for the occasion. The prophets also contributed their own perspectives and rhetoric to the communications they delivered.

The fundamental genre of prophetic speech is known as an oracle. *A judgment oracle* would have two parts. First there would be an indication of the present situation, often in the form of an accusation. The second part would be an announcement of impending divine judgment or verdict. Often the word *therefore* and a messenger formula would come between the two parts to introduce the judgment portion. A judgment oracle could be announced against an individual as well as to the people as a whole. An example of the two-part structure is the oracle from an anonymous prophet in 1 Kings 20:42 (translating closely to the Hebrew syntax):

> *Thus says Yahweh* (messenger formula):
> Because you have let go out of your hand the man
> whom I had devoted to destruction,
> *therefore*
> your life shall be for his life, and your people for his people.

Jeremiah 11:10b-11a provides an example of a judgment oracle against Israel (again in a literal translation).

> The house of Israel and the house of Judah have broken my covenant,
> which I made with their ancestors.
> *Therefore*
> *thus says Yahweh:*
> Look, I am going to bring disaster upon them that they cannot escape.

A positive message from God is termed a *salvation oracle*. Unlike the two-part judgment oracle, this genre did not have an introductory reason or statement of grounds. The prophet simply announced the comforting news (Isa 7:4-7; 14:25). A salvation oracle often comforted with the exhortation *Don't be afraid* (Isa 35:4; Jer 30:10).

At times, dramatic symbolic actions accompanied the delivery of Yahweh's word. These did not simply serve as a sort of visual aid but were thought of as bringing the events proclaimed into reality. These symbolic acts mimicked what was about to happen and made the oracle more vivid. Ahab's compliant prophet Zedekiah acted out the victory he was predicting for Ahab by charging around with animal horns (1 Kgs 22:11). During the reign of Solomon, the prophet Ahijah tore a cloak into pieces to accompany his warning that the nation would be divided into two kingdoms (1 Kgs 11:29-39). Without saying a word, Elijah threw his cloak over Elisha to enlist him as his follower (1 Kgs 19:19). Isaiah went about naked and barefoot for three years (Isa 20:2-4). Jeremiah smashed a pottery jug to illustrate God's judgment (Jeremiah 19). Ezekiel engaged in numerous peculiar actions such as laying siege to a brick representing Jerusalem, sleeping on one side for 390 days and then the other for forty days, and eating bread cooked with animal dung like an inhabitant of a besieged city (Ezek 4).

Prophets told *call stories* to authorize their vocation and encourage belief in what they announced. A call story emphasizes that the prophetic office is not a voluntary choice, and usually describes the prophet's initial objection to the divine call in order to make this point. The call stories of Isaiah (Isa 6:1-10) and Jeremiah (Jer 1:4-10) are characteristic examples.

In *vision reports*, prophets reported that they had been shown visions and then explained the meaning behind those experiences. Yahweh showed Jeremiah an almond branch that turned out to be a pun and a boiling pot tipped over (Jer 1:11-14). Amos saw visions of locusts, fire, a plumb line, and a basket of summer fruit, all of which presaged doom for the nation (Amos 7:1-9; 8:1-2). Jeremiah's vision of two baskets of figs contained a message for Judahites in exile (Jer 24). A dramatic vision of Yahweh's heavenly court experienced by Micaiah son of Imlah is recounted in 1 Kings 22.

Foreign nation oracles were directed against other nations and their rulers. They often cited violations of treaties or accepted norms of behavior. Collections of these appear in Isaiah 13–23, Jeremiah 46–51, and Ezekiel 25–32. Obadiah and Nahum consist entirely of denunciations against Edom and Nineveh respectively. The tightly structured foreign nation oracles in Amos 1–2 end with a shocking twist that attacks Judah and Israel for social injustice and violations of divine law. This genre of prophetic speech probably originated with oracles directed against foreign enemies in the context of war (for this context, see 1 Kgs 20:26-30; 2 Kgs 13:14-19). Even though Israel knew Yahweh as their national deity, the foreign nation oracles demonstrate their belief that Yahweh also controlled events in the international sphere.

Prophets also utilized forms of speech from other realms of life. For example, Isaiah 5:1-2 is a love song and Amos 5:2 is a dirge. Both Isaiah 1:10-17 and Amos 5:21-22 reuse typical priestly language to attack thoughtless reliance on sacrifice.

Chapter 15

Prophets and the Future

Prophecy is most often associated today with predictions about the future. The phrase "biblical prophecy" is commonly used to mean that events of our present day or our own near future were predicted accurately by ancient prophets. It would be more correct to say that the biblical prophets believed they were speaking Yahweh's words to their own contemporaries concerning current affairs and situations. Of course, the prophets' words of threat and promise would have had implications for the future of their audience in the relative short term. Warnings of punishment or assurances of well-being were directed to listeners of the prophet's own day and were intended to persuade their contemporaries to turn away from sin and evil, obey, or have confidence. Of course, later readers would also have applied those threats and promises to their own situations. This was certainly true of the authors of the New Testament. Early Christian believers applied much of what they read in the prophetic books to Jesus and to what they considered to be his mission as messiah. Early generations of Christians also looked forward to a time when all God's promises and judgments would be fulfilled, and they found confirmation of those hopes in the language of the prophets. However, the primary focus of the message of the Old Testament prophets was on the issues and crises of their own time. For this reason, an understanding of the historical context of each prophet (and the context of the later editors of the prophetic books as well) is vital.

Further Reading

Paul L. Redditt. *Introduction to the Prophets*. Grand Rapids: Eerdmans, 2008.

Thomas L. Leclerc. *Introduction to the Prophets: Their Stories, Sayings, and Scrolls.* New York: Paulist, 2007.

Chapter 16
THE ISAIAH SCROLL

Three Collections of Prophetic Material

The book of Isaiah was composed over a substantial period of time. The underlying foundations of the Isaiah scroll (chapters 1–39) are the words and career of Isaiah son of Amoz, who was a contemporary of Ahaz and Hezekiah in the last half of the eighth century. Isaiah attracted disciples (8:16-17) who remembered and collected his words. They believed that his message had continuing relevance for a future time (30:8-11). Those later followers of Isaiah (sometimes called the Isaiah School) also felt that it was completely appropriate to add responses to and reflections on Isaiah's threats and promises to the growing book. Some of this added material evidences perspectives that fit only with the exilic and post-exilic periods, generations later than Isaiah himself.

Biblical scholarship uses the designation *Second Isaiah* for Isaiah 40–55. The poems of this anonymous prophet only make sense in the context of a hope for the restoration of Jerusalem, something that came to fruition after the victories of the Persian king Cyrus in 539. The material collected in Isaiah 56–66 is called *Third Isaiah* and relates to life in Jerusalem some years after the initial return from Babylon. Nevertheless, the entire book of Isaiah displays similar themes and vocabulary, indicating that it was produced over time by a group that shared common theological ideas. For example, Jerusalem remains the focus of Yahweh's concern throughout Isaiah. A distinctive formula for the deity, *the holy one of Israel*, appears repeatedly in all three sections of the book (for example, 1:4; 41:14; 60:9).

Chapter 16

Isaiah Son of Amoz—Isaiah 1–39

According to the heading of the book (1:1), the career of Isaiah son of Amoz spanned the reign of four kings of Judah. Other internal headings provide evidence of a complex compositional process (for example, 2:1; 13:1; 30:6).

Chapters 1–12 concentrate on the prophet's call, judgment oracles, and interaction with King Ahaz. A refrain, pointing to Judah's incessant sin and God's ongoing anger and benevolence, unifies much of this material:

> Even then God's anger didn't turn away;
> God's hand was still extended. (5:25; 9:12, 17, 21; 10:4)

This refrain is absent from 6:11–9:7, which consists of a mixture of prose and poetry and relates to Isaiah's call and events during the crisis of 734–732.

Isaiah 13–23 consists of oracles announcing judgment against Babylon and numerous other nations. Several of these relate to events connected to Assyria's foreign policy. Chapters 28–33 are positive oracles of salvation that are connected with the 701 revolt of Hezekiah against Assyria. Chapters 36–39 are narratives about Isaiah taken up and reused from 2 Kings 18:13–20:19. Isaiah however lacks 2 Kings 18:14-16 and adds a thanksgiving song attributed to Hezekiah in Isaiah 38:9-20. Chapters 34–35 are similar in tone to Second Isaiah and appear to have originated from the exilic period. Isaiah 24–27 is often called the *Isaiah Apocalypse* and also stems from a later period.

Isaiah and History

Isaiah was the father of two sons to whom he gave symbolic names: *Shear-yashub* (7:3) and *Mahar-shalal-hash-baz* (8:3). It seems likely that Isaiah performed his prophetic mission as a staff member of the royal court, since his call as a prophet took place in the Jerusalem temple (6:1) and narratives about him portray face-to-face encounters with kings Ahaz and Hezekiah. The first-person account in chapter 6 of his call to become a prophet (or perhaps a prophet with a different message) is dated to the end of the fifty-two-year reign of King Uzziah (Azariah). The year of Uzziah's death cannot be determined with any certainty but is often given as 742 or 733.

The prophet's encounter with Ahaz and related oracles (Isaiah 7–8, chapter 17, parts of chapter 28) are set in the context of the events of 734–732 and the threatening behavior of King Pekah of Israel and King Remaliah of Aram (Damascus). Historians usually put together the portrayal of events from 2 Kings 16:5-9 and the narrative of Isaiah 7 in order to achieve a fuller picture of the so-called Syro-Ephraimite War. According to this reconstruction, the forces of Israel (Ephraim) and Damascus

(Syria) attacked and besieged Jerusalem in order to depose Ahaz and replace him with a puppet king who would support their revolt against Assyria. Isaiah's admonitions to Ahaz were intended to prevent him from seeking help from Assyria, but Ahaz lacked trust and faithlessly paid tribute anyway. Assyria devastated Damascus and Israel as Isaiah had predicted. This reconstruction may be justified, but Isaiah actually says nothing about submission to Assyria on the part of Ahaz or about any gift to the king of Assyria. Isaiah gives Ahaz no direct advice about foreign policy. Isaiah's promise of salvation, calling for faith and confidence on the part of Ahaz, focuses on the king's fear (7:2). The opposite of fear is faith (7:4, 9; 8:6), but what faith was to mean as far as submission to Assyria was concerned is not specified in Isaiah.

Isaiah 18 and 20 come from a period some twenty years later and reflect the situation of a rebellion by Ashdod against Assyria in 714–711, which involved the possibility that King Hezekiah might join in an anti-Assyrian conspiracy. The most dramatic of the events covered in Isaiah are those that took place in 701. In that year, Hezekiah's rebellion against Sennacherib culminated in a devastating Assyrian attack on the cities of Judah and the presence of an Assyrian army outside the walls of Jerusalem. (See 14.3, HEZEKIAH AND SENNACHERIB IN 701 BCE.) Jerusalem was spared and Sennacherib withdrew. Numerous oracles in Isaiah refer to these events (for example, 10:16-19; 29:1-8; 30:27-33).

A Message of Judgment

The story of Isaiah's prophetic call is staged as a dramatic vision in Isaiah 6. Isaiah seems to be in the Jerusalem temple, with its great doors and altar of glowing coals of incense sending forth clouds of smoke. But in his vision Isaiah is also aware of another dimension. He finds himself in the throne room of Yahweh while an assembly of the heavenly cabinet is in session. Yahweh is enthroned and surrounded or flanked by unearthly winged beings. Isaiah should die, because no human can see Yahweh and live (Exod 33:20; Judg 13:22), but a red-hot altar coal cauterizes the impurity and sin of his speech so that he may speak as Yahweh's prophet. Yahweh asks the assembly for a volunteer messenger, and Isaiah speaks up: *I'm here; send me!* However, his assignment turns out to be shockingly negative. Isaiah's words will not convert the people but will dull their mind (Isa 6:10; Hebrew: "fatten their hearts").

In common with the statements of other prophets of the eighth century, the first six chapters of Isaiah proclaim Yahweh's displeasure over Judah's misbehavior. There are caustic descriptions of social injustice. The upper classes take bribes and do not defend the interests of the orphan and widow (1:21-23). Yahweh engages in a lawsuit against the people and accuses them in open court of crushing and stealing from the poor (3:13-15). Upper-class women walk haughtily, decked out in jewelry and finery (3:16-24). The rich have taken over the ancestral property of their poorer neighbors and party day and night (5:8, 11-12). In the absence of any commitment to social justice, Judah's worship of Yahweh is empty and fruitless (1:11-17):

> I can't stand wickedness with celebration!
> I hate your new moons and your festivals. . . .
> Even when you pray for a long time,
>   I won't listen.
> Your hands are stained with blood. (1:13b-14, 15b)

Yahweh's special choice (election) of Israel has become a failure because the nation has proved less loyal and intelligent than even cattle and donkeys (1:2-3). To make this point, Isaiah imitates the style of a love song in 5:1-7. The image of a vineyard represented erotic love (Song 1:6, 14; 8:12) but also was a traditional metaphor for Israel (Isa 27:2-6; Ps 80:8-16). The lament of the love song is that Israel has never produced the good grapes that Yahweh expected, but only yielded fruit like that of wild vines (CEB: *rotten grapes*). In Isaiah 5:7, two puns point to a negative end for Israel's relationship with Yahweh. Instead of the justice (Hebrew: *mishpat*) that Yahweh expected to see, there was bloodshed (*mispakh*), and instead of righteousness (*tsedeqah*), Israel's behavior gave rise to the outcry of the oppressed (*tseʿaqah*).

A Remnant Will Survive

In Isaiah, the threat of judgment is modified by the concept of a surviving *remnant*. Israel's fate would be doom and disaster, marked by hunger and thirst, a breakdown in leadership and the social system (3:1-7; 4:1), and defeat (3:25-26). And yet Isaiah also proclaims that, on the other side of judgment, there will be a better state of affairs for the remaining few who survive. *Remnant* in the book of Isaiah is a double-edged concept. It portrays both the completeness of the coming destruction and the promise of something positive for whoever lives through the coming catastrophe. For example, in his call story in chapter 6, Isaiah's negative prophetic assignment must last until Judah becomes like a cut-down tree and only a stump remains to show where it once flourished (6:11-13). Yet the last sentence of 6:13 sparks hope: *Its stump is a holy seed.* The notion of remnant also appears in the symbolic name of Isaiah's son *Shear-yashub*, meaning *the remaining few will return* (or *survive*; 7:3). This encodes both a negative threat (when catastrophe strikes, only a few will remain) and a positive hope (a few will return and turn away from sin). In the events of 701, the city of Jerusalem remained as a remnant among the general destruction of the rest of the land (1:7-9). Doom is certain, but beyond that, the future is in Yahweh's hands (10:20-23).

Yahweh's Choice of Jerusalem

Isaiah is permeated by two theological traditions characteristic of Judah's religious life. The *Zion tradition* focuses on Yahweh's special, protective relationship with Jerusalem. Probably going back to beliefs current in Jerusalem long before it fell under Israelite control, the Zion tradition affirms that Yahweh in some sense dwells in the Jerusalem temple and can be counted on to defend the city against all enemies. This confidence is expressed in Psalms 46, 48, and 76. When kings and mythic forces gather against Jerusalem, Yahweh as Divine Warrior will defend the city and defeat its foes.

The Zion tradition appears in the narrative of Isaiah 7 concerning the events of 734–732. Isaiah insists that King Ahaz must not be afraid in the face of the threat posed by the two enemy kings, Pekah and Rezin. Ahaz must instead have faith, because Yahweh will not let their plans succeed (7:4-9). Prophetic words were sometimes backed up by confirming signs. In this case it is the birth of a baby that will confirm the doom soon to fall upon Israel and Damascus: *The young woman is pregnant [or "will conceive"] and is about to give birth to a son, and she will name him Immanuel* (7:14).

Immanuel means *God is with us*, a creed-like statement found in the Zion song Psalm 46:7, 11 (also Isa 8:10). Perhaps Isaiah intended to point to a still-unborn child of some woman in Ahaz's own royal family or among the palace household. In any case, before this child ever reached a certain age, Ahaz's problem would be solved. Yet Yahweh's solution involved the arrival of the king of Assyria, a prospect comforting and threatening at the same time (7:15-17). Another symbolic name given to another baby, a newly born son of Isaiah, further confirms Yahweh's ominous promise of deliverance by the Assyrian army. He is named *Maher-shalal-hash-baz* (*spoil hastens, plunder hurries*), which describes the rapid onset of military action and the taking of booty. Before this child can speak his first words, both of Ahaz's enemies will have been conquered and despoiled (8:1-4). However, although the tool of Yahweh's action in history, brutal Assyria can be counted on to exceed its commission and will itself be punished in the end (10:5-19).

16.1. ISAIAH 7:14

Because of the way the New Testament uses this verse, its translation has been enmeshed in controversy. The Septuagint Greek translated the Hebrew word for *young woman* (or *woman of marriageable age*) with a word that almost always meant *virgin*. Following the implications of this move by a Greek translation, Matthew 1:23 quoted Isaiah 7:14 in order to illustrate the

> virginal conception of Jesus and his continued presence with humanity (*God with us*). As a result, the King James Version opted to translate Isaiah 7:14 as *Behold, a virgin shall conceive, and bear a son*. This remained the standard translation until the mid-twentieth century, when the Revised Standard Version of 1952 recognized that this was inaccurate and misleading.

Some years later in 701, the Zion tradition played a major role in Isaiah's interactions with King Hezekiah. As he contemplated revolt against Assyria, Hezekiah seems to have engaged in negotiations with Egypt. In that context, Isaiah insisted that the Zion tradition implied that engaging in an alliance with Egypt would be futile, faithless, and unnecessary (30:1-5; 31:1-5). As Hezekiah's revolt against Sennacherib unfolded, Isaiah delivered oracles promising that Jerusalem would not be captured and that the Assyrians would fail (30:27-33; 31:8-9). In Isaiah 29:1-8, Jerusalem (alluded to under the name *Ariel*) is portrayed as being distressed and besieged at first, but then delivered by Yahweh's awesome visitation. That Jerusalem actually did escape capture by Sennacherib gave great prestige to Isaiah and meant that his words would be remembered, recorded, and reapplied to future situations. The deliverance of Jerusalem also seemed to justify the truth of the Zion tradition and convinced many that they could trust Yahweh to protect the city under any and all circumstances.

Yahweh's Promise to David

Isaiah also interacts with a second significant set of beliefs involving Yahweh's unbreakable relationship with the dynasty of David. This idea is expressed in 2 Samuel 7:11-16 and Psalm 89:19-37, for example. Psalm 2, a coronation hymn, proclaims that Yahweh has appointed the royal ruler of Judah as king on the *holy mountain* of Zion and adopted him as son (2:6-7). Isaiah 9:1-7 reflects this David tradition. The poem is usually understood against the background of the defeat of Israel in 732 and the resulting conversion of large portions of Israel into Assyrian provinces. The place names cited in v. 1 appear to refer to those annexed territories. Isaiah 9:6 sounds like an announcement made at the enthronement of a new king, quite possibly Hezekiah. His status as son (perhaps God's adopted son) is declared in 9:6 as though this were the moment of his birth. He receives special throne names describing his characteristics. This king is to advocate for justice, and great victory is anticipated, like Gideon's triumph *on the day of Midian* (9:4; see Judg 7:15-25).

The ideal Davidic king is also portrayed in Isaiah 11:1-9. This ruler is not merely a descendent of David but a brand-new David. He is a new start from David's father Jesse. He possesses gifts from Yahweh's spirit that make it possible for him to rule as defender of the needy, guarantor of true justice, and one who reigns in a time of paradisiacal peace. The language of Isaiah's acclamation is so magnificent that it seems eschatological, referring not to the horizon of present events but to a far-off future.

Second Isaiah—Isaiah 40–55

The disciples of the prophet Isaiah continued to preserve and reflect upon his words for generations. About a century and a half after Isaiah, an anonymous prophet now called Second Isaiah produced lyric oracles that addressed an audience living in that later era. These poems responded to the stresses and hopes of the Jewish community that had been forcibly resettled in Babylonian territories after the fall of Judah. Second Isaiah reapplied some of the themes and language of Isaiah son of Amoz and used them to promise that those distressed exiles would return home to Jerusalem. This prophet reflected on how long-standing traditions of God's special bond with Israel, such as the exodus and promises concerning Zion and David, would now be gaining new meaning. God was about to perform a new exodus, leading the people back home. Second Isaiah applied God's special relationship to Zion not only to the city of Jerusalem but to the community as a whole. In a similar way, God's everlasting covenant with David would be fulfilled in the whole people. Salvation was at hand.

Look Homeward

After a generation or two, life for many of those displaced exiles had become bearable, even comfortable. Yet a desire to return fueled resentment and longing, as may be seen in Psalm 137, which originated among the exiles in this period. Current events inflamed their hopes. Many, including Second Isaiah, could see that the Babylonian Empire, misruled by the inept Nabonidus, was near collapse. In contrast, the Persian king Cyrus II (559–530) was winning a string of decisive victories and was poised to move against Babylon. Second Isaiah perceived that Yahweh's purposes lay behind the successes of Cyrus. Yahweh had *anointed* (that is, appointed and authorized) Cyrus so that Jerusalem and its temple could be rebuilt (44:28; 45:1-8). The prophet proclaimed that Yahweh had summoned Cyrus to carry out Yahweh's purpose and march against Babylon (48:14-15). Yahweh roused Cyrus from his homeland north and east of Babylon and empowered his swift victories (41:2-4, 25). Isaiah 45:2-3 portrays Yahweh's address to Cyrus promising him the fruits of victory:

> I will shatter bronze doors;
> I will cut through iron bars.
> I will give you hidden treasures of secret riches.

Second Isaiah describes the defeat of Babylon in chapter 47, picturing the city as a humiliated royal princess. These hopes were justified when Cyrus captured the city of Babylon in October 539.

The Beginning and Conclusion of Second Isaiah

Second Isaiah begins with a dialogue (40:1-11) that appears to take place in the administrative council of Yahweh (see 1 Kings 22 and Isaiah 6) and functioned as the prophet's call story. Plural imperatives in 40:1-2 urge messengers from the council to comfort God's people and speak with compassion to Jerusalem. The time of punishment is over. Then a voice from the assembly commands a road-building project through the wilderness, intended to facilitate Yahweh's approach to rescue the exiles (40:3-5). In 40:6-8, a voice calls upon someone to call out and another figure (the prophet himself according to some textual witnesses) asks about the content of what is to be proclaimed. The reader is assured that, despite the fleeting nature of human existence, Yahweh's word is permanent and trustworthy. In 40:9-11, Jerusalem is urged to proclaim to all the cities of Judah that Yahweh is coming to shepherd the exiles home.

Chapter 55 concludes Second Isaiah and revisits the themes set forth in the introduction at Isaiah 40. The audience is urged to hear God's word of promise and encouragement as though it were an invitation to a satisfying and delightful feast offered without cost (55:1-3a). They are to seek out God to turn away from sin now while there is still a chance (55:6-7). Doubts should be set aside because God's intentions transcend human logic (55:8-9), and God's word is certain to accomplish God's purpose (55:10-11). God promises the nation a permanent covenant and a jubilant return home (55:3b-4; 12-13).

"I Am Yahweh; There Is No Other"

In place of the old, Yahweh promises a new thing so wonderful that the audience ought to forget the old traditions of exodus, creation, Zion, and David (43:18-19; 48:6-8). The return to Jerusalem will be a new and more wonderful exodus, with water in the desert (43:16-21; 48:20-21; 49:9-12). Some of Israel's old mythic stories had portrayed Yahweh's act of creation in terms of a battle with primeval chaos monsters. Reflecting on these, Second Isaiah describes the homeward return of those ransomed by Yahweh as a new creation and Zion as a new Eden (51:3, 9-11). The covenant with David, seemingly negated by the fall of Judah's kings, is converted into an everlasting covenant promised to the whole nation (55:3). Yahweh's promises to Zion are reaffirmed (51:16; 52:1). Yahweh has not forgotten Jerusalem:

> Can a woman forget her nursing child,
>> fail to pity the child of her womb?
>>> Even these may forget, but I won't forget you. (49:15)

Second Isaiah represents a significant development in the religious outlook of the Bible. In earlier portions of the Old Testament, the existence of other gods was taken for granted, even if they were not to be worshipped by Israel. Yahwism was not yet a monotheistic religion. The term *henotheism* is sometimes applied to this worldview in which one god is worshipped, but the existence of other gods is not denied. In the poetry of Second Isaiah, however, no divinity except Yahweh has any power or effective reality as a god. Only Yahweh has demonstrated control over the events of history to deliver Israel, and only Yahweh has been able to predict what has come to pass (41:26; 43:10-13; 44:6-8). Only Yahweh can claim to have created not only light but even darkness, and can bring about both prosperity and doom (45:7). Yahweh is first and last (48:12-13). This theological stance comes very close to the modern concept of *monotheism*. Yahweh is the only god worthy of the name.

Four Servant Songs

Scattered in four places within Second Isaiah are poems that speak of one called Yahweh's servant: 42:1-4; 49:1-6; 50:4-9 [or 11]; and 52:13–53:12. These texts have attracted interest and excited controversy, particularly because some authors of the New Testament perceived in them a prefiguration of the person and mission of Jesus. The Old Testament uses the title *servant of Yahweh* for Moses, Joshua, and David to indicate that they furthered God's rule and purposes in a way analogous to the service of a royal official. Prophets were also Yahweh's servants (2 Kgs 17:23; Jer 7:25). Second Isaiah (outside of the servant songs) uses the designation *servant* to refer to Israel (41:8-9; 44:1-2, 21; 45:4; 48:20), and this is also the case in 49:3 within the second servant song.

In 42:1-4 God presents the servant and outlines his duties and the manner in which he will carry them out. God sounds like a king introducing a new court official. This servant figure advances justice in a gentle style. In the following verses 5-9, Yahweh speaks directly to the servant to describe his mission and provide assurance. The servant in this text can be understood as either Israel or the prophet Second Isaiah himself.

In 49:1-6, the servant speaks as a prophet and gives a first-person account of his call from the womb and his ministry. As is the case with many biblical prophets, he complains that his efforts have been without success. Yahweh renews his prophetic commission and extends his role beyond Israel to be a light to the nations outside Israel. Verse 3 identifies this prophetic servant as Israel.

In 50:4-9 (and perhaps 10-11), the servant portrays himself as a perfect and uncompromising prophet. He has a tongue trained to comfort and an ear that listens to Yahweh's message. This prophet has remained faithful and so encountered resistance and violence. He is certain that Yahweh will aid and vindicate him. Such biographical specificity gives the impression that these words reflect the experiences of Second Isaiah himself.

Isaiah 52:13–53:12 is the most influential and also the most difficult of the servant songs. Issues of translation impact the way readers have understood it. The poem is a dramatic dialogue. Yahweh speaks first in 52:13-15. The servant was once despised as one disfigured, but will succeed and astound kings and nations. In 53:1-9, others speak of their experiences with this servant. There was nothing in his appearance or background to cause us to esteem him, they say. The suffering he experienced caused some to see him as one rejected by God, but we perceive that he bore his afflictions and wounds in solidarity with us. We were guilty of rebellion and crime, but he suffered unjustly, and in some fashion this has led to our healing. Although innocent, he is now as good as dead and buried. His experience was analogous to a sacrificial sin offering (52:10; CEB: *restitution*). As the poem reaches 52:11-12, the speaker becomes Yahweh. The poem ends on a positive note. Because the servant's mission led him to the brink of death in solidarity with sinners, Yahweh intends to exalt him to high status. In this way, Yahweh's positive words in 53:12 circle back to the positive divine announcement of 52:13 and round off the poem. Over the centuries, Judaism and Christianity have differed sharply over the interpretation of the last servant song. The New Testament consistently applies the text to Jesus as a suffering messianic figure (Matt 8:17; Luke 22:37; Acts 8:32-35; 1 Pet 2:21-22, for example). Judaism tends to see the servant as Israel. Perhaps it is best to acknowledge that there are so many difficulties and enigmas in this passage that a number of understandings are possible and legitimate.

Third Isaiah—Isaiah 56–66

Isaiah 56–66 is conventionally labeled as Third Isaiah, although these chapters do not display the same unity of authorship and thought as Second Isaiah does. The prophetic poems that make up Third Isaiah represent reflections on the themes and theology of the two earlier portions of the book. Most often Third Isaiah is dated to about a generation after Second Isaiah. Third Isaiah addresses an audience living in Jerusalem and Judah. This audience has experienced a period of vain waiting for God's wonderful promises to be fulfilled. The contrast between extravagant expectations and mundane, bleak reality has created an eschatological fervor.

The Isaiah Scroll

History provides little help in clarifying the background of the concerns reflected in Third Isaiah. There are few specific hints in the text and little is known about the decades immediately after the return from Babylon in any case. Isaiah 60:13 and 66:1 suggest that the project to rebuild the temple is underway, which indicates a date around 520–515. The poems reflect disillusionment, economic hardship, and ineffectual political and religious leadership (56:9-12). There appears to be disagreement over who should be allowed to make up the worshipping community. Some people are engaging in unorthodox, private religious practices. The audience faces outside opposition from those who live in Samaria and from the Edomites who have occupied large swaths of Judean territory to the south (63:1-6). Third Isaiah sharply contrasts the religious or political faction it supports with other groups it judges to be misguided.

Chapters 60–62 constitute the core of this final section of Isaiah. In spite of the disappointing present situation, these chapters proclaim a message of salvation and promise. Jerusalem will be enriched by foreigners and made illustrious. In a poem patterned on the servant songs of Second Isaiah, joyful good news of restoration is announced to Zion, specifically to the poor, the brokenhearted, and captives (61:1-4). The core chapters 60–62 are preceded in chapter 59 by a lament poem that complains about widespread legal injustice and oppression. Yet the speaker is confident that Yahweh will act to redeem Zion in the role of Divine Warrior (59:15b-20).

Third Isaiah explores the theme of who ought to be included in the worshipping community, urging the audience to move past narrow exclusiveness to welcome foreigners who are committed to the covenant (56:3-8). Even eunuchs are to be admitted, in spite of the prohibition of Deuteronomy 23:1-3. Third Isaiah reflects a more open attitude than that advocated in Ezra and Nehemiah. Following Israel's venerable prophetic tradition, Third Isaiah urges the audience to keep the Sabbath (58:13-14). It condemns mechanical and self-interested religious observance and calls for social justice instead (58:2-7; see also 66:1-4). Disgraceful cultic practices are condemned (57:5-10; 65:3-4).

Overall, in spite of all its compositional complexity, the message of Third Isaiah is optimistic. God will act to create new heavens and a new earth of joy and peace with Jerusalem as its center (65:17-25; 66:5-13, 22-23).

> Celebrate with Jerusalem. . . .
>   that you may drink and be refreshed from her full breasts. . . .
> As a mother comforts her child,
>   so I will comfort you;
>   in Jerusalem you will be comforted. (66:10-11, 13)

Chapter 16

The Isaiah Apocalypse—Isaiah 24–27

The section Isaiah 24–27 is usually designated as the Isaiah Apocalypse. These chapters contain themes that are common to later apocalyptic writings such as Zechariah 12–14 and Daniel 7–12. This apocalyptic unit seems to have been included to serve as a summary conclusion to the foreign nation oracles found in Isaiah 13–23. It portrays a universal judgment that ravages the entire earth. It recycles the chaos monster imagery of ancient myth (27:1). The doom of an unnamed unrighteous city (24:10-13; 25:2; 26:5; 27:10; Babylon?) is contrasted with the fate of Jerusalem (25:6-10a; 26:1-2). Most propose a late date for the Isaiah Apocalypse because of what appears to be a promise of a resurrection of the dead in 26:19 (also 25:8). The concept of resurrection appeared in Jewish thought only in the Hellenistic period (for example, Dan 12:2-3, 13). However, it is possible to see this language as a metaphor for the nation's revival.

Further Reading

Marvin A. Sweeney. "Isaiah 1–39." In *The Fortress Commentary on the Bible: Old Testament and Apocrypha*. Minneapolis: Fortress, 2014.

Shalom M. Paul. *Isaiah 40–66: Translation and Commentary*. Eerdmans Critical Commentary. Grand Rapids: Eerdmans, 2012.

Chapter 17
CATASTROPHE AND EXILE: JEREMIAH AND EZEKIEL

The Book of Jeremiah

Jeremiah was called to his prophetic office as a young man and was active for about forty-five years. He was a member of a priestly family living in Anathoth in the tribal territory of Benjamin, a few miles northeast of Jerusalem. The priestly line of Abiathar had been exiled to Anathoth in favor of priests tracing their origin back to Zadok (1 Kgs 2:26-27). It seems likely that Jeremiah's family was deprived of its full priestly office when King Josiah closed down all sites for sacrifice outside Jerusalem. For this reason, it is not surprising that Jeremiah was sharply critical of the established Jerusalem power structure. In keeping with a northern theological orientation that would be expected of someone living in Benjamin, the exodus tradition is central to Jeremiah's proclamation. In contrast, he makes little or no mention of the David or Zion election traditions. Jeremiah often echoes the covenant language and marriage imagery of the northern prophet Hosea. Jeremiah has a reputation as the "weeping prophet." Thus, *jeremiad* means a prolonged lament or complaint.

The Septuagint translated a form of Jeremiah somewhat shorter than the edition found in Jewish and Western Christian Bibles. This Greek version displays a different arrangement of materials, most notably in regard to the placement of the foreign nation oracles of chapters 46–51. Most likely the Septuagint shape of Jeremiah represents the translation of an earlier stage in the development of Jeremiah than the expanded and rearranged Hebrew version.

Chapter 17

Three Types of Literary Material

Three sorts of content appear in Jeremiah: poetic oracles, biography, and prose sermons.

The *poetic oracles* mostly originated with the prophet himself. Oracles of judgment dominate chapters 1–25. In contrast, messages of hope and comfort are collected into chapters 30–31. These encouraging chapters are usually called *the book of consolation* (CEB: *scroll of comfort*; see 30:2). The poetic materials also include the prophet's own personal laments, which are found embedded in various places in 11:18–20:18. Oracles against foreign nations make up chapters 46–51. Jeremiah 36 reveals how some of this poetic material, originally delivered in oral form, came to be written down. Baruch son of Neriah worked as scribe and secretary for Jeremiah (for example, Jer 32:9-15). According to chapter 36, in 605 Jeremiah asked Baruch to write down Jeremiah's judgment oracles dating from the start of Josiah's reign (627) until then. The originally oral nature of these words was preserved in that they were dictated aloud by the prophet (36:4, 6). Baruch then read them aloud to the people and to the royal court. After this scroll was burned by King Jehoiakim, Baruch was instructed to produce a second scroll containing all those words and others as well (36:32). It is significant that the fundamentally oral nature of Jeremiah's words is so strongly emphasized (36:17-18, 32). The transition from living, oral prophetic messages into written form must have been a revolutionary phenomenon.

Biographical materials about Jeremiah's career as prophet constitute a second genre of material. Chapters 26–29 narrate various incidents involving other prophets and important figures. These incidents are carefully dated. In addition, chapters 34–44 recount events that took place during the reign of Judah's last king, Zedekiah, and after the fall of Jerusalem in 586. Chapter 52, which describes the fall of Jerusalem and subsequent events, was reproduced from 2 Kings 24:18–25:30.

A third type of material consists of *prose discourses* or *sermons* that restate Jeremiah's message in terms of Deuteronomistic theology in vocabulary characteristic of Deuteronomy. An example is Jeremiah's temple sermon and the other content of 7:1–8:3. The temple sermon incident is retold in chapter 26. Standing at the gate of the Jerusalem temple, Jeremiah warns the people that they cannot rely on Yahweh's presence in the temple to protect the city from enemy destruction. Speaking for Yahweh, Jeremiah insists that instead of relying on this false premise, the people must instead repent and cease violating Yahweh's commandments. Other prose sermons are 11:1-14; 16:1-13; 17:19-27; 18:1-12; 21:1-10; 25:1-14; 35:1-19; and 44:1-14. These provide evidence that Jeremiah's words were later revised by editors influenced by Deuteronomy.

Five Periods of Jeremiah's Career

Reported events and many of Jeremiah's oracles can be coordinated with the history of the period. It is helpful to divide Jeremiah's career into five periods:

627–622—first part of the reign of Josiah

622–609—silence after Josiah's religious reform

609–597—the reign of Jehoiakim

597–586—the reign of Zedekiah

after 586—following the fall of Jerusalem

The *first period* extends from Jeremiah's call as prophet (evidently in 627) up to the religious reform of Josiah in 622. Chapter 1 presents Jeremiah's call story. In spite of Jeremiah's objections, Yahweh commissions Jeremiah to speak a hard message. He will be in constant conflict with his audience (1:18-19). A vision of an almond branch communicates through wordplay that Yahweh is watching to perform the divine word (1:11-12; in Hebrew, *almond* sounds like *watching over*). During this first phase of his ministry, Jeremiah delivers oracles of judgment calling for repentance (chapters 1–6), sounding much like the earlier northern kingdom prophet Hosea. Jeremiah threatens Judah with an impending attack by an unnamed "foe from the north," illustrated by his vision of a boiling pot (1:13-15). This theme of impending enemy attack dominates most of chapters 4–6.

During a *second period* (622–609) Jeremiah appears to remain silent after Josiah closes down local sites of sacrifice and terminates the worship of alien gods. Jeremiah's prophetic activity resumes after Josiah dies in 609.

A *third period* of Jeremiah's activity (609–597) begins with the accession of Jehoiakim, and is presented in chapters 7–20, 25–26, and 36. Jeremiah's temple sermon (chapters 7 and 26) is delivered at the start of Jehoiakim's reign. At first Jehoiakim is a puppet of the Egyptian king who appointed him to replace his younger half-brother Jehoahaz. After Babylon defeats Egypt at Carchemish in 605, Jehoiakim becomes a vassal of the Babylonian king Nebuchadnezzar (604–562). A few years later, Jehoiakim shifts to a policy of resistance toward Babylon. In quick succession, Jehoiakim dies, Jerusalem falls to the Babylonians in 597, and Jehoiakim's son and immediate successor Jehoiachin is deported along with elements of the royal court.

The *fourth period* covers events between 597 and 586. Much of chapters 21–24, 27–29, and 37–39 relate to this period. The new king, Zedekiah, treacherously hosts a summit of regional nations in 593 in order to coordinate resistance to Babylon (27:3). Jeremiah advocates a policy of continued compliance with Babylon, but other political and prophetic elements in Judah support rebellion. During this period,

Jeremiah sends a letter to those who were deported to Babylon (chapter 29). He counsels them that there can be no hope of an immediate return home. They should settle down to life in exile and, in fact, support the welfare of their new home. Several years later, Zedekiah does rebel. This results in a terrible siege of Jerusalem, and famine ravages the city. However, when Jeremiah's longstanding prediction of catastrophic defeat is about to come true, he unexpectedly looks beyond coming doom to a future hope, as reported in chapter 32. Jeremiah arranges to purchase a tract of family land back home in Anathoth, which is now under Babylonian control. This prophetic sign communicates that someday ordinary life will resume in the homeland. The Babylonians break through the city wall, and Zedekiah is captured. About a month later the temple is burned and at least part of the wall razed.

A *fifth period* at the end of Jeremiah's career is reported in Jeremiah 40–44. These chapters describe the last events of Jeremiah's career. The Babylonians have appointed Gedaliah to govern Judah from the city of Mizpah in Benjamin. He institutes land reform policies (40:7-12). But Gedaliah is murdered by a royalist faction. Fear of the likely Babylonian reaction to this act of rebellion drives some to seek refuge in Egypt. One of those groups takes Jeremiah with them to Egypt, where he presumably spends the rest of his life. Chapter 44 portrays a scene that seems to indicate that Jeremiah's prophetic efforts had been a failure. Jeremiah denounces those with him in Egypt for worshipping gods other than Yahweh (44:1-14). They respond in 44:15-19 that they have learned a lesson from recent events. As long as they were worshipping those other gods, things went well. Their present misfortune only began when they stopped that long-standing practice and turned to worship Yahweh alone. So they intend to continue making offerings to the Mesopotamian goddess called the Queen of Heaven, that is, Ishtar the goddess of war and fertility.

Jeremiah as an Individual

Jeremiah is presented as a human and vulnerable prophet. At one point some people from his hometown Anathoth conspire to kill him (11:21-23). At another time, the temple official Pashhur has Jeremiah beaten and publically exposed in the stocks for a day (20:1-2). Chapter 38 reports that after Jeremiah prophesies that Jerusalem will be handed over to the Babylonians, certain royal officials seek to have him executed. They throw Jeremiah into a cistern, where he is left to die. He is rescued by another royal official, but Jeremiah remains under guard until the besieged city falls. Jeremiah is also opposed by rival prophets who support the royal administration. Jeremiah 27–28 reports on public conflict between Jeremiah and the prophet Hananiah. Jeremiah 16:1-9 reveals how completely Jeremiah's life is consumed by his prophetic calling. He is not to marry or have children. He is not to engage in ceremonies of mourning. An important element of the prophetic office is closed off when Yahweh prohibits him from interceding for the people (14:11-12).

Jeremiah's personal response to the tragedy of his life is reflected in a series of laments or confessions. There are seven of these: 11:18-23; 12:1-6; 15:10-21; 17:14-18; 18:18-23; 20:7-12; and 20:14-18. In Jeremiah 20:7 the prophet express his despair in strong, almost offensive terms, using language that borders on accusing Yahweh of sexual assault:

> Yahweh, you enticed me, and I was taken in.
> You were too strong for me, and you prevailed.
> Now I'm laughed at all the time;
> everyone mocks me. . . .

Verses 14-15 continue:

> Cursed be the day that I was born.
> May the day my mother gave birth to me not be blessed.
> Cursed be the one who delivered the news to my father,
> "You have a son!"

In a powerful statement of divine concern for Israel, Yahweh also laments in 12:7-13 and 14:17-18:

> My eyes well up with tears;
> I can't stop weeping—day and night,
> because my virgin daughter, my people,
> have suffered a crushing blow and are mortally wounded. (14:17)

The Book of Ezekiel

Ezekiel was a priest taken into exile in 597. He lived in a settlement called Tel-abib on the Chebar canal in Babylonia. After five years, in 593, Ezekiel experienced his first prophetic vision. Thirteen chronological notices in Ezekiel pinpoint events by reference to the years of the exiled King Jehoiachin. Ezekiel engaged in his prophetic role for twenty-five years. For the first six years he preached a message of judgment and doom on Jerusalem. Then his message switched to one of hope for the future. Ezekiel appears to have had a hand in the literary shaping of his words, and the book is characterized by first-person narratives.

Ezekiel's priestly background is evident. He criticizes cultic and theological misdeeds rather than social sins. His vision of the future involves a restored temple. He displays a knowledge of priestly lore and of the myths of ancient West Asia. Ezekiel follows priestly theology in envisioning Yahweh's presence in the Jerusalem temple in terms of Yahweh's *glory*, the manifestation of divine splendor in terms of light. Ezekiel's prophetic career is marked by graphic visions and bizarre prophetic acts. His book employs complex allegories and uses intense language that sometimes approaches indecency. It is as though the situation of his audience is so critical that Ezekiel has to pull out all the stops to get their attention.

In some ways Ezekiel appears to follow the older prophetic model embodied by the ninth-century prophets Elijah and Elisha. Like earlier prophets who were marked by the activity of divine spirit (1 Sam 10:10; 11:6; 19:23), Ezekiel too falls under the spell of Yahweh's spirit (Ezek 2:2; 3:12, 24; 11:5). His visions and prophetic experiences take place while *Yahweh's power* [hand] *overcame him* (1:3; 3:14, 22; 8:1; 33:22; 37:1; 40:1), like the spirit possession experienced by Elijah and Elisha (1 Kgs 18:46; 2 Kgs 3:15). As with Elijah (1 Kgs 18:12; 2 Kgs 2:16), the spirit transports Ezekiel to other places, such as to the far-off temple in Jerusalem (Ezek 3:14; 8:3; 11:1, 24; 37:1; 43:5).

Call and Vision—Ezekiel 1–3

Ezekiel's call as prophet in 593 appears to coordinate with a regional summit hosted by King Zedekiah in order to discuss resistance against the Babylonians. Ezekiel's call or commissioning story is a first-person account of his vision of Yahweh's throne-chariot while in exile in Babylon by the Chebar canal (chapter 1). The energetic, flamboyant description of what Ezekiel sees is impossible to resolve into a clearcut picture, but it is apparent that this wheeled flying object is both the war chariot of Yahweh and the throne of Yahweh as cosmic ruler. It is accompanied by traditional features of Yahweh's appearance in a theophany (storm, glowing cloud, lightning, and thunderous sound). The motive force of its four wheels is provided by unearthly winged beings that are part human and part animal. The word *like* is repeated incessantly (over twenty times in chapter 1) in order to communicate that the vision and its description are mere approximations of the actual, incomparable, transcendent reality they imperfectly represent. As the vision unfolds, the very figure of Yahweh seated on the throne almost materializes, but yet remains cloaked by color and fire and brightness. Ezekiel never actually sees Yahweh. No, *this was how the form of Yahweh's glory appeared* (1:28). Yahweh's presence on the cosmic chariot throne is on the move. But what can this mean? The book will provide some answers in chapter 10.

Ezekiel falls on his face and is commissioned as a prophet in 2:1–3:11. In 2:1 and 3:1 and throughout the book, Yahweh repeatedly addresses Ezekiel as *human one* (CEB; NRSV: *mortal*; KJV: *son of man*). Perhaps this form of address is meant to emphasize that Ezekiel is a human being in contrast to the heavenly creatures he has just observed and to signal the prophet's solidarity with his audience. Yahweh encourages Ezekiel to persist in the face of what will prove to be an unresponsive and hostile audience. Ezekiel is handed a scroll containing words of lament and doom, written on both sides (that is, completely full). Commanded to eat it, the prophet finds it to be *sweet as honey*. In contrast to Jeremiah, who agonizes over the message he has been given to speak, Ezekiel appears to accept it wholeheartedly. Nevertheless, his audience will not be receptive. Judah has not learned the lesson of its conquest by Babylon in 597 and remains a *household of rebels* (2:6). Ezekiel will butt heads with them and must have a forehead hard as *diamond* (3:8).

Ezekiel's commissioning continues in 3:12-21. Carried off by the spirit to the exiles of Tel-abib, he sits stunned for seven days. Yahweh appoints him to the task of *lookout*. Like a sentinel on a city wall, Ezekiel is to warn of approaching danger. His audience may live or die depending on how they react to his warning, but Ezekiel will be held accountable to sound the alarm, whatever the response to this may be (3:17-21).

A Message of Judgment—Ezekiel 4–32

The career of Ezekiel extended from his call in 593 to at least 573. As presented in the book of Ezekiel, it is divided sharply into two parts. Chapters 4–32 threaten doom on Judah and Jerusalem. From chapter 33 on, the message becomes one of comfort and hope. The dividing point between these two different proclamations is the decisive second fall of Jerusalem to the Babylonians in 586, or more accurately, the moment some months later when a refugee from the debacle comes to Ezekiel bearing this news (33:21-22).

Ezekiel communicates the seriousness of the crisis unfolding in Jerusalem by performing a number of dramatic prophetic acts as commanded by Yahweh. He portrays the impending siege of the city using a brick and an iron plate (4:1-3). He lies first on one side and then the other to represent how long Israel and Judah will be punished (4:4-8). He acts out the cooking and eating of someone in the starving city—graciously allowed, as a priest, to cook with animal dung instead of ritually unclean human dung (4:9-17). He manipulates the hair of his shaven head and beard and a sword to illustrate Yahweh's thoroughgoing judgment (5:1-4). Later, Ezekiel acts out the plight of one escaping a doomed city and forced into exile with meager baggage (12:1-7). He eats and drinks while quaking with fear to illustrate how the people will react to the destruction of their land and cities (12:17-20).

Transported back to Jerusalem by the spirit (chapter 8), Ezekiel perceives four scenes of what is happening there. Taken to the temple, Ezekiel sees an idolatrous statue, images on the walls of a secret room housing an improper rite practiced by prominent citizens, ritual weeping for the Babylonian god Tammuz, and worship of the sun in the temple courtyard.

Chapter 17

The vision of Yahweh's throne chariot, described in chapters 1–3, is picked up again as a sign of Jerusalem's coming doom. Yahweh's presence in the temple, embodied by Yahweh's glory, cannot remain in the face of such rebellion (8:6). The first stage of Yahweh's departure from the temple is portrayed in 9:3 as the divine glory moves to the temple doorway. Ezekiel 10:1, 4-5 picks up the topic and associates Yahweh's glory with the chariot throne of Ezekiel's earlier vision. This is the flying object that Ezekiel had seen in Babylon (10:15, 20, 22). God's glory moves to the main east gate of the temple (10:18-19). Then the wheels and the glory leave the city and pause at the Mount of Olives to the east (11:22-23). The import of this stage-by-stage movement is clear: Yahweh has abandoned Jerusalem and its temple to their fate and is traveling eastward to be present with the exiles in Babylon.

The crisis comes to a head when King Nebuchadnezzar of Babylon begins his siege of Jerusalem (24:1). According to Ezekiel 24:15-24, Yahweh commands a further prophetic act of Ezekiel when the prophet's wife dies. Ezekiel is not to engage in any of the standard acts of mourning for her, even though she has been *the delight of his eyes* (24:16). The explanation Ezekiel is to give to those who question this behavior is that Yahweh is about to undo the holiness of the temple, which is *the delight of their eyes* (24:21). Ezekiel is struck mute, and will only speak again when he receives the news that Jerusalem has been captured (24:25-27). Ezekiel's inability to speak is one of the numerous puzzles in this book. Yahweh first announces this in 3:26-27, and yet Ezekiel continues to speak prophetic words. One solution is to interpret Ezekiel's experience as an inability to speak except under Yahweh's direct mandate.

Israel's History of Sin

Ezekiel uses allegories to speak of Israel's history of sin. An allegory about two eagles and a vine in chapter 17 alludes to events on the international scene leading up to the destruction of Judah. Other allegories speak of a lioness (19:1-9), a vine (19:10-14), a forest (20:45-49), and a cooking pot (24:1-14).

Two allegories use a negative view of the sexuality of women to portray the sinfulness of the people. Both of these are told in lurid language. In chapter 16, Jerusalem acts as a faithless wife. She was born of an Amorite father and Hittite mother and left untended in an open field. When she grew to womanhood, Yahweh married her, treated her well, and provided lavish clothing, jewelry, and choice food. But Jerusalem betrayed Yahweh her husband, using what he had provided to facilitate her adulteries with foreign nations. Worse than any prostitute, she paid her lovers rather than the other way around.

In chapter 23, one reads of two sisters, Oholah (Samaria, capital of the northern kingdom) and Oholibah (Jerusalem). Both had earlier engaged in licentious behavior in Egypt and both become Yahweh's wives (*they became mine*, 23:4). Oholah had sex with Assyrians and was slain by them, just as Samaria was destroyed by Assyria. Her younger sister Oholibah (Jerusalem) did not learn from this but in fact acted even worse. Her sex partners were Assyrians and then Chaldeans (that is, Babylonians). So Jerusalem too will be punished by the nations that have been her lovers.

Ezekiel 18 speaks of individual responsibility and represents a significant development in religious thought. Yahweh cites a current aphorism asserting that the present generation is being punished for the misdeeds of their parents: *When parents eat unripe grapes, the children's teeth suffer* (18:2). This expresses the theology of transgenerational or corporate punishment prevalent in Old Testament thinking (for example, Exod 20:5; 34:7). Yahweh insists to Ezekiel that the fate of every person will depend on their own deeds and decisions. Examples describing three successive generations—first righteous (18:5-9), then sinful (18:10-13), and then righteous again (18:14-18)—illustrate that the behavior of parents does not determine their children's fate, either for good or ill. The sinner who turns away from sin will live; the righteous who backslides into disobedience will die (18:21-24).

A Message of Hope—Ezekiel 33–39

Beginning with chapter 33, the message of Ezekiel reverses from one of threatened doom to a comforting announcement of future hope. The arrival of the news that Jerusalem has fallen (33:21-22) marks this change in what the prophet proclaims. Yahweh promises new actions that will prevent a recurrence of the national tragedy that has happened. According to chapter 34, God will serve as a new and proper shepherd for the people, rescuing and feeding them in place of their former selfish leaders (shepherds). *You are my flock, the flock of my pasture . . . and I am your God* (34:31). Yahweh promises to give the people a new heart and a new spirit (36:26-27). This new heart will be living flesh, not stubborn stone like their former hearts. The new spirit will cause them to obey God's law so that the ancient motto of the covenant can become true once more: *you will be my people, and I will be your God* (36:28).

To confirm the promise of national restoration for a people who are as good as dead, Ezekiel reports another vision of spirit transport (37:1-14). A valley of dry bones, apparently the long-dead remains of a great battle, provides a symbol of the whole house of Israel, completely without hope (37:11). Ezekiel declines to answer God's rhetorical question as to whether the bones could ever live again and is then commanded to speak an oracle to the bones that triggers their return to life. The first stage of this process of revival is incomplete. The bones rearticulate and develop sinews, flesh, and skin, but still have no breath, which is to say no life. A second oracle to breath (or spirit) is required to cause them to stand up and live. The imagery then shifts from unburied bones to the dead in their graves (37:12-13), but the point is the same. God will bring the whole of Israel, exiles of both the northern and southern kingdoms apparently, back to life from the death of their peoplehood and return them to their own soil.

Utopian Vision—Ezekiel 40–48

The book concludes with a utopian vision of a newly restored temple and new rules for it (chapters 40–46), along with a new ecology of fertility and new arrangement of the land (chapters 47–48). Ezekiel had earlier described the departure of Yahweh's glory from the old temple (chapters 8–11). Now Ezekiel sees that glory returning permanently to a restored and improved temple (43:1-5). Fourteen years after the former one had been destroyed, Ezekiel is given a guided tour of this temple. The detailed description of its ground plan and measurements reveal that this building is as much a fortress as it is a place for religious activity. A massively thick perimeter wall and military-style gates are intended to separate the holiness of the temple from the common or ordinary state of affairs outside (42:20). Foreigners who might profane the temple are excluded (44:6-8). A special buffer district surrounds the sanctuary (45:1-8; 48:8-22). Rigorous rules protect the temple's holiness (45:10–46:24). Renewed fertility of the homeland pours out from this temple as a river runs from it down to turn the Dead Sea into fresh water, engendering fertility along its course (47:1-12). New and idealized tribal boundaries replace traditional ones (48:1-7, 23-29).

Further Reading

Louis Stulman. *Jeremiah*. Abingdon Old Testament Commentaries. Nashville: Abingdon, 2005.

Margaret S. Odell. *Ezekiel*. Smyth & Helwys Bible Commentary. Macon, GA: Smith & Helwys, 2005.

Chapter 18
PROPHETS OF SOCIAL JUSTICE: AMOS, HOSEA, AND MICAH

Amos

Amos was a Judahite who spoke to the northern kingdom of Israel in the last part of the reign of Jeroboam II. Thus, he overlapped with the earlier part of Hosea's period of activity. The words of both Amos and Hosea reflect a serious gap in social power and wealth between the upper and lower classes. New economic forces included centralized royal tax gathering, vocational specialization encouraged by growing urbanization, and a shift from an economy facilitated mostly by barter to one that used money (in the form of silver, though not yet in the form of coins). These developments led to a concentration of wealth in the hands of the elite and a corresponding disempowerment of small landowners. In difficult times, the rich made loans in the form of money to tide over small farmers. Those who defaulted on loans suffered the loss of ancestral land that their families had owned for generations. Impoverished debtors and their family members were enslaved by their creditors or worked as daily wage laborers. In contrast, the rich were able to assemble large estates.

Amos was from the village of Tekoa south of Bethlehem. He identified himself as a herdsman and farm laborer who trimmed sycamore trees (by scratching the unripe fruits to enable them to ripen; 7:14). The judgment oracles of Amos focused on social and economic injustices during a period of prosperity enjoyed by the affluent classes. An account of his dramatic encounter with the royal administration sets the scene for his career (7:10-17). Amaziah, the presiding priest of the northern kingdom shrine at Bethel, reports to King Jeroboam that Amos has been publically announcing the king's impending violent death and impending destruction and exile for the kingdom. Amaziah then challenges Amos's authority to function as a prophet at the royal sanctuary of Bethel. He demands that Amos go back home to Judah and make his living as a prophet there. Amos retorts in 7:14 that he is no professional prophet in the sense that Amaziah means: *I am not a prophet, nor am I a prophet's son*. Rather his authority to speak derives from a direct call by Yahweh.

Fig. 14. This is the impression of a seal reading, "belonging to Shema, servant of Jeroboam." It was discovered at Megiddo and subsequently lost.

In 3:3-8, Amos argues that Yahweh has compelled him to prophesy. A series of rhetorical questions establishes the principle that events have causes. Appointments lead to meetings. The warning blast of the sentinel's trumpet causes fear in the city. Indeed, it is Yahweh who causes all disasters (a common theological assumption of the time) and reveals them to prophets. Therefore, prophets like Amos speak because they are compelled to by Yahweh.

A Society under Judgment

The burden of Amos's message is that Israel is a society under judgment. Amos 1:3–2:8 opens the book with a stunning rhetorical move. Seven oracles proclaim judgment on neighboring nations surrounding Israel because of behavior that violated accepted norms. Each stanza is introduced by a step-up pattern that builds suspense: first three crimes and then four. Six foreign nations are accused of atrocities, actions that one would call war crimes today. Next, Judah is accused of violating Yahweh's law. The original audience made up of citizens of Israel would have certainly been pleased up to this point in the address, but then shocked by the conclusion that follows in 2:6-8. Yahweh condemns Israel as well on account of its oppression of the poor and its sexual misdeeds. The striking accusation of 2:6—*They have sold the innocent for silver, and those in need for a pair of sandals*—refers to the practice of forcing those who could not pay their debts into slavery. The shocking message is that Yahweh will judge Israel as if it were merely any other nation, and its social and economic inequities are put on the same moral level as war crimes. Other passages in Amos also undermine Israel's claim for special treatment from Yahweh. The exodus, for example, certainly means that Israel has a special relationship with Yahweh, but this relationship also means that Yahweh will hold them especially accountable for their misdeeds (3:1-2). Over time Yahweh has tried to teach Israel its lesson, sending famine, drought, the destruction of crops, pestilence, and other catastrophes, but the people have never repented and turned back (4:6-11). Israel dare not become self-satisfied or complacent because of the exodus, because Yahweh has worked in a similar way with other peoples in history (9:7-8).

Amos uses colorful language to criticize the influential and wealthy for their treatment of the disempowered poor. For example, 4:1-3 addresses the rich women of the capital city Samaria. Though now they live a pleasant life, sleek as well-fed cows, they will be dragged off into exile. Amos 6:1-6 makes bitter fun of the lifestyle enjoyed by the new leisure class of both kingdoms. They lounge about on fine furniture, eat and drink at lavish banquets entertained by music, and rub fine ointments into their bodies, but they do not care about the coming catastrophe.

Amos 5:10-15 denounces the absence of justice shown to the poor and demands that Israel *establish justice at the city gate* (5:15). The open space at the gate was the place where legal matters were adjudicated. The justice system has been corrupted by the power of money taken in bribes. Yahweh's law was intended to protect the weak, but now the needy are pushed away when they seek justice.

Empty Religion

Amos charges that the way Israel is practicing its religion is empty and worse than useless. People lie down beside the altar atop the clothing of those they have defrauded, in violation of divine law (Exod 22:26-27), and the wine used in worship has been bought with oppressive legal fines (Amos 2:8). Israel imagines that sacrifice and ritual will keep Yahweh on their side (4:4-5). In truth, however, Yahweh cannot tolerate this sort of worship (5:21-23). Yahweh wants not religious ritual but justice:

> But let justice roll down like waters,
>   and righteousness like an ever-flowing stream. (5:24)

Amos censures Bethel, Gilgal, and Beer-sheba, some of Israel's most popular sites for sacrifice and pilgrimage, as sites of sin (4:4; 5:5), and attacks the invocation of divinities associated with Samaria, Dan, and Beer-sheba (8:14).

Israel interpreted the traditional concept of the *Day of Yahweh* in a positive sense and looked forward to its coming. Amos reversed this and instead proclaimed that the Day of Yahweh would be a day of darkness and judgment (5:18-20). Two graphic vignettes describe its impact. It will be like someone who escapes a lion only to run into a bear, or someone who takes refuge in a house and pauses to lean against a wall, only to be bitten by a snake hiding there.

18.1. THE DAY OF YAHWEH

The concept of the Day of Yahweh was an ancient one, with roots in both the religious calendar (perhaps as an annual celebration of Yahweh's enthronement as cosmic king) and the theology of the Divine Warrior. Originally understood as Yahweh's victorious intervention in history in order to protect Israel from its enemies, prophets such as Isaiah and Amos reversed the Day of Yahweh into an image of divine judgment and anger directed against Israel. The Day of Yahweh, in both its positive and negative sense, also appears as a significant theme in Joel, Obadiah, Zephaniah, and Malachi. Similar expressions such as *that day, on the day of,* and the like, are also used in the prophets to refer to the moment of God's decisive intervention.

Five Visions of Doom

Amos 7, 8, and 9 report five visions that depict Yahweh's judgment on Israel.

- Amos is shown a plague of locusts. Prophets often interceded for the people. Amos does so and Yahweh relents and calls off the punishment (7:1-3).

- Next, Amos is shown a cosmic annihilating fire. Once more Yahweh yields to intercession on the part of Amos (7:4-6).

- A third vision discloses God determining the structural integrity of a wall with a plumb line. The import of this is that Israel is warped, and so its shrines and the present royal dynasty are doomed. This time Amos remains silent. (7:7-9).

- After an interlude, a fourth vision serves as a visual play on words. Amos is shown a basket containing produce of the summer harvest (*qayits*), corresponding to the end (*qets*) that is coming upon Israel (8:1-3).

- In the fifth vision, Yahweh's judgment is complete, involving the total annihilation of the nation. Yahweh appears standing next to the altar of what seems to be a temple and commands that the building fall on the people. No one is to escape; every last survivor is to be hunted down by an outraged God (9:1-4).

Hope on the Other Side of Judgment

Like several other prophetic books, Amos has been edited into a pattern in which judgment comes first and then is followed by promise. Thus, the book concludes with assurances of rebuilding, renewed abundance, and restoration (9:11-15). Earlier in the book, the phrase *on that day* had been used to introduce an announcement of judgment (2:16; 8:3, 9, 13), but in 9:11, in contrast, the expression introduces a promise. Since the words of Amos emphasize total destruction, many scholars contend that these positive statements must come from a later time. Another indication of this is that Amos 9:11 promises the restoration of the Davidic kingdom, which would not fall until more than a century had passed.

Hosea

The first three chapters of Hosea describe his bizarre marriage and family life, which is interpreted as reflections of Yahweh's fractured relationship with Israel. Hosea 4–14 is a complex of prophetic oracles arranged into a repeated pattern of judgment (chapters 4–10), promise (chapter 11), judgment (chapters 12–13) and promise (chapter 14).

Hosea's oracles demonstrate remarkable poetic creativity based on metaphors. Israel's love is like morning mist (6:4). Unstable Israel is compared to a stubborn cow (4:16) or a half-baked loaf of flatbread (7:8). Israel is a silly dove strutting back and forth between false hopes (7:11) and an untamed ass *wandering alone* (8:9). Plotting princes are like a hot oven (7:6-7). Israel is like a defective bow that cannot shoot straight (7:16). God damages Israel like a *moth* and *decay* (5:12). Yahweh is *like a lion* to Israel (5:14; 13:7) or an angry mother bear (13:8). Samaria's kings will perish *like a chip of wood* on the water's surface (10:7). *Because they sow the wind, they will get the whirlwind* (8:7).

Historical and Social Background

Hosea functioned as a prophet in the northern kingdom during the last quarter century of the nation's independent existence. During his career, from about 750 on, Israel underwent a series of crises. Up until the end of the reign of Jeroboam II (about 745), Assyrian weakness had allowed Israel to enjoy a period of peace. This was a time of prosperity, at least for the more favored elements of the population. This period came to an end when the Assyrians took steps to reassert their control of Syria-Palestine under the assertive Tiglath-pileser III (744–727), Shalmaneser V (726–722), and Sargon II (721–705).

In the decade between 746 and 737, royal power in Israel shifted back and forth several times. Kings who favored resistance to Assyrian pressure alternated with regimes supported by groups who favored a policy of accommodation. The tribute required to comply with Assyrian demands was costly, but resisting Assyrian military power was hazardous. Jeroboam's successor Zechariah was murdered after six months in favor of Shallum. After only a month, Shallum was replaced by Menahem, who followed a policy of accommodation, levying an onerous tax to pay tribute. However, his son Pekahiah was soon killed in a coup and replaced by Pekah, who returned to a policy of resistance. Yahweh's complaint in Hosea 8:4 describes this unsettled pattern: *They set up kings, but not through me.* The first great crisis came in 734–732, when Pekah rebelled against Tiglath-pileser III with disastrous results. Israel lost large portions of its territory. Israel's new (and last) king, Hoshea, reinstated a policy of compliance for a time, but Israel's existence as an independent state ended with the fall of the capital Samaria to Assyria in 722 (or 720). Hosea 13:16 vividly anticipates the horror of this calamity.

The Hebrew of Hosea is difficult and most likely features distinctively northern linguistic characteristics. Hosea references traditions about the patriarchs and election that reflect his northern background, such as a positive view of the wilderness experience (2:14-15; 9:10) and Jacob seen from the perspective of the Elohist tradition (12:2-4). After the fall of Israel, the traditions connected to Hosea were transmitted to Judah, apparently by refugee immigrants from the northern territories.

Hosea and Gomer—Hosea 1–3

It is not possible to construct a biography of Hosea. However, his atypical marital history and family life was of great interest to those who preserved traditions about him. The book seems to speak of two relationships. Chapters 1–2 concern Gomer, Hosea's wife and the mother of his children. Chapter 3 refers to *a woman who has a lover* (3:1). This may refer to a second woman and not to Gomer. In any case Hosea's marriage and children in chapter 1, the divorce and reconciliation portrayed in chapter 2, and Hosea's acquiring and sheltering a notorious woman in chapter 3 are all treated as symbolic analogies to Yahweh's fraught relationship with Israel.

In chapter 1, Yahweh commands Hosea to marry a woman with a reputation for sexual license. He is to give their three children symbolic names. Although the children are called *children of prostitution* because of her background, nothing untoward is ever reported about Gomer's behavior in chapter 1. It is the names of her children by Hosea that matter. Each is treated as a negative symbol. *Jezreel* was the site of a bloody assassination in the coup that brought Jehu to the throne of Israel (2 Kings 10). The name Jezreel thus predicts the end of the dynasty of Jehu. The names of the girl *No Compassion* and the boy *Not My People* signal the breakdown of the covenant relationship between Yahweh and Israel. Yahweh is negating the standard covenant formula: *you are not my people, and I am not your God* (v. 9; see Deut 29:13; Jer 7:23; and so forth).

In chapter 2, Hosea's marriage to the mother of his children takes on a negative character. The language shifts from prose description to an extended poetic metaphor describing the divorce and punishment of Israel as an adulterous wife, followed by the prospect of reconciliation. Prostitution, painted in the most negative of colors, serves as a metaphor for Israel's infidelity with other gods (*lovers*, 2:5, 10; *the Baals*, 2:13). Israel's threatened punishment is presented in shocking language (2:3, 10). This disturbing metaphor must be read carefully in order to prevent its poetic language from being taken as something that supports domestic violence. Israel's punishment is not total, however, but concludes with Yahweh's continuing fidelity. Yahweh reconstructs the covenant relationship by taking Israel back to "the good old days" in the desert, charming Israel with tender words (2:14-15). The very name Baal will no longer be spoken by Israel, who from now on will address Yahweh not as *My lord* (equivalent to *my Baal* in Hebrew), but as *My husband* (2:16-17). The negative names of the three children are reversed and revoked (2:22-23; *Jezreel* means *God sows*). The standard covenant formula is in effect once again: *I will say to Not My People, "You are my people"; and he will say, "You are my God"* (v. 23).

Gomer may or may not be the woman whom Hosea purchases and shelters in the first-person account in chapter 3. If so, is this a parallel to chapter 1 retelling the beginning of their marriage? Or is this an episode that took place after the events of chapters 1 and 2? In any case, chapter 3 narrates a symbolic, prophetic act that prefigures Israel's future. Just as the woman is kept isolated from relational contact for a time, so too Israel will be deprived of its political and religious institutions for a period. After this interval of isolation, they will return to Yahweh *in the latter days* (3:5).

Hosea's peculiar dealings with women may be understood in terms of the non-standard behaviors that were expected of prophets. Odd actions were understood to be evidence of the authenticity of their office. Marrying a prostitute and paying for and housing a notorious woman in a platonic relationship would certainly be seen as odd activities. Perhaps this is what lies behind the saying preserved in Hosea 9:7: *The prophet is a fool, the spiritual man is mad!*

Judgment Oracles

Hosea 4:1 begins an extensive collection of prophetic proclamations with the phrase *Yahweh has a dispute with the inhabitants of the land.* The word *dispute* (Hebrew: *rîb*) is considered a legal term by some scholars, meaning an indictment in a formal legal proceeding, if such formal complaints were presented among the elders at the city gate. In the chapters that follow, Israel is accused of a long catalogue of misdeeds in the realm of religion and politics. Israel's behavior is summed up as an absence of *faithful love* (Hebrew: *ḥesed*). The term *faithful love* is used throughout the Old Testament to refer to covenant fidelity, which may be defined as the mindset required to remain in a covenantal relationship. Hosea often refers to an absence of *faithful love* or the need for it (6:4, 6; 10:12; 12:6). In Hosea 4:2, the prophet points to five of the Ten Commandments as a standard for covenant behavior. In ancient covenant documents, the verb *know* was often used to describe the loyalty expected of vassal kings as they acknowledged their overlord. Hosea summarizes Israel's covenant disloyalty as the absence of the *knowledge of God* (4:1, 6; 5:4). Yahweh desires *faithful love* and relational *knowledge* more than sacrifice (6:6).

Connecting back to the complexities of his relationship with Gomer, Hosea uses the metaphor of sexual infidelity to portray Israel's misbehavior, which is labeled as prostitution (4:12; 5:3-4; 6:10; 9:1). Hosea focuses particularly on sinful behavior in the political realm. Instead of relying on Yahweh, Israel has sought out foreign alliances with Assyria or Egypt (5:13; 7:11). Israel has relied on its kings and changed them often (8:4; 13:10-11). Political infighting has reached a fever pitch, hot as an oven (7:3-7).

The Problem with Religion

Israel's practice of religion was not the solution but part of the problem. Hosea attacks both prophets and priests for failing to perform properly (4:4-6). Israel is using images in worship, including the bull calf images at Bethel and Dan (8:5-6; 10:5; 13:2). Hosea also criticizes Israel's worship behavior at other venerable sanctuaries of the northern kingdom: Gilgal, Beth-aven (a derogatory allusion to Bethel), Mizpah, and Mount Tabor (4:15; 5:1).

A desire for the fertility of one's field, flock, and family was a central aim of religion in ancient societies. For the average Israelite, it must have seemed that worship of the god Baal was the best way to attain this goal (2:8; 13:1). Although the details are in dispute, some fertility rituals involved sexual activity at local hilltop shrines (4:13-14). Hosea's critique of Israel's infidelity in terms of *prostitution* was thus a fitting image. Specially sanctified women were involved somehow in these sacrifices (4:14, CEB: *consecrated workers at temples*), but the nature of their duties remains unclear. Translating this office as *temple prostitute* (NRSV) is more specific than can be justified.

Israel's practice of religion is futile because it actually obscures the reality of Israel's sin and prevents genuine repentance. In 6:1-3, Hosea caricatures Israel's fruitless, cheap, and easy repentance. Those who speak proclaim that Yahweh can be counted on to heal them and see this as something as certain as the arrival of springtime rain. Yahweh's response in 6:4-6 reflects puzzlement and internal turmoil: *What will I do with you?* Israel's repentance is as thin as mist. All Yahweh wants is covenant love, but all Israel is willing to give is sacrifice. In 8:11-12, Yahweh similarly complains that Ephraim's never-ending multiplication of altars has only brought about even more corrupt behavior and that Israel is treating God's extensive legal instructions as though they were something completely unrelated to their lives.

Yet Yahweh Still Loves Israel

To teach Israel the lesson it must learn, Yahweh will take away the good gifts Israel has enjoyed. This divine plan of education by deprivation is communicated in chapters 2 and 3. In the divorce proceedings, Israel's husband Yahweh takes back her food and clothing because she has treated them as though they were gifts from Baal (2:8-13). In chapter 3, Hosea isolates the woman he has acquired In order to to keep her from sexual contact, symbolizing that Israel will lose its political and religious institutions for a time. The nation will face war and defeat (10:14-15).

For the most part, Hosea emphasizes Yahweh's hurt and anger. Yet a few passages speak of Yahweh's willingness to continue the relationship with Israel. One example of this is a promise of renewal stated in 14:4-8:

> I will be like the dew to Israel;
> he will blossom like the lily. (14:5)

The most striking of these positive statements is 11:1-9, in which Yahweh takes the role of the loving parent of a recalcitrant child. Yahweh rescued this son from Egypt, taught him to walk, embraced him, and fed him. In spite of all this, Israel is rebellious and deserves nothing but punishment. But amazingly, 11:8 takes the reader right into God's inner emotional life.

> How can I give you up, Ephraim?
> How can I hand you over, Israel? . . .
> My compassion grows warm and tender.

Yahweh comes to realize that the threatened total annihilation, though well deserved, simply cannot take place. Yahweh's feelings of warm affection make this impossible.

Micah

Background and Structure

The superscription (1:1) attributes this compendium of prophetic materials to Micah of the Judahite town of Moresheth, dating it to the reigns of Jotham, Ahaz, and Hezekiah. This would mean that Micah overlapped with the career of Isaiah. Under the shadow of Assyrian power, Judah experienced three great crises during this period.

- In 734–732 Israel and Damascus put pressure on Judah, and Israel was defeated and partially dismembered by Assyria.
- In 722 or 720, the northern kingdom fell to Assyria.
- In 701, the Assyrian king Sennacherib devastated the countryside of Judah and threatened Jerusalem.

With respect to the catastrophe of 701, the towns listed in Micah 1:10-15 (including Moresheth) seem to trace the path of the Assyrian army as Sennacherib advanced from the southwest through the Shephelah up toward Jerusalem.

In contrast to Isaiah, who focused on Jerusalem and Yahweh's positive relationship to it, Micah's rural background appears to have given him a different perspective and a more jaundiced view of the capital city. Whereas the amazing rescue of Jerusalem from Sennacherib in 701 was a marvelous event for its citizens, the rural population of Judah must have suffered immensely as the Assyrians devastated the countryside, destroyed Lachish, and captured the dozens of other towns about which Sennacherib brags. (See 14.3, HEZEKIAH AND SENNACHERIB IN 701 BCE.)

Micah is carefully structured and divides into two parts: chapters 1–5 and 6–7. Each of those divisions is further subdivided into a negative section of indictments and pronouncements of destruction (1:2–3:12 and 6:1–7:7) and a positive section announcing deliverance (4:1–5:15 and 7:8-20). Micah describes himself in 3:8 as a prophet who declares *wrongdoing* and *sin*. For this reason, it is often thought that the positive oracles of salvation could not have been spoken by him, but were added later as the book grew. Micah 4:1-3 and Isaiah 2:2-4 preserve the same oracle promising peace and describing the central role that Jerusalem will play in God's plan.

God Demands Justice

Like Amos, Hosea, and Isaiah, Micah preached a message loaded with social critique. For example, 2:1-2 proclaims doom on those who plan ahead to seize unjustly the ancestral property of others. The powerful are appropriating the land of those who have fallen into debt (2:8-9). However, Yahweh claims a personal, covenantal relationship with those who are being exploited and led astray, calling them *my people* (2:9; 3:2-3, 5).

Micah's oracles in 2:6-11 reveal that he has a conflicted relationship with his fellow prophets. Some leaders are demanding that no one should preach negative words of accusation and doom because no disgrace seems to be approaching, but Micah condemns this stance. In light of the injustice that is going on, Micah sarcastically describes the sort of prophet who would be acceptable and appropriate to this audience. This would be a prophet who preaches empty lies in exchange for *wine and liquor* (2:11).

Micah attacks official corruption and exploitation (3:1-11). Yahweh's key demand from Judah's leaders is that they practice justice (3:1, 8, 9). Rulers are supposed to know justice, but instead these leaders devour the people *like meat in a kettle* and *build Zion with bloodshed* (3: 3, 10). Prophets proclaim messages for personal gain and priests teach for money (3:5, 11). In the realm of commerce too, God cannot forget or tolerate dishonesty (6:10-11).

Yahweh's requirement for social justice may be heard most clearly in the ringing declaration that concludes 6:1-8. Yahweh is portrayed as bringing a legal indictment (*rîb*) against Israel. After calling the mountains and the foundations of the earth as witnesses, God reviews a long history of redeeming and protecting those who are addressed as *my people*. Micah then quotes rhetorically what someone might ask concerning sacrificial obligations in light of Yahweh's accusations (6:6-7). The prophet insists that God does not want more religion. The audience already knows that what God requires is—

> to do justice, embrace faithful love, and walk humbly with your God. (6:8)

Micah's severe oracle announcing the destruction of Jerusalem into a heap of ruins would be long remembered:

> Zion will be plowed like a field,
> > Jerusalem will become piles of rubble,
> > > and the temple mount will become an overgrown mound. (3:12)

This word was in direct opposition to the popular Zion theology that promised that Jerusalem was inviolable and that Yahweh would always defend it. Jeremiah 26:18 attests that these words of Micah were still remembered a century later and could be quoted in order to defend Jeremiah when he threatened the same fate for Jerusalem.

A Ruler from Bethlehem

The announcement of salvation in Micah 5:1-5a is well-known in Christian circles. The Gospel of Matthew applies its reference to a ruler from Bethlehem to the birth of Jesus (Matt 2:5-6). The original historical background of the oracle cannot be determined. Nevertheless, the concern of the passage is a threatened collapse of the Davidic royal line. In a context of a siege, the present ruler (CEB: *judge*) is humiliated (5:1). A new ruler (using a different word) is promised, who will bring security and peace. This ruler originates in David's native town Bethlehem (1 Sam 17:12), not in Jerusalem. Therefore, he is not just another Davidic king, but actually a new David. The new ruler is lauded in terms that echo the Davidic ideology of royal psalms such as Psalms 2 and 72. He corresponds to the ideal of a shepherd king, an image common throughout the ancient world. Perhaps this promise originated in the humiliation of Hezekiah during the Assyrian siege of 701, or in the fall of Jerusalem in 586 and the end of the Davidic kingship. Jewish interpretation of this unit has traditionally stressed the hardships to be suffered by Israel (associated with *she who is in labor*; 5:3) before the messiah comes.

Further Reading

Carol J. Dempsey. *Amos, Hosea, Micah, Nahum, Zephaniah, Habakkuk.* New Collegeville Bible Commentary. Collegeville, MN: Liturgical Press, 2013.

James D. Nogalski. *Introduction to the Hebrew Prophets.* Nashville: Abingdon, 2018.

Carolyn Sharp. *The Prophetic Literature.* Nashville: Abingdon, 2019.

Chapter 19
JUDAH IN THE ORBIT OF ASSYRIA, BABYLON, AND PERSIA

Zephaniah

Zephaniah explores the negative and positive consequences of the coming *Day of Yahweh*. The superscription identifies him as a prophet in the reign of Josiah. Attacks on problematic worship practices suggest a career before Josiah's religious reformation in 621 (1:4-6, 8-9). The book consists of brief, independent oracles on several topics, but unity is provided by the overarching theme of the decisive day when Yahweh will act. The enemies that endanger Jerusalem (3:15) cannot be identified, although mention of Nineveh's desolation in 2:13-15 suggests that Assyria is meant. As is true for some other prophetic books, Zephaniah was edited so that judgment oracles come first (1:2–3:8) and promises of deliverance appear at the end (3:9-20).

Judah is addressed in the first section, 1:2–2:3. Like Amos, Zephaniah reverses the Day of Yahweh from a hoped-for day of great victory and rescue to a day of punishment (1:7, 14). This cataclysm will be universal (1:2-3), but it is also directed specifically against the religious infidelity of Judah and Jerusalem (1:4-6). The refrains *on that day* (1:9, 10) and *at that time* (1:12) punctuate Yahweh's punishment of Jerusalem. Verses 14-18 describe the nearing Day of Yahweh in intensely negative terms.

Zephaniah 2:4-15 catalogues nations that have been Judah's enemies: the Philistine cities, Moab and Ammon, far-off African Cushites, and finally Nineveh. The gods of foreign nations will each bow to Yahweh from their own territory (2:11). An unnamed city (no doubt Jerusalem) that has not listened to or trusted in Yahweh is denounced in 3:1-7.

Zephaniah concludes with announcements of a positive future in 3:9-20. The refrains *on that day* and *at that time*, which had previously introduced punishment (see 1:9, 10, 12), now point instead to beneficial developments (3:11, 16, 19, 20). One of these promises is surprisingly universal. The language of foreigners will be purified so that they can invoke Yahweh, and even those beyond the rivers of far-off Cush will bring sacrifices (3:9-10). The book ends with joy. Zion is called upon to sing and rejoice (3:14) because Yahweh *is in your midst* (3:15, 17). The Divine Warrior Yahweh is Israel's victorious king, and Yahweh too will join the joyful song (3:17).

Nahum

The *scroll* (see 1:1) of Nahum celebrates the fall of the Assyrian capital Nineveh. The prophet is either anticipating this event or is reporting on it soon after it took place. Nineveh fell to the Babylonians and Medes in 612, although Assyria remained a significant military power until 609. Mention of Assyria's conquest of the Egyptian city of Thebes in 664 indicates that Nahum was composed after that date (3:8-10). Yahweh's power and splendor as Divine Warrior means that Yahweh controls world events and that Assyria deserved its punishment.

A damaged acrostic poem seems to lie behind 1:2-8. (Each line of an acrostic poem begins with a successive letter of the Hebrew alphabet.) The presumed acrostic goes only as far as the first half of the alphabet. Language similar to Exodus 34:6-7 introduces the theme of Yahweh's character: *a jealous and vengeful God . . . very patient but great in power* (Nah 1:2-3). Images describing the approach of the Divine Warrior extol Yahweh's might in 1:3-6 (wind and storm, effects on the sea and rivers, quaking mountains). Chapter 1 ends with the thrilling arrival of a messenger who proclaims peace brought about by the fall of Nineveh (1:15).

Chapter 2 reports the destruction of Nineveh in dramatic and realistic terms. Chariots race, and the city wall is attacked (2:4-5). The river gates are breached and the city is flooded (2:6, 8). Treasuries are plundered (2:9). Assyrian palace art often invoked the lion as a symbol of imperial power, but in 2:11-12 the lion image is turned against Assyria.

Most of chapter 3 is a satirical lament over the fate of Nineveh, the *city of bloodshed*. Multiple images describe the destruction of the city. Verses 2-3 depict chariots and piled-up corpses. A brutal image in 3:4-7 compares Nineveh to a humiliated prostitute (CEB: *whore*) and *mistress of sorceries*. The archetypical war crime of smashed babies is invoked in 3:10 (see 2 Kgs 8:12; Ps 137:9; Isa 13:16; Hos 10:14; 13:16). Nineveh is like a ripe fig ready to fall (3:12) and like locusts that first multiply but then fly off and disappear (3:17). The fall of the king of Assyria is universally applauded:

> All who hear the news about you clap their hands over you.
> Who has not suffered from your continual cruelty? (3:19)

Habakkuk

The topic of Habakkuk is the crisis of faith caused by the prevalence of injustice and oppression. Why does God permit such evil things, and why does God delay in righting them? The despairing prophet engages in dialogue with Yahweh, and Yahweh responds with instructions to wait in faith. The date of composition is uncertain. Habakkuk 1:6-11 mentions rousing the Chaldeans (that is, Babylonians), which suggests a date somewhat before the defeat of Judah in 597.

The book falls into three parts, distinguished by different literary forms. Habakkuk 1:2–2:4 is a dialogue between the prophet and Yahweh. The remainder of chapter 2 is a series of five woe oracles, each introduced by the word *doom* (CEB; NRSV: *alas*). Chapter 3 incorporates a psalm of confidence into the book.

In the first part, the prophet and Yahweh engage in two rounds of question-and-answer dialogue. In 1:2-4, the prophet complains of confusion and a breakdown of law and justice. Yahweh responds in 1:5-11, pointing to a plan to stir up the *bitter and impetuous* Chaldeans. In 1:12-17, Habakkuk protests that Yahweh is too pure to make use of such a treacherous and wicked nation. The Babylonians are like those who ruthlessly overfish people and nations and are overstepping the bounds of what should be permissible. So in 2:1, Habakkuk challenges God. He intends to take a stubborn stand at his sentinel post to wait for a response. God does reply in 2:2-4, telling Habakkuk to write down the prophetic vision in a way that can easily be seen, so that it will be preserved for its certain fulfillment. Even if deliverance seems delayed, wait for it, because the proud and greedy will eventually go too far.

The precise import of 2:4b is obscure. According to CEB, there is a contrast between those who do not *do the right thing* in 2:4a and the righteous person of 2:4b, who lives faithfully (*honestly*). As understood by the NRSV, 2:4b offers a general principle for coping with the challenges and enigmas of life that are so distressing for Habakkuk. A righteous person can survive by faithfully holding on to confidence in the reliability of God and trusting God's plan.

The second part, 2:5-20, is a taunting song consisting of five doom or woe sayings asserting that the Babylonians will eventually fall victim to their own greed. These taunts focus on an emblematic individual (*an arrogant man*; 2:5) whose behavior exemplifies the offenses for which the Babylonians are notorious. These are greed

(2:6-8), building projects (2:9-11), towns founded on bloodshed (2:12-14), degrading neighbors (2:15-17), and senseless idolatry (2:18-19). Each behavior receives its comeuppance, and balance is restored.

The third part, chapter 3, reproduces a psalm of trust, complete with performance directions in 3:1 and 3:19b and even the notation *Selah* in 3:3, 9, and 13 (perhaps indicating a musical interlude). Yahweh is the Divine Warrior, who approaches from the southern mountains to rescue Israel (Judg 5:4-5; Ps 68:7-8; Nah 1:3-5). Yahweh is ready to employ weapons of pestilence and plague and the arrows of lightning. The effects of this arrival on the natural and human world are disruptive. Sun and moon freeze. At the end, even though nothing positive is happening yet (Hab 3:17), Habakkuk trusts in God's intention to save the people and will wait (as commanded in 2:3) for calamity to fall on the enemy (3:16).

Obadiah

This is the shortest book in the Old Testament. It reports nothing about Obadiah except his name. These oracles appear to have originated relatively soon after the fall of Judah. Obadiah attacks Edom for its hostile behavior when Judah fell to the Babylonians. Moreover, in the Babylonian period, Edomites moved northward into territories in the south part of what had been Judahite territory. The eponymous ancestor of Edom was Jacob's brother Esau, but Edom did not live up to its brotherly responsibilities (Obad 10, 12). Edom's actions are condemned elsewhere as well (Ps 137:7; Lam 4:21-22). For Obadiah the *Day of Yahweh* is a positive concept. Nations will themselves suffer the evil they have inflicted on Israel (Obad 15-16). *On that day* retribution will fall on Edom (v. 8), because of their behavior *on the day* that Jerusalem fell (vv. 11, 12, 13). Israel will reoccupy its lost territories and exiles will return from distant lands (vv. 19-20). The positive future of Mount Zion is contrasted with the fate of Mount Esau (vv. 8, 9, 17, 19, 21).

Haggai

The prophets Haggai and Zechariah were contemporaries, active in the early days of the restoration of Jewish life in Jerusalem and the reconstruction of the temple. Haggai records oracles delivered during the first several months of that rebuilding project. It culminates with the day on which the laying of the temple's foundation was celebrated. The book records four prophetic announcements and dates each precisely within the second year of the Persian king Darius I (521–486). The first oracle is dated to mid-August of 520 and the last two to a single day in mid-December of the same year.

Table 6. Significant Persian Rulers

Cyrus II (the Great)	539–530
Cambyses	529–522
Darius I	521–486
Xerxes (Ahasuerus)	485–465
Artaxerxes I	464–424
Darius II	423–405
Artaxerxes II	404–359
Darius III	335–331

Displaced Jews began returning to Jerusalem soon after Cyrus the Great took over Babylon (about 538). Times were difficult at first, marked by economic difficulties and political tension between those newly returned and those who had remained in the land. Consequently, serious work on rebuilding the temple did not begin for eighteen years (Hag 1:2). Because the succession of Darius I had been opposed by rival factions and claimants, it was vital for him to stabilize the frontiers of his empire. This meant that attention had to be paid to the province of Yehud (Persia's designation for Judah) on the border with Egypt. The two leaders of the restored Jewish community were Zerubbabel, a grandson of the late king Jehoiachin, and Joshua, who held the office of high priest.

Haggai addresses his first oracle to Zerubbabel and Joshua (1:1–15a). It is structured by the refrain *Take your ways to heart* in 1:5 and 7. Prosperity has been lacking because temple reconstruction has not yet begun, even though the citizens of Jerusalem have been building fine houses for themselves. Yahweh commands: *Rebuild the temple so that I may enjoy it* (1:8). It still takes three weeks to get the project started (1:15a).

The second oracle is delivered in the early stages of temple rebuilding as encouragement (1:15b–2:9). Apparently the new temple seems unimpressive compared to what people remember about the previous one. Yahweh promises that treasure from other nations will fill the new temple and make it magnificent.

The third section of the book raises the issue of the purity of the new temple (2:10-19). Yahweh tells Haggai to ask the priests for two rulings on matters of ritual law concerning holiness and purity. Their first answer is that a holy thing does not make an item of food holy when it comes into indirect contact with it. The second judgment is that the touch of a ritually unclean person will make such food unclean.

The point being made is that impurity will remain rampant among the people until the temple can be rebuilt and put into operation.

The fourth oracle (2:20-23) takes place on the same day as the third, on the day when the temple foundation is laid and celebrated (2:18). It is directed to Zerubbabel, whose potential political future is attracting hopeful attention on the part of the people. Perhaps an independent monarchy could be restored under Zerubbabel as scion of the Davidic dynasty. Haggai's words seem to hint at just such an outcome. Zerubbabel is designated as Yahweh's chosen *signet ring* (2:23). In fact, Zerubbabel never became king and would soon disappear from the scene, probably removed by the Persian authorities as a threat. The temple was finally finished in 515.

Zechariah

First Zechariah—Zechariah 1–8

Zechariah is a composite book. Like the scroll of Isaiah, it contains materials from more than one prophet. Chapters 1–8 comprise the visions and oracles of Zechariah, who was a contemporary of Haggai. Eight so-called night visions make up chapters 1–6. In these visions, the prophet first describes what he saw or was shown to him. A divine messenger appears to explain the significance and meaning of what is being presented, and usually the prophet and messenger engage in questions and answers. Chapters 7 and 8 collect other oracles of threat and promise.

Zechariah's first vision entails four riders patrolling on horses (1:7-17). Its message is that Yahweh is returning to Jerusalem in compassion, the temple will be rebuilt, and prosperity will ensue. The second vision is of four horns, symbols of the power of the nations that have troubled Israel, and four *metalworkers* who will destroy those horns (1:18-21). In the third vision (2:1-5) Zechariah sees a man setting out to measure the size of Jerusalem. However, it turns out that no measuring is necessary, because restored Jerusalem will be so populous that a standard city wall would not be appropriate. Rather Yahweh will protect it as a wall of fire.

Chapter 3 reports a fourth vision portraying a dramatic scene in Yahweh's heavenly court. The topic is the suitability of Joshua to serve as high priest. Apparently his birth and life in an impure foreign land is seen as an impediment. The Satan (CEB: *the Adversary*), who serves as prosecutor in Yahweh's courtroom, is ready to accuse Joshua, but Yahweh rebukes the Satan before this can take place. Joshua is purified by being dressed in clean vestments, so that he may perform his priestly duties.

The fifth vision (chapter 4) also deals with the question of leadership in the restored community. Yahweh designates Zerubbabel for greatness. The episode referred to in 4:7-10, involving *capstone, foundation*, and *plumb line* (better: "inscribed metal tablet") portrays the laying of the temple's foundation (mentioned also in Hag 2:18). Zerubbabel presides over this ceremony. The vision itself is of a lampstand in the form of a bowl with seven indented spouts for wicks. Two olive trees channeling oil stand to either side. They represent Zerubbabel and Joshua as leaders who are closely associated with Yahweh. The high priest and civil leaders would continue to share governance roles during the Persian period.

The sixth vision, of a huge flying scroll, points to a reformation of the people's behavior (5:1-4). The little drama of the seventh vision signifies that the land's wickedness is removed (5:5-11). Wickedness in personified as a woman, and she is carried far away by two women with wings. The final vision is of four patrolling chariots (6:1-8). It indicates that Yahweh controls all nations, even those to the north, who were traditionally the people's enemies.

Zechariah 6:9-14 reports an enigmatic incident with political overtones. Zechariah is commanded to prepare a crown (a symbol of high honor) for the priest Joshua, and this eventually ends up as a dedicated memorial in the temple. However, the prophetic oracle associated with this act concerns not Joshua but Zerubbabel. Without being named, Zerubbabel is designated with the messianic title *Branch* (6:12-14; see also 3:8). This one is identified as the temple builder and he will rule from his throne. The priest is beside him so that they work closely together. As things turned out, expectations centered on Zerubbabel came to nothing. Although Zechariah 4:9 seems to predict that he would finish the temple reconstruction, he is not mentioned when this event is reported in Ezra 6:13-18.

Zechariah 9–11 and 12–14

Zechariah 9–11 and 12–14 are two complex collections of prophetic material from a period later than Zechariah himself. Each begins with the heading *A pronouncement. The word of Yahweh*. (Malachi 1:1 begins the same way.) These units are difficult to date, but both are late enough to display some of the characteristics of apocalyptic literature. Zechariah 9:13 speaks of war involving the Greeks. They probably stem from sometime in the late Persian period.

These chapters gather images picturing Yahweh's conflict against foreign nations that will result in a future age of peace and restoration. Community leaders are indicted, one example being the shepherds who appear in chapter 11. The first collection of chapters 9–11 is mostly poetic. Themes of doom dominate, and the figure of Yahweh as the Divine Warrior dominates. The second collection, chapters 12–14, consists mostly of visions, and the theme of promise dominates. Its central topic is the day of Yahweh's action, designated by the repeated phrase *on that day* (12:3, 4, 6, and so forth). Zechariah 9:9-10 is well-known because of its use in the New Testament Gospels. It portrays Jerusalem's coming king, who is victorious and also humble and peaceful.

Malachi

When read directly after Zechariah, it can be seen that Malachi represents the last of three successive units with the heading *A pronouncement. The word of Yahweh* (Zech 9:1; 12:1). It is possible that this little book was once transmitted together with Zechariah. *Malachi* means "my messenger." It is likely that this is not actually a proper name but a repetition of the expression translated as *my messenger* in Malachi 3:1. The topics discussed in the book's question-and-answer format suggest a date after the reconstruction of the temple (3:10) and before the reforms of Nehemiah in 445. Quotations attributed to the audience indicate that disappointment over failed promises has led to skepticism. Does Yahweh really love us (1:2-3)? *Where is the God of justice* (2:17)? *Serving God is useless* (3:14). Malachi engages in dialogue with his audience over these issues.

The prophet highlights a problem with the system of temple sacrifice on which the nation's relationship with God depended. Substandard sacrifices are being offered and priests are failing in their duties (1:6-8, 10; 2:8). But in the coming future, a purified priesthood will be able to offer pleasing sacrifices (3:2b-4). The prophet reveals a strikingly universal perspective about worship. In contrast to the priests who are despising Israel's God, pure offerings are being (or will be) offered to Yahweh throughout the world, since Yahweh's name is (or will be) honored everywhere (1:11, also see 1:5).

The covenant is of central concern. By teaching the people improperly, the priests have corrupted Yahweh's covenant with Levi (2:4-9). The nation as a whole has profaned the covenant by faithless cheating and its practice of divorce (2:10, 14). The book of Malachi motivates its call to return to God and remain faithful in a variety of ways. God is father and creator of all (2:10). God will judge those who commit injustice (3:5). If you stop deceiving God by cheating with respect to proper offerings, prosperity will rain down on you (3:8-12). A day of judgment and deliverance is coming (4:1-3).

Before judgment takes place, God will send someone designated as *my messenger. . . . The messenger of the covenant*, who will cleanse the priesthood (3:1, 3). At the end of the book, this messenger is identified with Elijah. Since Elijah did not die but was carried up to heaven (2 Kgs 2:11), he could be expected to return as a herald of the future. As the final book of the prophetic corpus, the concluding verses of Malachi wrap up the whole of the (torah) Instruction and the Prophets, the first two sections of the Hebrew Bible canon. Readers are called on to remember the teachings of Moses the teacher (4:4) and alerted to the coming of Elijah the prophet (4:5-6).

Joel

Joel is a call to repentance, because the catastrophic Day of Yahweh is at hand. The book cannot be dated, although the late Persian period is often suggested as its time of composition. Joel alludes to the words of earlier prophets, particularly Isaiah, Amos, Obadiah, and Micah. A striking example of this is Joel 3:10, which reverses the well-known peace imagery of swords beaten into plowshares (Isa 2:4 and Mic 4:3) into a call for rearmament. The language of the Day of Yahweh appears in Joel 1:15; 2:1-11; and 2:30–3:16. It is marked by terrifying heavenly portents (2:30-31). These images of *blood and fire and columns of smoke*, darkened sun and reddened moon, anticipate features found in apocalyptic literature. In Joel's case, however, they appear to reflect the natural effects of a dust storm kicked up by the dry desert wind.

Joel is organized according to the two-part pattern found in other prophetic books. Joel 1:1–2:17 portrays disaster and doom and calls for lament and turning away from drunkenness due to trauma. Then the topic changes abruptly, and 2:18–3:21 proclaims positive promises for the future. The approaching Day of Yahweh devastates harvests and livestock (1:15-18). In 2:1-11 the Day is a described in terms of a military assault merged with images of a locust invasion. The prophet urges: *Blow the horn in Zion*, first in order to warn of the coming attack (2:1) and then a second time to call the entire nation together for a ceremony of repentance (2:15). The second half of Joel looks to the future. God will provide peace and abundance (2:18-26) and send the prophetic spirit on men and women of all ages and classes (2:27-29). God will bring judgment upon the nations who have been Judah's enemies (3:2-15).

Jonah

Jonah is different in character from the other prophetic books. In genre it is a short story (or novella), similar to Ruth or Esther. The author takes the name *Jonah, Amittai's son* from prophetic tradition as a prophet from the past era when Assyria and the northern kingdom still existed (2 Kgs 14:25). Jonah focuses not on the shortcomings of Israel but on the issue of Yahweh's relationship to foreign peoples. Foreign sailors prove to be courageous and insightful, and even cry out to Yahweh and offer sacrifice. The hated Assyrians engage in an extraordinary ceremony of repentance at the very moment they hear Yahweh's threat, consisting of but a single sentence. The narrative unfolds in a series of episodes: call and flight (1:1-3), on the ship (1:4-16), inside the fish (1:17–2:10), inside Nineveh (3:1-10), and Jonah's dialogue with God (4:1-11).

The Story

The first episode begins with a standard opening, but immediately has a twist. Jonah gets up as commanded, but flees in the opposite direction from Nineveh. Tarshish was at the far western edge of the world known to the audience. Jonah's goal is to flee from Yahweh (stated twice in 1:3) by leaving Israelite territory, but it turns out that even heading out to sea (a place of rebellious chaos) cannot accomplish this. The reader is not yet told the reason for Jonah's disobedience.

Ironic contrast is drawn between the prophet and the pagan sailors (1:5-16). They pray and take action (jettisoning cargo and casting lots); Jonah sleeps and must be encouraged to pray. The sailors have a fairly good idea of what is going on and are willing to hear Jonah out. His claim in 1:9, *I worship Yahweh . . . who made the sea and the dry land*, sounds ironic. Even after Jonah has told them to throw him overboard, these admirable sailors first row hard to avoid doing that, then confess Yahweh's effective power and ask for understanding. They sacrifice to Yahweh and make solemn promises. Jonah may claim to *worship Yahweh*, but these pagans really do. The *great fish* (1:17) echoes the mythic sea monsters of ancient lore (Pss 74:14; 104:25-26), but Yahweh is in charge and *provided* it.

The author has recycled a previously existing psalm of thanksgiving and put it into Jonah's mouth (chapter 2). Its traditional lament language suits his situation: *belly of the underworld*, *the depths*, and overwhelming waters. Jonah has neither turned away from rebellion nor obeyed, but Yahweh nonetheless orchestrates his rescue.

The action restarts in 3:1-2 with a repetition of Yahweh's command from 1:1-2. This time Jonah responds properly. The (unhistorical) fabulous size of Nineveh increases the entertainment value of the story and intensifies the marvel of its instant and complete repentance. The king and people of Nineveh are portrayed in a completely positive light. They do not need *forty days* (3:4), but react immediately. Their turn away from sin is extraordinary, far beyond what would be considered normal. Even the domestic animals fast and wear mourning clothes, and the king commands everyone to stop evil and violent behavior. The pagan population of Nineveh share with the pagan sailors a belief in the possibility of divine rescue. *Who knows?* We might *not perish* (1:6 and 3:9). Responding to their change of behavior, God rescinds the planned destruction.

After this narrative climax, chapter 4 explores the significance of what has happened. It turns out that Jonah refused to go to Nineveh because he was concerned about what was likely to result from Yahweh's gracious nature. Jonah's anger is deeply ironic, given that he is quoting a proverbial formula about Yahweh's benevolent character that is repeated numerous times in the Old Testament (for instance, Exod 34:6): *you are a merciful and compassionate God* and I do not like that. God's merciful character not only undercut Jonah's desire for Nineveh's destruction but meant that his prophetic prediction did not come true. The story concludes with more humor. God reveals the inner workings of divine mercy to Jonah by rapidly providing a shrub to shade Jonah, a worm to kill it, and a desiccating wind to increase Jonah's misery in the hot sun. Jonah is sorry and angry that the shrub is gone, and God draws out the comparison. Jonah had been outraged at God's mercy toward a huge city, but now is angry because God destroyed a mere bush. God concludes with a rhetorical question: *Can't I pity Nineveh?* It contains 120,000 clueless human beings, to say nothing of all those animals!

The Lesson of Jonah

Jonah uses humor and irony for a didactic purpose. It was commonly thought that Yahweh's election (choice) of Israel was an exclusive matter. The book of Jonah insists that God cares about foreigners too, and that gentiles are capable of faith, concern for neighbor, and changing their lives. Yahweh is not just Israel's national god and not concerned only with the affairs of one people.

Jonah also explores the question of divine justice. Assyria was the textbook example of an evil nation. It had oppressed and destroyed many peoples, including Israel. Nineveh is serving as a proxy for the imperial realm that was in control when Jonah was written, most likely the Persian Empire. If Yahweh is a just God, why has judgment not been visited on the oppressive, imperialist foreigners who dominate us?

Further Reading

James D. Nogalski. *Introduction to the Hebrew Prophets*. Nashville: Abingdon, 2018.

Carolyn Sharp. *The Prophetic Literature*. Nashville: Abingdon, 2019.

Ehud Ben Zvi. *Signs of Jonah: Reading and Rereading in Ancient Yehud*. Journal for the Study of the Old Testament Supplement Series 367. Sheffield, UK: Sheffield Academic Press, 2003.

Part V
WRITINGS

Chapter 20
PSALMS

The Book of Psalms is a collection of Israel's religious poetry. It is the longest book in the Bible, with the most words and chapters. Its Hebrew title describes its contents as *songs of praise* (*tehillim*), rendered in Greek as *psalmoi*. The 150 psalms represent liturgical songs originally used in temple worship along with other poems of various types that originated and were used outside the temple in public and private settings. Psalms is sometimes called the "hymnbook of the Second Temple," although this description tells only part of the story.

Shape and Composition

By their very nature, individual psalms are difficult to date. Tradition has assigned the bulk of them to the authorship of King David, but this attribution is untenable. The headings of many psalms (Psalms 3–41, 51–70, and others) use the expression *of David*, but this seems originally to have indicated not authorship but that they belonged to a collection of psalms whose theme was David as Yahweh's chosen servant. *Of David* means "belonging to the David collection."

The earliest psalms reflect standard poetic conventions known to us from Ugaritic literature, indicating composition in the early monarchic (or even premonarchic) period. Psalm 29, for example, employs language about storm and primordial waters that was used to glorify Baal in Canaanite mythology. Psalm 68 uses similar imagery to extol Yahweh as the awesome Divine Warrior who rides on the clouds, echoing a common way of speaking about Baal (68:4). Psalms that mention royal affairs or ideology, such as Psalms 2, 18, 45, and 110, originated and were first used during the monarchy period, although they continued to be prized and used in later periods. Some psalms, such as 126 and 137, unmistakably refer to Judah's forced resettlement (exile) in the Babylonian period and restoration under the Persians. Other psalms stem from the Second Temple (Persian and perhaps Hellenistic) period.

The book of Psalms in its present form is structured into five books on the analogy of the five books of the Torah (Psalms 1–41, 42–72, 73–89, 90–106, and 107–150). A nearly uniform doxology (poetic praise of God) concludes each of the five books. This can be seen in the closing verses of Psalms 41, 72, 89, and 106. The expression *hallelujah* (praise Yahweh) appears with increasing frequency near the end of the book of Psalms and stands out especially at the beginning and end of each of the last five psalms. Psalms 1 and 2 seem to work together as an introduction to the book as a whole. Psalm 1:1 and Psalm 2:12b create brackets around the two poems by repeating the phrase *truly happy*. Psalm 1 praises God's law and calls for constant meditation on it. The theme of Psalm 2 is kingship, which points to the hope for a future ideal king. These topics represent two of the most important themes in Psalms.

There is persuasive evidence that earlier collections of psalms lie behind the shape of the present book. For example, Psalms 3–41 (now Book I) all have the heading *of David*. Psalms 42–89 (now Books II and III) all use the designation God (*Elohim*) instead of the proper name Yahweh for the deity, and are therefore called the Elohistic Psalter. In fact, Psalm 14 and Psalm 53 are equivalent poems, but the editorial process has changed Yahweh in Psalm 14 to God in Psalm 53. The statement of Psalm 72:20 indicates that it concluded an earlier collection: *The prayers of David, Jesse's son, are ended*. Psalms 120–134 make up a group of songs that were sung by pilgrims going up to Jerusalem. Each of these psalms is headed *A Song of Ascents* (NRSV; CEB: *pilgrimage song*). Many scholars postulate that the long acrostic psalm about God's torah (instruction) (Psalm 119) wrapped up an earlier collection that consisted of Psalms 1–119, and which was later expanded.

The titles and headings that begin most psalms are also part of the editing process. These headings may assert traditional ideas about authorship (Psalm 72, Solomon; Psalm 90, Moses; the Levitical families of Korah and Asaph). Some are musical notes indicating the type of song and musical instruments for accompaniment (Psalms 22 and 55). Because David was increasingly seen as the author of the Psalms, a number of these headings suggest circumstances in his life that might have occasioned their composition. Psalm 3 and 51 are examples of this. Psalm 56 is notable for having accumulated several different kinds of heading material.

Songs of the same genre as those collected in Psalms appear in other Old Testament books. For example, Jonah's prayer voiced while inside the great fish is a psalm of thanksgiving repurposed for its new setting. David's words in 2 Samuel 22 are also found as Psalm 18. Other examples are 1 Samuel 2:1-10 (Hannah's Song), Isaiah 38:9-20 (prayed by Hezekiah), and Habakkuk 3.

Psalms as Poetry

Poetry in biblical Hebrew is characterized by the presence of terse language and parallelism in meaning between lines. Short lines are paired together with *and* or simply set out side by side. These paralleled lines are intended to be connected in some way. Sometimes the two short lines are nearly equivalent in meaning or opposed to each other. At other times, the relationship is less direct. The second line may offer an alternative perspective on the first, as though instructing the reader to consider the first line in light of the second. This more general relationship might be stated as "*x*, and what is more *y*."

Synonymous parallelism, in which meaning is repeated, is the easiest type to grasp.

> Heaven is declaring God's glory;
>   the sky is proclaiming his handiwork. (Ps 19:1)
> Who can ascend Yahweh's mountain?
>   Who can stand in his holy sanctuary? (24:3)

Similar to this is antithetic or contrast parallelism.

> Yahweh is intimately acquainted with the way of the righteous
>   but the way of the wicked is destroyed. (1:6)
> God, listen to my prayer;
>   don't avoid my request! (55:1)

It is common that an element will be left out of one of the lines, so that what is repeated is highlighted while what is skipped over is de-emphasized.

> The earth is Yahweh's and everything in it,
>   the world and its inhabitants too. (24:1)

It what is often called synthetic parallelism, the first line leads to the second line or connects to it in some other, less obvious way.

> Whenever I am in trouble, I cry out to you,
>   because you will answer me. (86:7)

It is often up to the reader to supply the connection.

> Do you work wonders for the dead?
>   Do ghosts rise up and give you thanks? (88:10)

Parallelism can be used to build metaphorical sentences.

> Mountains surround Jerusalem
>   that's how Yahweh surrounds his people. (125:2)

There can be complications to the simple two-line pattern. The opening of Psalm 29 reflects a stair-step pattern that builds up to a conclusion (29:1-2). Parallelism may extend over several verses as in Psalm 29:3-5 (what *Yahweh's voice* does). Repeated refrains appear in Psalm 136 and in Psalm 46:7 and 11. The presence of such a refrain in both Psalm 42:5, 11 and Psalm 43:5 shows that these two are really a single poem that has been divided into two. Psalms 8 and 118 each begin and end with the same words. Several psalms are acrostic poems, in which each line begins with a successive letter of the Hebrew alphabet. Psalm 9 and Psalm 10 together constitute a single, somewhat imperfect acrostic, and Psalms 25, 34, 37, 111, 112, and 145 are other examples. Psalm 119 consists of 22 sections of eight verses each. The verses of each section begin with the same Hebrew letter in alphabetical order. Using this pattern may have helped with the task of memorization, but also communicates the qualities of completeness, artistic beauty, and intellectual sophistication.

The imagery of psalms can be powerful and pleasing. Yahweh is a shepherd (23:1). A wise person is like a flourishing tree (1:3), but the wicked are blown away like dust (1:4). Opposites sometimes appear side by side to indicate totality (*merismus*): *one day . . . one night* (19:2; 22:2).

Laments and Thanksgiving Psalms

One can better understand and appreciate the psalms though a knowledge of their various types or genres and the purposes for which they were initially used.

Laments were intended to motivate God to act in favor of the distressed person (or community) who prayed them. The situation and prayer of Hannah as recounted in 1 Samuel 1 provides an example of when a lament would be employed. The situations described in laments are portrayed colorfully, but are nonetheless generic so that the poem can be used by a variety of sufferers. Typical troubles include sickness, false accusations, harassment by enemies, abandonment by God, and guilt over sin. Petitioners promise that they will offer sacrifice and praise God in the worshipping congregation in order to motivate God to take action (22:22; 54:6). Laments tell a story. They describe the sufferer's plight and rehearse appeals made to God. Sometimes they conclude with an assurance that God has heard and has acted.

For example, Psalm 22 is a prayer for an individual whose problems center on physical sickness (22:14-15) and who is being maligned and oppressed by others (22:6-8, 12-13, 16-18). Past prayers seem to have been to no avail (22:1-2), yet the one who prays nevertheless expresses trust in God's reliability (22:3-5) and nurturing character (22:9-10; the image is of a midwife). In the end, the petitioner expresses confidence in divine rescue (22:21b-24) and describes the sacrifice and praise that will ensue when this takes place (22:25). Other characteristic lament psalms include Psalm 7 (false accusation), Psalm 51 (sin and guilt), and Psalm 59 (enemies). Psalms 79 and 80 are laments intended to be prayed by the community as a whole in response to national disaster.

Laments sometimes feature imprecations and curses against enemies. Many modern readers find these disturbing (for example, Pss 21:9-10; 58:7-9; 109:6-19; 137:9). Such enemies may have been those who took petitioners' sufferings as evidence of wickedness and who accused them without cause and spread rumors. It is sometimes proposed that those identified as enemies were people thought to be causing sickness and adversity by working magic. In communal laments, the enemies are foreign foes.

Thanksgiving psalms were used after God had answered prayer through a lament. In temple worship these songs accompanied the offering of a thanksgiving sacrifice that had been previously promised by the sufferer. A story of divine rescue makes up the core of a thanksgiving psalm. Psalm 116 is a good example. The previous plight is described with generalized and intense language (116:3), the former plea of the one now offering thanksgiving is noted (116:4), and God's deliverance is described (116:8-9). A confession of faith in Yahweh's power and willingness to deliver is proclaimed (116:5-7), and the thanksgiving sacrifice is announced (116:12-14, 17-19). Other typical examples of thanksgiving psalms are Psalms 30, 32, 34, 92, 118, and 138. Psalm 124 is a community song of thanksgiving.

Fig. 15. A reconstruction of a stone altar from Beer-sheba with horns on its corners (see Ps 118:27, for example). These probably were intended to be symbols of power. The original was a little over five feet (1.6 m) in height.

Chapter 20

Hymns

Hymns express praise to Yahweh. Hymns were a feature of temple worship. In Psalm 100:4 worshippers are exhorted:

> Enter his gates with thanks;
> enter his courtyards with praise!

Hymns often begin with a call for praise addressed to worshippers. Then reasons for offering this acclaim are given, grounded in the character and rule of Yahweh. Inspiration for praise may be found in the wonders of creation (as in Psalm 104) or in Yahweh's history of fidelity with Israel (as in Psalm 105). Psalm 33 is typical. Verses 1-3 direct the audience to joyful, musical praise of Yahweh. Then the following verses offer reasons (*because*; 33:4, 9) based on creation and history. Psalm 117 is the shortest psalm and is a compact hymn:

> Praise Yahweh, all you nations!
> Worship him, all you peoples!
> Because God's faithful love toward us is strong,
> Yahweh's faithfulness lasts forever!
> Praise Yahweh!

At the end of the book, Psalms 146–150 are all hymns. The well-known Hebrew expression *hallelujah* often occurs in hymns. This means *praise Yahweh* (*yah* or *jah* is a shortened form of Yahweh).

Enthronement Psalms

An *enthronement psalm* is a special category of hymn with the kingly rule of Yahweh as its topic. Its most characteristic phrase is *Yahweh reigns* (or *Yahweh has become king*; CEB: *Yahweh rules*). The original setting in life for these psalms may have been an annual festival of enthronement celebrated in the temple. Although such a festival is never actually mentioned in the Old Testament, these psalms provide some evidence for a liturgical renewal of Yahweh's kingship, seen as the consequence of Yahweh's creation victory over chaos. Such a celebration might have been thought to guarantee the stability of the created world for the upcoming year. Psalm 82 portrays God as king in the midst of the heavenly council of subordinate gods. God judges and sentences the gods, because they have not provided justice for the marginalized, weak, and poor, but instead have favored the wicked. Psalm 47 celebrates God as king enthroned over the nations (47:2, 8), mounting up to rule accompanied by liturgical acclamation:

> God has gone up with a joyous shout—
> Yahweh with the blast of the ram's horn. (47:5)

Yahweh's reign and enthronement as creator, judge, and victorious Divine Warrior are the themes of Psalms 93, 96, 97, 98, and 99.

Royal Psalms

Royal psalms focus on the king of Judah and his special relationship to Yahweh. Royal marriage is celebrated in Psalm 45. Prayer for the anointed king's success in warfare is the topic of Psalm 20. In Psalm 18, the king offers thanksgiving that Yahweh has granted him victory (18:31-45, 50). Psalm 72 is a prayer for the welfare of the king, whose mission is to do justice and whose long reign brings abundance. Probably utilized as part of a new king's enthronement ritual, Psalms 2 and 110 describe the king's close relationship to Yahweh, using mythic language. According to Psalm 2, the king is Yahweh's *anointed one*, installed by Yahweh in Jerusalem and defended from the plots of enemy kings. Yahweh even addresses the king with a formula of divine adoption:

> He said to me, "You are my son,
> today I have become your father." (2:7)

In Psalm 110, Yahweh assures the king of victory and promises high royal honor and eternal priesthood.

> Sit right beside me [NRSV: *at my right hand*]
> until I make your enemies a footstool for your feet. (110:1)
>
> You are a priest forever in line with Melchizedek. (110:4)

The kings of Judah exercised a role in temple worship. In the centuries after the abolition of Judah's kingship, these royal psalms came to be understood in terms of a divinely promised ideal king, the coming messiah (that is, *anointed one*).

20.1. MESSIAH

Beliefs surrounding Yahweh's promise to the Davidic dynasty continued to play a role in later Jewish and eventually Christian thought. The term *messiah* (anointed) derives from the practice of installing kings and other special persons such as priests by anointing them with olive oil. This title is applied to kings in the royal psalms (2:2; 18:50; 20:6; 28:8; 89:38, 51). By the Hellenistic period, the term *messiah* was employed to speak of a hoped-for future leader, who would be sent by God to inaugurate a time of peace and prosperity. Prophetic promises were interpreted in light of this expectation and applied to the messiah. Both the Qumran community and the emerging Christian movement connected the language of divine sonship to the messianic concept. The New Testament reflects this by using the title Son of God for Jesus. The New Testament Greek also features the title "Son of Man" (KJV; CEB: *Human One*) from a wooden translation in the Septuagint of the Aramaic in Daniel 7:13 (more accurately *one like a human being*). This title had messianic connotations concerning an expected future human leader. *Christ* (Greek *christos*) is a translation of *messiah* or "anointed one."

Zion Songs

In Psalm 137 from the exilic period, the deportees who sit *alongside Babylon's streams* are goaded with the demand, *Sing us a song about Zion* (137:3). Several psalms have Yahweh's special relationship to and protection of Jerusalem as their theme. (*Zion* is a poetic designation for Jerusalem.) Psalms 87 and 122 are examples of Zion songs, which express the joy of living and worshipping in Jerusalem. Psalms 46, 48, and 76 celebrate a conviction that, because Jerusalem is Yahweh's dwelling place, Yahweh may be counted on to protect the city against all enemies. This theme of Zion's inviolability is conveyed by mythic language and motifs associated with Yahweh as Divine Warrior. Chaotic forces and enemy kings attack the city, but are shocked and defeated.

> God is in that city. It will never crumble.
> God will help it when morning dawns (46:5)
>
> Look: the kings assembled themselves,
>   advancing all together—
> when they saw it, they were stunned;
>   they panicked and ran away frightened. (48:4)

The idea that Jerusalem could never be conquered must have been strengthened by Jerusalem's unexpected escape from Sennacherib's assault against Hezekiah in 701.

The prophet Jeremiah preached strongly against the indifference to imminent danger produced by this belief (Jeremiah 7, 26).

Psalms 15 and 24, called *gate liturgies*, reflect the ethical requirements for entrance to temple worship using a question-and-answer format.

> Who can ascend Yahweh's mountain?
> Who can stand in his holy sanctuary? (24:3)

Songs of Trust

Songs of trust express confidence in God's providence and protection. They are characterized by images of security, sheltering, and feeding. According to Psalm 11, Yahweh is the refuge of the righteous against the wicked. In Psalm 23, Yahweh is a nurturing shepherd. Psalm 131 uses the engaging image of a calm and quiet *weaned child* snuggling with its mother in order to express trust. Other songs of trust are Psalms 16, 27:1-6, and 62.

Wisdom and Torah Psalms

Another category of psalms promote wisdom and obedience to divine instruction (*torah*). Psalms 1 and 112 use contrast and metaphor to celebrate wise obedience and rebuke disobedience. Psalms 127 and 128 emphasize the prosperity and happiness that come with obedience, particularly in regard to the blessing of having numerous children. Psalm 37 offers advice about Yahweh's vindication of the wise and righteous and the inevitable fall of those who do wrong. Its expressions of wisdom are similar to those found in the book of Proverbs. Psalm 119 is a massive appeal to honor the torah and keep it perfectly. Almost every verse of this poem contains the word *law* (CEB: *instruction*) or a synonym for it.

Further Reading

J. Clinton McCann. *A Theological Introduction to the Book of Psalms*. Nashville: Abingdon, 1993.

James L. Crenshaw. *The Psalms: An Introduction*. Grand Rapids: Eerdmans, 2001.

William P. Brown. *Seeing the Psalms: A Theology of Metaphor*. Louisville, KY: Westminster John Knox, 2002.

Chapter 21
OPTIMISTIC AND PESSIMISTIC WISDOM: PROVERBS AND JOB

Wisdom

Israel saw the acquisition and practice of wisdom as the key to a productive, happy, and long life. The Hebrew word for wisdom could be used of the skill of an artisan or magician. So wisdom in the biblical sense may be defined as skill in living. This attribute can be taught through proverbial advice. Wisdom had two settings in Israelite culture. In ordinary life, especially in rural towns, certain experienced men and women were recognized as wise. Village wise women are mentioned in 2 Samuel 14:2 and 20:16. This folk wisdom was crystallized into commonplace proverbs. The other venue of wisdom was government and the royal court. It appears that young men were trained in wisdom in some formal way to prepare them for administrative careers. As an indication of such a school setting, the instruction of Proverbs is sometimes directed at *my son* (for example, Prov 2:1; 3:1-2). Wisdom materials were collected by scribes under royal patronage.

Proverbs

The book of Proverbs gathers together both poems about wisdom and individual short aphorisms. Chapters 1–9 and 31 represent longer wisdom poems that pursue various themes. The bulk of chapters 10–30 consists of individual proverbs. These proverbs are pithy two-line poetic observations on reality and lessons intended to improve the lives of those who learn and practice them.

Chapter 21

The compositional history of Proverbs is indicated by headings that introduce originally independent or added units (1:1; 10:1; 22:17 [NRSV]; 24:23; 25:1; 30:1; 31:1). Proverbs 25:1 serves as the title for chapters 25–29 and reveals that one phase of this collection process took place during the reign of Hezekiah. Frequent observations about kings and advice on how to behave with reference to them also point to the monarchy period (for example, 16:13; 20:2; 22:11). The book of Proverbs probably achieved its final shape in the Persian period. Conventionally, Israel attributed its wisdom literature to Solomon (see 1 Kgs 4:32), just as it credited law to Moses and psalmody to David.

Wisdom was an international phenomenon, and there are parallels between Proverbs and Mesopotamian and Egyptian wisdom literature. A striking example of such interconnection is Proverbs 22:17–24:22, which is indirectly related to the Egyptian work *Instruction of Amenemope*. The reference to *thirty sayings* in Proverbs 22:20 alludes to the thirty chapters of that work.

Wisdom is a grammatically feminine noun in Hebrew (*hokmah*), so it was natural to personify it as a woman. In Proverbs 1:20-33, personified Wisdom speaks out publically and with authority as a woman who appeals for the attention of those who have much to learn (CEB: *clueless people*; 1:22). The female figure of Wisdom is praised in 3:13-18. A young man is to call her sister and friend (7:4). She builds a house and invites those who need wisdom to her banquet (9:1-6). Personification is taken further in Proverbs 8, where Wisdom speaks out publically to invite people to learn how to be wise and to promote the benefits she offers. In 8:22-31, Wisdom is portrayed in transcendent terms as a figure who was involved is some way with Yahweh's act of creation. Her opposites are the *mysterious woman* (NRSV: *loose woman*) who would lead the student of wisdom astray (2:16-19; 5:3-14, 20) and Woman Folly (NRSV: *foolish woman*) who calls out to passersby in order to lure them to their doom (9:13-18).

Two core principles are advanced in Proverbs. The first is the correlation between acts and their consequences. This act-consequence relationship is built into the nature of reality.

Laziness brings poverty;
 hard work makes one rich. (10:4)

Those who dig a pit will fall in it;
 those who roll a stone will have it turn back on them. (26:27)

The other distinctive theme of Proverbs is that God is the ultimate source of wisdom and is in charge of events.

Yahweh gives wisdom;
 from his mouth come knowledge and understanding. (2:6)

Optimistic and Pessimistic Wisdom: Proverbs and Job

A person's steps are from Yahweh;
> how then can people understand their path? (20:24)

Therefore, *the beginning of wisdom is the fear of Yahweh* (9:10; also 1:7; 15:33). In the Old Testament, fear of God means both respect for and obedience to God.

Wisdom can be discovered in the ways of the human and natural world (30:18-19), so the person seeking wisdom should observe plants and animals and even the weather (6:6-8; 25:14; 27:18; 28:15; 30:24-31). The wise person is one who knows about the vagaries of human nature. Proverbs teaches that people can be prideful (16:18) and quarrelsome (26:21). Rich people have more friends than the poor (14:20), but poverty with love is better than riches with hatred (15:17). Deprivation motivates hard work (16:26). Two heads are better than one (27:17). Proverbs regularly points to the stock character of the fool, who is dangerously impervious to wisdom.

Safer to meet a bear robbed of her cubs
> than fools in their folly. (17:12)

The capacity to balance wise speech and timely silence is a characteristic of the wise person.

Words spoken at the right time
> are like gold apples in a setting of silver. (25:11)

A sensitive answer turns back wrath
> but an offensive word stirs up anger. (15:1)

Fools who keep quiet are deemed wise;
> those who shut their lips are smart. (17:28)

Proverbs pays a great deal of attention to women. Some of this advice is hostile and negative and serves as a reminder that Israelite society was very male-oriented.

The constant dripping on a rainy day
> and a contentious woman are alike. (27:15)

Like a gold ring in a pig's nose
> is a beautiful woman who lacks discretion. (11:22)

In contrast, Proverbs 31:10-31 celebrates the ancient patriarchal ideal of a good wife. She is hard-working and a good businesswoman. She is single-minded in her devotion to others. Her husband gains public respect. On a different note, Proverbs 5:15-19 urges the husband to remain faithful to his wife, whose sexuality is celebrated.

Chapter 21

Job

Background and Composition

Job is concerned with the question of theodicy, that is, the theological problem of God's justice. The foundation of mainstream wisdom literature, as expressed in Proverbs, was that one could count on a reliable relationship between a person's acts and the consequences that would result. The world made sense, and the application of wisdom could reliably be counted on to bring about prosperity and happiness. However, Job reflects a more skeptical stream of ancient international wisdom thought and literature, one that investigated the issue of undeserved suffering and the apparent failure of divine justice. Parallels to Job exist in Sumerian, Old Babylonian, and Egyptian wisdom literature. The closest known equivalent to Job is *The Babylonian Theodicy* from about 1000 (*COS* 1.154:492–95; *ANET* 601–604). This work is an extended poetic dialogue between a sufferer and his friend over the lack of correspondence between piety and one's lot in life. The friend asserts that the motivations of the gods are unfathomable, but that punishment will ultimately be visited on the wicked.

As a literary exposition of a universal wisdom theme, the book of Job cannot be coordinated with actual history. Job lives in the unidentifiable eastern land of Uz, perhaps in Edom. In Ezekiel 14:14, 20, Job is cited with Noah and Daniel as one of three proverbial righteous worthies of ancient times (see 24.1, NOAH, DAN(I)EL, JOB). Although Job's timeless literary character makes the work difficult to date, the Babylonian or Persian period is usually suggested. The destruction of Judah's national life in the fall of Jerusalem and the exile would naturally have generated anxiety about the causes of suffering, its meaning, and the debatable nature of God's justice.

There is a stark difference in character between the narrative portions that introduce and conclude Job and the poetic dialogues that make up the core of the book. The outer framework of the book comprises an older folktale recounting how Job's innocent and faithful suffering was rewarded in the end with a "happy ending" (1:1–2:13 and 42:7-17). A poetic conversation about suffering and divine justice has been set into this frame (chapters 3–37). These speeches by Job and his dialogue partners are followed by Yahweh's eventual responses to Job and Job's two subsequent statements of submission (38:1–42:6). This process of composition means that there are noticeable differences in outlook between the framing story and the dialogues. The positive ending, in which Job receives back all he has lost and more, undercuts the opinion advanced in the central section that God does not reward and punish people based on their virtue. The name Yahweh is used in the folktale, but the dialogue poems use other divine names instead. In the dialogues, Job's interlocutors represent various positions consistent with theological orthodoxy and mainstream wisdom. Job, in contrast, repeatedly calls God's just nature into question. However, in the end, God unexpectedly disparages the opinions of the friends: *you haven't spoken about me correctly as did my servant Job* (42:7, 8).

21.1. SATAN

The ordinary meaning of the Hebrew word *Satan* is simply the common noun *adversary*. In 1 Samuel 29:4, the Philistines apply this word to David (NRSV: *he may become an adversary to us in the battle*). In early Old Testament texts, Satan was not yet used as a proper name, and a definite article was used to indicate that a particular adversary was intended: *the Satan*. Satan was conceived of as part of Yahweh's governing administration and was one of the subordinate divine beings that made up Yahweh's royal council. In the prologue to Job, Satan assembles with the members of this group and raises questions about Job's integrity (Job 1:6-12; 2:1-6). Satan performs much the same function in accusing the high priest Joshua in Zechariah 3:1-2. These texts do not represent Satan as rebelling against God or advocating evil. Indeed, many Old Testament texts assert that God is responsible for everything that happens, positive or negative (Isa 45:7; Amos 3:6 as translated by NRSV).

Satan eventually developed into a mechanism for defending God against the idea that God was in some way responsible for evil. Second Samuel 24:1 states that Yahweh *incited David* to take a forbidden census. However, when the author of Chronicles used that text as a source, he reported instead that Satan (now used as a proper name without a definite article) was responsible for that incitement (1 Chr 21:1).

Persian religion was dualistic in some of its forms, assigning responsibility for good to the god Ahura Mazda and evil to a sort of anti-god, Angra Mainyu. This outlook may have influenced Jews in the Persian and Hellenistic periods to conceive of Satan as a rebellious, anti-God force. Satan appears in this way in the Pseudepigrapha and the New Testament. (Pseudepigrapha, meaning "falsely named as to authorship," refers to a category of ancient religious books, mostly Jewish in origin and mostly composed before the end of the second century CE.) The crafty snake in the Garden of Eden story is never identified with Satan in the Old Testament.

The Narrative Frame

The framing narrative sets up the problem of Job's suffering, which results from a discussion in the heavenly council of Yahweh. Satan (CEB: *the Adversary*) acts as a sort of prosecuting attorney, spying out the human world. Ironically, it is Yahweh who first spotlights Job as a righteous paradigm (1:8). Yahweh is thus the initial cause of Job's becoming Satan's target, and Yahweh authorizes a step-by-step obliteration of Job's property, servants, and children. Yet Job remains faithful. In a second meeting of Yahweh's heavenly cabinet, Yahweh again raises the issue of Job with Satan (2:3) and gives Satan the authority to strike at Job's own physical health. Beset with disgusting and painful sores and urged by his wife to curse God and die, Job still refuses to *sin with his lips* (2:10). Job's three friends arrive and sit with him until he initiates a dialogue about suffering and the question of divine justice.

As the book approaches it conclusion, the folktale narrative picks up again in 42:7. Yahweh restores to Job twice the property he has lost and blesses him with seven sons and three daughters in order to compensate for those who were killed. Job's beautiful daughters have wonderfully attractive names: Dove, Cinnamon, and Cosmetics Jar (42:14). Job dies happy at the age of 140. Modern readers may find this conclusion too pat and object that a new batch of children cannot really make up for the ones who died, but ancient readers seem to have accepted this as a happy ending. It is important to note that 42:11 unashamedly acknowledges Yahweh's responsibility for Job's suffering.

The Dialogues

Job 2:11-13 introduces Job's three friends, Eliphaz, Bildad, and Zophar, who seem to come from Edom and Arabia, lands famous for wisdom. After a week of silence, Job initiates the dialogue with explosive words. He curses the fact of his birth and wishes he were in the realm of the dead. Job 3:11-19 describes what the hollow and meaningless existence of the dead was thought to be like.

> ### 21.2. HONORING THE DEAD
> Although it was considered unorthodox by the prophets and the final editors of the Old Testament, honoring and maintain-

> ing relationships with dead ancestors was a feature of popular Israelite religion. Deuteronomy 26:13-14 points to a practice of offering food and drink to the dead. Jeremiah 16:5-9 condemns participation in the funeral banquet or *marzeaḥ*. This mourning rite involving eating and drinking is known from Ugaritic sources. Such strong condemnation suggests that rituals involving deceased ancestors remained popular. Tradition located the graves of ancestors such as the patriarchs and matriarchs, Rachel (1 Sam 10:2), Joshua (Josh 24:30), Gideon (Judg 8:32), and Samson (Judg 16:31). This is evidence for a practice of pilgrimage to and veneration of the tombs of ancestral heroes. A monument marking the burial spot of two revered prophets provides another example (2 Kgs 13:20-21; 23:17-18).

The long poetic interchange between Job and his interlocutors is reminiscent of a philosophical panel discussion. A variety of perspectives on suffering and explanations for it are explored. Is human innocence really possible? What does divine justice look like? Job speaks out first. He is followed by his three friends, one after the other. Then a fourth speaker joins in. This is Elihu, who arrives on the scene unexpectedly. Finally and climactically, God speaks, and does so with such power that Job simply admits defeat. At first, Job and his three friends take turns in a nicely structured sequence. However, this orderly structure breaks down at the end of the third repetition of the cycle:

Job (chapter 3) / Eliphaz (chapters 4–5) / Job (chapters 6–7) / Bildad (chapter 8) / Job (chapters 9–10) / Zophar (chapter 11)

Job (chapters 12–14) / Eliphaz (chapter 15) / Job (chapters 16–17) / Bildad (chapter 18) / Job (chapter 19) / Zophar (chapter 20)

Job (chapter 21) / Eliphaz (chapter 22) / Job (chapters 23–24) / Bildad (chapter 25) / Job in three individual speeches (chapters 26–31)

Zophar does not speak in the third round. Instead, what are designated as Job's last words (31:40) are followed by the surprising appearance of a new character, Elihu. He holds forth in chapters 32–37, rebuking both Job and the friends. Elihu extols God's justice, goodness, and grandeur using arguments similar to those of Job's friends.

Chapter 21

The arguments of the three friends overlap with one another and cannot easily be summarized. Eliphaz observes that no person can ever be completely righteous and defends the causal relationship between acts and their consequences.

> Think! What innocent person has ever perished?
> > When have those who do the right thing been destroyed? (4:7)

Bildad also defends God's justice and insists on the certainty of the act-consequence relationship. It is the wicked and not the righteous who suffer. Job's children must have been notable sinners to be treated so brutally by God.

> If your children sinned against him,
> > then he delivered them into the power of their rebellion. (8:4)

The innocence that Job is claiming is nothing but an illusion.

> How can a person be innocent before God;
> > one born of woman be pure? (25:4)

Zophar asserts that Job is suffering for his own sin. Job should face the fact of his sin and repent.

> If you make your mind resolute
> > and spread your palms to him, . . .
>
> Then you will lift up your face without blemish;
> > you will be secure and not fear (11:13, 15)

Job passionately rejects the arguments of his friends concerning his own lack of innocence and the reliability of God's justice. Job asserts that human goodness does not reliably lead to prosperity, nor is there any coordination between misbehavior and misfortune.

> Why do the wicked live,
> > grow old, and even become strong? (21:7)

> It's all the same;
> > therefore, I say God destroys the blameless and the sinners. (9:22)

Job insists on his own virtue and innocence.

> I put on justice, and it clothed me,
> > righteousness as my coat and turban (29:14)

He wishes that God would just leave him alone.

> Why not look away from me;
>> let me alone until I swallow my spit? (7:19)

Job repeatedly expresses the wish that he could state his complaint directly to God (for example, 13:3, 20-28; 23:3-7; 31:35-37). Yet Job also supposes that even if God were to appear to him, God would simply overwhelm him with divine power and intensity.

> If I were to call and he answered me,
>> I couldn't believe that he heard my voice.
>
> Who bruises me with a tempest . . . ? (9:16-17)

And this is exactly how things turn out as the book comes to a close. Yahweh answers Job twice out of a whirlwind (38:1–40:2 and 40:6–41:34).

In essence Yahweh's response to Job is: I have created all the marvels of the cosmos, and you do not have any standing to question me. Yahweh offers two poetic descriptions of creation's wonders. These come as rhetorical questions that challenge Job. Do you have the capacity and understanding to do what I have done and am still doing as creator and overseer of the cosmos? Yahweh's response to Job is overwhelming and rhetorically powerful, but still never really answers Job's questions about justice and the reason for his suffering. Nevertheless, after each of these intense divine speeches, Job responds briefly to submit and declare an end to his defiance (40:3-5; 42:1-6).

> I have indeed spoken about things I didn't understand,
>> wonders beyond my comprehension. (42:3)

Creation in Job

The created world portrayed in Yahweh's final speeches is orderly and full of mysteries that humans can never understand. These two poems use concepts that Israel shared with the mythic thought world of neighboring cultures. In creation, Yahweh shut in the chaotic sea with doors and clothed it with clouds after it had burst forth from the primordial womb (38:8-9). Two monstrous beings, Leviathan and Behemoth, are invoked as wonders beyond human control. Behemoth (40:15-24), described as *the first of God's acts* (40:19) is not just an ordinary hippopotamus (as has been traditionally understood), but a primordial monster. In both the Bible and Ugaritic literature, Leviathan (41:1-34) is the great sea monster who was defeated by the divine creator (Job 3:8; Ps 74:13-14; Isa 27:1). Yet Yahweh can fish for it and treat it like a pet (Job 41:1, 5; see Ps 104:26).

Chapter 21

Further Reading

Leo G. Perdue. *The Sword and the Stylus: An Introduction to Wisdom in the Age of Empires.* Grand Rapids: Eerdmans, 2008.

Gerald H. Wilson. *Job.* New International Biblical Commentary. Peabody, MA: Hendrickson, 2007.

Chapter 22
THE FIVE SCROLLS

The Five Scrolls

In the Jewish canonical tradition, the books of Song of Songs, Ruth, Lamentations, Ecclesiastes, and Esther are grouped together as the Five Scrolls (*Megillot*). Although customs vary in different Jewish communities, each of these books is linked to a religious observance. Song of Songs, with its references to new growth and springtime, is read on Passover (April). Ruth is associated with Shavuot or Weeks (May–June), which celebrates the end of the grain harvest that is an important feature of the book. Lamentations is associated with the observance of the destruction of the First and Second Temples on the Ninth of Av (July–August). Ecclesiastes is coupled with Sukkot or Booths (September–October). A central feature of Purim (March) is the reading of Esther in the synagogue with much animation on the part of the congregation.

Song of Songs

Song of Songs celebrates human erotic love. The title signifies "the greatest of all songs." Another designation is Song of Solomon, which highlights the tradition that he was its author (Song 1:1). Isaiah 5:1-7, Ezekiel 33:32, and the heading of Psalm 45 witness to the performance of love songs in Israel. The inclusion of Song of Songs in the canon was facilitated and justified by a tradition of allegorical interpretation in Jewish and Christian circles. Its description of human love was understood as a metaphor for the reciprocal love relationship between God (as the male lover) and Israel or the church. Alternatively, the woman was sometimes construed as an image of the human soul.

Chapter 22

The book is dominated by the speeches of two lovers, punctuated with observations by others. The woman speaks first (1:2-7), expressing desire for her lover and describing herself, perhaps teasingly, as suntanned: *Dark am I, and lovely* (1:5, 6). Some scholars, however, think she is speaking as a North African woman. Throughout the book, she describes a strong sexual charge between the two lovers (1:12-14; 2:4-6; 8:1-3). He is handsome and desirable (2:3; 5:10-16). She recounts two night episodes or dream sequences. In 3:1-4 she searches for her lover and finds him. In 5:2-7, a potential encounter of the lovers is unfulfilled and ends in violence. She invites him to consummate their love (4:16; 7:11-13; 8:14). The male lover in turn describes her physical beauty and desirability (1:9-11, 15; 2:2; 4:1-15; 5:1; 6:4-9). Song 7:1-8 pays tribute to her by cataloging the beauty of various features of her body.

Two groups provide commentary. The *daughters of Jerusalem* praise the woman and tease her with prompting questions (5:9; 6:1). She speaks to them in a repeated refrain, urging that the relationship of love not move too quickly (2:7; 3:5; 8:4), but also asking them to communicate her desire to her beloved (5:8). Her *brothers* make up a second group of speakers. They are protective about her sexuality (8:8-9; compare 1:6).

Repetition brings unity to an otherwise diffuse composition. The refrain *Who is this?* appears in 3:6; 6:10; and 8:5. A declaration of reciprocal love, *I belong to my lover and he belongs to me*, is spoken by the woman with variations in 2:16; 6:3; and 7:10. She invokes her mother's house twice as the place where they may be intimate (3:4; 8:2). A vineyard is an image of her sexuality, negatively in 1:6 and positively in 8:11-12.

Metaphors are intriguing and engaging. The woman's sexual inviolability is an enclosed garden (4:12) and a wall (8:9-10). *His banner raised over me is love* (2:4). Many metaphors have to do with animals and the fertility of vineyards, gardens, flowers, fruits, and trees. Her eyes are doves (1:15). He is a gazelle (2:9). She is a rose of Sharon (2:1). He is an apple tree (2:3). Springtime is the time for love (2:10-13). The erotic impact of these images is sometimes direct and intense (4:11; 5:4-5; 7:8).

Whether the Song of Songs is read as a celebration of the relationship between God and humanity or of human passion, it testifies to the power of love:

> For love is as strong as death,
>   passionate love unrelenting as the grave.
> Its darts are darts of fire—divine flame!
> Rushing waters can't quench love;
>   rivers can't wash it away. (8:6-7)

Ruth

Ruth is a short story about loyalty in human relationships and Yahweh's hidden role in fostering it. The primary relationship is that between Naomi and her daughter-in-law Ruth. The bond between these two women leads to a marriage relationship between Ruth and Boaz. Naomi also has a relationship to her dead husband Elimelech that requires her to make provisions to continue his lineage and inheritance.

Ruth is often dated to the Persian period, but this is uncertain. The book accepts the assimilation of foreigners like the Moabite Ruth into Judah. This attitude stands in sharp contrast to the xenophobia of Ezra–Nehemiah. Ruth is concerned with the continuity of the Davidic royal line (Ruth 4:18-22). The Jewish canon places Ruth within the Writings. The Christian canon places it after Judges, in line with the book's narrative setting (1:1) and its concern for David's ancestry that points forward into the book of Samuel.

As a short story, Ruth moves in a series of episodes from the statement of problems to eventual solutions. The timetable moves from the start of the barley harvest (1:22) to the close of the wheat harvest (2:23) and then to the time of threshing (3:2). The major narrative problems belong to Naomi. As a widow without living sons, she is without access to material security. In ancient Israel, a woman participated in society's benefits through her relationship to men (fathers, husbands, and sons). A second problem for Naomi is that the family inheritance of her deceased husband Elimelech has been estranged and his name will drop out of memory because their two sons have died without heirs. Naomi blames her troubles on God (1:13, 20-21).

Her speech to the people of Bethlehem sums up her situation: *Don't call me Naomi [Pleasant], but call me Mara [Bitter], for . . . I went away full, but Yahweh has returned me empty* (1:20-21).

Naomi's Problems and Ruth's Loyalty—Ruth 1

The first chapter sets up Naomi's problems, but also introduces the intrepid and loyal character of Ruth. Ten years after her own husband's death, Naomi's sons die. In the world of storytelling, this might be expected, since Ruth's husband was named Mahlon (Sickness) and Orpah's husband, Chilion (perhaps Fragility). In the normal course of affairs, Ruth and her sister-in-law Orpah could only find economic security in their mother's house or with a new husband (1:8-9). Naomi's speech declaring that she is too old to have sons that Ruth and Orpah could marry (1:11-13) subtly introduces the custom of levirate marriage. A widow without a son was to be married to her dead husband's brother (or other relative) in order to have a son by him, who would be considered the son of the dead man for inheritance purposes. This relative would be the *redeemer* (Hebrew: *go'el*). In the case of Ruth (and Naomi), a respected citizen named Boaz will turn out to be one of those who could become a *go'el* (2:20; 3:12-13).

In her pledge of loyalty to Naomi, Ruth, the foreign Moabite, promises that Naomi's god will now become her god, and she takes an oath in Yahweh's name (1:16-17). Ruth's stance reflects the ancient notion that each land and people had their own god and that to move into Yahweh's territory meant to come under Yahweh's divine authority. Glimmers of hope for a good outcome show through the overall gloom of chapter 1 in Naomi's wish that Yahweh might deal faithfully with the younger women (1:8) and the statement that the famine in Judah has been reversed (1:1 and 6).

Hope on the Horizon—Ruth 2

Chapter 2 introduces Boaz to readers, but it is not revealed that he is a potential redeemer until 2:20. Nonetheless, at least he turns out to be a solution to the problem of food security for the two women. Ruth takes the initiative in suggesting that she engage in gleaning during the harvest (2:2). The custom of gleaning, picking up unharvested grain after the reapers have passed, served as a sort of social safety net for the poor (Lev 19:9-10; Deut 24:19). Ruth proves to be a polite and diligent worker (Ruth 2:6-7, 13, 17). The potential for a levirate marriage solution is hinted at by repeated references to Boaz's relationship to Elimelech (2:1 and 3) and in the tantalizing comment that *by chance, it happened* that Ruth was gleaning in Boaz's field (2:3). Could Yahweh be involved in this happy coincidence? The possibility of a levirate marriage becomes explicit in 2:20. Naomi seems to have some kind of stratagem involving Boaz in mind when she tells Ruth to *go out with his young women* and not to glean *in another field* (2:22). It is promising that Ruth has *found favor* in the eyes of Boaz (2:2, 10, 13). Boaz has complimented Ruth on her loyalty (2:11) and has been kind and protective (2:8-9; 14-16). Yet there is a serious obstruction to the desirable outcome of a levirate marriage in that nothing more in the way of a relationship develops between Ruth and Boaz. Boaz seems unaware of the ironic implications of the blessing he has spoken to Ruth: *May you receive a rich reward from Yahweh, the God of Israel, under whose wings you've come to seek refuge* (2:12).

Weeks pass (2:23). Boaz needs to be made aware of his potential to function as redeemer.

A Solution, Almost—Ruth 3

Naomi, however, has a plan. When harvests concluded, the grain had to be threshed (beaten or trampled to separate the grain from hulls) and winnowed (thrown up in the air so that the wind could blow the husks away). This process took place on a *threshing floor*, which was a high, level area outside of town. Boaz would be sleeping out there by his grain piles to protect them. Naomi's strategy, outlined in 3:3-5, is a dangerous one and depends of the good character of Boaz. The worrisome implications of Ruth's bath and perfume and lying down beside Boaz in a dark, deserted place are obvious. The moment of highest tension comes when Ruth reveals her identity and in effect ask Boaz to marry her: *Spread out your robe [or wing] over your servant, because you are a redeemer* (3:9).

For a man to spread his robe over a woman was to claim her in marriage (Ezek 16:8). Ruth's words echo what Boaz wished for her in 2:12.

Boaz compliments Ruth on her faithfulness (*ḥesed*) in seeking a redeemer and not just any husband (3:10). Significantly, he calls her *a woman of worth* (3:11). This expression of high social status is the feminine equivalent of what Boaz is called in 2:1: *a man of worth*. He is saying that Ruth would make a proper wife for him. She is not a mere immigrant or servant (contrast 2:10, 13). Boaz protects her reputation (3:14) and indicates his intentions with a gift to Naomi (3:15, 17). Naomi's problem is almost solved, but a snag still remains. Boaz is one of the redeemers and is willing to act, but it turns out that there is another male relative who has first claim on Ruth and the property of Elimelech (3:12-13). Will that closer relative take on the role of redeemer and acquire the land of inheritance and Ruth?

A Happy Ending—Ruth 4

Legal processes took place in public in the open area near the town gateway. Boaz's enactment of the rights and responsibilities of being redeemer required a quorum of ten elders to serve as witnesses. They must observe and be ready to testify to a verbal exchange and a visible dramatic action. Boaz's first statement of the situation to the other potential redeemer carefully omits any reference to Ruth (4:3-4). The dramatic tension rises when the other man agrees to serve as redeemer. However, when Boaz lays out the whole situation, the other candidate withdraws. He takes off his sandal to signal publically that he is relinquishing his option to acquire the property and Ruth (4:7-8). Boaz speaks his intentions before the witnesses and the deal is done. Naomi's problem is solved. The marriage of Ruth and Boaz is intended to preserve the dead man's name for his inheritance so that the name of the dead man might not be cut off (4:10).

Good wishes and the actual marriage follow. Ruth will be like Rachel and Leah, the fertile wives of Jacob, and like Tamar who began the family line that led to David. Ruth's baby boy Obed is designated as Naomi's son for genealogical purposes, and she validates this claim publically (4:16). Verses 18-22 establish the genealogical link to David.

Chapter 22

The Theology of Ruth

The concept of covenant loyalty (*ḥesed*) is central to Ruth, and the word appears three times. First, Ruth demonstrates this loyalty as a widow to her dead husband and to Naomi (1:8; CEB: *deal faithfully*) by remaining with Naomi when she returns to Judah. Second, Yahweh is faithful to both the living (Naomi, Ruth) and the dead (their husbands) in that Boaz is a potential *redeemer* (2:20). Third, Boaz declares that Ruth has acted faithfully by seeking marriage with him as redeemer and not some young man (3:10).

From start to finish the human actors wish for (1:8-9; 2:12; 4:11-12) and point to (1:6; 2:20) God's gracious activity. In the end, Yahweh gets credit for the happy ending (4:13-14), just as Yahweh was blamed at first for Naomi's tragedy (1:13, 21). Unlike most other places in the Old Testament, however, the stage for God's activity is not creation, history, or the fate of the nation, but ordinary life. Yahweh works in the context of sustenance, social interaction, marriage, and birth. God's activity in Ruth is hidden and takes place behind the scenes. Ruth simply happens *by chance* on a certain field (2:3). Yahweh lets her get pregnant (4:13). Yet in the end it is really human loyalty, determination, courage, and character that bring about the desired outcome.

Lamentations

The fall of Jerusalem to the Babylonians in 586 was the ultimate national catastrophe for Judah and a traumatic experience for its inhabitants. Those trapped in the besieged city suffered terrible famine, which led to horrifying acts of inhumanity (Lam 2:20; 4:3-10). About a month after Babylonian troops first broke through the city's defenses, a Babylonian official burned the royal palace, the temple, and other important structures. At least portions of the city's defensive wall were torn down.

Lamentations is a collection of five poems that grieve over the fall of Jerusalem and the subsequent deportations of many of its prominent citizens. These poems were probably originally sung in public commemorations, such as described in Zechariah 7:1-7; 8:19. These observances may originally have taken place at the site of the destroyed temple (Jer 41:4-5). In the Christian canon, Lamentations follows Jeremiah, acknowledging the tradition that he was its author.

Three of the five poems begin with the traditional language of a dirge (for example, 2 Sam 1:19; Isa 1:21). Their initial Hebrew word is usually translated *How!* or *Alas!* (Lam 1:1, 2:1, 4:1; CEB: *Oh, no!*) In fact, this word serves as the title of the book in Hebrew. Four of the poems (chapters 1–4) are alphabetic acrostics. Chapter

5 is not a formal acrostic, but it does have 22 lines, which is the number of letters in the Hebrew alphabet. Using the tightly structured form of an acrostic may have been a way of moderating the emotional turmoil of those who utilized these poems. In Hebrew, the poetic meter of chapters 1–4 is of a sort that was generally employed in mourning songs, featuring lines with three stresses in the first part and two in the second part (*qinah* meter).

Lamentations 1 portrays the plight of the ruined city, contrasting its previous situation with its present affliction.

> Once a queen over provinces,
>   she has become a slave. (1:1)

Jerusalem is a once-majestic woman who is now disgraced and humiliated. She has been abandoned by all because of her misdeeds. Verses 1-11 portray her ordeal. Then Zion speaks out for herself in 1:12-22. Chapter 2 pictures the city's physical destruction and explicitly says that Yahweh is the one who caused this catastrophe. The horrors of the siege are reflected in chapter 4:

> The hands of loving women
>   boiled their own children
>   to become their food. . . . (4:10)

In chapter 5 the approach shifts to that of a communal lament psalm. The nation's sufferings are described in order to motivate God to act on its pleas for mercy.

The mood is almost completely pessimistic except for chapter 3, where some glimmer of hope is allowed to show through in 3:21-33. Whatever hope is possible can rest only on Yahweh's faithful and merciful character, as repeatedly confessed in the Old Testament (for example, Exod 34:6-7; Ps 103:8; Jonah 4:2):

> Certainly the faithful love of Yahweh hasn't ended;
>   certainly God's compassion isn't through! (Lam 3:22)

Lamentations would have helped the nation come to terms with questions raised by the catastrophe of 586. The book acknowledges that what happened was the just judgment of God. It is significant that Lamentations never mentions the Babylonian enemy by name. God is the true cause of these troubles. The appropriate response to what has happened is hesitant repentance.

> Return us, Yahweh, to yourself.
>   Please let us return! . . .
> Unless you have completely rejected us,
>   or have become too angry with us. (5:21-22)

Chapter 22

Ecclesiastes

The Hebrew name of this book is *Qoheleth*, a word denoting someone who gathers an assembly or who speaks or leads in an assembly. This is translated as "Preacher" or "Teacher," the one who speaks (for example, 1:1-2; 12:10). The Christian canon places Ecclesiastes among other books attributed to Solomon. Ecclesiastes is difficult to date, but features similar to Epicurean and Stoic philosophy suggest the early Hellenistic period.

In format, the book is a royal testament, that is, the supposed words of a king who imparts a legacy of wisdom in a first-person, autobiographical style. However, Ecclesiastes does not advocate the standard approach to wisdom that promoted it as a way to live a full and satisfying life. Instead, the Teacher emphasizes the contradictions of human existence and limits on what can be known. The philosophy of the Teacher is based on thoughtful observation of how life actually works. Variations on the assertion *I have seen* appear throughout the book (1:14; 3:10, 16; 4:1; 6:1; 10:5, 7, and so forth). Ecclesiastes seeks to correct simplistic views about wise living.

The author takes on the persona of Solomon (1:12), Israel's definitive possessor of wisdom (1 Kgs 4:29-34; Proverbs). The Teacher begins by recounting his quest to discover what is of value and profit in life. He considered the value and role of wisdom in the affairs of life (1:12-14). Then he pursued pleasure and the magnificence he could achieve as king (2:1-11). In the end these experiences taught him that neither wisdom nor self-indulgence can lead to anything but futility. This disappointing truth is summed up repeatedly with a word that is traditionally translated as *vanity* (for example, 1:2, 14; 2:11; CEB: *pointless*). This word means insubstantial breath or vapor and occurs over thirty times in Ecclesiastes. The vanity formula provides brackets for the book:

> Perfectly pointless, says the Teacher, . . .
>   everything is pointless. (1:1; 12:8)

All is empty and futile because, in spite of what traditional wisdom teaches, one's acts and one's fate do not reliably correspond: *The righteous person may die in spite of their righteousness; then again, the wicked may live long in spite of their wickedness* (7:15; see 9:2-3, 11).

People work hard and then have to leave their property to another person:

> Sometimes those who have worked hard with wisdom, knowledge, and skill must leave the results of their hard work as a possession to those who haven't worked hard for it. (2:21; see 6:2)

Experience shows that there is no lasting profit or gain in hard work or in any endeavor (1:3; 2:11; 3:9; 5:15-16).

There is a fitting time for everything, and what is appropriate to do depends on what time it is (3:1-8). There is

> a time for loving and a time for hating
> > a time for war and a time for peace. (3:8)

Traditional wisdom taught that it is advantageous to understand what to do at the proper time. However, the human tragedy is that one can never actually know in what sort of time one is living at any given moment (3:11; 8:6-7; 9:12).

In the end the fact of death robs life of meaning (3:20-21; 9:3-6): *the same fate awaits everyone* (9:3). This point is made poignantly in 12:1-7. The physical degeneration of old age robs life of its pleasures, and then you die.

The Teacher is skeptical and pessimistic, but still has advice to share. Life may be pointless, but live it to the fullest anyway. Eat with enjoyment and drink with a merry heart; enjoy the work you have been given to do and the prosperity God has granted you (2:24; 5:18; 8:15; 9:7-10). Appreciate the goods things that come from God by delighting in them (3:12-13). Two epilogues were added later to soften the book's skepticism and unconventional approach. One says Teacher was wise and gathered and honestly evaluated many sayings that are provocative and stimulating (12:9-11). The other says the bottom line of all this wearisome study is to revere God and keep God's commandments (12:12-14).

Esther

The story of Esther is inextricably linked to the exuberant festival of Purim, which celebrates the deliverance of the Jewish people from annihilation by intolerant enemies. It is striking that Esther (in its Hebrew Bible version) never mentions God directly. Esther was probably composed in the late Persian or early Hellenistic period. There is no reason to treat this melodramatic tale of palace intrigue, full of exaggerations and improbabilities, as a historical report. Nevertheless, details about Persian court life and administration have been incorporated in order to supply verisimilitude and an atmosphere of exotic foreignness. Esther provides an etiology for the festival of Purim. The day of reckoning for the Jews and their enemies is determined by casting a lot (*pur*), giving the holiday its name (3:7; 9:24, 26). Two letters sent out near the end of the book enjoin the celebration of Purim on Jews throughout the Persian Empire (9:25-26, 31-32).

22.1. PURIM

Purim is mentioned in 2 Maccabees 15:36 as Mordecai's Day. It takes place on the fourteenth day of Adar (or on the fifteenth day in Jerusalem, based on an interpretation of 9:18-21). Purim is marked by the boisterous reading of the scroll of Esther in the synagogue, wearing costumes, distributing gifts of food, and dispensing charity. In the public reading of the Esther scroll, the name of Haman the villain is "blotted out" by raucous noisemaking. The names of his ten sons in Esther 9:7-10 are traditionally read together in a single breath to indicate that they died simultaneously.

Esther features an intriguing cast of characters.

Ahasuerus, king of Persia, is usually identified with the historical Xerxes I (485–465). He reveals himself as weak and detached from the affairs of his empire.

Vashti, the queen of Ahasuerus, refuses to parade her beauty before a party of the king's guests. She thus loses her position and opens the way for Esther to take her place.

Mordecai, a wise Jew and royal official, is a kinsman and foster parent of the orphan girl Esther.

Esther, the beautiful queen and secret Jew, is at first fearful and compromising, but rises to the occasion in order to save her people.

Haman, the villain, is descended from those who were hereditary enemies of the Jews.

Zeresh, Haman's wife, gives her husband advice.

The Plot of Esther

The complex plot opens with the story of how Esther becomes queen by replacing Vashti (1:1–2:18). The two Jewish heroes are introduced. The reader learns of matters that will be important for the story: the king's dangerous anger and drinking habits (1:10-12), the irrevocability of *the laws of Persia and Media* (1:19), and the efficient Persian postal system (1:22). The humorous byplay concerning threats to the state of marriage in the empire (1:16-22) makes it clear that Ahasuerus needs better advisors (like Mordecai). Future problems are foreshadowed by the secret of Esther's Jewishness (2:10).

In 2:19-23, Mordecai discovers an assassination plot directed against the king and communicates this to the king through the agency of Queen Esther. Even though his deed is recorded, it is not rewarded.

Chapter 3 introduces Haman and his plot to destroy the Jews on a day he determines by lot. His hostility is triggered by Mordecai's refusal to bow to him as required by a royal decree. Haman belongs to a group who are hereditary enemies of the Jews (the Agagites), and his anger at Mordecai morphs into a plan to destroy all the Jews. Couriers are sent out with instructions to annihilate all Jews on the thirteenth day of the month of Adar.

In chapter 4, Mordecai learns of this and sends an appeal to Esther to intercede to save her people. However, there is a problem. She is not permitted to go to the king without his invitation, on pain of death, and he has not summoned her for a month. Encouraged by Mordecai, however, she resolves to take the chance: *Even though it's against the law, I will go to the king; and if I am to die, then die I will* (4:16).

In chapter 5, she presents herself, and the king admits her. When he asks her to name her request, Esther does not immediately ask for the Jews to be saved. It cannot be that simple, because *the laws of Persia and Media* can never by changed (1:19). Instead Esther invites the king and Haman to a banquet. Yet at that banquet she does nothing but invite them to a second banquet. The story is designed to tease the reader and create dramatic tension.

Before the climactic second banquet, however, two significant developments occur. Haman is advised by Zeresh to erect a seventy-five-foot-high stake (CEB: *pointed pole*) on which to impale Mordecai (5:14). Meanwhile, as recounted in chapter 6, the sleepless king discovers the record of how Mordecai saved his life. When the king asks Haman for advice on how properly to honor a royal favorite, Haman thinks that he himself is meant and suggests a display of public acclaim. Ahasuerus then orders Haman to perform this honor for Mordecai, and Haman is humiliated.

Chapter 7 recounts Esther's second banquet, at which she makes her request, revealing that Haman is the one behind the plan to kill the Jews. A misunderstanding (7:7-8) leads to Haman's immediate impalement on the stake he had prepared for Mordecai. In chapters 8 and 9, the danger to the Jews is averted. The king gives royal authority to Mordecai, and Mordecai sends out an edict that permits the Jews to engage in a pre-emptive strike against those who were authorized to destroy them by the previous, irreversible royal decree. On the very day set for their own annihilation, the Jews are able to massacre their enemies. They do this on the thirteenth day of Adar and then celebrate on the fourteenth day, which is when most Jews observe Purim. However, in the capital city Susa the slaughter continued for two days, so that rest and celebration took place on the fifteenth. For this reason, Jews in Jerusalem (and a few other cities thought to have been walled since the days of Joshua) celebrate Purim on the fifteenth of Adar.

Chapter 22

Additions to Esther

The Septuagint form of Esther incorporates additions to the earlier text preserved in the Hebrew Bible. This longer Esther is the version represented in the Catholic and Orthodox canons. The supplementary material (Additions to Esther) consists of six units. These report a revelatory dream granted to Mordecai, copies of two decrees from the royal administration, back-to-back prayers by Mordecai and Esther, a highly dramatized version of Esther's unbidden appearance before the king, and finally a notice that Mordecai's dream was fulfilled. With these additions and some other small changes, the resulting version presents a more dramatic and more conventionally religious story. The two Jewish heroes pray before Esther goes before the king. God clearly influences events. Esther is shown to be someone concerned with keeping Jewish law and who detests having to sleep with the uncircumcised king.

Further Reading

Linda Day. *Esther*. Abingdon Old Testament Commentaries. Nashville: Abingdon, 2005.

Judy Fentress-Williams. *Ruth*. Abingdon Old Testament Commentaries. Nashville: Abingdon, 2012.

Chapter 23
EZRA–NEHEMIAH AND 1 AND 2 CHRONICLES

Ezra–Nehemiah

Ezra–Nehemiah is a single book in the Jewish canonical tradition and in the Septuagint. Christians of the third and fourth century CE were responsible for its division into two books. It depicts the struggles of those Jews who returned from deportation to revive their religious and community life. When Cyrus the Great completed his takeover of the Babylonian Empire in 539, those Jews who had been deported to Babylon had lived there for fifty or sixty years. Many had adjusted to life there and some had prospered. Some of these expatriates, however, took the opportunity offered by the new Persian regime to return to Jerusalem and the province of Yehud (Judah). There they rejoined other worshippers of Yahweh who had remained in the land. The returnees sought to impose their vision of Yahwism on the local population. This vision emphasized genealogical purity and conformity to a version of divine instruction and worship that had been preserved by the priests of the exile community. This group of returnees was able to rebuild the temple and institute worship there relatively quickly, by 515, but further progress was hampered by poverty, internal dissension, and the hostility of outsiders. These included rival Yahweh worshippers who lived to the north in the area of Samaria. Given these obstacles, the city wall of Jerusalem could not be rebuilt until 445.

23.1. CYRUS CYLINDER

Sometime after he completed his conquest of Babylon in 539, Cyrus sponsored a dedicatory building inscription reviewing and celebrating his actions. The Cyrus Cylinder is a piece of effective propaganda in which Cyrus presents himself as the liberator of Babylon. He claims that the god Marduk chose him for this task and supported him. His army treated the population of Babylon well. He was welcomed with joy. He returned the divine images that had been carried off from their shrines by his incompetent and impious predecessor, Nabonidus. Some exiled peoples were allowed to return to their homeland (*ANET* 315–16; *COS* 2.124:314–16). This policy of repopulating subjugated territories would have increased tax revenues and boosted stability in those regions. In a decree presented in Ezra 1:1-4, Cyrus commands deported Jews to return to Jerusalem and rebuild its temple. Rather than being a copy of an actual proclamation, this text appears to be a literary representation of the policies of Cyrus as reflected in the Cyrus Cylinder. In contrast, the decree of Ezra 6:3-5 that concerns the reconstruction of the temple is more likely to be genuine.

Fig. 16. Cyrus Cylinder. Following the long-standing practice of instituting reform policies at the beginning of one's reign, after conquering Babylon Cyrus the Great commissioned this inscription to serve as a foundation deposit within an important temple there. Although the cylinder itself was hidden from sight, its text would have been widely disseminated for propaganda purposes.

Ezra–Nehemiah was written in about 400 BCE in order to encourage the restored community led by those who had returned from Babylon. The book upholds their legitimacy and divine election. They are not to despair over their lack of power or the hostility of neighboring peoples. They are to adhere to the priestly instruction of Moses that had been brought back from Babylon. Ezra–Nehemiah advocates an exclusivist point of view. The faithful community must remain pure and remain apart from other groups. Because marriage involves extensive social and religious contact between families, mixed marriages must by avoided and even dissolved.

The outlook of Ezra–Nehemiah is similar to that of 1 and 2 Chronicles. A significant difference, however, it that Chronicles has a moderately positive view of the northern kingdom of Israel, whereas Ezra–Nehemiah totally disparages the northern Yahwists of Samaria. Its opinion is that the only true worshippers of Yahweh are members of the Jewish community centered on Jerusalem. The book called 1 Esdras is part of the Protestant Apocrypha, but it is not among the deuterocanonical books of the Catholic canon. Its narrative parallels 2 Chronicles 35–36, Ezra, and Nehemiah 8:1-13.

Ezra–Nehemiah as History

The historian who composed Ezra–Nehemiah used numerous sources. Many of these documents are clearly genuine, but some appear to be later reconstructions. These include:

- copies or imitations of official documents: Ezra 1:2-4; 6:3-5.

- letters: Ezra 4:8-22; 5:7-17; 6:6-12; 7:12-26; Neh 6:2-9.

- inventory lists: Ezra 1:9-11; 8:26-27.

- rosters and census rolls: Ezra 2:1-70 [= Neh 7:6-73a]; 8:1-14; 10:18-43; Neh 3:1-32; 9:38–10:27; 11:3-24, 25-36; 12:1-26.

Some of these texts are in Aramaic, which was the language of the Persian imperial government.

Much of Nehemiah reproduces a source document that scholars call the Memoirs of Nehemiah. This is a first-person account of Nehemiah's public career, intended to justify his public actions. The Memoirs of Nehemiah lies behind Nehemiah 1–7; 11:1-2; 12:31-43; and 13:4-31. The final words of the document are, *Remember me, my God, for good*, that is to say, "to my credit." It is generally thought that this is a genuine autobiographical account produced by Nehemiah himself.

There are several historical problems in Ezra–Nehemiah. First, the documents quoted in Ezra 4:6-23 are out of place chronologically. The context of chapters 3–6 describes the rebuilding of the temple. However, the communications reproduced in 4:6-23 actually refer to opposition to rebuilding the wall of Jerusalem, something that did not take place until many years later. Second, there is a chronological gap of over fifty years between the completion of the temple at the end of Ezra 6 (515) and the start of Ezra's mission in Ezra chapter 7 (458). This half century is simply collapsed into a simple *After this* (7:1).

Third, the author seems to have been in error in portraying the missions of Ezra and Nehemiah as overlapping occurrences. Ezra and Nehemiah appear together when Ezra reads out the instruction of Moses (Neh 8:9; also in 12:26, 36). However, the date of Ezra's commission was most likely 458 (Year 7 of Artaxerxes I) and that of Nehemiah's appointment was definitely 445 (Year 20 of Artaxerxes I). If Nehemiah had indeed been in attendance when Ezra read out the instruction, Ezra would have waited thirteen years after his arrival before carrying out the most important task of his commission. It seems likely that Nehemiah's two terms as governor did not begin until after the mission of Ezra had concluded. It should be noted that some scholars maintain that Ezra was appointed much later, in 398 by Artaxerxes II (404–359). Neither Ezra nor Nehemiah is mentioned in any extra-biblical sources.

Rebuilding the Temple—Ezra 1–6

Ezra–Nehemiah presents the history of the restoration of the Jewish community in three episodes. In the first of these, Sheshbazzar and then Zerubbabel rebuild the temple at the instigation of Cyrus (Ezra 1–6). An edict of Cyrus permits the Babylonian Jews to return to Jerusalem, commands the rebuilding of the temple, and returns captured temple vessels (Ezra 1:2-4). *Sheshbazzar the prince of Judah* (1:8, 11) serves as leader of this first returning group. It is generally thought that this is a reference to Shenazzar, who was a son of King Jehoiachin, although this assumption is hardly certain. The leader mentioned more often in the events surrounding temple rebuilding is Zerubbabel, who was one of Jehoiachin's grandsons. Sacrificial worship begins immediately on a rebuilt altar (3:2-4), and in the second year of the return (537) some sort of foundation ceremony takes place (3:8-13). However, it would not be until 520 that serious construction work began. The temple was completed and dedicated in 515 (Ezra 5–6). This Second Temple, with later expansions to the courtyard area, would remain the epicenter of Jewish worship until it was destroyed in 70 CE.

Ezra Proclaims the Law—Ezra 7–10, Nehemiah 8–10

After approximately fifty years, the second episode in the story of Ezra–Nehemiah begins when the Persian king Artaxerxes I commissions the priest Ezra in

458 BCE to create a purified community through promulgating divine law. These events surrounding Ezra's mission are described in Ezra 7–10 and Nehemiah 8–10. According to Ezra 7, Ezra is commissioned by the king to lead back another group of returnees, regularize temple worship, and promulgate and enforce the law of God and the law of the king. This assignment is consistent with Persian imperial policy in regard to the religion of its subject populations. When he arrives, Ezra confronts the problem of mixed marriages between Jewish men and foreign wives. He appoints an investigative commission and calls a public assembly, which leads to a mass divorce (Ezra 9–10).

The climax of Ezra's activity takes place when Ezra publically reads out the torah of Moses (CEB: *Instruction scroll from Moses*) to an inclusive national gathering in Jerusalem (Nehemiah 8). Levites are described as providing an explanation and interpretation of the law for the common people (8:7-8). This may imply simultaneous translation from Hebrew into the more commonly understood Aramaic. The identity of Ezra's instruction document remains uncertain, although it has traditionally been equated with the Torah portion of the Hebrew Bible. It probably refers to some version of the legal elements of the Priestly Writing (P) now incorporated into the Pentateuch. This event is followed by a celebration of the Feast of Booths and a ceremony of fasting and confession (Nehemiah 9).

Nehemiah Rebuilds the Wall—Nehemiah 1–7 and 11–13

The third episode has been partially interleaved with matters concerning Ezra in the compositional structure of Ezra–Nehemiah. It begins when Artaxerxes I appoints Nehemiah as governor. He is tasked with rebuilding Jerusalem and its wall (Neh 2:1-8). Nehemiah served as governor from 445 to 433 and then served a second term. Upon his arrival, Nehemiah engages in a nighttime inspection of the derelict wall and devises a plan to reconstruct it (2:11–3:32). Individual family groups in the city are given responsibility for work on designated sections. They work alongside crews from the rural areas of Judah. Those rural work parties may have been paid by the elite Jerusalem families responsible for those sections.

Persian authorities may have encouraged the refortification of Jerusalem so that it could serve as a strong point to strengthen the approaches to Egypt. A revolt in Egypt against the Persian administration had begun about 460 and had been supported by Athens. However, Nehemiah's project is understandably opposed by Sanballat, governor of the province of Samaria immediately to the north, and leaders of other neighboring population groups. This threat of outside intervention forces Nehemiah to delegate some of his personnel to provide military protection and obliges the workers to keep weapons near to hand (Nehemiah 4). Nehemiah also has to alleviate the economic distress of the non-elite classes needed to labor on the wall

(Nehemiah 5). These low-income people have had to borrow from the rich in order to survive and pay their taxes. As a result, they are losing their lands and falling into debt slavery. Nehemiah negotiates a remission of debts and an end to the practice of taking property and persons as pledges when lending money. He makes some personal economic sacrifices as well. In the end, in spite of various attempts to stop the project and undermine his authority, Nehemiah succeeds in completing the wall in a mere fifty-two days, even if the city's population remains small in comparison with the size of the fortified city (Nehemiah 6–7).

To solve this problem, Nehemiah devises a plan to increase the population of Jerusalem by resettling some of the outlying populace into the city (Nehemiah 11). Nehemiah 13 reports on other reforms in his second term, involving an equitable distribution of temple resources to its personnel, curbing violations of the Sabbath for commercial purposes, and dealing with the continuing problem of intermarriage with foreigners. Unlike Ezra's earlier draconian measures, Nehemiah's response does not require the dissolution of mixed marriages already in effect, but bans intermarriage in the future. Marriage to outsiders has resulted in some children being unable to speak *the language of Judah* (13:24), so limitations on the practice must have seemed necessary to protect ethnic and religious identity. However, opposition to intermarriage represents only one side of biblical tradition. For example, Ruth was a Moabite but was celebrated as David's great-grandmother.

Later Developments in the Persian Period

Two of Nehemiah's opponents, Sanballat the governor of the province of Samaria and Tobiah (Neh 2:10; 6:14), would prove to be particularly significant for future developments. Both of these men were Yahwists. Sanballat is mentioned in a significant extra-biblical source, the Elephantine papyri, along with his sons Delaiah and Shelemiah. According to Nehemiah 13:28, one of his daughters had been married into the family of the high priest. His descendants seem to have remained in control of Samaria up to the beginning of the Hellenistic period. Tobiah was connected to the high priestly family and was important enough to have a room in the temple compound (Neh 13:4-5, 7). His designation as *the Ammonite* indicates that the power base of his family was in the area east of the Jordan. It seems likely that it was descendants of this Tobiah who emerged in the following centuries as the Tobiads, a powerful Jewish family from the Transjordan area.

Surprisingly little is known about developments in the province of Yehud in the century after Nehemiah. The sequence of its successive governors and high priests can only be reconstructed with some guesswork. The Elephantine papyri, which date from about 495 to 399, reveal the existence of a military settlement of Jews in Egypt.

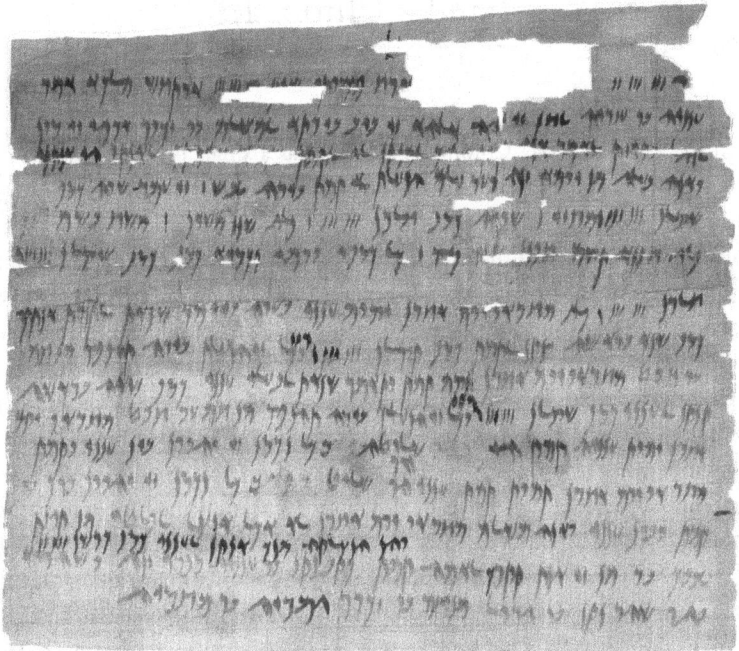

Fig. 17. The Elephantine papyri provide insight into Jewish life in the Egyptian diaspora. This marriage document, dated in 449, is a request by one Ananiah to the father of Tamut for her hand in marriage. It was folded into a linen wrapper and secured with a mud seal.

23.2. ELEPHANTINE PAPYRI

Displaced Jews formed a community on the island of Elephantine in the Nile River, which became a Persian military garrison under the Persian king Cambyses starting about 525. A large collection of documents from this community, consisting of Aramaic letters, contracts, and literary texts, reveals information about the social and religious life of those fifth-century diaspora Jews. The community had its own temple and priesthood and engaged in the worship of Yahweh in association with other divinities. In 410 the temple was destroyed by Egyptian neighbors, and the community appealed to the religious and political authorities in Jerusalem for permission to rebuild it. Permission was granted, but the community was abandoned a few years later.

Chapter 23

1 and 2 Chronicles

Sources and Audience

In the Hebrew Bible, Chronicles is treated as a single book and is part of the Writings portion of the canon. The Christian canon treats it as a book of history and so places it in chronological order between Kings and Ezra. Its Hebrew name is better rendered as "The Events of the Days." Chronicles dates from the first half or middle of the fourth century. Its ideology of openness to northern Yahwists suggests that it was composed some time after the more exclusivist Ezra–Nehemiah. Its final verses, 2 Chronicles 36:22-23, are identical to Ezra 1:1–3a.

Chronicles retells the history of the monarchy from the perspective of the Jerusalem community in the Persian period. The author (called the Chronicler) revised and rewrote material from Samuel and Kings in order to express a distinctive theology. This re-presentation of national history focuses on the kingdom of Judah. Chronicles utilized a text of Samuel and Kings that was somewhat different from the one preserved in the Hebrew Bible. The book also contains quotations from and allusions to the Pentateuch and prophets (notably Isaiah, Jeremiah, and Zechariah). Selections from the book of Psalms are reproduced in 1 Chronicles 16 and 2 Chronicles 5:13; 7:3.

The Chronicler was selective in using Samuel and Kings as a source. For example, the Chronicler focused on positive items about David as temple builder and victor, but left out negative items such as his adultery with Bathsheba and the rebellions of his sons. Thus, the negative material about David from 2 Samuel 9–20 was excluded. In addition, the story of the northern kingdom was left out for the most part unless it intersected with the history of Judah. The Chronicler may have had access to other source material in addition to Samuel–Kings. For example, supplementary information given about Rehoboam's forts (2 Chr 11:5-10) and Hezekiah's water tunnel (2 Chr 32:30) appears to be reliable.

In addition to this source material, Chronicles also incorporates dramatic scenes featuring theologically weighted speeches by significant characters. These speeches and prayers set forth the Chronicler's distinctive theology. Speeches and a prayer of David establish him as the most significant actor in the establishment of the temple (1 Chronicles 22; 28; 29). An address to a northern army by the Judahite king Abijah criticizes the rebellion of the northern kingdom and highlights the fidelity of Judah (2 Chr 13:4-12). A message by Hezekiah to the north calls for reunification of the two kingdoms under Davidic leadership (2 Chr 30:6-9). Speeches by prophets warn kings about impending judgments. For example, King Asa is urged by one Azariah son of Oded to reform worship in Judah (2 Chr 15:1-7). A seer named Hanani scolds

King Asa for his reliance on a foreign alliance (16:7-9). Familiar prophets also appear, such as Elijah (2 Chr 21:12-15), Isaiah (2 Chr 32:20), and Jeremiah (2 Chr 35:25). However, like Azariah and Hanani, other prophets featured in Chronicles are otherwise unknown, for example, Jehu (2 Chr 19:2) and Oded (2 Chr 28:9). No doubt in imitation of the practice of the book of Kings, Chronicles cites written sources to lend authority to the narrative. These include citations of supposed works by Samuel, Nathan, and Gad (1 Chr 29:29), Shemaiah and Iddo (2 Chr 12:15), Isaiah (2 Chr 26:22; 32:32), and others. It is generally agreed that these citations are literary constructions rather than genuine sources.

Chronicles was primarily directed to the Jewish community in and around Jerusalem in the Second Temple period. It spoke a strong message of encouragement and identity. In addition, Chronicles had a message for the adherents of Yahweh in the north part of the land (Samaria), who did not acknowledge the legitimacy and religious authority of the Jerusalem community. With this group in mind, Chronicles stresses that true Israel is a single people and that in the past some northerners had been part of the temple community. For example, loyal northerners come to worship at Jerusalem after the division of Solomon's kingdom (2 Chr 11:13-17). King Abijah of Judah speaks to a northern kingdom army, condemning their ancestors for their rebellion against the house of David and abandonment of proper worship. He concludes with a call for them not to resist the southern kingdom (2 Chr 13:4-12). The people of Samaria dutifully obey the prophet Oded and return thousands of captives taken from Judah (2 Chr 28:8-15). Hezekiah invites northern tribes to participate in his great Passover in Jerusalem and makes special arrangements to welcome them (2 Chr 30:1-11, 18-20). Josiah acts in a similar fashion (2 Chr 35:17-18).

Organization

Chronicles has four major divisions. First Chronicles 1–9 consists of genealogies and lists that reach back to Adam and come down (in some cases) to the time of the original readers. These genealogies give the book a universal scope, incorporate the history of the northern tribes, and connect the present audience to the story that Chronicles will tell.

The second section, 1 Chronicles 10–29, describes David's successes and his preparations for the building and organization of the temple. Chronicles gives David a large degree of credit for the establishment of the temple, one that is at least equal to that granted Solomon. David gathers building materials and organizes workers and personnel needed for worship. He prepares for what Solomon will do, and then Solomon does everything that his father planned. David's contributions to the temple are bracketed by the prayers he offers in 1 Chronicles 17:16-27 and 29:10-19.

The third major section of Chronicles consists of 2 Chronicles 1–9. These chapters recount Solomon's completion of the temple and its dedication. Characteristically, the negative judgments made in 1 Kings 11 concerning Solomon's wives and his apostasy are omitted.

The fourth segment, 2 Chronicles 10–36, tells the story of the kings of Judah, focusing on their policies concerning worship and the temple. Numerous narratives are reported that have no parallel in the book of Kings.

- King Abijah addresses the people of the northern kingdom and then wins a victory over them thanks to Yahweh's intervention (2 Chronicles 13).
- King Asa repulses a huge Ethiopian invasion (chapter 14).
- Jehoshaphat engages in reform, and Yahweh routs an invading Moabite and Ammonite force (chapters 19–20).
- King Uzziah violates the sanctity of the temple and is punished (26:16-21).
- Judahite captives are returned by northern Israelites at the urging of the prophet Oded (28:9-15).
- Much space is given to reporting Hezekiah's religious reform efforts (chapters 29–31).
- Wicked King Manasseh is captured by the Assyrians, but repents and is restored (33:10-19).
- The account of Josiah's Passover is enlarged and his death explained as divine punishment (chapter 35).

Chronicles ends on a positive note when Cyrus announces permission for the exiles to return home and his intention to rebuild the temple. He is doing these things, he proclaims, at the command of *the God of heaven* (2 Chr 36:23).

The Theology of Chronicles

The Chronicler uses what is often called the "doctrine of retribution" to explain events. A better name for this concept is the act-consequence relationship. This notion argues for a precise correspondence between one's behavior and one's destiny. Routinely and inevitably, the unrighteous suffer and the pious are rewarded. Thus, in Chronicles, obedient and reforming kings have numerous children, engage in impressive building projects, win victories, and receive tribute. In contrast, disobedient kings are defeated, suffer from disease, and experience conspiracies. Chronicles justifies the amazingly long reign of the disobedient king Manasseh by reporting that he repented of his corrupt conduct (2 Chr 33:10-19). The early violent death of the obedient king Josiah is explained by altering what 2 Kings 23 reports. In

2 Chronicles 35:20-24, the Egyptian king Neco takes the role of being a spokesperson for God and warns Josiah off. So in opposing Neco, Josiah is actually guilty of failing to heed God. The prophet Oded's words to Asa summarize the concept of the act-consequence relationship:

> Yahweh is with you as long as you are with him. If you seek him, he will be found by you; but if you abandon him, he will abandon you. (2 Chr 15:2).

However, even in Chronicles, this principle is not always followed through mechanically. Divine punishment is sometimes withheld if the warning of a divine messenger or prophet is followed by repentance, as proves true for David (1 Chr 21:15-19), Rehoboam (2 Chr 12:5-8, 12), and Asa (15:1-8).

The Chronicler celebrates worship, which is described in terms of joyful song, prayer, and praise. Joyful celebrations mark important turning points of Israel's history (1 Chr 12:38-40; 29:20-22; 2 Chr 7:8-10; 20:27; 30:26). Even warfare is treated as a liturgical activity (20:18-22).

The temple and its holiness are matters of central concern for the Chronicler. Solomon builds a separate palace outside Jerusalem for his Egyptian wife in order to move her away from holy space (2 Chr 8:11). When King Uzziah attempts to burn incense within the temple, he is struck by leprosy and must hurry out of the holy space of the temple (2 Chr 26:16-21). Chronicles also advocates for what are seen to be proper roles and privileges for Levites and priests. The respective roles of priests and Levites are clearly distinguished, evidently as a way of protecting the Levites from encroachments on their privileges on the part of the priests. Levites are divided into families that each have specific tasks (1 Chr 15:16-23). They serve as singers who lead the people in praise, doorkeepers who guard the holiness of the temple, and liturgical assistants. They also carry the ark (1 Chr 15:2; compare 2 Chr 35:3). The Chronicler traces this sharp demarcation in responsibility back to Moses and David. The privileges of the priests go back to Moses and Aaron, but it is David who puts the Levites in charge of song and service.

Further Reading

Erhard S. Gerstenberger. *Israel in the Persian Period: The Fifth and Fourth Centuries BCE*. Atlanta: SBL Press, 2011.

Chapter 24
DANIEL

Alexander the Great and His Successors

After two centuries of relative stability under the Persian Empire, the Jews in the homeland and in the diaspora came under the rule of the Greeks and began to be influenced by Hellenistic culture. The book of Daniel and the two books of Maccabees arose out of this fundamental change in the balance of power. The Macedonian (Greek) ruler Alexander (336–323) was able to destroy the Persian Empire in a series of victories between 334 and 331. He spent the winter of 332–331 in Egypt, where he founded the city of Alexandria and was declared to be a god by an oracle. Even after the death of the last Persian king Darius III (330), Alexander pushed eastward with his army to the verge of India before returning west. He died in Babylon in 323 at the age of thirty-two. Nothing is known about any direct interactions with Judea, but in 331 Samaria rebelled against his decision to reduce its administrative status, and the city was destroyed. In its place, Shechem became the cultural and religious hub of those north of Judea who worshipped Yahweh (Samaritans). At some uncertain date, possibly already in the fifth century, a temple for the worship of Yahweh had been built on Mount Gerizim near Shechem.

Alexander's generals divided his empire among themselves. A complex series of battles and conspiracies resulted in a relatively stable situation by around 275. Of the competing dynastic kingdoms that emerged, two are important for an understanding of events in Palestine. The successors of Ptolemy I (323–283; the *Ptolemies*) ruled the rich and stable territory of Egypt and (until 200) Palestine. A dynasty founded by another general, Seleucus I (312–281, the *Seleucids*), controlled Syria, Mesopotamia, and territory farther east. In territories ruled by these Hellenistic kings, including Palestine, many local elites adopted elements of prestigious Greek culture. The Jews of Alexandria grew into a substantial minority. The needs of this large Greek-speaking community led to the translation of the Hebrew Bible into Greek, a project that probably began in the reign of Ptolemy II (283–246). The rival Ptolemaic and Seleucid kingdoms continued to dispute hegemony over Palestine in a series of wars. Incidents of these convoluted wars are summarized in allegorical form in Daniel 11. In 200 (or perhaps 198) the Seleucid king Antiochus III (223–187) defeated Ptolemaic forces at Panias north of the Sea of Galilee (later Caesarea Philippi). At this point, Judea and Jerusalem fell under Seleucid rule. About a decade later, Rome, which was extending its power into the eastern Mediterranean area, blocked Antiochus III from further attempts to expand his territory. Interference in Jerusalem affairs by the next Seleucid king, Seleucus IV (187–175) set up an unstable situation that led to the oppressive actions of his successor, Antiochus IV (175–164). The tyranny of Antiochus provides the background for Daniel.

The events to which Daniel reacts are reported in 1 Maccabees 1–3 and 2 Maccabees 4–9. The focus of Jewish outrage was the introduction of alien religious observances into the Jerusalem temple by Antiochus. Daily sacrifices to Yahweh were suspended (Dan 11:31; 12:11). Sacrifices to the Greek deity Zeus Olympius were offered on a supplementary altar constructed over the temple altar. Daniel refers to this installation as the *desolating monstrosity* (CEB; NRSV: *abomination that desolates*; 9:27; 11:31; 12:11). Those pagan sacrifices began in late 167. Moreover, Seleucid authorities restricted Torah study, Sabbath observance, and circumcision. Altars were erected outside Jerusalem, and Jews were forced to participate in unlawful sacrifices.

Shape and Date

Daniel combines a collection of folktales describing resistance to an oppressive state (chapters 1–6) with the genre of apocalyptic literature promising that God will bring to an end the current brutal regime (chapters 7–12). The book offered inspiration and reassurance to Jews undergoing persecution. The apocalyptic portion of Daniel relates directly to the policies of the Seleucid Greek king Antiochus IV and his persecution of the Jews of Palestine between 167 and 164. Daniel can be dated accurately to 164. The book accurately reports the events of Antiochus IV's reign in the form of "predictions" actually made after those events had taken place. (This literary strategy is a common feature of apocalyptic literature.) However, its supposed prediction of the circumstances of the death of Antiochus gets the location of that event wrong (11:45). Consequently, this erroneous prediction must have been made before Antiochus died in 164. This circumstance pinpoints the date of Daniel to just before the death of Antiochus and just before the nearly contemporary restoration of proper worship in the Jerusalem temple, which took place in Kislev (December) 164.

Table 7. Seleucid Rulers in the Maccabean Period

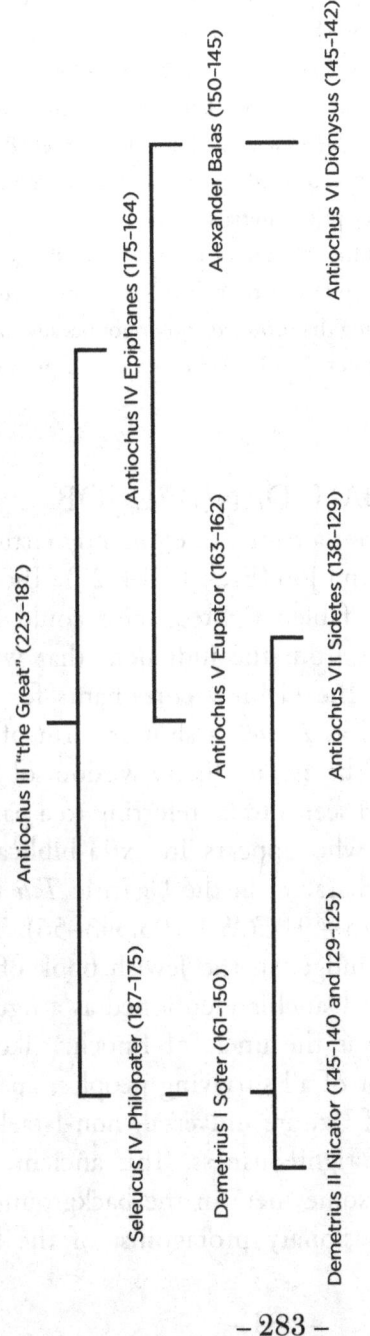

Alexander Balas falsely claimed to be a son of Antiochus IV. Diodotus Trypho murdered Antiochus VI and then contended for the throne 142-138.

The narratives in the first six chapters are presented in the third person, and the apocalyptic visions are mostly recounted in the first person. The narrative sections of Daniel are related to the apocalyptic portions. Both are reactions to the persecution by Antiochus IV. In addition, Daniel's interpretation of the statue in Nebuchadnezzar's dream (chapter 2) describes the same four successive world empires that appear in chapters 7–8. Daniel was written in the two languages current among Jews of the period: Aramaic (2:4b–7:28) and Hebrew (1:1–2:4a and chapters 8–12). This shift in language cannot be adequately explained and does not correspond to the book's division into narrative and apocalyptic materials.

Daniel is placed in the Writings section of the Hebrew Bible since it appeared centuries after the Torah and Prophets sections had been completed. In the Christian canon Daniel is placed among the prophets, no doubt because of the apocalyptic predictions presented in chapters 7–12. Daniel is called a prophet in Matthew 24:15.

24.1. NOAH, DAN(I)EL, JOB

Ezekiel twice mentions a trinity of eminently virtuous persons: Noah, Dan(i)el, and Job (Ezek 14:14, 20). The prophet asserts that even their fabled righteousness could not save anyone but themselves from the judgment that will strike Judah and Jerusalem. The Hebrew consonants for the second name can be read as *Danel*, a shorter form of Daniel. Ezekiel also alludes to the extraordinary wisdom of Dan(i)el in Ezekiel 28:3. Ezekiel seems to be referring to a past iconic figure of that name, who appears in extra-biblical literature. This Danel is a character in the Ugaritic *Tale of Aqhat* (as *Dani'ilu*; *ANET* 143–49; *COS* 1.103:343–56). There he is a wise and upright judge. In the Jewish book of *Jubilees* (second century BCE), Danel is mentioned as a figure from primeval times who was the uncle of Enoch. Like Dan(i)el, Noah, as progenitor of all surviving peoples, and Job, as resident of the land of Uz, are universal, non-Israelite worthies known for their righteousness. This ancient, legendary Danel/Daniel lies somewhere in the background of the righteous, wise, and visionary protagonist of the book of Daniel.

Daniel

Tales of Encouragement—Daniel 1–6

The stories about Daniel and his companions probably circulated independently before being attached to the reports of his visions. Daniel is portrayed as a hero of the Babylonian Exile under Nebuchadnezzar in the first part of the sixth century. This setting is several centuries before the events concerning Antiochus IV that serve as the background for the apocalyptic section. In their present form, these six tales of valiant fidelity were intended to motivate resistance to Antiochus. With respect to genre, they are court legends, describing the exploits of Jews who have risen to important roles in a foreign royal administration. The stories of Joseph (Genesis 37–50) and Esther are other examples of this genre.

Daniel 1 describes how Daniel and his companions achieve positions in the court of Nebuchadnezzar. Their insistence on keeping Jewish dietary laws makes them healthier than those who eat palace rations. The four young men prove to be wiser than any of the king's magicians. They receive Babylonian names, and Daniel is named Belteshazzar (1:7).

Daniel 2, 4, and 5 demonstrate that Daniel is more insightful than the king's other advisors. In chapter 2, the servants of Nebuchadnezzar prove unable either to describe the content of his dream or to interpret it. Daniel, however, receives a nighttime vision. He goes to the king and reveals that the king has dreamed of a great statue made from five materials in descending value from head to toes and that this statue was crushed by a stone of nonhuman origin. Daniel then interprets the dream in terms of four successive world empires. The first is the Babylonian Empire of Nebuchadnezzar. Then follow Media, Persia, and Greece in turn. The fourth kingdom degenerates into a brittle mixture of iron and clay that represents the divided realms of Alexander's successors. These kingdoms will be destroyed and replaced by a permanent kingdom set up by God. In chapter 4, Nebuchadnezzar tells the story of a second dream. He sees a colossal tree at the center of the earth that provides sustenance and shelter. But it is chopped down by heavenly decree. When consulted, Daniel applies this to Nebuchadnezzar's ruling power. This power is soon brought low by an affliction that causes him to engage in bizarre and antisocial behavior for a time. Chapter 5 recounts the well-known incident of the handwriting on the wall, which materializes during a feast hosted by King Belshazzar. Once again the wise men of Babylon cannot interpret the omen. Daniel reveals the answer to the puzzle. The Babylonian Empire has been weighed on the scales of history and does not measure up. It will be defeated and divided among the Medes and the Persians (5:24-28). That same night King Belshazzar is killed and the kingdom is given over to another royal power.

The fictional nature of these tales is underscored by two historical errors. Belshazzar did exist but he was a son of Nabonidus, not Nebuchadnezzar. He was never actually king of Babylon. Daniel 5:30-31 says that Darius the Mede (an unhistorical character) captured Babylon from Belshazzar, but it was Cyrus the Persian who did this.

24.2. WRITING ON THE WALL

In Daniel chapter 5, King Belshazzar hosts a feast. Historically, this is Bel-shar-usur, son of Nabonidus. He served as coregent for Nabonidus when the latter was unavailable in northwestern Arabia (perhaps between 549–543).

The writing on the wall read: *mene, mene, tekel, and parsin* (Daniel 5:25). Unlike the king's sages, Daniel could read the writing and interpreted it as an omen of doom for the Babylonian Empire. The surface meaning of the phrase has to do with units of weight: a mina, a mina, a shekel, and two paras (which were half-minas or half-shekels). But the true meaning of the omen is under the surface and is based on wordplay (5:26-28):

God has numbered [*mena*] the days of your rule. It's over! . . .

you've been weighed [*tekilta*] on the scales, and you don't measure up. . . .

your kingship is divided [*perisat*] and given to the Medes and the Persians [*Paras*].

Daniel chapters 3 and 6 recount conflicts between the Jewish courtiers and their rivals in the court. Chapter 3 begins as Nebuchadnezzar erects a huge golden image and demands that everyone worship it. Shadrach, Meshach, and Abednego refuse, and their rivals inform on them. Thrown into a raging furnace, they survive unharmed. The plot of chapter 6 is somewhat similar. Daniel violates the command of King Darius by praying toward Jerusalem to his own God. Betrayed by his rivals, he is thrown into a pit full of lions and sealed up there. Intervention by a divine messenger saves Daniel, and his opponents and their families are killed by the lions instead. After each of these two episodes the king extols Daniel's God (3:28-29; 6:25-27).

Apocalyptic Visions—Daniel 7–12

In the second half of the book, Daniel appears as an apocalyptic seer and reports his visionary experiences. The three separate accounts in chapters 7, 8, and 10–12 largely overlap in regard to the historical events that they embrace. Using different symbols, they each describe the success of Alexander the Great in destroying earlier imperial dominions and how his rule was then superseded by the regimes of the Ptolemies and the Seleucids. Antiochus IV arises and institutes his oppression and persecution of the Jews and their religion. His sovereignty will soon be broken by God's intervention in history and a wonderful future will ensue. Chapter 9 reinterprets Jeremiah's prophecy of a seventy-week period of exile in a way that brings its consummation down to the period of Antiochus IV.

Apocalypticism emerged in the Jewish thought world in the last centuries BCE, in part as a response to persecution and religious disillusionment. Apocalyptic literature is characterized by revelations about the heavenly world and impending divine judgment. Typically a renowned figure from the past receives visions, and the meaning of these is communicated to him by supernatural beings such as angels. Events are determined beforehand. The apocalyptic promise is that God will soon break into the normal course of history and bring to a dramatic end the powers that oppose God and God's people. Visions granted the apocalyptic seer may accurately describe historical events in the form of "predictions" supposedly made in the distant past when the seer lived. However, from the perspective of the actual author and the original audience, who lived years later, those purportedly predicted events have really already taken place. Claimed accuracy in foretelling events that had already taken place served to authenticate the real predictions offered by the apocalyptic writer. Daniel's visions, supposedly received in the sixth century BCE, are understood to be sealed up for a future time (8:26), that is to say for the time of the original readership in the year 164. Thus Daniel's visions accurately "forecast" the fall of the empires of Babylon, the Medes, the Persians, and Alexander, along with the division of Alexander's realm and the persecutions instituted by Antiochus IV, because those things have already come to pass.

Judgment on the Beasts—Daniel 7

Chapter 7, the dramatic vision of four mythic beasts rising from the sea, is the thematic center of Daniel. It links back to Nebuchadnezzar's dream of a statue in chapters 2 and its portrayal of a succession of four world empires superseded by a fifth, ideal kingdom. Daniel's dialogue with an otherworldly interpreter helps clarify the symbolism of his vision (7:16-27). When interpreted against the background of the reign of Antiochus IV, the identity of the symbolic animals and reported events becomes relatively clear, although not all details can be explained with certainty:

- The lion with wings is the Babylonian Empire.
- The bear is the realm of the Medes.

Chapter 24

- The leopard with four wings and four heads is Persia. Persia's four most notable kings were Cyrus, Cambyses, Darius, and Xerxes.
- The ten-horned monster is the worst of them all. This represents the Hellenistic kingdoms, and its ten horns successive kings, probably the Seleucid rulers before Antiochus IV.
- The small horn with eyes and a big mouth speaking with arrogance is Antiochus IV (7:8, 11, 24-25). He is described as persecuting the Jews and undermining Jewish law about festivals and Sabbath.

Antiochus had usurped the throne from the son of his brother, and his accession was marked by controversy and violence. Antiochus took the epithet Epiphanes (resplendent; one manifesting divine power) and on some of his coins styled himself explicitly as "King Antiochus, God Manifest."

In 7:9-14, the emergence of the beasts and of the little horn is followed by a dramatic scene that takes place before the wheeled chariot throne of God (as earlier described by Ezekiel). God is titled as the *ancient one*, envisioned in physical terms, and surrounded by myriads of attendants. God's court is sitting for judgment. The last beast is destroyed. As is common in the Bible, a use of the passive voice indicates God's action. Then a figure with a human form, *one like a human being*, arrives before the throne. The Aramaic expression for this figure, taken word for word, is "one like a son of mankind." In other words, in contrast to the four kingdoms in the form of beasts, he resembles a member of the human race. Universal dominion is given to him. Verse 18 explains that he represents *the holy ones of the Most High*, most likely the pious Jews who are resisting Antiochus (but perhaps militant angels). The order of future events is reviewed in 7:21-22 and 26-27. Persecution will seem to triumph, but God will intervene. Divine judgment will deliver worldwide dominion *to the people, the holy ones of the Most High* (7:27), again most likely the faithful Jews to whom the book of Daniel is directed.

The emergent Christian movement utilized and reinterpreted the imagery of Daniel to express its own apocalyptic expectations, most notably in the book of Revelation. Later readers of Daniel would reinterpret the fourth and final beast as the Roman Empire, which was the oppressive regime of their own time. In addition, interpretive developments in both Judaism and Christianity would understand the human-looking figure arriving in 7:13-14 as a future transcendent judge or messianic figure. In the New Testament, this became the Human One (CEB; NRSV: *Son of Man*) who would return as a heavenly judge and was identified with Jesus (for example, Mark 13:26; 14:62).

A Ram and a Goat—Daniel 8

Daniel's second vision and its interpretation by the divine messenger Gabriel covers the same events as those portrayed in chapter 7. Alexander (the goat) overcomes the Medes and Persians, but is in turn replaced by four of his generals. The focus is on a small horn, which symbolizes Antiochus IV. His impious acts against the temple and persecutions will be defeated by divine power.

Daniel's Final Vision—Daniel 10–12

Daniel's final vision is set in the early years of the Persian Empire. The history leading up to the tyranny of Antiochus IV is gone over again (Dan 10:2–11:20), but this time in much greater detail. A century's worth of complicated interactions between the Ptolemies (*the southern king*) and the Seleucids (*the northern king*) are covered (11:6-19). The ups and downs of the career of Antiochus IV are detailed in 11:21-39, with an emphasis on his numerous misdeeds. A striking feature of these descriptions is that heavenly, angelic forces play a role in the struggles of human peoples (10:13, 20-21). Beginning at 11:40, the author shifts from a retelling of completed events disguised as predictions, and moves into making forecasts concerning the future doom of Antiochus. The predicted location of the death of Antiochus between the Mediterranean Sea and Jerusalem is inaccurate (11:45). Antiochus died in Persia in 164.

Daniel 12:2-3 stands out among Old Testament texts in promising resurrection and eternal life or eternal disgrace to some of the victims and some of the perpetrators of the persecution of Antiochus. Apparently, the idea behind this resurrection concept was that, if true justice is to be achieved, there must be a reward for those who were martyred on account of their obedience to God's law and a special punishment for those who committed such atrocities.

24.3. PERSIAN RELIGION

In their inscriptions, the kings of the Persian Empire refer to the will and order of the god Ahura-Mazda. It is clear that some early form of what we call Zoroastrianism today (after its founder) was their personal religion. However, the question of any official role for the religion of Ahura-Mazda in the Persian Empire is uncertain. It is thought that Persian religious ideas influenced developing Jewish thought, but the extent of such influence is a controversial matter. Alleged traces of Persian ideas are actually more visible in Jewish literature from the Hellenistic and Roman periods than in the Persian period itself. The chief problem is that our knowledge about Persian religion at the time of the Persian Empire remains extremely limited and imperfect. The various elements appearing within Zoroastrian written sources (the Avestas) are nearly impossible to date. Nevertheless, striking parallels exist between concepts characteristic of the Zoroastrian faith and developments that took place in Jewish thought leading into the New Testament and rabbinic Judaism.

Zoroastrianism reflects an ongoing cosmic conflict or dualism between good and evil. The high god Ahura-Mazda is entirely good and benevolent, but is opposed by powers that are evil and malignant. This opposition centers in a transcendent and personalized power of evil, Angra Mainyu. This figure is analogous to later portrayals of Satan in the Old and New Testaments. Malignant beings (demons, *daewas*) are opposed by benevolent ones (angels, the Amesha Spenta). Both Zoroastrianism and later Judaism teach a universal resurrection of the dead to face final judgment. Both religions also exhibit an emphasis on matters of purity.

Timetables

Daniel displays a concern for predicting the schedule for God's impending acts of intervention. Daniel 9:2, 24-27 revisits Jeremiah's prediction that the exile would last seventy years (Jer 25:11-12; 29:10) and recasts the timetable as seventy weeks of years, that is seven times seventy or 490 years. In an approximate way, this recalculation brings the culmination of Jeremiah's prediction down to the period of the oppression of Antiochus IV. The persecution by Antiochus is understood to be the last half of this last week of years, that is the three-and-a-half-year duration of his lawless actions (Dan 9:26-27). In agreement with this, 7:25 and 12:7 specify the extent of time before the crimes of Antiochus are brought to an end as three-and-a-half years, poetically expressed as *a period of time,* [two] *periods of time, and half a period of time.* Daniel 8:13-14 refers to a slightly shorter period of 1150 days. The pagan altar that Antiochus had erected in the temple (the *desolating monstrosity*; 9:27; 11:31; 12:11) remained in place for three years from December 167 to December 164. At the end of the book there are successive attempts to update this chronology when fulfillment was delayed (12:11, 12).

Additions to Daniel

The Greek tradition of Daniel contains three supplements that are not present in the Hebrew Bible. The first of these additions consists of two songs that appear in connection with the story of Daniel's three companions in the fiery furnace, between Daniel 3:23 and 3:24. These are the Prayer of Azariah and the Song of the Three Young Men. Azariah is Abednego's Hebrew name (Dan 1:7). Azariah prays after the three companions are thrown into the furnace (Pr Azar 3-22). Then after an angel has cooled the inside of the furnace, all three young heroes join together in praising God (Pr Azar 29-68). In genre the Prayer of Azariah is a communal lament. The Song of the Three Young Men puts together two hymns of praise. These three poems are similar to laments and hymns in the book of Psalms.

The second addition is the story of Susanna, which is designated as chapter 13. In some ways it is similar to a modern detective story in the sense that the young Daniel is able to uncover the truth about a crime by means of shrewd cross-examination. The righteous woman Susanna has been falsely accused of adultery by two elders who have failed in their attempt to seduce her. Daniel shows precocious wisdom by exposing their false testimony. He interrogates them separately and uncovers a critical discrepancy in their statements.

A third addition, Bel and the Dragon, appears as chapter 14. These two episodes demonstrate Daniel's extraordinary wisdom and testify to the futility of idol worship. Daniel exposes the priests of the idol Bel as frauds. Then Daniel kills a great dragon by feeding it a concoction that causes it to burst open. As a result of this, Daniel is thrown into a den of hungry lions (an alternative version of the story recounted in Daniel 6). At God's command, the prophet Habakkuk is carried from Judea with food for Daniel. Miraculously, the lions do not eat Daniel and he is released.

Further Reading

Carol A. Newsom. *Daniel*. Old Testament Library. Louisville, KY: Westminster John Knox, 2014.

Part VI

APOCRYPHAL / DEUTERO-CANONICAL BOOKS

Chapter 25
SPELLBINDING TALES AND PROFOUND WISDOM

Tobit

Tobit is similar in form and outlook to the short stories Esther and Judith. These three books reflect on issues raised by existence in the diaspora. How should Jews navigate life in the context of foreign culture? Tobit seems to have been written during the Hellenistic period. A relatively late date is indicated by its author's confusion about the proper succession of Assyrian kings (1:15). Tobit undergoes persecution because of his piety (1:16-20), but the book's silence about the calamity created by Antiochus IV suggests that it was composed before that crisis emerged, probably between the mid-third and early second centuries. Evidence from Qumran shows that Tobit was originally composed in Aramaic.

Cultural Background

The plot of Tobit rests in part on two folktale motifs that appear elsewhere in world literature. First, Sarah is an example of the "dangerous bride" with a jealous demon lover who kills her suitors. The demon Asmodeus has killed her seven husbands, each before the marriage could be consummated. In another folktale motif, that of the "grateful dead," a person buries an unburied corpse and is subsequently aided by a mysterious figure, often the ghost of the person who was buried. In Tobit this helper is an angel in disguise. Tobit refers to the Assyrian courtier Ahikar and his son (1:21-22; 14:10). These two were characters of a popular Mesopotamian story.

Angels and demons became increasingly important in Jewish religious thought in the Persian and Hellenistic periods. In Tobit the angel Raphael (*God heals*) serves as an intermediary between the world of God and human affairs. Raphael acts as a communicator and messenger. He instructs Tobias about how to save Sarah and how to heal Tobit (6:4-9; 11:4). He teaches Tobias and Tobit about the practice of wise piety (12:6-10). The angel moves the action of the story along by reminding Tobias of his father's instructions about marriage (6:16). He transmits the prayers of Tobias and Sarah up to God and carries out God's commissions to test Tobit and bring healing to him and Sarah (3:17; 12:12-14). After revealing his true identity, Raphael ascends back to God (12:15-21). Conversely, Sarah's troubles are caused by the demon Asmodeus, who must be driven off and incapacitated (3:8; 8:3).

Tobit as Literature

Tobit is set in what for its earliest readers would be the distant past, in the time of the Assyrian Empire, at the time when inhabitants of the northern kingdom had been forcibly deported to Mesopotamia. The story plays out on two levels, the earthly world and the heavenly realm. A nesting series of four problems is expounded in chapters 1–7 (Tobit's lack of money, his blindness, Tobias's need for a wife, and Sarah's predicament with the demon). These problems are solved in the climatic chapters 8–9. The demon is exorcised, the wedding is celebrated, and the deposited money is recovered. Blind Tobit is healed in chapter 11.

The author makes skillful use of irony and humor. Irony is at work when Tobit, who has lost everything because of his acts of piety, advises his son that God rewards good deeds (4:7) and expresses his confident wish that God's angel will accompany Tobias and Raphael on their journey (5:17, 22). Raphael's assumed name Azariah (5:13) means "Yahweh has helped." It is hard to miss the humor when Raphael proves himself to be such an accomplished liar in chapter 5 or when Sarah's father Raguel arranges to have a grave dug for Tobias while he and Sarah are in the wedding chamber—and then has it filled in before anyone can see it (8:9, 18). The charming detail of the dog that accompanies Tobias and Raphael on their journey from beginning to end (6:2; 11:4) is intriguing. Nothing else is said about this dog, and there is no really satisfying explanation for its presence.

The Narrative Structure of Tobit

Chapter 1 introduces themes that will develop in the unfolding narrative. The reader learns of Tobit's altruism, his money deposited in Media, and his courage in burying the dead. In a preliminary rehearsal of what will follow, Tobit loses all and then regains all (1:20 and 2:1). Chapter 2 recounts Tobit's blindness, a shockingly unfair result of his concern for others. This undeserved tragedy is emphasized when Tobit's wife, Anna, rebukes him for his obsessive commitment to righteousness.

Chapter 3 recounts a providential "coincidence." The fates of Tobit and Sarah, both of whom suffer unjustly, are intertwined when undeserved reproach leads each of them to pray for death. Tobit prays to die because of his distress and false insults from his wife (3:1-6). On that very same day, Sarah plans to commit suicide and prays to die because of undeserved insults (3:7-15). The two prayers come together at God's throne at the same time, and Raphael is sent forth to answer both (3:16-17). Correspondence between the destinies of Tobit and Sarah continues. At the very moment that Tobit goes back to his house, Sarah comes down from her room (3:17), and on that same day Tobit remembers about the money he has deposited with Gabael (4:1).

Preparing for death, Tobit gives his son Tobias final advice and ethical instruction in chapter 4, and informs him of the money on deposit in Media. Tobias is to find a wife from his own people (4:12-13). In chapter 5, preparations are made for Tobias's journey to recover the ten talents of silver. Tobias objects that there are obstacles to this undertaking in that he will not be recognized and does not know the way from Nineveh to Rages. But Tobias is provided with what he will need: a written receipt and, after much discussion, the assistance of a protector and guide in the shape of Raphael.

In chapter 6, Raphael provides Tobias with other things he will turn out to need. Raphael also reveals what really lies behind their journey to Rages by way of the home of Raguel in Ecbatana. It becomes fairly obvious where the story is headed when Raphael reveals the special properties of this fish's internal organs for driving away demons and for healing blindness (6:7-9). Raphael also reveals the advantageous prospect of a marriage between Tobias and Sarah and instructs Tobias on how to proceed on his wedding night (6:11-13, 17-18).

Chapters 7, 8, and 9 represent the narrative climax, in which the interlocking problems of a wife for Tobias, the murderous demon, and acquisition of the money are resolved in turn. After a delaying conversation and copious tears that increase the narrative tension (7:1-8) and a rehash of Sarah's problem (7:11), Tobias and Sarah are married. Raguel and Sarah's mother Edna express both hope and despair about the likely outcome (7:11-12, 16; 8:9-12). In chapter 8, all goes well. The demon is driven off. The newlyweds pray and then fall asleep together. In the morning a two-week wedding feast commences. Tobias sends Raphael off to recover the money (chapter 9). Back home, Tobit and Anna are waiting for Tobias and (typically) arguing about his fate, while the wedding feast and a protracted farewell scene are taking place (chapter 10). In chapter 11, Sarah, Tobias, and Raphael finally return. Tobit's sight is quickly restored and celebrations ensue.

In chapters 12–14, the import of story is explored and loose ends are wrapped up. Raphael reveals himself and disappears (chapter 12). Tobit utters a hymn of praise that reflects the diaspora situation, calls for turning away from sin on the part of

Israel, and predicts the restoration of Jerusalem (chapter 13). As Tobit draws near death, his last words predict the fulfillment of what the prophets have predicted. Nineveh will fall, and Samaria and Jerusalem will be made desolate. In the end, scattered Jews will return to a glorious Jerusalem.

Judith

Judith seems to have been composed in the late second or early first century BCE. Judith was probably first written in Hebrew, but all surviving versions go back to a Greek translation. Judith is a short story similar to Esther and Tobit. Its romantic character and lack of historical reliability is indicated by the imaginative setting described in chapter 1. Nebuchadnezzar was not king of the Assyrians nor was his capital Nineveh. His Median opponent, the exotically named Arphaxad, is not a historical character. In Judith 2:1, the story is set in the eighteenth year of Nebuchadnezzar, actually the year he conquered Jerusalem (587/586). But at the same time it also takes place soon after the return from exile (4:3), that is, after 539. The events reported in 3:8 sound like a reflection of the atrocities committed by Antiochus IV in the mid-second century. Readers are entertained by exotic foreign touches like presenting earth and water as a symbol of surrender and archers on horseback (2:7, 15).

The Story

The plot of Judith moves from a dire threat to Jerusalem and the town of Bethulia, set up in chapters 1–7, to a solution to this crisis produced by the wisdom and courage of Judith, which unfolds in chapters 8–16. The narrative problem begins with Nebuchadnezzar's ultimatum and the western campaign led by Holofernes (chapters 1–3). He threatens Judah, which reacts with prayer and penitence (4:8-12) and an order to block the northern approaches to Jerusalem (4:6-7). The narrow pass at Bethulia would be the key to any successful Assyrian advance. Thus, a war that covers the whole western empire and threatens the safety of Jerusalem and its temple narrows down to the endurance of one small town and to one intrepid woman (7:1; 8:32). The town of Bethulia is not known outside the book of Judith. Its name reflects the Hebrew word for young woman, while Judith is a feminine form of Jew or Judean.

There is a pause in the action in chapters 5–6. The Ammonite leader Achior is expelled from the camp of Holofernes for suggesting that God will not let the Israelites be defeated if they remain faithful. He is turned over to the citizens of Bethulia to share their fate. In chapter 7, the situation grows even more dire as the army of

Holofernes encamps against Bethulia, captures its only source of water, and cuts off access to the town. Thirst drives the town rulers to decide on a surrender to the enemy after five days unless God rescues them.

It is only with chapter 8 that a resolution to this crisis begins, with the introduction of Judith and her willingness to take action. Judith is pious and wise (8:4-8). She rebukes the town elders and tells them that the oath of surrender they have taken displays a lack of faith (8:11-17). Although asked only to pray for rain, Judith goes further and announces that she will take matters into her own hands (8:32-34). However, she reveals nothing to the elders (or to the readers) about what her plan will entail. Judith's prayer in chapter 9 asks for success and hints at what she has in mind when she reviews the violent vengeance that her ancestor Simeon took on the occasion of the rape of his sister Dinah (9:2-4; Gen 34:25-31). Judith will use *lying words* and *the hand of a woman* to bring down the foe (Jdt 9:10, 13). For Holofernes to die by the hand of a woman would be a humiliating disgrace (Judg 4:21; 9:53-54).

In Judith 10:1-10, Judith prepares herself and organizes her maid and a bag to hold her ritually pure food. This bag will serve as an important part of her plan. The effect of her beauty on the enemy camp is emphasized, but it actually seems to make things even worse for the Israelite cause (10:14, 19, 23). In chapter 11, Holofernes and Judith engage in a conversation marked by deceit and veiled truth on her part. Judith falsely states that the Jews of Bethulia plan to commit an egregious sin that will cause God to hand them over to Holofernes. To establish her escape route, she states that she will go outside the camp each night to discover through prayer when this sin will be committed. There is irony and double meaning:

> I won't lie to you.... If you follow the instructions of your female servant, God will accomplish something great through you, and my master's plans won't fail. [Is her master Holofernes or God?] ... God sent me to accomplish things with you that will amaze the whole world. (11:5-6, 16)

In chapter 12, after three days of going outside the camp each night to pray and bathe, Judith is invited to a banquet by Holofernes. Holofernes plans to seduce her into having sex (12:12, 16). She reclines before him to dine and drink wine, and deceives him with ironic words: *Today is the best day of my life since the day I was born* (12:18).

The climax comes in chapter 13. Holofernes has gotten dead drunk, and Judith is left completely alone with him. After a brief prayer, she uses his sword to cut off his head, and her maid puts it into her food bag. Judith pulls down the bed canopy (13:9-10a). She and her maid execute the escape plan without incident and are admitted to Bethulia. The severed head and canopy are visible proof that *the Lord struck him down by the hand of a woman!* (13:15; see 9:10). Judith carefully assures everyone that Holofernes never actually had sex with her. He was undone only by the beauty of her face (13:16).

The effects of her exploit are described in chapters 14 and 15. Judith takes charge of military strategy. Achior converts and is circumcised. When the Assyrians discover the headless body of their commander, they flee in panic and are cut down in a fashion reminiscent of the classic victories described in Joshua and Judges. Then like Miriam in Exodus 15:20, Judith leads the women in a victory dance and sings a song of praise.

> Her sandal captured his eyes;
> her beauty captured his heart,
>   and the sword sliced through his neck. (Jdt 15:9)

Wisdom of Solomon

The Jewish diaspora community of Alexandria, the chief city of Hellenistic and Roman Egypt, was large and influential. There is little question that Wisdom of Solomon (or the book of Wisdom in Roman Catholic usage) originated from within that environment. The author writes excellent literary Greek and displays a background in Greek rhetoric and philosophy. An Egyptian environment is indicated by the author's hostility to Egyptians in the exodus story and attacks on the idolatry and animal worship that Jews saw as characteristic of Egyptian religion. Wisdom of Solomon is difficult to date because it refers to no external events. Many scholars think that its vocabulary and strong condemnation of idolatry hints at a period after the Roman conquest of Egypt about 30 BCE. On the other hand, it may have been composed as late as the early first century CE, when tensions between Alexandrian Jews and their neighbors reached dangerous levels. The author adopted the identity of Solomon, the biblical patron of wisdom (9:7-8).

In the context of Hellenistic cultural domination, Wisdom of Solomon advocates resistance to assimilation. It defends Jewish monotheism and morality as a philosophical stance superior to the religion and lifestyle of Gentiles. One can be educated in Greek thought and yet still remain a Jew who takes pride in a noble heritage. Readers are urged to seek for and understand the true nature of wisdom. Following the lead of Proverbs 8:22-31 and Sirach 24:1-22, wisdom is personified and exalted.

Structure

The book divides into three parts, with transition sections. First, chapters 1–6 urge rulers to seek after wisdom and practice justice. The unjust are contrasted with

Spellbinding Tales and Profound Wisdom

the righteous, who are rewarded with immortal life (5:15-16). The second, central section consists of chapters 7–10, in which wisdom is lauded as God's gift. Chapters 7 and 8 are presented as a first-person account of a lifelong relationship between wisdom and Solomon (see 7:5, 7). Chapter 9 consists of a prayer for wisdom spoken by King Solomon, reflecting on his prayer for wisdom recounted in 1 Kings 3 (see Wis 9:7-8). Chapter 10 discloses how wisdom protected seven righteous heroes of the Old Testament, starting with Adam and ending with Moses. Wisdom was active in the exodus, leading Israel through the Red Sea and drowning the foe.

The third section, chapters 11–19, focuses on the exodus story and reframes it to demonstrate how God used control of the elements of the natural world to free Israel and punish Egypt. The figure of wisdom does not appear in this last part of the book. Seven antitheses portray seven punishments against the sinful Egyptians and seven corresponding benefits for Israel.

- The Nile turned to blood and was undrinkable, but Israel was given water in the desert (11:6-14).
- The very same irrational animals worshipped by the Egyptians caused them torment, but quail gave Israel the chance to feast (11:15-16; 12:23-27; 16:1-4; this is interrupted at two points by other material).
- Egyptians were killed by flies and locusts, but Israel was delivered by the bronze serpent (16:5-14).
- Thunderstorms descended on the Egyptians, but manna fell upon Israel (16:15-29).
- Darkness terrified the Egyptians, but light in the pillar of fire guided Israel (17:1–18:4).
- The firstborn of Egypt were destroyed, but Aaron protected Israel from deadly plague (18:5-25).
- The Egyptians drowned in the Sea, but Israel passed through unharmed (19:1-9).

Themes

Much space is devoted to condemning and mocking the worship of images and animals. Chapters 13–15 explore the supposed origin and negative consequences of idolatry and expose its folly. Imagine a woodcutter who cuts down a tree and makes it into something useful, burns some to cook his food, and then shapes a leftover, crooked stick from it into a wooden idol and prays to it (13:11-19). Or imagine one who navigates over raging seas and yet prays to a piece of wood more fragile that the ship on which he sails (14:1).

Wisdom of Solomon portrays survival after death in terms of the immortality of the soul, not a resurrection as in other late Jewish texts (Daniel 12, Isa 26:19). In Greek thought, immortality was considered to be a natural, intrinsic quality of the human soul (see Wis 8:19-20), but Wisdom of Solomon emphasizes that immortality is God's reward for the righteous.

> The souls of the righteous are in the hand of God,
>   and no torment will ever touch them....
> For though in the sight of others they were punished,
>   their hope is full of immortality. (3:1, 4 NRSV)

Wisdom is extolled as God's throne companion (9:4, 10). She lives with God and is a partner in God's works (8:3-4). She plays a role in the workings of the cosmos and guides the events of history. In 7:22b–8:1, the author lists twenty-one characteristics of wisdom, derived mostly from Greek philosophy.

> She pervades and embraces everything because she is so pure. Wisdom is the warm breath of God's power. She pours forth from the all-powerful one's pure glory.... She's a mirror that flawlessly reflects God's activity. She's the perfect image of God's goodness. (7:24b-25a, 26)

Wisdom is the mother of all good things (7:12). The female persona of wisdom is stressed when Solomon seeks her as a bride and companion (8:2, 9, 16).

Sirach

The Wisdom of Jesus, Sirach's son (see 50:27), was composed in Palestine around 180 BCE. Jesus is the Greek form of the Hebrew name Joshua. In Christian tradition the book is sometimes called Ecclesiasticus (that is, belonging to the church) because it is frequently used in teaching and worship. Generally, the author is called Ben Sira (following Hebrew), and the book's title shortened to Sirach. According to the book's prologue, the author's grandson moved to Egypt in 132 BCE and subsequently translated the work into Greek. Although Sirach was known only in this Greek translation until the end of the nineteenth century, manuscript discoveries have made most of Sirach available in its original language of Hebrew. Ben Sira expresses opinions that would eventually become hallmarks of the later Sadducee party, namely that there is no life after death (41:1-4) and that humans enjoy free will (15:11-20). He strongly supports temple leadership and ritual.

Advice and Wise Teaching

The author speaks of his purpose as one who has belatedly gathered up fruits of wisdom for the benefit of others.

> I was the last to keep vigil,
> > as one who gathered the leftovers after the grape pickers. . . .
> Understand that I haven't labored for myself alone,
> > but for all those who are seeking instruction. (33:16, 18)

For the most part, Sirach consists of proverbs presented in a loose order, along with prayers and poems. Following the precedent of Proverbs, Sirach brings together the practice of wisdom and obedience to God's law by joining them together as *the fear of the Lord*.

> Fearing the Lord is Wisdom's crowning garland,
> > sprouting forth peace and restorative health. . . .
> Fearing the Lord is Wisdom's root,
> > and her branches yield a long life. (1:18, 20)

Ben Sira wrestles with the correlation between divine mercy and divine justice (5:4-7; 16:11-14). He mirrors the honor-and-shame culture that pervaded the ancient world, according to which an honorable reputation determined one's social status and public standing. This theme appears throughout the book, but is particularly evident in 3:2-11; 10:19–11:6; 41:17–42:8.

Sometimes Ben Sira's advice is thoroughly practical, touching on table manners (31:12–32:13), religious duties (18:22-23; 34:21-31; 35:1-13), and the value of consulting a physician (38:1-15). He teaches good financial practice (14:3-19; 29:1-20; 31:1-11). He promotes a "tough love" approach to raising children (7:23-26; 30:7-13; 42:9-14). Much attention is paid to the relationship between the sexes—from a thoroughly male perspective (9:1-9; 23:16-27; 25:16-26; 26:1-18 [19-27]; 36:26-30). One of the more positive statements about women is:

> A wife's charm will delight her husband,
> > and her skill will put fat on his bones. (26:13)

Travel is a valuable experience (34:9-13). Ben Sira continues a typical wisdom theme by reflecting on the topic of silence and speech (19:4-17; 20:1-8, 18-20; 28:12-26).

> Never repeat something that you've heard,
>   and you will not lose anything. . . .
> Have you heard some word?
>   Let it perish along with you.
> Have courage! It won't make you burst. (19:7, 10)

In Praise of Wisdom

Chapter 24 praises wisdom as a transcendent figure who praises her own merits *in the assembly of the Most High* (24:2). She emanated from God's mouth, circled the cosmos as an indication of her sovereignty over it, and then sought a place to call home (24:3-7). At God's command, wisdom found her home among Israel and resided in Jerusalem, where she was associated with temple worship (24:8-12). She grew there, like a tall and fragrant tree, and now invites all who will to eat her fruit and obey wisdom (24:13-22).

> Come to me, you who desire me,
>   and take your fill of my produce. . . .
> Those who eat of me will hunger for more,
>   and those who drink of me will thirst for more. (24:19, 21)

Some elements of wisdom's self-description in Sirach 24 are similar to claims that the goddess Isis makes about herself in Egyptian religious literature.

Let Us Praise the Famous

Chapters 44–50 catalogue famous and intrepid worthies from the past—all men. The selection follows the order of the three-fold Hebrew canon. Chapters 44–45 celebrate figures from the Torah, and 46:1–49:12 cover the Former and Latter Prophets. Nehemiah (49:13) is the only representative from the Writings section. An addendum (49:14-16) gathers up six other characters from Genesis, and the tribute concludes in chapter 50 with the high priest Simon II (Simon the Just), who was in office from about 219 to 196. His eminence is stressed by a vivid description of his splendid appearance and a description of his duties in the temple ritual. In this section, Ben Sira shows his interest in priestly matters by focusing on the priests Aaron, Phinehas, and Simon and on figures who built and reformed the temple (David, Solomon, Hezekiah, Josiah, and Zerubbabel).

Baruch

Baruch son of Neriah was Jeremiah's scribe. According to Jeremiah 43:1-7, he was forcibly taken to Egypt with Jeremiah in about 582. The book of Baruch, however, locates him in Babylon. It purports to be a letter sent by him to members of the Jerusalem community who had not been exiled. Inconsistencies and historical errors in the introduction establish that Baruch originated at a later time. Neither the Sud River nor a high priest named Jehoiakim are otherwise known (Bar 1:4, 7). Belshazzar was not the son of Nebuchadnezzar (1:11-12).

Baruch was probably composed in Hebrew, but is now known only in Greek translation. It consists of three originally independent units, which were brought together by an introduction (1:1-14) that makes them into a letter. The three sections may have been composed at different times, but the work as a whole is usually dated to the late second or early first centuries. In the Roman Catholic and Orthodox canons, Baruch is placed between Jeremiah and Lamentations.

The first unit of the letter proper begins as a prayer of repentance (1:15–3:8). The exile was God's punishment for disobedience, and the Jews may hope that God will restore them as repentant people. Confession is followed by a plea for deliverance. Portions of this section are very similar to the prayer found in Daniel 9:4-19, and direct literary dependence is likely.

> Lord our God, we have sinned. We were ungodly. We have broken all of your commandments. . . . Lord, listen to our prayer and our pleading. For your own sake, set us free. . . . (Bar 2:12, 14)

The second unit, Baruch 3:9–4:4, is a poem that links Mosaic instruction with wisdom. Wisdom is elusive and hard to get hold of, but it has appeared on earth in the form of *the scroll containing God's commandments* (4:1).

The third unit is a poem of consolation (4:5–5:9). Personified Zion speaks in 4:9-29, urging her children to take courage and cry out to God. Then she is comforted with a promise that her exiles will return:

> The children you sent away are coming.
>   By the holy one's word,
>   they are coming from the east
>   and the west,
>   rejoicing in God's glory. (4:37)

In the canonical tradition of the Catholic Church, the Letter of Jeremiah is appended to Baruch as chapter 6. The Letter of Jeremiah forms a separate book in Orthodox canons. This epistle was supposedly sent by Jeremiah to the Jewish diaspora in the East and is modeled after the prophet's letter to exiles in Jeremiah 29:1-23. It vehemently attacks and mocks idolatry.

Further Reading

David A. deSilva. *The Apocrypha*. Nashville: Abingdon, 2012.

David A. deSilva. *Introducing the Apocrypha: Message, Context, and Significance.* 2nd ed. Grand Rapids: Baker, 2018.

Benedikt Otzen. *Tobit and Judith*. Sheffield, UK: Sheffield Academic Press, 2002.

Daniel J. Harrington. *Jesus Ben Sira of Jerusalem: A Biblical Guide to Living Wisely.* Collegeville, MN: Liturgical Press, 2005.

Chapter 26
1 AND 2 MACCABEES

1 Maccabees

The two books of Maccabees are separate works, not a single book divided in two like 1 and 2 Kings or 1 and 2 Chronicles. First Maccabees was written in the late second or early first century BCE in order to support the cause of the Hasmonean dynasty. The Hasmonean rulers were descendants of the Maccabees. They ruled in Palestine as an independent kingdom from 110 to 63 and then as a client kingdom under Roman hegemony from 63 to 40. The last event reported in 1 Maccabees is the changeover in rule from Simon to his son John Hyrcanus I that took place in 134.

First Maccabees exists in a Greek translation of a lost Hebrew original. The author quotes supposedly official documents, which may or may not be genuine, but which are basically accurate in what they report. Following the common practice of Greco-Roman historians, the author composed speeches for important characters to deliver. The book displays a positive attitude toward the Romans, whose support for the Maccabean movement is described in 12:1-4 and 15:15-24 and in the treaty cited in chapter 8. The content of this treaty is thought to be basically authentic. Events are dated according to the Seleucid Era, which was the standard calendar at that time. Year 1 of the Seleucid Era was 311. Equivalent years in today's calendar are provided in the footnotes of modern versions. The first-century CE Jewish historian Josephus utilized 1 Maccabees as a source.

First Maccabees is basically a family history, recounting military exploits and religious observances. It reports on *the family of those men through whom deliverance was given to Israel* (5:62). The account spans three generations:

- Mattathias (died about 165; chapter 2)
- His sons

- ○ Judas (died 160; 3:1–9:22)
- ○ Jonathan (died 143; 9:23–12:53)
- ○ Simon (died 134; 13:1–16:17)
- John Hyrcanus, son of Simon (16:18–23).

The history of this period is complex, which makes it difficult for anyone not conversant with the period to follow the story of either 1 or 2 Maccabees. Readers should rely on a good study Bible to help untangle the various Seleucid kings, military leaders, intrigues, and battles involved. First Maccabees covers the period between 169 and 134, while 2 Maccabees begins earlier, in about 180, and concludes in 161. Events before 1 Maccabees opens are outlined below in the discussion of 2 Maccabees.

Persecution by Antiochus IV Epiphanes

Aspects of Greek culture led to developments offensive to more orthodox Jews, such as the establishment of a gymnasium in Jerusalem where men engaged in athletic events naked. Antiochus IV engaged in a moderately successful invasion of Egypt in 169. This was followed by an abject failure in 167 (something not mentioned in 1 Maccabees). In 167 he plundered the temple and instituted religious practices there that were appalling to orthodox Jews. He had a *disgusting and destructive thing* (CEB; NRSV: *desolating sacrilege*; traditionally *abomination of desolation*) erected over the temple altar for the purpose of offering improper sacrifice (1 Macc 1:54; see also Dan 9:27; 11:31; 12:11). The first of these sacrifices took place on 25 Kislev 167. He destroyed scriptural books and criminalized possession of them. He forbade circumcision. These repressive policies led to the martyrdom of many who resisted. Antiochus IV also had a citadel built, overlooking the temple area. Meanwhile, through political intrigue, murder, and bribery, the high priesthood had fallen into the hands of a certain Menelaus (in office about 172–162). This change was seen as scandalous by many faithful Jews, because Menelaus was from a priestly family other than that of the Zadokites, from which the high priests had traditionally come. This development is reported only in 2 Maccabees.

Antiochus IV set up altars where pigs and other unclean animals were sacrificed (1:47, 54) and demanded that Jews living outside Jerusalem participate in pagan sacrifice at those illicit altars. In the town of Modein, the priest Mattathias resisted, killing both a compliant Jew and a royal representative. Heading up into the hills, Mattathias led the first round of a Jewish revolt against the Seleucids. He and his followers dismantled pagan altars, killed renegade Jews, and enforced circumcision. After his death, leadership of the rebellion fell to his oldest son, Judas, nicknamed the Maccabee (perhaps meaning the Hammer).

Table 8. The Maccabee Family in 1 and 2 Maccabees

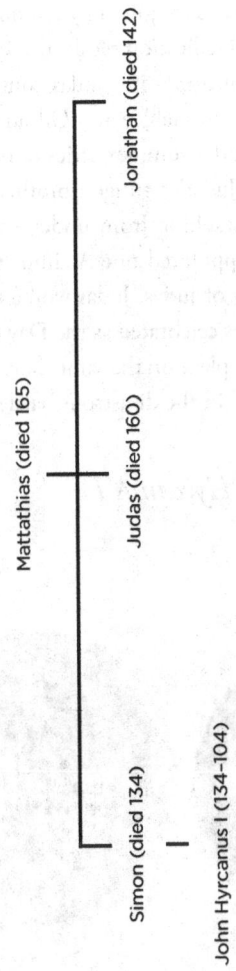

Chapter 26

Judas the Maccabee

Judas won victories at Beth-horon, Emmaus, and Beth-zur (3:1–4:35). This put him in the position to move into Jerusalem, recapture the temple, and purify and dedicate it. This rededication is said to have taken place exactly three years after the temple's desecration, on 25 Kislev 164. The defiled altar was removed and the stones stored away *until a prophet should arise who could say what to do with them* (4:46). A new altar was built of unhewn stones as required by Exodus 20:25 and Deuteronomy 27:6. The festival of Hanukkah or Dedication recalls this event and celebrates various traditional stories connected with it (4:36-59). Judas continued to be successful and was able to rescue endangered Jews in Galilee and Gilead (chapter 5). Antiochus IV died in Persia in 164 (chapter 6) and a complex series of battles ensued. One notable scene portrays the heroic death of Judas's youngest brother Eleazar, who was crushed to death by the elephant he was stabbing from underneath (6:43-46). The current Seleucid king, Demetrius I, had appointed one Alcimus to the high priesthood (in office 162–159). He was an enemy of Judas. Judas won a significant victory over the general Nicanor (7:26-50). This was celebrated as the Day of Nicanor until that festival merged with Purim, which took place on the same date. Finally, Judas was defeated by the general Bacchides and killed in the disastrous battle of Elasa in 160 (9:1-18).

Jonathan, Simon, and John Hyrcanus I

Fig. 18. The Seleucid king Antiochus VII Sidetes (139–129) gave permission for the Jewish authorities to mint coinage. This small bronze coin struck by John Hyrcanus I reads: "Yehohanan [John] the high priest and the Council of the Jews." It features a double cornucopia and a pomegranate as symbols of abundance.

Judas was succeeded by his brother Jonathan (160–142). Playing off rival candidates for the Seleucid throne, Jonathan was able to secure the high priesthood for himself in 152 (10:18-21). After various battles and intrigues, Jonathan was tricked, captured, and put to death by Trypho, at the time a supporter of one of the claimants for the Seleucid throne (12:39-48). Jonathan's brother Simon (142–135) came next and was able to gain independence from the Seleucid king Demetrius II (son of Demetrius I; 13:31-42). Simon became high priest in place of Jonathan. Good relations between Simon and the Seleucid king (now Antiochus VII, brother of Demetrius II) eventually collapsed, and Simon's son John Hyrcanus won a victory over a Seleucid general at a place called Kedron in 137 (15:38–16:10). Simon and two sons were later slain by treachery at a banquet in 134 (16:11-17). Simon's only surviving son John Hyrcanus I (134–104) took the reins of leadership and became high priest. Near the end of his reign, Hyrcanus captured Samaria after a year-long siege. His rule initiated the Hasmonean period.

26.1. Samaria

Samaria was the most important city of the central highlands, first as capital of the northern kingdom of Israel and then as an administrative capital during succeeding centuries of domination by foreign powers. King Omri had founded the city of Samaria as his new capital (1 Kgs 16:23-24). It retained this status until the Assyrian conquest. Samaria then gave its name to the Assyrian province (*Samerina*) that was formed out of the territory that had remained to Israel after the debacle of 734–732. In the Persian period, authorities located at Samaria opposed efforts to revitalize Jerusalem, as reported in Ezra and Nehemiah.

In 331, the inhabitants of Samaria assassinated an administrator of Alexander named Andromachus, and a Greek army was sent to punish the city. Some citizens fled, carrying with them a collection of administrative documents known today as the Samaria papyri. They were killed by Alexander's army in a cave north of Jericho in the Wadi ed-Daliyeh, where their skeletons and the documents were discovered in 1962. This catastrophe caused the center of gravity for northern Yahwism (eventually, the Samaritans) to shift from the city of Samaria to Shechem. Samaria regained importance under Roman rule and

> the kingship of Herod the Great. Herod engaged in impressive building projects there and renamed the city Sebaste in honor of the emperor Augustus.

2 Maccabees

Second Maccabees tells of how God defended the sanctity and purity of the Jerusalem temple when it was successively threatened by three enemies. The book advocates the celebration of Hanukkah in two introductory letters that precede the historical narrative (1:1-9 and 1:10–2:18): *So now you should keep the Festival of Booths in the month of Kislev* (1:9).

These cover letters indicate that the composition was sent to the Jewish diaspora in Egypt. The date cited in the first letter is 124, which provides an approximate date for the book's completion.

2 Maccabees as History

Second Maccabees supplements the historical witness of 1 Maccabees, but is less restrained and more interested in recounting miraculous and wonderful tales. Second Maccabees begins in about 180 during the reign of Seleucus IV (187–175), who was the brother and predecessor of Antiochus IV. It concludes in 161 with the victory of Judas the Maccabee over the enemy general Nicanor, which was celebrated for a period of time as the Day of Nicanor (15:36). Sometimes 2 Maccabees reports events in a different sequence from that of 1 Maccabees, and it is not always clear which of the two is correct. The compiler of 2 Maccabees abridged an earlier five-volume work by one Jason of Cyrene, which is now lost (2:23). He states as his purpose:

> to provide something amusing for those who want to read, to make it easy for those inclined to commit facts to memory, and to offer something useful to all those who happen to pick up the scroll. (2:25)

Greek was the original language of 2 Maccabees. In 11:16-38, the author quotes four archival letters that are commonly accepted as authentic. Unlike the relatively sober 1 Maccabees, 2 Maccabees incorporates numerous spectacular supernatural events. It uses melodramatic language in order to arouse the emotions of readers and draw them into the drama of what is being reported.

The second introductory letter (1:10–2:18) initiates the topic of the rededication of the temple celebrated as Hanukkah by recounting a colorful story about the death of Antiochus IV (1:13-16). It then cites precedents for temple rededication, including legendary accounts about Nehemiah rekindling the temple's altar fire (1:18-36) and Jeremiah hiding the ark and altar for safekeeping (2:1-8).

26.2. Hanukkah

The name Hanukkah derives from the Hebrew verb *to dedicate*. Hanukkah is not mentioned in the Hebrew Bible, but only in 1 and 2 Maccabees. According to 1 Maccabees 4:36-59 and 2 Maccabees 10:1-8, after they regained control of the temple, the Maccabees purified and rededicated the sanctuary over an eight-day period. They lit the lamps on the temple lampstand, *which illuminated the temple* (1 Macc 4:50). A law was decreed to celebrate this event every year on the twenty-fifth of Kislev (4:59). The holiday is also known as the Festival of Lights. John 10:22 mentions Hanukkah as the Feast of Dedication.

A later legend preserved in the Talmud and elsewhere recounts that nearly all the olive oil needed for the lamps had become impure. Only a single sealed container remained pure, but this was only enough to last a single day. Miraculously, that supply of undefiled oil kept the Temple *menorah* (lamp) burning for eight days until a new supply could be prepared.

Customs for the celebration of Hanukkah vary in different Jewish communities. A standard practice is for the household to set out a special Hanukkah menorah in a visible place. Each night, the number of lights kindled on its candles or oil lamp wicks is increased one by one until eight are burning on the last night. An auxiliary branch holds the *shamash* or servant candle that is used to kindle the other lights.

The Succession of High Priests

Because 2 Maccabees begins about a decade earlier than 1 Maccabees, it describes the crisis caused by the impact of Greek culture in Jerusalem, which the author interprets as disrespect for God's law (4:9-17), and the political intrigues that surrounded the succession of the high priests. The legitimate high priest, *Onias III*, was deposed and supplanted by his brother *Jason*, who attaining office in 175 by offering an enormous bribe to the newly enthroned Antiochus IV (4:7-9). In 171, Jason sent one *Menelaus* (the brother of an enemy of Onias III) as an envoy to the Seleucid court. Menelaus took this opportunity to offer an even more generous bribe to the king, who in turn appointed him as high priest (4:23-26). This appointment was widely seen as scandalous because, although Menelaus was a priest, he was not of the proper Zadokite priestly family, for which the high priesthood had previously been reserved. (Some popular and introductory works suggest Menelaus was not even a priest, but it is generally accepted that this misreads the evidence about his brother Simon in 3:4).

Menelaus arranged to have the deposed Onias III assassinated (4:30-34). Menelaus and his brother were guilty of plundering the temple of its vessels, but he was able to avoid the consequences of his crime by means of a well-placed bribe (4:39-50). Menelaus was put to death in 162 by the Seleucid king Antiochus V (13:3-8). *Alcimus*, an opponent of Judas, was the next high priest (162–160 or 159; see 1 Maccabees 7, 9; 2 Maccabees 14). After his death, the office remained vacant until the Maccabee brothers *Jonathan* (152–142) and then *Simon* (142–134) were appointed. Simon's son *John Hyrcanus* served as high priest from 134–104; 1 Macc 16:24). The issue of non-Zadokite high priests continued to be a matter of controversy, giving rise to the sectarian Qumran movement, which abandoned the Jerusalem temple, its priesthood, and its liturgical calendar.

God Defends the Temple

The core subject matter of 2 Maccabees is God's defense of the temple's sanctity against three successive assaults.

- The first of these attacks (3:1–40) was an aborted attempt by Heliodorus, an agent of the Seleucid king, to plunder the temple treasury (about 178). He was stopped by divine intervention, being attacked by a vison of a supernatural horse and rider and two angels.

- The second assault consisted of the policies of Antiochus IV against Jewish religious life (4:1–10:9). Particulars of this persecution are described in dramatic language in 6:1–11. Antiochus's threat to the temple was ended when Judas recaptured and purified it (10:1–9).

- The third assault on Jerusalem was the campaign of the Seleucid general Nicanor (10:10–15:36). This is represented as a threat to the temple (14:33, 15:17). Before the battle against Nicanor (in 161), Judas encouraged his troops by recounting a dream or vision in which Onias III and Jeremiah acknowledge Judas as God's champion (15:11–16). Nicanor was defeated and found dead. His body was treated with what the author understands to be well-deserved disrespect.

Judas is the central character of 2 Maccabees and is described as the ideal warrior. He prays before and after battle and is careful about religious observances. His father Mattathias and his brothers do not appear in 2 Maccabees at all. Nothing is reported about his death, nor is there any mention of the serious defeat he suffered the year following his victory over Nicanor (the battle of Elasa in 160, reported in 1 Macc 9:1-18).

Heroic Martyrdom

Second Maccabees celebrates a theology of heroic martyrdom and suffering (6:12–7:42; 14:37-46) in order to encourage religious fidelity. Three emotionally powerful stories make this point. First, the old man Eleazar refuses to eat sacrificed pork and, after a noble speech, dies on the rack (6:18-31).

> In this manner he died, and his own death left behind a most noble and memorable example of virtue not only for the youth but also for the majority of his nation. (6:31)

Second, seven brothers in turn refuse to commit the same apostate act and are tortured to death horribly, one by one. Each of them speaks intrepid and defiant last words (7:1-41). Their mother watches, and when her last son is put to the test, she urges him to resist. At the end, she too dies. Third, the leader Razis determines to die with nobility rather than fall into enemy hands, and commits a most gruesome and drawn-out suicide (14:37-46).

These stories of heroic martyrdom are told in the context of a belief in resurrection. Eleazar testifies to the possibility of divine punishment after death (6:26). Several of the seven brothers and their mother proclaim their confidence in a bodily resurrection to everlasting life (7:9, 11, 14, 23). The writer attributes the courage of Razis to his belief that his body would be restored in the resurrection (14:46). Judas indicates his belief in resurrection by arranging for sin offerings intended to atone for his troops killed in battle and by praying for them (12:39-45).

Later Jewish Religious Works

A number of ancient Jewish religious works fall outside the scope of this volume, although they are sometimes printed in Bibles directed at ecumenical audiences. Some of the books discussed below are recognized as canonical or deuterocanonical scripture in the Greek and Russian Orthodox churches: 1 Esdras, 2 Esdras, Prayer of Manasseh, Psalm 151, and 3 Maccabees. In addition, 1 and 2 Esdras (as 3 Esdras and 4 Esdras) and the Prayer of Manasseh appear in a (non-canonical) appendix to the Latin Vulgate Bible.

First Esdras reproduces portions of 2 Chronicles, Ezra, and Nehemiah and narrates events from the Passover celebrated by King Josiah to the reading of the torah by Ezra (selections from 2 Chronicles 35 to Nehemiah 8). First Esdras 3:1–5:6 is an independent narrative recounting a debate among three bodyguards of King Darius, one of whom is Zerubbabel, over what thing is strongest. Wine, the king, and women are contenders, but the final conclusion is that truth is strongest of all.

The *Prayer of Manasseh* is a penitential poem placed in the mouth of Manasseh king of Judah. According to 2 Chronicles 33:10-17, Manasseh repented of his evil ways while in exile and was restored to his throne.

Psalm 151 concludes the Septuagint version of the book of Psalms. Its previously lost Hebrew original appears in a Psalm scroll from Qumran in a form longer than the Greek version.

Third Maccabees actually has nothing to do with the Maccabees. It tells of events that supposedly took place in the reign of the Hellenistic king of Egypt, Ptolemy IV (221–204). Ptolemy makes an unsuccessful attempt to enter the Jerusalem temple. Most of the book reports on his vicious persecution of the Jews of Egypt. In the end Ptolemy relents.

Second Esdras appears in the Bible of the Russian Orthodox Church (as 3 Esdras). The Jewish core of the book (chapters 3–14) consists of seven apocalyptic visions supposedly experienced by Ezra that respond to the situation of the Jews after the Roman destruction of the temple in 70 CE. Chapters 1–2 and 15–16 are of Christian origin and stem from an even later period.

Fourth Maccabees does not have any canonical status. It is a philosophical treatise composed in Greek proclaiming that reason is always superior to the emotions and that reason is compatible with Mosaic law. To prove its point, the book retells the martyrdom stories of Eleazar and of the seven sons with their mother from 2 Maccabees.

Further Reading

Daniel J. Harrington. *The Maccabean Revolt: Anatomy of a Biblical Revolution.* Michael Glazier, 1988.

CHRONOLOGY OF SIGNIFICANT EVENTS

about 1208	first mention of Israel in an extra-biblical source by Pharaoh Merneptah
about 1175	Philistines settle in southern Palestine
10th century	Saul, David, and Solomon
about 930	kingdoms of Israel and Judah established
about 925	Pharaoh Shishak invades Israel and Judah
about 880	Omri builds Samaria, captures territory from Moab north of the Arnon river
853	Battle of Qarqar, Ahab and allies block the advance of Assyrian King Shalmaneser III
841	rebellion of Jehu, Jehu begins paying tribute to Assyria
740 and 738	Menahem pays tribute to Assyria
734–732	Israel and Damascus threaten King Ahaz of Judah
732	Megiddo and Gilead become Assyrian provinces
722 or 720	fall of the northern kingdom, Samaria becomes an Assyrian province, deportations
701	Sennacherib invades Judah, captures Lachish, and threatens Jerusalem
664	No-Amon (Thebes) in Egypt falls to the Assyrian King Assurbanipal
622/21	religious reform of King Josiah
612	Nineveh destroyed
609	Pharaoh Neco kills Josiah at Megiddo
605	Battle of Carchemish, Babylon becomes dominant in the region at the expense of Egypt
597	Jerusalem falls to the Babylonians, deportations
593	Zedekiah involved in regional summit to plan resistance to Babylon
586	Jerusalem captured by Babylonians, temple destroyed, deportations
582	further deportations
561/560	King Jehoiachin is released from prison in Babylon
539	Cyrus overcomes the Babylonian Empire, some Jews return to Jerusalem
525	Persian King Cambyses captures Egypt
520–515	construction of the Second Temple
458	mission of Ezra begins

Chronology of Significant Events

445–438	Nehemiah serves as governor
333	conquests of Alexander the Great begin
331	Samaria destroyed by Alexander
200	Battle of Panias, Palestine shifts from Ptolemaic to Seleucid control
167	desecration of temple by Antiochus IV begins
164	temple purified and rededicated
63	Roman commander Ptolemy enters Jerusalem, Roman dominance begins

VOCABULARY

acrostic—a poem in which succeeding lines or groups of lines begin with the letters of the Hebrew alphabet in order. Psalm 119 is an example.

Ammon—kingdom east of the Jordan River. Today its chief city, Rabbath-ammon, is Amman, the capital of Jordan.

apocalypse, apocalyptic—a genre of literature (noun) and description of a worldview (adjective) concerned with revelations about end times or a future age. Daniel 7–12 is an apocalypse, and earlier prophetic texts like Zechariah 1–6 and Isaiah 24–27 exhibit apocalyptic features.

Apocrypha—seven Jewish religious works composed in the Hellenistic and Roman periods included in the Roman Catholic and Orthodox canons, but not considered part of the Bible by Protestants and Jews. See *deuterocanonical books*. The term *Apocrypha* may also describe other Jewish religious books (some included in Orthodox Bibles) often printed in Bibles for ecumenical audiences: 1 Esdras, Prayer of Manasseh, Psalm 151, 3 Maccabees, 2 Esdras, and 4 Maccabees.

apodictic law—an absolute command or prohibition lacking reference to specific situations or cases (see *casuistic law*).

Aramaic—a language related to Hebrew, used as an international means of communication from about 600 BCE on. Portions of Daniel and Ezra are written in Aramaic.

ark—a box or chest. The traditional translation for two different Hebrew words: (1) the boat built by Noah, and (2) a box that concretized Yahweh's presence by functioning as a throne or footstool and served as a container for holy objects (CEB: *chest*).

Baal—a divine title, meaning "lord" or "owner," used for the Canaanite storm and fertility god Hadad and for deities worshipped at local shrines in Palestine.

Vocabulary

Booths—seven-day festival beginning on 15 Tishri (September–October) and marking the harvest of grapes, olives, and other summer fruits. *Sukkot* in Hebrew.

Canaan—ancient designation for territory west of the Jordan and running northward into Phoenicia and Syria. Israel inhabited the southern portion of Canaan.

canon—an authoritative list of revered and authoritative religious books.

casuistic law—a conditional legal statement in an "if . . . then" format. A situation is described in greater or lesser detail, and then consequences are stated.

cherub (plural *cherubim*, a Hebrew cognate)—transcendent winged guardian beings. Cherubim guarded the entrance to Eden (Gen 3:24), and cherub images overshadowed the ark (covenant chest) and decorated the temple.

circumcision—removing the foreskin (prepuce) from the penis. This custom was widely practiced in the ancient Near East. For Israel circumcision on the eighth day served as a sign of the covenant relationship to Yahweh and as an ethnic marker.

codex (plural *codices*)—a book made up of pages bound together with text on both sides of each page, as opposed to a rolled-up scroll with text on its inside surface.

covenant—a formal agreement between two parties, consisting of obligations and promises. Beginning with the eighth century, Israel conceptualized its relationship with Yahweh in terms of a covenant with stipulations offered to them by the deity. The covenant concept in some contexts was probably modeled on ancient royal grants and international treaties.

Covenant Code—Exodus 20:22–23:19, the earliest collection of laws in the Old Testament.

Day of Atonement/Day of Reconciliation—an annual ceremony, described in Leviticus 16, intended to purify the tabernacle or temple and remove sin as an obstacle to the relationship between Yahweh and Israel. It is observed on 10 Tishri (September–October).

Day of Yahweh—the time of Yahweh's decisive intervention in human affairs to deliver and punish. The concept originated in liturgical and military contexts and was central to the message of prophets like Joel, Amos, and Zephaniah.

Dead Sea Scrolls—manuscripts and manuscript fragments of a religious nature discovered in the mid-twentieth century in caves on the west side of the Dead Sea. See *Qumran*.

Decalogue—the Ten Commandments, from the Greek for "ten words."

Vocabulary

deuterocanonical books—designation for seven books traditionally considered part of the OT canon of the Roman Catholic Church. The term recognizes that these were authoritatively defined as part of the Roman Catholic Bible by the Council of Trent (1546). See *Apocrypha*.

Deuteronomistic History (DH)—a connected history of Israel in the land composed under the theological influence of Deuteronomy. It consists of portions of Deuteronomy followed by Joshua through 2 Kings.

diaspora—dispersion of Jews from Judah. This began about 600 BCE to Babylon and Egypt. Jewish emigration continued into the Mediterranean and West Asia.

divine council—in ancient West Asian thought, an assembly of gods or transcendent beings, modeled after the court of human kings, and presided over by a ruling god such as El or Yahweh.

Documentary Hypothesis—the widely held premise that the Pentateuch was formed by an editorial process that incorporated earlier source documents (J, E, D, P). The classic, granular form of this compositional model has come under increasing scrutiny in recent decades.

Edom—kingdom and region south of Moab and the southern end of the Dead Sea. Edomites (later Idumeans) encroached into the southern part of Judah's territory in the early sixth century.

El—ruling god of the Ugaritic pantheon. The historical relationship between El and Yahweh in Israelite religion is disputed, but their names, characteristics, and worship sites seem to have merged together over time.

Elohim—the generic word for God in Hebrew, for the most part used to designate Yahweh.

endogamy—marrying within one's kinship group or ethnicity. Marriage within one's clan was a standard but not exclusive practice in biblical times. Deuteronomy registers strong opposition to intermarriage with Canaanites. In the Persian period, marriage with non-Jews was seen as increasingly problematic.

Enuma Elish—an epic poem lauding the Babylonian god Marduk as the one who vanquished the sea goddess Tiamat and created the world and humanity.

eschatology—concepts connected to expectations of an end time.

etiology—a statement of origin that explains the existence and characteristics of something such as a name, topographic feature, custom, ritual, or sanctuary site.

fable—an instructive story in which animals or plants are the dramatic characters.

Vocabulary

Fertile Crescent—cultural and economic zone consisting of an arc of fertile territory stretching northward from Palestine and Syria and then eastward and southward through Mesopotamia.

Five Scrolls—short books in the Writings section of the Hebrew Bible, associated with religious observances: Song of Songs, Ruth, Lamentations, Ecclesiastes, and Esther. Hebrew: *Megilloth*.

form criticism—the study of oral and written literary genres (forms) and their typical structures, intentions, and usage in social settings (German: *Sitz im Leben*).

Former Prophets—the first division of the Prophets portion of the Hebrew Bible: Joshua, Judges, 1 and 2 Samuel, and 1 and 2 Kings.

Gilgamesh Epic—classic Mesopotamian tale about the hero Gilgamesh and his failed quest for the secret of eternal life. Traveling with his companion Enkidu, he encounters Utnapishtim, survivor of the universal flood.

Hanukkah—eight-day celebration of the rededication of the temple by Judas Maccabeus in 164 BCE, beginning 25 Kislev (November–December).

Hebrew Bible—the canonical scriptures of Judaism consisting of twenty-four books divided into *Torah*, Prophets (*Nebiim*), and Writings (*Kethuvim*). See *Old Testament* and *Tanak*.

Hellenization—the process by which Greek culture (Hellenism) and language came to dominate the societies of the eastern Mediterranean and West Asia after the conquests of Alexander the Great.

henotheism—the religious worldview in which one god is worshipped, but the existence of other gods is not denied.

Holiness Code—the independent legal source emphasizing the holiness of Yahweh and Yahweh's people preserved in Leviticus 17–26.

Horeb—the name for Mount Sinai in Deuteronomy and the Elohist document.

Immanuel—child whose birth and early years served as a sign of God's support for Judah and King Ahaz during the crisis of 734–732 (Isa 7:10-17). The name means "God is with us."

Isaiah Apocalypse—an example of apocalyptic literature incorporated into the scroll of Isaiah as chapters 24–27.

Israel—the northern kingdom of Israel, consisting of areas to the north of Judah, Galilee, and territory east of the Jordan. Jacob is given this name in Genesis 32:28 as the eponymous ancestor of the twelve tribes. The name Israel also expressed the common identity claimed by people of both Judah and the northern kingdom and by their descendants.

Vocabulary

Judah—the dominant tribe in the southern region known during the Roman period as Palestine. Judah became the name of the southern kingdom with its capital in Jerusalem and governed by the house (dynasty) of David. In the Persian period the region was called Yehud and later, Judea.

Latter Prophets—the second division of the Prophets portion of the Hebrew Bible: Isaiah, Jeremiah, Ezekiel, and the book of the Twelve.

Levites—members of the tribe of Levi who functioned as religious specialists, particularly those groups with support roles who had lower status than priests.

manna—extraordinary food (bread) provided to Israel by Yahweh in the traditions of the desert wandering.

Marduk—chief god of the Babylonian pantheon and the city of Babylon.

Masoretic text—the text of the Hebrew Bible preserved through the efforts of the Masoretes, who were textual scholars active between about 600 and 950 CE.

Mesopotamia—territory defined by the Tigris and Euphrates rivers and their tributaries.

messiah—"anointed one," pertaining to the practice of setting royal and priestly leaders by a ceremony of anointing. In later Christian and Jewish thought, a future royal leader sent by God.

Midian—territory located in the northwestern part of the Arabian Peninsula. Biblical tradition reports that the Midianites were enemies of Israel in pre-monarchic times.

Moab—kingdom and region east of the Dead Sea and north of Edom. Moab's core territory was bounded on the north by the Arnon River, but sometimes extended further north into territory contested by Israel.

myth—a narrative set in the time of origins in the remote past that expresses aspects of a culture's fundamental worldview. Myths feature interactions among gods in the realms of sexuality and conflict. Understood more broadly, myth refers to expressions of elemental realities though unempirical, non-historical, poetic discourse.

Old Testament—the first part of the Christian Bible, consisting of books inherited from Judaism and contrasting with the New Testament. See *Hebrew Bible*.

ostracon (plural, *ostraca*)—an inscribed piece of broken pottery, which served as the writing material for everyday notes and records.

parallelism—the basic building block of Hebrew poetry. Two consecutive lines work together so that the second restates, reshapes, or develops the first.

Vocabulary

Passover—festival commemorating the exodus of Israel from slavery in Egypt. Passover begins on 14 Nisan (April–May).

Pentateuch—the first five books of the Bible (the Torah). Greek: "five books."

Philistines—non-Semitic ethnic group that migrated from the Aegean area and settled in the coastal area of southern Palestine in the early twelfth century.

prophet—religious intermediary who delivered messages from the deity. Prophets performed acts of power to authenticate their words. A prophet might also be called a seer or a man of God.

Pseudepigrapha—a category of ancient religious books, mostly Jewish in origin and mostly composed before the end of the second century CE.

Purim—festival on 14 Adar (February–March) commemorating the rescue of the Jews of the Persian Empire and validated by the story told in the book of Esther.

Qumran—ruins near the west shore of the Dead Sea inhabited by the community that produced the Dead Sea Scrolls.

redaction criticism—study of the editing processes that resulted in biblical literature achieving its final forms.

Reed Sea—frequent translation in modern versions for the body of water crossed by Israel in the exodus. Traditionally the Red Sea, based on a Greek Septuagint identification.

sacrifice—the transfer of an animate or inanimate entity from the human realm to the realm of God in order to change or maintain some relationship or situation. The sacrifice of animals could result in a communal meal.

Samaria—city constructed by King Omri in the highlands of Ephraim to serve as the capital of the kingdom of Israel. Samaria eventually became the name of the surrounding region.

Sea Peoples—inclusive term for the various Aegean-area groups (including Philistines and others) who migrated, sometimes violently, into the eastern Mediterranean at the beginning of the Iron Age (about 1200).

Second Temple Period—the six centuries during which the temple built under the leadership of Zerubbabel was in use: 515 BCE to 70 CE.

Septuagint—translation of the Hebrew Bible into Greek made by the Jews of Egypt. This process began about 250 BCE. The Septuagint and translations of it served as the Bible of most Christians in early centuries.

servant songs—four poems sharing the figure of the servant of Yahweh as a common topic. They are incorporated into the second part of the book of Isaiah (42:1-4; 49:1-6; 50:4-11; 52:13–53:12).

Vocabulary

Sheol—the realm of the dead in the underworld. Sheol is not a place of punishment but a place of weakness, emptiness, and futility. CEB: *grave* or *death*.

Sinai—the whereabouts of the mountain of lawgiving is uncertain, but it is usually understood to be in the southern part of the Sinai Peninsula, traditionally Jebel Musa (mountain of Moses; site of the monastery of St. Catherine). Another possibility is in Midian, east of the Sinai Peninsula and south and east of Palestine. See *Horeb*.

son of man—in Daniel 7:13-14, the human being who succeeds the four beasts of world empire and is given universal dominion. CEB: *one like a human being*.

suzerainty treaty—a form of international treaty in which a powerful king (the suzerain) and a lesser king (the vassal) agree to an unequal relationship involving stipulations, blessings, and curses. Some scholars think biblical writers utilized features of the suzerainty treaty to conceptualize the relationship (covenant) between Yahweh and Israel.

tabernacle—portable tent shrine of the wilderness period that embodied the functions of the Jerusalem temple building. CEB: *the dwelling*. See *tent of meeting*.

Tanak—acronym denoting the Hebrew Bible from the first letters of its three divisions: *Torah*, *Nebiim* (Prophets), and *Kethuvim* (Writings).

tell—mound formed by long-standing occupation of a town or city and marking its site. Arabic (Hebrew: *tel*).

tent of meeting—name associated with one of the traditions that made up the final depiction of Israel's portable shrine, emphasizing Yahweh's presence there to facilitate communication with Moses. CEB: *meeting tent*.

Tetragrammaton—a designation for the personal name of Israel's God, Yahweh, which points to its four consonants (YHWH). There is uncertainty about what vowel sounds should be used to pronounce it, and many Jews have scruples about uttering the sacred name. Greek: "four letters."

theodicy—literature and thought that explores the problem of divine justice and human suffering.

theogony—a mythic explanation of present reality that describes the origin of a multitude of gods through divine genealogy.

theophany—the appearance of a deity to humans. The tradition of a manifestation of God or transcendent being designated the location of a shrine. Poems portray the arrival of Yahweh as Divine Warrior to save Israel (for example, Deut 33:2-3; Judg 5:4-5, Hab 3:3-7).

Vocabulary

Tiamat—in Babylonian religion, the goddess of the primeval salt water of the sea. In *Enuma Elish*, Marduk defeats her in the form of a sea dragon and then fashions heaven and earth from her body.

trickster—The trickster may use a disguise, engage in deceptions, and tell lies. Jacob, Tamar, and Ehud are prime examples.

Ugaritic—language of texts from the city of Ugarit on the coast of Syria that are important for an understanding of Canaanite religion and culture.

Weeks—springtime agricultural festival marking the wheat harvest. The name refers to seven weeks after a formal marking of the start of the barley harvest during Passover. Today it is celebrated on 6 Sivan (May–June). *Shavuot* in Hebrew. *Pentecost* (referencing fifty days) in Greek.

Yahweh—the personal name of the God of the Old Testament. Modern versions print this as LORD with small capital letters.

Zion—poetic name for Jerusalem.

www.ingramcontent.com/pod-product-compliance
Lightning Source LLC
Chambersburg PA
CBHW012128010526
44113CB00042B/2658